The Critical Response
to Jack London

Jack London, Glen Ellen, California, ca. 1905

The Critical Response to Jack London

Edited by
SUSAN M. NUERNBERG

Critical Responses in Arts and Letters, Number 19
Cameron Northouse, Series Adviser

GREENWOOD PRESS
Westport, Connecticut • London

Library of Congress Cataloging-in-Publication Data

The critical response to Jack London / edited by Susan M. Nuernberg.
      p.   cm.—(Critical responses in arts and letters, ISSN
1057–0993 ; no. 19)
   Includes bibliographical references and index.
   ISBN 0–313–28927–1 (alk. paper)
   1. London, Jack, 1876–1916—Criticism and interpretation.
I. Nuernberg, Susan M. II. Series.
PS3523.046Z6217 1995
818′.5209—dc20   95–15448

British Library Cataloguing in Publication Data is available.

Library of Congress Catalog Card Number: 95–15448
ISBN: 0–313–28927–1
ISSN: 1057–0993

First published in 1995

Greenwood Press, 88 Post Road West, Westport, CT 06881
An imprint of Greenwood Publishing Group, Inc.

Printed in the United States of America

The paper used in this book complies with the
Permanent Paper Standard issued by the National
Information Standards Organization (Z39.48–1984).

10 9 8 7 6 5 4 3 2

Copyright Acknowledgments

The editor and publisher gratefully acknowledge the following for permission to use copyrighted materials:

Photograph of Jack London, Glen Ellen, California, ca. 1905. Reproduced by permission of The Huntington Library, San Marino, California.

Jack London to "Mr. Revision Editor" at *Youth's Companion* February 5, 1902. This item is reproduced by permission of The Huntington Library, San Marino, California.

Clell Peterson, "The Theme of Jack London's 'To Build a Fire,'" *American Book Collector* 17 (November 1966), 15-18. Reprinted by permission of the author.

Earle Labor and King Hendricks, "Jack London's Twice-Told Tale," *Studies in Short Fiction* 4 (1967), 334-41. Copyright by Newberry College. Reprinted by permission.

James M. Mellard, "Dramatic Mode and Tragic Structure in 'To Build a Fire,'" *Four Modes: A Rhetoric of Modern Fiction* by James M. Mellard (New York: Macmillan, 1973), 260-64. Reprinted with permission of the author.

Charles E. May, "'To Build a Fire': Physical Fiction and Metaphysical Critics," *Studies in Short Fiction* 15 (1978), 19-24. Copyright by Newberry College. Reprinted with permission.

Charles Child Walcutt, "Jack London: Blond Beasts and Supermen," *American Literary Naturalism, A Divided Stream* by Charles Child Walcutt (Minneapolis: University of Minnesota Press, 1956), 97-103, by permission. Copyright 1956 by The University of Minnesota.

James R. Giles, extract taken from "Beneficial Atavism in Frank Norris and Jack London," *Western American Literature* 4 (Spring 1969), 20-23. Reprinted with permission.

Tony Tanner, "Books: *The Call of the Wild*," *Spectator* July 16, 1965, 80-81. Reprinted by permission of the journal.

For Hensley C. Woodbridge

Editor of the *Jack London Newsletter* 1967-1988

Contents

Series Foreword

Critical Responses in Arts and Letters is designed to present a documentary history of highlights in the critical reception to the body of work of writers and artists and to individual works that are generally considered to be of major importance. The focus of each volume is basically historical. The introductions to each volume are themselves brief histories of the critical response an author, artist, or individual has received. This response is then further illustrated by reprinting a strong representation of the major critical reviews and articles that have collectively produced the author's, artist's, or work's critical reputation.

The scope of *Critical Responses in Arts and Letters* knows no chronological or geographical boundaries. Volumes under preparation include studies of individuals from around the world and in both contemporary and historical periods.

Each volume is the work of an individual editor, who surveys the entire body of criticism on a single author, artist, or work. The editor then selects the best material to depict the critical response received by an author or artist over his/her entire career. Documents produced by the author or artist may also be included when the editor finds that they are necessary to a full understanding of the materials at hand. In circumstances where previous, isolated volumes of criticism on a particular individual or work exist, the editor carefully selects material that better reflects the nature and directions of the critical response over time.

In addition to the introduction and the documentary section, the editor of each volume is free to solicit new essays on areas that may not have been adequately dealt with in previous criticism. Also, for volumes on living writers and artists, new interviews may be included, again at the discretion of the volume's editor. The volumes also provide a supplementary bibliography and are fully indexed.

While each volume in *Critical Responses in Arts and Letters* is unique, it is also hoped that in combination they form a useful, documentary history of the critical response to the arts, and one that can be easily and profitably employed by students and scholars.

Cameron Northouse

Acknowledgments

———————————

My acknowledgment goes to the late Russ Kingman, founder of the Jack London Foundation and of the Jack London Research Center in Glen Ellen, California, who is the spiritual father and inspiration of all London scholarship produced since 1972. He is one of the great men of the world; he saw what needed to be done in the world of Jack London and did it tirelessly and selflessly.

There are many people at the University of Wisconsin-Oshkosh who need to be recognized for helping with this book. I would like to thank the university's faculty development board, the dean of the College of Letters and Science, Michael Zimmerman, and chairs of the English Department, Stanley Larson and Estella Lauter, for their support of this project. My appreciation goes to the Libraries and Learning Resources staff, especially Erin Czech, Nicholas Dvoracek, and Marsha Tuchscherer for their great assistance on this book. In addition, I want to thank James Russo for his fine work on this book as my student assistant.

My gratitude also goes to Earle Labor, Wilson Professor of American Literature and Director of the Jack London Research Center at Centenary College of Louisiana, to Winnie Kingman, Executive Director of the Jack London Foundation and of the Jack London Research Center in Glen Ellen, California, and to I. Milo Shepard, executor of the Jack London Estate, for their many helpful and thoughtful suggestions for this project.

And lastly, my love and appreciation to Ali, Mabel and Pie Nuernberg for their patience.

Chronology

1876   Born January 12 in San Francisco, California, and named John Griffith Chaney by his mother, Flora Wellman, who had been deserted by her common-law husband, professional astrologer/lecturer William Henry Chaney, when she informed him of her pregnancy. On September 7 Flora Wellman Chaney marries Civil War veteran and widower John London; her child is renamed John Griffith London.

1878   To escape the diphtheria epidemic that has almost claimed Jack and his stepsister, Eliza, John London moves his family across San Francisco Bay to Oakland, where he manages a grocery store and sells to local markets the produce he grows.

1881   The Londons move to a twenty-acre farm in Alameda.

1882   JL begins schooling in Alameda.

1886   After living on farms in San Mateo County and in the Livermore Valley, the Londons buy a house in Oakland. JL is introduced to the world of books in the Oakland public Library.

1891   Graduates from Cole Grammar School and begins working in Hickmott's Cannery. With $300 borrowed from his former wet nurse, "Aunt Jennie" Prentiss, he buys the sloop *Razzle-Dazzle* and becomes an oyster pirate on San Francisco Bay.

1892   Joins the California Fish Patrol in Benecia as a deputy patrolman.

1893   Serves as able-bodied seaman aboard sealing schooner *Sophia Sutherland* on eight-month (January-August) voyage to the Bering Sea via Hawaii, the Bonin islands, and Japan. Upon returning to California, works in jute mill. "Story of a Typhoon Off the Coast of Japan" wins first prize ($25.00) in contest for young writers sponsored by the *San Francisco Call*.

1894   Works as coal heaver in local electric railway power plant. In April joins Kelly's Army, the western contingent of Coxey's Army of the Unemployed, in its protest march to Washington. In late May leaves the Army in Hannibal, Missouri, to tramp on his own. Heads east after visiting Chicago World's Fair grounds. Arrested for vagrancy in Niagara; returns to California after thirty days in Erie County Penitentiary.

1895   Attends Oakland High School, where he publishes short stories and articles in *The High School Aegis*. Falls in love with Mabel Applegarth, who will become the model for Ruth Morse in *Martin Eden*.

1896   Joins the Socialist Labor Party, achieving notoriety as the "Boy Socialist" of Oakland. Leaves high school and, after intensive cramming for entrance examinations, is admitted to University of California.

1897   Leaves university because of lack of funds. After unsuccessful writing efforts, takes job in laundry at Belmont Academy (where Frank Norris had been a student twelve years before). With brother-in-law, Captain James H. Shepard, journeys to Alaska in late July to join Klondike Gold Rush. Spends winter in cabin on Split-Up Island in Yukon Territory.

1898   Suffering from what appears to be scurvy, rafts down Yukon River from Dawson to St. Michael on the Bering Sea (June 8); works his way home as coal stoker, arriving in Oakland in late July. Begins intense regimen to become a professional writer.

1899   "To the Man on Trail" published in Christmas issue of the *Overland Monthly*. "An Odyssey of the North" accepted by *Atlantic Monthly* (published in January 1900). In December meets Anna Strunsky.

1900   Meets Charmian Kittredge in March. On April 7 marries Bessie Maddern. Publishes first book, *The Son of the Wolf*.

1901   Daughter Joan born, January 15. JL commissioned by Hearst
       newspaper syndicate to cover Third National Bundes Shooting Festival,
       his first journalism assignment. Runs unsuccessfully for mayor of
       Oakland on the Socialist ticket. On December 27 George Brett,
       president of Macmillan Company, writes to solicit book-length mss. JL
       elected secretary of the Economic League (with Oakland Public Library
       Director Frederick Irons Bamford as president). Publishes *The God of
       His Fathers*.

1902   Begins friendship with poet George Sterling, model for Russ Brissenden
       in *Martin Eden*. On April 28 signs contract with Macmillan to publish
       Children of the Frost. Spends six weeks (August-September)in the East
       End of London composing *The People of the Abyss*. Second daughter,
       Bess (Becky), born, October 20. Publishes first novel, *A Daughter of
       the Snows*, as well as *Children of the Frost* and *Cruise of the Dazzler*.

1903   Falls in love with Charmian Kittredge and separates from Bessie
       London. Publishes *The Kempton-Wace Letters* (co-authored with Anna
       Strunsky), *The Call of the Wild*, and *The People of the Abyss*.

1904   Reports on Russo-Japanese War in Korea and Manchuria for Hearst
       (January-June). Divorce suit filed by Bessie London, who names Anna
       Strunsky as co-respondent. Publishes *The Faith of Men* and *The Sea-
       Wolf*.

1905   Runs (unsuccessfully) as Socialist candidate for mayor of Oakland.
       Moves to the Sonoma Valley town of Glen Ellen, where he purchases
       the 129-acre Hill Ranch, the beginning of his 1500-acre "Beauty
       Ranch." In October starts socialist lecture tour throughout the Midwest
       and East, including Harvard. Granted divorce on November 18;
       marries Charmian Kittredge the following day in Chicago. Publishes
       War of the Classes, and *Tales of the Fish Patrol*.

1906   Resumes socialist lecture tour after honeymoon in Jamaica. After
       appearances at Carnegie Hall, Yale, and the Universities of Chicago
       and North Dakota, cancels lecture tour because of illness and returns
       to Glen Ellen in mid-February. Starts building the schooner *Snark* for
       projected seven-year voyage around the world. Reports San Francisco
       earthquake for *Collier's*, April 18. Publishes *Moon-Face and Other
       Stories*, *White Fang*, and *Scorn of Women*.

1907   After repeated delays, *Snark* sets sail from Oakland on April 23, bound
        for Hawaiian Islands; arrives at Pearl Harbor on May 20. Leaves
        Hawaii on October 7, sailing to Marquesas Islands and Tahiti.
        Publishes *Before Adam*, *Love of Life and Other Stories*, and *The Road*.

1908   Returns to Oakland from Tahiti to attend to financial affairs (Mid-
        January). Resumes *Snark* voyage in April, sailing to Samoa, Fiji
        Islands, New Hebrides, Solomon Islands, and Australia. Hospitalized
        with unidentified tropical ailments in Sydney, Australia, on November
        29 and forced to abandon cruise. Publishes *The Iron Heel*.

1909   Returns to Glen Ellen, via Ecuador, Panama, and New Orleans,
        arriving home on July 24. Publishes *Martin Eden*.

1910   Hires Eliza London Shepard as ranch manager in February; expands
        Beauty Ranch to nearly 1,000 acres. Visits friends at the artists' colony
        in Carmel. Agrees to buy several story outlines from Sinclair Lewis at
        $5.00 apiece. Daughter Joy born June 19; dies June 21. JL reports
        Johnson-Jeffries fight in Reno, Nevada, July 4. Discusses plans to
        build "Wolf House" with architect Albert Farr. Publishes *Lost Face*,
        Revolution and Other Essays, *Burning Daylight*, and *Theft: A Play in
        Four Acts*.

1911   With Charmian and valet Nakata, spends summer driving four-horse
        wagon to Oregon and back. Departs on December 24 for two-month
        trip to New York. Publishes *When God Laughs and Other Stories*,
        Adventure, *The Cruise of the Snark*, and *South Sea Tales*.

1912   On March 1 sails from Baltimore with Charmian aboard the barque
        Dirigo for five-month voyage to Seattle around Cape Horn. Returns to
        Glen Ellen in early August. Signs five-year fiction contract with
        Cosmopolitan. Publishes *The House of Pride and Other Tales of
        Hawaii*, *A Son of the Sun*, and *Smoke Bellew*.

1913   Operated on for appendicitis, July 8; informed by surgeon that kidneys
        are diseased. "Wolf House" destroyed by fire, August 22. Attends
        Grauman's Imperial Theatre in San Francisco for premier of Hobart
        Bosworth's *The Sea-Wolf*, first feature-length film produced in
        America, on October 5. Publishes *The Night-Born*, *The Abysmal Brute*,
        John Barleycorn, and *The Valley of the Moon*.

1914   On January 9 travels to New York to discuss business affairs. Leaves
          with Charmian, April 16, for Vera Cruz to report on Mexican
          Revolution for *Collier's*. Following attack of acute dysentery, returns
          to Glen Ellen in June. Publishes *The Strength of the Strong* and *The
          Mutiny of the Elsinore*.

1915   After severe rheumatism attack in February, sails to Hawaii hoping to
          improve health. Returns to Glen Ellen in July and sails back to Hawaii
          in December. Publishes *The Scarlet Plague* and *The Star Rover*.

1916   On March 7 resigns from Socialist party. Returns from Hawaii in late
          July. On September 3 visits California State Fair in Sacramento, where
          he is stricken again with rheumatism. Dies November 22 of "Uraemia
          following renal colic." *The Acorn-Planter: A California Forest Play*,
          The Little Lady of the Big House, and *The Turtles of Tasman* are
          published.

Introduction

Jack London's Literary Reputation

Susan M. Nuernberg

Readers seeking to learn about Jack London encounter many wide-spread myths and highly embellished accounts of his life and work in supposedly reliable sources of information such as biographies and encyclopedias. In spite of the vigorous campaign waged during the past twenty years by the late Russ Kingman, founder of the Jack London Foundation and Research Center in Glen Ellen, California, to set the record straight,[1] the myth-making process is perpetuated, perhaps unwittingly, by readers relying on information about London that was inaccurate from the beginning.

The prevailing myths are that London was one of the most autobiographical of American writers, that he committed suicide, that he wrote obsessively about his own illegitimacy, that he was a writer of dog stories and adventure tales for adolescent boys, that he was a racist, a womanizer, an alcoholic, and a hack writer, and that he contradicted himself and was confused in his thinking about socialism, individualism, scientific materialism, and idealism.

While there is always a grain of truth in any myth, none of the above accurately describes London. Readers who reject London as a mess of contradictions should realize that he was true to his own experiences, and those who reject him as a hack writer should know that he is highly esteemed abroad as a great writer. Those who reject him for being a racist should know that he based his ideas on the most advanced scientific theories of the period. Those who reject him as an adventure-story writer for boys should know that he wrote a wide variety of prose and fiction. And those who look for parallels between his fiction and his life should look instead for his philosophy of life, that view of his own which characterizes all that he wrote and which allows us to account for his tremendous success and popularity as a writer.

Readers are always astonished to discover that, in addition to being one of the most popular and highest paid authors in America during his lifetime (1876-1916), London has been the best-selling American writer in the world. He has been translated more extensively (in over eighty languages) than any other American or English novelist of the twentieth century. Editions of his complete works abound in various major languages exclusive of English.

His largest audience resides in the world beyond the United States where his reputation as a great imaginative writer, thinker, and social critic is well established. The French literary scholar, Roger Chateauneu, identifies London as the Homer of the United States and places *The Road* along side of the *Odyssey*. Do Duc Duc, a Vietnamese writer, notes that London is called the "Gorky of the United States." Leon Trotsky, a leader in Russia's October Revolution in 1917, declared in 1937 after reading *The Iron Heel* that London "saw incomparably more clearly and farther than all the social-democratic leaders of that time taken together."[2] It is ironic that London should be regarded more highly outside of the United States than within it.

Jacqueline Tavernier-Courbin argues that "the major reason why London has been contemptuously dismissed by literary critics in America is the fact that he claimed a little too loudly that he was writing for money, thus projecting the image of a mercenary writer that did not tally with an idealized vision of a writer's vocation."[3] She is certainly correct in observing that critics have taken at face value London's open acknowledgments that he was a "vendor of brains," that he would rather dig ditches any day than write if only it paid as well, and that he devoted two hours a day to writing and ten to farming when in fact he was a serious writer committed to his craft.

While struggling to succeed as a writer, London carefully scrutinized the stories being published in magazines as well as the very structure of the publishing industry itself. His own break came about as a consequence of a shrewd decision he made early in 1899 to allow James H. Bridge, editor of the *Overland Monthly*, to publish a series of his Yukon tales featuring the Malemute Kid as protagonist for a paltry sum of $7.50 each.[4] The *Overland* was a San Francisco-based magazine that focused primarily on California subjects and authors. Under its original editorship of Charles Warren Stoddard, Ina Coolbrith, and Bret Harte it had been the prestigious magazine of the Far West. After its revival in 1883, however, it was unable to pay its authors competitive rates because it lacked the large advertising revenues of a mass circulation magazine like *McClure's* and deep subscriptions to draw upon as did the finest quality literary magazines, namely *Atlantic Monthly* and *Harper's*.

In a letter of February 28, 1899, to his friend Mabel Applegarth, London explained his understanding of the situation:

> The *Overland* prints forty pages of advertisements at thirty dollars per page, while *McClure's* prints one hundred pages at three hundred dollars per page; yet printing plates, paper, mail service, etc. cost just as much for the *Overland*. The only thing the *Overland* could scale down was the writers, and these it had to.[5]

In lieu of competitive compensation, Bridge offered London a prominent place in the pages of the *Overland* with a guarantee that newspapers and reviews would "puff" him and put his name before the public. London accepted this offer explaining in the same letter to Mabel Applegarth, "You can readily see how valuable this would be—putting future employment into my hands from publications which could afford to pay well." This is precisely what happened a short six months later. London submitted one of his Malemute Kid stories, "An Odyssey of the North," to the *Atlantic* in June of 1899 and received $120 for it instead of the customary $7.50 from the *Overland*. Furthermore, a number of magazine editors became interested in London's writing after seeing this story in the January 1900 issue of *Atlantic* including Samuel S. McClure, who asked to be given first glance at whatever London wrote. McClure's publishing house, McClure, Phillips & Co., subsidized the writing of London's first novel, *A Daughter of the Snows*, by paying an advance against royalties of $125 per month. Ultimately, McClure rejected the novel, and London eventually worked off his debt to McClure, Phillips & Co. by sending them material for publication in *McClure's*.

The advertising revolution wreaked havoc upon the makers of editorial policy in the United States at the turn of the century. In the late 1890s when London was seeking publishers for his early short stories, a number of cheap monthlies including *McClure's*, *Cosmopolitan*, and *Munsey's* already had discovered the formula for mass circulation by reducing prices below costs of production and recouping themselves through advertising revenue. The formula also demanded that the contents be slanted to reflect the interests and problems of the average reader. Frank Munsey estimated that the magazine-buying public tripled from approximately 250,000 to 750,000 readers between 1893 and 1899 as a result of the introduction of the 10-cent magazine. A high circulation justified high advertising rates and this in turn led to high advertising revenue, making it possible to sell a magazine, like a newspaper, for less than its cost of production. While many magazines such as the *Saturday Evening Post* insisted on editorial independence, many others like *McClure's* relied on the principle of "minimum offense." This tended to make the large-circulation magazine an exploiter rather than a discoverer of fresh talent or new ideas.

London thoroughly understood this. He explained in the *Writer*, a Boston-based monthly magazine that gave help to beginning authors, that "the magazine editor must consult first and always the advertisers and the reading public; he must obey the mandates of the business department, and . . . [not] the promptings of his heart. Trade is trade."[6] One of the most perplexing questions dogging the critical response to London's work is: Did he slant the contents of his work to reflect the interests and problems of the average reader so as to give a minimum of offense or did he embrace the ideas and attitudes expressed in his writing?

London refused to present to the public an image of himself as being above financial reward for his work because he was intellectually honest. He firmly believed that his strength had always come from being candid and from being true to himself. For him intellectual honesty meant knowing as much as possible of life and being true to it all. It meant that he had to develop a big view, not a limited one, but one big enough to let life reveal itself to him. It was up to London to adjust his philosophy to accommodate life, rather than to reject those aspects of life that didn't fit into a particular view. He was constantly educating himself, and his views evolved in response to his experiences. He was not afraid to appear contradictory because he was being true to an evolving self, a dynamic self. Knowledge was a quest for him; he had no use for the received opinions, unquestioned and unexamined ideas of the world such as Ruth Morse in *Martin Eden* embraces. London meant what he said, and readers who fail to understand his perspective find him confusing.

London always remained true to the experiences that made him. After completing eighth grade at age fourteen in 1890, he began supporting himself as a manual laborer. He worked at a canning factory, as an oyster pirate in the San Francisco Bay, and then as an able-bodied seaman on a sealing-ship. He found little work during the 1893 depression, and in 1894 he "beat" his way east on freight trains. All across the country London "battered on the drag" and "slammed back gates" or "shivered" in box cars and city parks with homeless people who told him their life stories. He learned from them that hard physical labor had sapped their strength and left them in a "shambles" at the "bottom of the Social Pit." When no longer able to work, due to injury, illness, or old age, they had been replaced by younger and stronger men eager for work. As London listened to their stories, a terror seized him. He saw in his mind's eye that he too would end up at the bottom of the Social Pit when his strength ran out. He resolved to forgo any more "hard work" and to earn his living by writing.

He returned to Oakland, joined the American section of the Socialist Labor Party, and studied hard. Without having graduated from high school, he passed the entrance exams for the University of California at Berkeley but left after one semester to join the Klondike gold rush to the Yukon Territory of Canada where he learned an awful lot of information for future use in the writing game. It was only after his return to Oakland in the summer of 1898 that he began to write on a full-time basis. His daughter Joan notes his fondness for saying that "It was in the Klondike that I found myself. There nobody talks. Everybody thinks. You get your perspective. I got mine."[7] By 1916, London had published forty-three books including nineteen novels, sixteen volumes of collected stories, five volumes of sociological essays and autobiographical sketches, and three plays. Eight additional volumes appeared posthumously between 1917 and 1963.

When London first approached his editor at Macmillan, George P. Brett, about publishing his tramp essays in book form as *The Road*, he was told to deal with more uplifting subjects than the life of the tramp.[8] London replied that his strength had always come from being candid and from being true to himself, and that he saw *The Road* as no exception to the rule. He wrote to Brett: "I have always insisted that the cardinal literary virtue is sincerity, and I have striven to live up to this belief."[9] London was intellectually honest. He was not just interested in advancing his own career as a writer, he wanted to express life as he had experienced it and encountered those who found it shameful. He stood behind *The Road* and was not ashamed to acknowledge what he had experienced.

London also went out of his way to demystify the process through which a writer achieved distinction, flatly denying that genius, talent, or inspiration were required. Rather, as he wrote in 1899, it took an individual "philosophy of life," or a view of one's own, to make the world want to sit up and listen to what a writer has to say. He went on to explain:

> And it must be understood that such a working philosophy enables the writer to put not only himself into his work, but to put that which is not himself but which is viewed and weighted by himself. Of none is this more true than of that triumvirate of intellectual giants—Shakespeare, Goethe, Balzac. Each was himself, and so much so, that there is no point of comparison.[10]

Although the French writer Chateauneu places London in the company of great artists including Shakespeare, Chekhov, and Van Gogh among others, American readers tend not to go this far, generally limiting their comparisons of London to Kipling. London, like the other intellectual "giants," wrote about life as he saw it. He passionately wanted to see life, all of it. He strove to know life inside and out, not just some pretty little corner of it. He wanted to understand how it all worked together, how everything was related. He was not afraid of what he would find. He thought each of his stories was a piece of life and that they were true to life because he had seen things like them himself. Many readers are like Sitka Charley in "The Sun-Dog Trail" who "saw life in pictures, felt life in pictures, generalized life in pictures; and yet he did not understand pictures when seen through other men's eyes and expressed by those men with color and line upon canvas." To Sitka Charley, London's narrator explains, "'Pictures are bits of life. . . . We paint life as we see it.'"[11] In the narrator's opinion, pictures and stories are true to life in that they are without beginning and without end. They end in understanding only when they are recognized as pieces of life.

The critical response to Jack London is characterized by a lack of consensus over how to interpret the meaning as well as the theme of London's works. It appears that many readers have failed to perceive London's point of view just as Mrs. Eppingwell failed to catch Freda's in "The Scorn of Women" because "there are some points of view which cannot be gained save through much travail and personal crucifixion. . . ."[12] Presumably, London came closer to universality in his philosophy of life than did those of his critics who had not experienced the harshness of poverty, the brutality of exploitation, or the degradation of illegitimacy encountered by the young London.

Much of the critical debate over *The Call of the Wild* centers around interpretations of the dog, Buck. Does he represent human behavior or London's theories of animal behavior? In London's philosophy, all species must live under the same law of life, and all are subject to the same processes of evolution. In his dog stories, London exploited the idea that differences in animals and humans are merely a matter of degree and not of kind. Buck may be capable of rudimentary reason, but his real advantage over the human dwellers of modern civilization is the free reign he gives his instincts. Early reviewers wrote that *The Call of the Wild* signifies the appeal (and in Buck's case, the triumph) of barbarian life over civilized life. They found it a sympathetic yet unsentimental story of a dog. The range of themes discovered in it include toil and suffering, the spiritual and material conflict that rages between civilization and savagery with the savage being within us, an allegory in which people are simply the fatalistic forces in society representing the force of dishonesty, of the club, of selfishness, pettiness, cruelty, kindness, love and grief. Others interpreted it not as allegory but as a study of animal nature.

Discussions of *The Sea-Wolf* tend to focus on the Nietzschean notion that all human behavior could be reduced to a single principle, the will to power. Whether London meant to attack the popular misconception of Nietzsche's idea of the superman as a man of strength, virility and genius or to create in Wolf Larsen an example of the superman as anti-social, aloof, and doomed has been the subject of much debate. In a letter of November 5, 1915, to Mary Austin, London wrote, "Lots of people read *The Sea-Wolf*, no one discovered that it was an attack upon the superman philosophy."[13] Some early reviewers saw this work as a tale about the initiation of an effete scion of civilization into manhood. In this view, Larsen is classified as a man absolutely devoid of moral sense and human sympathy, or as a reversion to the primordial type of the stone age and yet paradoxically possessed of a cultured mind with an appreciation of Spencer and Huxley. Apparently not all early reviewers were well enough acquainted with contemporary philosophy to accurately evaluate works reflecting ideas such as determinism, evolution, and naturalism even though they bandied these terms about in their reviews. Others dismissed *The Sea-Wolf* as a good tale of life on the high seas, as a conflict of man with the elements. Many found *The Sea-Wolf* full of excessive brutality like other stories of London's. One of the more sophisticated early reviews, the *Argonaut*, saw

Sea-Wolf as a subtle, brilliant satire of Nietzsche's Superior Man declaring that Larsen embodies Nietzsche's ideas and is opposed by exponents of "slave morals" in persons of Van Weyden, Thomas Mugridge, and Maud Brewster. According to this view, London is illustrating a theory; the hero of the book is Larsen, not Van Weyden; and the appeal of the book is the deep, true-running instinct to side with the strong man.

London's political novel *The Iron Heel* has been endlessly debated. Trotsky praised the "audacity" and "independence" of the book's historical foresight, and saw the novel as London's passionate effort to shake those who were lulled by routine to see what approached. London is, according to this view, bringing the tendencies rooted in capitalism—of oppression, cruelty, bestiality, betrayal to their extreme expression—not lusting in violence as others imagined. Trotsky said that London had imagined the ominous perspective of the alliance between finance capital and labor aristocracy more fully than the revolutionary Marxists like Lenin and Rosa Luxemburg. He also said London is a far-sighted optimist, not a pessimist, and that he manifests remarkable freedom from reformistic and pacifist illusions. In London's picture of the future there remains no trace of democracy and peaceful progress. It is precisely the picture of fascism. In 1907 London already foresaw and described a fascist regime as the inevitable result of the defeat of the proletarian revolution. By contrast other reviewers denied that the country could come to such an era of bloodshed and they insisted that problems could be peacefully settled. Or they belittled the work by calling Everhard a tiresome windbag and by accusing London of having a bloodthirsty imagination.

How did London react when his efforts missed fire? He told Mary Austin that he did not worry about it: "I go ahead content to be admired for my red-blood brutality and for a number of other nice little things like that which are not true of my work at all."[14] The lack of consensus suggests that London put himself into his work along with his views and opinions of that which was not himself, like other great writers whose works continue to intrigue readers around the world.

The critical response to London throughout the twentieth century in America has relied too heavily on biographical interpretation which has tended to exaggerate the consequences of London's alleged preoccupation with his illegitimacy. London's discovery at age twenty-one that he most likely was the spurned son of William H. Chaney, an astrologer, has generally been seen as the most traumatic factor in the development of his personality and his artistic consciousness. This concept was set forth in Irving Stone's biographical novel, *Sailor on Horseback* (1938), and subsequently restated with varying degrees of emphasis by Richard O'Connor ("underneath the picaroon was a man tormented by the act of his illegitimate birth"), Kenneth Lynn ("not all the money or all the whiskey in the world could gainsay the shameful fact of his illegitimacy"), Kevin Starr (who argues that London's "blatant, schizoid Anglo-Saxonism compensated for the meanness of his own origins"), E. L. Doctorow (who writes of Buck's decivilization to the savage wolfhood of his ancestors that, "It is perhaps [London's] fatherless life of bitter self-reliance in late-nineteenth-century America that he transmutes [in *The Call of the Wild*]"), and by Andrew Sinclair who claimed that London "could hardly admit to himself the blow of finding out that nobody would own up to fathering him. . . . He could feel no gratitude in the face of such a denial by his presumed father, such a false start from his true mother." In Sinclair's mind, this caused London to reject "their worlds of spiritualism and astrology, mysticism, and nonsense," and to embrace "positivism and rationalism" with the result that London became "more proud and isolated than ever, absolutely determined to impose his identity on an indifferent world."[15]

In fact by the time he was twenty-one years old, London had already discovered Karl Marx, joined the American section of the Socialist Labor Party (in April of 1896) and developed a class consciousness. Through his socialist acquaintances and his own life experiences London had learned that working people could not improve conditions through individual efforts nor as individuals could they combat the system which exploits them. London rejected the "nonsense" of spiritualism, astrology and mysticism, not because nobody would own up to fathering him, but because the philosophy of scientific materialism made more sense to him. Regarding the question of London's illegitimacy, James Lundquist sounded a sane note when he commented: "that London went through inner tortures because of what he learned about William H. Chaney cannot be doubted; that he got over them in fairly good shape has not been stressed enough."[16]

London, as we all know, was not born into the cultured class that produced some of the most highly esteemed writers of his age such as Henry James and Edith Wharton. There is a stigma attached to Jack London within American literary circles because he lacks a middle-class background and a conventional education, and because he was an outspoken Socialist who dared to criticize bourgeois society. Although London's own life was his best adventure story, the tendency to read London's works as autobiography has helped to keep London's status marginal within the canon of American letters because it serves, among other things, to constantly remind readers of London's questionable origins, his seedy past, his lack of formal education, his racist ideas and his contradictory life-style. And if few biographies of London have been translated into foreign languages, even less foreign criticism has been translated into English, leaving American readers largely unaware of his reputation abroad.

In contrast to the excessive reliance on quasi-autobiography to explain London's fiction within American literary circles, the information about London's life available to foreign readers is limited to those few biographies, including Stone's *Sailor on Horseback* and Kingman's *Pictorial Life of Jack London*, that have been translated into other languages. As a result, foreign critics tend to de-emphasize the autobiographical aspect of London's work and to place a higher value on his purely literary accomplishments than American critics have.

We can explain the discrepancy between London's international reputation and the low status generally accorded him at home by recalling that America's literary intelligentsia share neither a working-class perspective nor a commitment to socialist humanism which is a major tradition in Europe predating Karl Marx and Jack London. Moreover, America lacks a public sector as found in Europe that would support art founded in this tradition. That sector is made up of literary professionals (teachers, professors, writers, editors and book reviewers) and a class of rich, educated individuals who have traditionally sought social recognition not only through wealth but through the acquisition of literature and art. Given the high cultural value traditionally placed within certain sectors of European society on art and literature, it is possible to understand why London's greatest tribute comes to him from outside of the United States.

London's place in the history of American letters has yet to be established. There may be some justification for this given that his works fit neatly into no traditional literary category and that he avowedly wrote only for money. Nevertheless, if a writer continues to give satisfaction to large numbers of people for a long enough period, it becomes impossible for critics to avoid him. London lived during a period of great social, political, industrial, and scientific change, and he recorded the contradictions of life during those times with intellectual honesty. His works are a record of his times and worthy of serious consideration.

This collection of criticism on Jack London is the first to appear in over a decade and unlike earlier collections of essays[17] on the works of London, this volume is designed specifically to document London's critical reception in the United States from an historical perspective. The individual works that serve as foci for these critical selections represent milestones in London's career as a writer.

"To Build a Fire" is London's most widely read and often-anthologized short story. Many readers continue to think of London as a writer of thrilling adventure stories for boys although he was never satisfied to write uplifting stories with happy endings designed to please the juvenile reader of periodicals such as *Youth's Companion* even if they did pay their authors well. Published in Boston with a circulation of more than half a million, *Youth's Companion* was typically wholesome in content, intending to "warn against the ways of transgression" and to encourage "virtue and piety." On December 15, 1901, London submitted a story fitting this description to *Youth's Companion* and was paid $50 for it. This story, "To Build a Fire," was later rewritten by London to his own satisfaction and sold to *Century Magazine* for $400. This later version of "To Build a Fire," which has neither an uplifting moral nor a happy ending, is now considered by most critics to be a masterpiece of short American fiction. London initially gained fame for his Klondike tales which, like "To

Build a Fire," demonstrate his strong narration, fresh fictional subject, and ability to create atmosphere. Analyses of this story have tended to focus on the differences between the various versions of the story, especially major differences such as the dog and the man's death, on the Darwinian theme of the primitive struggle for survival, and on elements of naturalism in the tale.

A Daughter of the Snows (1902), because it is London's first novel, figures prominently in any study of the development of London's craftsmanship, style, and ideas. London himself regarded the novel as a failure because it lacked unity. Two aspects of this novel that critics have routinely faulted are its blatant Anglo-Saxon chauvinism and its improbable heroine. In a seminal review of the novel, Julian Hawthorne called the book an indictment of civilization itself. Hawthorne saw promise in London because he was a writer with hopes of reconstructing society and mankind. Hawthorne identifies the theme of the book as the attempt to draw a woman unhampered by the absurdities of modern conventions, with courage to act on her own convictions. However, he also noted that London was unaware that a thing which might actually occur in real life is not necessarily possible in fiction.

The Call of the Wild (1903) and *The Sea-Wolf* (1904) are London's two best sellers[18] which have sold millions of copies and are still widely read and discussed. *The Call of the Wild* was serialized in the *Saturday Evening Post* between June 20 and July 18, 1903, and published in book form by Macmillan in July of 1903. It was written following the summer of 1902 at which time London lived in the underworld of England's worst slum, the East End of London, where he researched and wrote *The People of the Abyss* (1903). London was so disgusted by the chronic conditions of misery, starvation, suffering, and the perpetual lack of shelter that he found even during a period of prosperity in England, that he declared, "If this is the best that civilization can do for the human, then give us howling and naked savagery."[19] Upon his return to the United States, London wrote *The Call of the Wild* in a short six weeks.

The Sea-Wolf, long recognized by many as one of the world's great sea novels, was serialized in the *Century Magazine* between January and November of 1904, and published in book form by Macmillan in October of 1904. London wrote much of this novel aboard his thirty-foot sloop, the *Spray*, while sailing up and down the San Francisco Bay and the Sacramento Delta. During the writing of this book, London left his wife, Bess, for Charmian Kittredge, whom he married in 1905. Discussions of this book invariably focus on the appearance of Maud Brewster half way through the book which may or may not correspond to changes in London's own life.

The Iron Heel was the *1984* of its day, and like Orwell's book, it is a dystopia. The difference is that while *1984* begins and ends with the dictatorship of "Big Brother," *The Iron Heel* reflects London's faith in the eventual triumph of the "Brotherhood of Man." Published by Macmillan in February of 1908,

The Iron Heel was embraced by some American socialists but rejected by others because of its refusal to portray the achievement of socialism as imminent.

The Valley of the Moon, considered by some to be America's first proletarian novel, reflects a working-class point of view and advocates a life style based on a return to nature and a life on "the road" not unlike that celebrated by great American writers from Walt Whitman to Jack Kerouac. Serialized in *Cosmopolitan* between April and December of 1913, and published in book form by Macmillan in October of 1913, *The Valley of the Moon* is a California novel and a perfect example of London's later writings. The title refers to Sonoma County, California, which is the site of London's 1400-acre Beauty Ranch where he lived, wrote, and farmed from 1905 until his death in 1916. The novel recounts the 1350 mile four-horse wagon trip to Oregon which Jack and Charmian made in 1911, and it gives a fictional account of the Carmel colony of artists of which London was a member. London felt a desire to live simply and close to nature and he believed that all people eventually wanted to return to the soil.

In addition, this collection contains a selection of general criticism in section seven representing a variety of critical approaches used to analyze literature in general and London's fiction in particular such as the psychological analysis of London's "The Red One" by the late James I. Kirsch who studied and was associated with Carl G. Jung from 1929 until Jung's death in 1961, and who founded the C. G. Jung Institute of Los Angeles.

Stephen Conlon's essay, "Jack London and the Working Class," focuses on *The People of the Abyss*, the sociological study London wrote of his stay in the East End slum of London, England. London considered that he had left more of himself in this book than in any of his others. Conlon sees it as a book about the working class written by a person who saw himself coming from that class.

Jacqueline Tavernier-Courbin's essay on humor in Jack London's fiction identifies elements of humor in many of London's stories. Tavernier-Courbin is the editor of *Thalia: Studies in Literary Humor,* which devoted a special issue to Jack London in 1992.

Roger Chateauneu's essay, "From the Abyss to the Summit," translated from French and appearing here for the first time in English, is the lead article in a special issue of *Europe* devoted to Jack London in celebration of America's bicentennial as well as the centennial of London's birth in 1976. It offers readers a glimpse of the reputation London enjoys abroad.

Margaret Guilford-Kardell reconstructs diary notes written by her uncle, Finn Frolich, a sculptor and a good friend of London's, in her article "Sea Dog and Sea Wolf at Play in the Valley of the Moon." It captures the spirit and character of London from an insider's viewpoint and seems to bring London to life for the present-day reader.

Section eight contains a selected reading list on London and a new bibliography of material in English on Jack London from 1981-1992 which updates the bibliography in Tavernier-Courbin's *Critical Essays*.

The brand-new essays appearing here for the first time include "Why the Man Dies in 'To Build a Fire'" by George Adams, a professor of English at the University of Wisconsin at Whitewater, my essay on "Jack London's Concept of New Womanhood" in *A Daughter of the Snows*," and "Call Forwarding" on *The Call of the Wild* by Dan Dyer, a middle-school English teacher in Aurora, Ohio. Two of the new essays in this collection have been contributed by international London scholars including "Looking Forward/Looking Backward: Romance and Utopia in *The Iron Heel*" by Christopher Gair, an instructor of American Literature at the College of St. Mark and St. John in Plymouth, England, and "*The Valley of the Moon*: A Reassessment" by Laurent Dauphin, a doctoral candidate at the Sorbonne in Paris. Their inclusion attests to the fact that foreign writers continue to produce some of the best criticism of London's work.

This anthology is designed to provide readers with a useful text for the study of London that brings together in one place new essays, an updated bibliography, a selected reading list, many hard-to-obtain early reviews, and key critical articles documenting the literary response to Jack London. The reviews and critical essays collected in this volume reveal much about the tastes of the period and indicate ways in which critical perceptions of London's work have changed during the twentieth century. Few contemporary readers commented, for example, on London's views of racial evolution which were the dominant views of that period. In most cases, London's critics shared his views of Anglo-Saxon racial superiority although these views are now thought by many to be nothing short of embarrassing. In like manner, many early readers claimed that London was inept at portraying believable female characters whereas most recent critics find him somewhat ahead of his time in portraying the new woman. When viewed within their proper context, critical assessments of London's ideas and accomplishments provide insights not only into London's literary merit, but into the intellectual milieu of late nineteenth and early twentieth century American culture as well. Although London continues to be widely read within the United States and abroad, his literary reputation is still subject to lively debate especially in academic circles.

The selections collected here indicate a tremendous revival of interest in London as a writer and a thinker during the past two decades. Although the momentum of this movement appears to be in full swing, it is impossible to determine at this time whether or not it will result in London's being accorded the status a writer like Herman Melville now enjoys in the canon of American literature. It is likely that London will continue to be the subject of serious scholarly and critical inquiries into American culture at the beginning of the twentieth century because his own life and works so fully express the contradictions and experience of what it meant to be an American at that pivotal time.

NOTES

[1] See Russ Kingman's *A Pictorial Life of Jack London* (Glen Ellen, CA: Jack London Research Center, 1979) and *Jack London: A Definitive Chronology* (Middletown, CA: David Rejl, 1992) for dependable and accurate information on the life of Jack London.

[2] Quotations are taken from the essays of these writers included in this anthology.

[3] "Jack London: A Professional," *Critical Essays on Jack London*, ed. Jacqueline Tavernier-Courbin (Boston: G. K. Hall, 1983), 2. See also Earle Labor's earlier essay on this subject in his *Jack London* (New York: Twayne, 1974), 83-89.

[4] These stories were collected and published by Houghton Mifflin in 1900 as *The Son of the Wolf*, London's first book.

[5] *The Letters of Jack London*, 3 vols., ed. Earle Labor, Robert C. Leitz, III, and I. Milo Shepard (Stanford: Stanford UP, 1988), 51.

[6] "The Question of a Name" [*The Writer*, December, 1900], reprinted in *Jack London: No Mentor But Myself*, ed. Dale L. Walker (Port Washington, NY: Kennikat Press, 1979), 19.

[7] Joan London, *Jack London and His Times* (New York: Doubleday, 1939; reprinted Seattle: U of Washington P, 1968), 146.

[8] For further information on London's tramp writings, see *Jack London on the Road*, ed. Richard W. Etulain (Logan: Utah State UP, 1979), 21.

[9] Letter to George P. Brett dated March 7, 1907, in *The Letters of Jack London*, 675.

[10] "On The Writer's Philosophy of Life" [*The Editor*, October, 1899], reprinted in *Jack London: No Mentor But Myself*, 7.

[11] Jack London, "The Sun-Dog Trail" (1905), *The Complete Short Stories of Jack London*. 3 vols., ed. Earle Labor, Robert C. Leitz, III, and I. Milo Shepard (Stanford: Stanford UP, 1993), II, 971.

[12] *The Complete Short Stories of Jack London*, I, 418.

[13] *The Letters of Jack London*, III, 1513.

[14] *The Letters of Jack London*, III, 1514.

[15] Richard O'Connor, *Jack London: A Biography* (Boston: Little, Brown, 1964), 158; Kenneth Lynn, *The Dream of Success* (Boston: Little, Brown, 1955), 79; Kevin Starr, *Americans and the California Dream 1850-1915* (New York: Oxford UP, 1973), 213; E. L. Doctorow, "Introduction," *The Call of the Wild* by Jack London (New York: Vintage Books/The Library of America, 1990), xvii-xviii; Andrew Sinclair, *Jack: A Biography of Jack London* (New York: Harper & Row, 1977), 37, 16.

[16] James Lundquist, *Jack London: Adventures, Ideas, and Fiction* (New York: Ungar Publishing, 1987), 6.

[17] See *Critical Essays on Jack London*, ed. Jacqueline Tavernier-Courbin (Boston: G. K. Hall, 1983); *Twentieth Century Literary Criticism*, ed. Dennis Poupard (Detroit: Gale Research Co., 1983); *Jack London: Essays in Criticism*, ed. Ray Wilson Ownbey (Santa Barbara: Peregrine Smith, 1978).

[18] See Joan London's new Introduction to her *Jack London and His Times* (New York: Doubleday, 1939; reprinted Seattle: U of Washington P, 1968), xii.

[19] Jack London, *The People of the Abyss* (New York: Macmillan, 1903), 115.

Feb. 5/02.

Dear Mr. Revision Editor: —

In reply to questions will state (1) — At 95 ℉, Vincent will match from inside pocket. It does not matter what he does with matches during first several attempts to build fire — not until he leaves that place and starts along the trail. Then insert, page 6, after "The frost had beaten him. His hands were worthless.", the following: "But he had the foresight to drop the bunch of matches into his wide-mouthed outside pocket. ~~Following this was the regular test.~~ Then, in despair, he slipped on his mittens and started to run up the trail," etc. etc.

(11) Take my word for it, that a man simply cannot build a fire with heavy Klondike mittens on his hands. I have seen

hundreds of such fires built in cold weather, and I never even saw a man attempt to build one fire with mittened hands. It is impossible. I have built a fire at 74° below zero, and I did it with my naked hands.

But the point with Vincent is that his wet feet are freezing. Had he not wet his feet, he could have simply kept right on traveling and never exposed his hands at all. But traveling or not, his feet _were_ freezing all the time.

It is an old Alaskan ~~Klondike~~ tragedy, this fire-building. I huy have traced a man, from his first careful attempts at a fire to his last wild & feeble attempt, & then found his stiff body — and this had been done more than ~~once~~.

You see, the time element must be considered. At such low temperature

3.

flesh freezes quickly. The fire also must be built quickly.

Why, I ran two hundred feet and back again, through the dead calm air at sixty-five below, and nipped my ear (exposed) so badly that it kept me awake that night, later turned black & peeled off all the skin.

In this connection, however, at top of page 5, after "waited the match," you might insert: "It is impossible to build a fire with heavy Alaskan mittens on one's hands; so I must bared size, gathered a sufficient number of twigs, and kindling the same, etc."

I do not know what kind of mittens you have in the East. Up North they are of fairly thick, pretty thick, mooseide (native-tanned) and they are warmly lined with flannel. It is impossible to strike a sulphur match & cherish the

xxxix

4.

slow-growing flame thereof with such mittens on one's hands. To attempted it with a punch would be to cause a healthy conflagration, wide-spread burns & much smoke —— three things which would effectually just a quietus on the fire.

I hope I have explained.

By the way. The "Companion," has always been prompt in paying. "To Build a Fire," was sent about the middle of December. I now learn from you that the story is already in make-up. This leads me to fear that check for same has probably gone astray, as I have received no word from the Corresponding Editor. Will you please ask him to look into the matter? Also, last of December, I sent "Companion," another story; "By the Slide. As with the other, I have had printed notice of its safe arrival, but nothing more.

Very truly yours,
Jack London.

To Build a Fire

Letter to "Mr. Revision Editor" at *Youth's Companion*

Jack London
56 Bayo Vista Avenue
Oakland, Calif.
Feb. 5/02.

Dear Mr. Revision Editor:

In reply to questions will state (I)—At go off, Vincent took matches from inside pocket. It does not matter what he does with matches during first several attempts to build fire—not until he leaves that place and starts along the trail. Then insert, page 6, after "The frost had beaten him. His hands were worthless.", the following: "But he had the foresight to drop the bunch of matches into his wide-mouthed outside pocket. There, in dispair, he slipped on his mittens and started to run up the trail," etc. etc.

(II) Take my word for it, that a man simply cannot build a fire with heavy Klondike mittens on his hands. I have seen hundreds of such fires built in cold weather, and I never even saw a man attempt to build one fire with mittened hands. It is impossible. I have built a fire at 74° below zero, and I did it with my naked hands.

But the point with Vincent is that his wet feet are freezing. Had he not wet his feet, he could have simply kept right on traveling and never exposed his hands at all. But traveling or not, his feet *were* freezing all the time.

It is an old Alaskan tragedy, this fire-building. They have traced a man, from his first careful attempt at a fire to his last wild & feeble attempt, & then found his stiff body—and this has been done more than once.

You see, the time element must be considered. At such low temperature flesh freezes quickly. The fire also must be built quickly.

Why, I ran two hundred feet and back again, through the dead calm air at sixty-five below, and nipped my ear (exposed) so badly that it kept me awake that night, later turned black & peeled off all the skin.

In this connection, however, at the top of page 5, after "waited the match," you might insert: "It is impossible to build a fire with heavy Alaskan mittens on one's hands; so Vincent bared his, gathered a sufficient number of twigs, and knocking the snow, etc."

I do not know what kind of mittens you have in the East. Up north they are of fairly thick, pretty thick, moosehide (native-tanned) and they are warmly lined with flannel. It is impossible to strike a sulphur match & cherish the slow-growing flame therof with such mittens on one's hands. To [have] attempted it with a bunch would be to cause a healthy conflagration, wide-spread burns & much smoke—three things which would effectually put a quietus on the fire.

I hope I have explained.

By the way. The *Companion* has always been prompt in paying. "To Build a Fire," was sent about the middle of December. I now learn from you that the story is already in make-up. This leads me to fear that check for same has probably gone astray, as I have received no word from the Corresponding Editor. Will you please ask him to look into the matter? Also, last of December, I sent *Companion*, another story: "Up the Slide.["] As with the other, I have had printed notice of its safe arrival, but nothing more.

Very truly yours,

Jack London

The Theme of Jack London's "To Build a Fire"

Clell Peterson

Judged simply by the number of times it has been selected by the editors of anthologies, "To Build a Fire" is Jack London's most popular and presumably his best short story. What merit editors find in it, I can only speculate; but I imagine that it is admired as a fine example of a suspenseful story with a strong theme presented in vivid, realistic detail. All this, of course, it is; and it is interesting to recall in this connection that, aside from the death of the protagonist, the story treats of precisely the range of experience that London himself had had in the northland. He too, in his relations with cold, dogs, fires, and all the rest of the exotic *mise en scene*, had never become more than a *chechaquo*; and writing within that narrow range of experience, he recreated a moment of truth about the Yukon more clearly and credibly than anywhere else in his fiction.

Valid as it is, however, an interpretation which halts at the careful contrivance of suspense, a strong theme—by which is meant, I suppose, the primitive struggle for survival—and precise, realistic details cannot explain the appeal of the story, which, like all serious fiction, hints at a depth and richness of meaning below the level of literal narration. In this paper I wish to discuss this "depth and richness of meaning," or theme, particularly in terms of the fable and the characters. To put the discussion into context, let me summarize the story even if its great popularity guarantees that most readers are familiar with it.

A man, whose name is not given, is traveling alone, except for an almost wild dog as companion, in the far north in the dead of winter. Although aware of the dangers of the journey, the man is confident. He is alert and careful; but even so he accidentally breaks through the surface of a frozen stream and gets his feet wet. When he fails in his attempts to build a fire to dry himself, he dies. His wolf-dog companion leaves the body to seek food and warmth with the dead man's companions waiting in camp.

The fable unfolds as a journey taken in the face of serious danger in which the conflicts between man and nature and between man and dog provide the drama. But I wish to consider here the journey itself, presented in the first sentence of the story in a passage that is both rhetorically impressive and charged with implication:

> Day had broken cold and gray, exceedingly cold and gray, when the man turned aside from the main Yukon trail and climbed the high earth-bank, where a dim and little-travelled trail led eastward through the fat spruce timberland.

These details, admirably foreshadowing the events of the story, tell how a man leaves the well-trodden path of the familiar world of men to follow a faint and difficult trail into a world of mysterious ("dim and little-travelled") but significant ("fat spruce timberland") experience. The very rhythms of the passage reinforce the meaning. The shifts from the initial iambic rhythm to anapestic and back to iambic follow the movement of the passage from the scene itself ("Day had broken . . .") to the first action ("turned aside") and to the second ("climbed the high earth-bank"). The double stress upon "earth-bank" emphasizes the boundary between the realms of familiar and unfamiliar.

The journey thus brilliantly announced is, as I have implied, more than a literal journey, although the hard, realistic surface of the narrative may obscure what ought to be obvious. The nameless man (his anonymity is significant) is a modern Everyman who, if not precisely summoned, nevertheless takes a pilgrimage the end of which "he in no wise may escape." At the realistic level, the direction of the journey is toward camp and safety, a return to the comfortable, sensual world of the known and familiar, but it becomes a journey into the unknown with the possibility of illumination as well as the risk of disaster. Hence another analogue, what Maud Bodkin, after Jung, has termed the archetypal theme of rebirth, suggests itself.

For Miss Bodkin, the rebirth theme consists of a double movement—downward toward disintegration and death and upward toward redintegration and life, but life greatly enriched. Jung terms this latter change "subjective transformation" and the result the "enlargement of personality." The pattern is similiar to what Toynbee calls "withdrawal and return." "The Rime of the Ancient Mariner" is a rich and exciting work employing this theme, whether formulated in Jung's or Toynbee's terms; but the theme is a common one in fiction, including London's. "The Story of Jees Uck" (1902), an obvious instance, tells of Neil Bonner, a spoiled young man who is forced by his father to leave the civilization that has corrupted him and to live in the northern wilderness. There he has experiences, including a liaison with Jees Uck, a native girl, which give him new insights and values. These he takes back to civilization where he becomes a prominent member of his society.

"To Build a Fire" is of this general type. The central character—like Neil Bonner and the Ancient Mariner—has a misconception that must be changed, for living in such ignorance is a kind of death. At the beginning of the story we are told "That there should be anything more to it than that [cold as a fact requiring certain simple precautions] was a thought that never entered his head." Extreme cold is a metaphor for a whole range of experiences beyond the man's awareness, and the point of the story is not that the man freezes to death but that he has been confronted with the inadequacy of his conception of the nature of things.

Neither the analogue of Everyman nor of the archetypal rebirth quite fits, however. The man, unlike Everyman, undergoes no redemption; nor, like Neil Bonner and the Ancient Mariner, does he return to civilization changed by the intensity and significance of his experience. He does not even have a moment of illumination as he dies. He comes nearest to insight when dying, he thinks, "When he got back to the States he could tell the folks what real cold was." The inadequacy of the vision is indicative; had he been capable of truly comprehending his experience, London implies, he might not have died. Inexact as the analogues are, however, they define the kind of story "To Build a Fire" is and show that its significance lies in something profound and universal in the fable.

Before turning to a discussion of the characters, I must call attention to several details of the setting that seem to me symbolic. The "dark hairline" of the main trail and the "pure snow" on the broad frozen Yukon suggest the narrow limits of the man's rational world compared with the universe beyond his knowledge and comprehension. The whiteness is not the whiteness of innocence but the blankness of the unknown, neither good nor evil but inexplicable, its meaning yet to be discovered. The events of the story take place in a world devoid of sunlight, of daylight, which is also the light of reason and common sense. Thus the absent sun, "that cheerful orb," represents the dominant qualities of the man which are useless in a sunless world where reason fails and common sense proves unavailing.

Although the man is the central character, it is valid to speak of both the dog and the man as characters. They are equally important to the story, and we know as much about one as the other. All we know of the man is that he is from the civilized land to the south and that he is both unimaginative and unreflective. He is not presented as young, strong, or heroic. The dog, his companion, is almost wild and retains its primitive instincts virtually intact.

London's point, that the man lacks imagination and does not think, would be obscure were it not for the careful contrast with the dog; for the man does think. Or, as London puts it, he is "quick and alert in the things of life." A common interpretation, I suspect, sees the man as a fool who dies for his folly, but a careful reading will disprove it. He is alert and attentive, and he handles himself well in a dangerous situation; but his thought is always practical and immediate, never looking beneath the surface of things. He reminds us of Peter Bell, for whom "A yellow primrose by a river's brim, A yellow primrose was to him, And it was nothing more." The vastness of the scene London describes so vividly, the unbroken white extending for thousands of miles, means nothing to the man. And yet we realize that his self-confidence is, on the whole, justified, and we cannot dismiss him simply as a fool.

The distinction between the man's thought and the dog's instinct is explicitly made in three places. One passage will serve for example: "The dog did not know anything about thermometers. Possibly in its brain there was no sharp consciousness of a condition of very cold such as was in the man's brain. But the brute had its instinct." The reiteration of the contrast between man and dog points to the theme. London's Everyman, not civilized in any very significant way, is nevertheless modern, sensual, rational man; and what London is saying is that modern man, in accepting reason as a guide to short-sighted ends, has allowed his primal instincts to atrophy. In exchange for increased authority in dealing with a constantly shrinking range of experience, he has ceased to feel the primitive pulse beat of his own life. His normal world is constricted, London writes, in language which is partly metaphorical, "within certain narrow limits of heat and cold;" and he neither knows nor reflects upon the incredible vastness of things outside that range and outside his control. Confident of his ability to manage within the narrow limits of his world, he does not think beyond to "man's place in the universe."

The theme, to say all this a little differently, springs from the contrast between our tidy, civilized world and the powerful forces beneath. Modern man reasons his way with false confidence, unaware that he may at any moment break through the shell of his comfortable, rational world into a universe of terrifying dimensions. The man in the story discovers these dimensions and forces, but the moment of illumination London seems to prepare us for never comes. The man dies with only a glimmering of insight.

In the story, breaking through the ice is both a realistic action with serious real consequences and a symbolic action which begins the destruction of the protagonist's confidence in a rationally ordered universe. In a different version of the fable (Crane's "Open Boat," for example), the protagonist would be plucked from disaster to emerge with an "enlargement of personality." London's grimmer story implies that man may have gone too far to save himself; and yet, if escape is possible, it may lie in surrendering upon occasion belief in reason and falling back upon the ancient, inarticulate guidance of instinct. The man does not comprehend this, but the reader does when he sees the dog's instincts save it.

A number of motifs occur repeatedly in London's fiction. Two of them, the struggle of man against nature and "love of life," appear in "To Build a Fire," comprise an interesting triad.

The first is also called "To Build a Fire," for London had already used the title for a story he sold to *Youth's Companion* in 1902. In the earlier story the man has a name, Tom Vincent, but no dog for companion; and he succeeds in building the fire that saves his life. Tom is typical of the triumphant Anglo-Saxons that figure frequently in London's fiction. He is "a strapping young fellow . . . with faith in himself" who takes pride in "mastering the elements" and who laughs "aloud in sheer strength of life."

He even imagines that he is stronger than the animals who crawl into hiding in the intense cold, but his confidence is soon shaken. The point London wants to make is simple and straightforward: "In the Klondike, as Tom Vincent found out . . . a companion is absolutely essential"; and Tom learned his lesson and "limped pitifully" back to camp with an "enlargement of personality," in Jung's phrase. But the fact that he did survive raises a question about London's thesis. In fact, Tom survived without a companion because "the love of life was strong in him" and would not let him sit down and die. "Love of life" in the story suggests both a tenacious clinging to mere existence and sheer joy in being young and strong; and although the ostensible theme is a practical warning about wilderness travel, a secondary theme celebrates human strength and endurance in opposition to nature.

The phrase "love of life" appealed to London and he uses it again as theme and title for a story published in *McClure's Magazine* in 1905. Two men, this time, are traveling through the perilous northern wilderness in late summer, on their way out with the gold that represents success in civilization. One man, unnamed, sprains his ankle—again the accident that brings ordinary man into direct contact with the dark forces of nature. His partner, Bill, callously deserts him, ironically as events prove, to save his own life. The deserted man, however, staggers and crawls for days. As he goes he sheds the emblems of man, first the useless gold and then the empty rifle and the knife. At the beginning of his journey he shoulders his pack and painfully straightens up "so that he could stand erect as a man should stand;" but the imagery shows his reversion to beast and then to mere living thing. He stalks ptarmigan "as a cat stalks a sparrow," and he attempts to eat grass "like some bovine animal." Eventually he reaches the shore of the Arctic Ocean where some members of a scientific expedition find "a strange object on the shore. . . . They were unable to classify it. . . . And they saw something that was alive but which could hardly be called a man. It was blind, unconscious. It squirmed along the ground like some monstrous worm."

Life itself had kept the man alive, "life in him, unwilling to die," the fear of dying "that is to life germane and that lies twisted about life's deepest roots." Life force and body become disassociated: "He was very weary, but it refused to die." The man survived by jettisoning his human qualities. The point is lightly underscored, for his quondam companion died on the trail, still carrying the sack of gold he would not give up even to save his life.

Whereas in "To Build a Fire" (1902), "love of life" is characteristically human, and specifically characteristic of London's heroic Anglo-Saxon adventurers, "Love of Life" suggest that the naked will to live has little to do with humanity and nothing at all with civilization. "To Build a Fire" (1908) carries the shift of theme a step further. The protagonist does not wish to die, but he lacks the "love of life" that would force him to struggle to the end. We infer that the instinct to cling to life at any cost, like an instinctive awareness of cold or other danger, has decayed in civilization.

The story, however, takes a final twist and ends as tragedy. Denied any significant awareness of his inadequate vision of the universe, the man nevertheless faces up to his own human limitations. The realization that his efforts to stay alive are futile and absurd steels him in "meeting death with dignity," a response quite impossible to the survivor in "Love of Life," and he succumbs to a death that is nothing but a "comfortable sleep."

The three stories are not, I think, random variations upon a theme. Rather they reflect the growth of London's thought and a movement from comic to tragic vision with an accompanying artistic development. The first story sees man and nature in opposition, with man, strong equally in youth and innocence, reaffirming the traditional myth of his dominion over nature. The second story, disillusioned and reflecting London's melancholy pondering of Haeckel and Spencer, places man squarely within a materialistic nature. The third story ambiguously suggests that man has been corrupted from nature and therefore pays occasionally a fearful consequence. Ignorant of his apostasy and unable to see quite where he has gone wrong, man nevertheless is capable of new insights and the tragic vision that both ennobles and conceals his fall from nature. The third story is not better simply because it is better written, for the second story is its equal in style if not, perhaps, in structure, but because it is London's serious, mature treatment of a favorite theme. All of the by now familiar details of his mythic northland gain new vigor from the insight that fuses them into a taut, highly charged, meaningful whole that justly deserves its reputation.

Jack London's Twice-Told Tale

Earle Labor and King Hendricks

While Jack London's fiction awaits a proper critical assessment, "To Build a Fire," that "brilliant little sketch whose prose rhythms . . . are still fresh," has firmly established itself as a perennial favorite among the world's readers.[1] In it London managed to combine those qualities which distinguish his best work: vivid narrative, graphic description of physical action, tension (*e.g.*, human intelligence *vs.* animal intuition, man's intrepidity *vs.* cosmic force, vitality *vs.* death), a poetic modulation of imagery to enhance mood and theme, and—above all—a profound sense of irony. It is therefore hardly surprising that his masterpiece of short fiction is still available in a dozen contemporary anthologies.

What is surprising is that London sold the same title to two magazines. The first sale was made in December, 1901, to *The Youth's Companion*,[2] a Boston weekly whose circulation exceeded a half-million and whose contributors included Thomas Hardy, Rudyard Kipling, William Dean Howells, Theodore Roosevelt, and Woodrow Wilson. London received fifty dollars for the story. Six years later, after he had become world-famous, *Century Magazine* paid $400 for "To Build a Fire." Following publication of the story in August 1908, *Century* Editor R. W. Gilder discovered that he had paid for, and foisted upon his readers, apparently soiled goods. Understandably indignant, he lost little time in notifying the author of this discovery. London, who had been cruising the South Seas aboard *The Snark*, sent the following reply:

Sydney, N.S.W., Australia
December 22, 1908

Dear Mr. Gilder:—

I have been sick for many weeks now, am just out of the hospital and pretty weak and wabbly, with a mass of correspondence piled up that almost gives me a collapse every time I look at it. Somewhere in that mountain of letters is a bunch of correspondence relating to "To Build a Fire." I cannot find it, and shall have to go on memory.

A long, long time ago I wrote a story for boys which I sold to the *Youth's Companion*. It was purely juvenile in treatment; its motif was not only very strong, but very true. Man after man in the Klondike has died alone after getting his feet wet, through failure to build a fire. As years went by, I was worried about the inadequate treatment I had given that motif, and by the fact that I had treated it for boys merely. At last I came to the resolve to take the same motif and handle it for men. I had no access to the boys' version of it, and I wrote it just as though I had never used the motif before. I do not remember anything about the way I handled it for juveniles, but I do know, I am absolutely confident, that beyond the motif itself, there is no similarity of treatment whatever.

I can only say that it never entered my head that there was anything ethically wrong in handling the same motif over again in the way I did, and I can only add that I am of the same opinion now, upon carefully considering the question. Please let me know how you feel about the matter.

Sincerely yours,
Jack London[3]

The most cursory reading of the two versions of "To Build a Fire" confirms London's defense: despite the similarity of motifs, the stories are radically different. Perhaps the most remarkable thing, in view of the circumstances of composition, is the recurrence of a few similar—and, at times, identical—phrases in both versions. In any case, London's reply would seem to have satisfied Gilder; for the matter was not pursued further.

But we wish to pursue it further here—for several reasons. First, by reprinting the earlier version of "To Build a Fire,"[4] unavailable now for more than sixty years, we may relieve the doubts of any scholars who have been puzzled by the story's multiple publication dates. Second, we believe that the first version is significant enough, especially in the light of renewed interest in London,[5] to warrant its presentation to SSF readers. Third—and most important—we hope to demonstrate by comparing the two versions, that Jack London was not merely a prolific hack but, contrary to modern critical opinion, an astute craftsman who understood the difference between juvenile fiction and serious literary art. The first "To Build a Fire," if we will grant the author his *donnée*, is a well-made boys' story; the second version is a classic for all ages. An appreciation of this distinction should not only enhance London's reputation but also sharpen our own insights into the ontological qualities of the short story as art form—a form whose aesthetic virtues have been too easily ignored by the critics.[6]

There are a number of interesting features about the first "To Build a Fire." It was written early in London's career, during a period of financial depression when he was frequently in the depths of despair. Certain autobiographical implications are fairly evident in the story: like its protagonist, London had been a robust "young fellow, big-boned and big-muscled, with faith in himself and in the strength of his head and hands;" also like Tom Vincent, the struggling young writer had found out, "not by precept, but through bitter experience," that—regardless of one's optimism, vigor, and self-confidence—man cannot travel alone; and London had furthermore, in his extremity, "set to work to save himself [by] heroic measures"—we need only to read his early letters to see how heroic these measures were.[7] The "love-of-life" theme, so crucial to Tom Vincent's survival, was equally crucial to Jack London's literary survival. As the Russian scholar Vil Bykov has suggested, for example, it is the "deep belief in man's abilities in the face of overwhelming odds" and the "life-asserting force [of] his writings"—not his socialism—which has made London the most widely read foreign writer in the Soviet Union.[8] Ironically, this raw vitality, which many of our own critics find objectionable, has helped to keep London's works in print at home as well as abroad.

Though London may have written the first "To Build a Fire" "for boys merely," he nevertheless worked his form to perfection. This form, one of the oldest types of short fiction, is the *exemplum*.[9] Because its primary function is moral edification, such structural elements as atmosphere and characterization are subordinated, in the *exemplum*, to theme; and what E. M. Forster has called the "mystery" of plot is sacrificed for the didactic explicitness of "story." London adheres closely to the conventions of his form by stating his moral at the outset ("a companion is absolutely essential") and reemphasizing it at the end ("*Never travel alone!*"). The narrative action is simple and direct; his "story" is an uncomplicated circle, moving from message through true-to-life illustration back to message. The tale's effectiveness depends upon two major factors: clarity of the statement and vividness of the illustration. Another important, if minor, factor is the attractiveness of his hero; Tom Vincent, notwithstanding his foolishness, is a sympathetic, clean-cut character—an admirable model for young men. The first "To Build a Fire" was, in short, one of the many fictional examples used by the editors of *The Youth's Companion* to vivify their weekly sermons to America's strenuous young manhood.

The second "To Build a Fire" is, as London himself indicated, an altogether different story. It is, for one thing, considerably longer than the earlier version (7,235 as compared to 2,700 words). Although expansion is of itself no criterion for artistic merit, in this case London obviously used his additional wordage for greater artistic effect, creating a narrative "mystery" and an "atmosphere" lacking in the first version. His awareness of the importance of such elements is revealed in one of his letters to a fellow writer: "Atmosphere stands always for the elimination of the artist, that is to say, the atmosphere is the artist; and when there is no atmosphere and the artist is yet there, it simply means that the machinery is creaking and the reader hears it."[10] Since Wayne Booth has recently explained in his *Rhetoric of Fiction* that there is really no such thing as "eliminating" the author from the work, perhaps we should paraphrase London's advice as follows: "The effect of certain kinds of fiction—particularly fiction informed by cosmic irony—depends heavily upon the evoking of mood; and mood is most effectively evoked through a skillful manipulation of setting and imagery, rather than through editorial comment by the author. In other words, rather than being "told," the reader must be made to hear, to see and—above all—*to feel*."

Examination of the opening paragraph of the second "To Build a Fire" reveals the devices through which London allows atmosphere to function as commentary:

> Day had broken cold and gray, exceedingly cold and gray, when
> the man turned aside from the main Yukon trail and climbed the high

earth-bank, where a dim and little-travelled trail led eastward through the fat spruce timberland. It was a steep bank, and he paused for breath at the top, excusing the act to himself by looking at his watch. It was nine o'clock. There was no sun nor hint of sun, though there was not a cloud in the sky. It was a clear day, and yet there seemed an intangible pall over the face of things, a subtle gloom that made the day dark, and that was due to the absence of sun. This fact did not worry the man. He was used to the lack of sun. It had been days since he had seen the sun, and he knew that a few more days must pass before that cheerful orb, due south, would just peep above the sky line and dip immediately from view.

By varied repetition of a textural motif, London achieves the same kind of hypnotic impact that Hemingway is said to have learned from Gertrude Stein: certain images recur and cluster to produce a mood that is at once somber and sinister ("cold and gray, exceedingly cold and gray . . . a dim and little-travelled trail . . . no sun nor hint of sun . . . intangible pall . . . a subtle gloom . . . day dark . . . absence of sun . . . lack of the sun . . . days since he had seen the sun"). The story's dominant symbolism, the polarity of heat (sun-fire-life) and cold (darkness-depression-death), is carefully adumbrated at the outset so that the reader *senses* the protagonist's imminent doom. We are subtly oppressed by that "intense awareness of human loneliness" that Frank O'Connor has identified with the short story, and we are reminded of that haunting statement from Pascal: "*Le silence eternal de ces espaces infinis m'effraie.*"[11] It is undoubtedly such scenes as this that prompted Maxwell Geismar to remark that "London's typical figure was a voiceless traveler journeying across the ghostly leagues of a dead world."[12]

Unlike Tom Vincent, the protagonist of this "To Build a Fire" is nameless. He is the naturalistic version of Everyman: a puny, insignificant mortal confronting the cold mockery of Nature as Antagonist. Yet, though nameless, he is distinguished by certain traits of character: the man is practical, complacent, insensitive, and vain—he must, for example, excuse to himself the impractical human act of pausing for breath; he is unawed by the mysterious other-worldness of his surroundings; caught in this weird *Urwelt*, he is foolish enough to put his faith in mere clock-time.

What has been hinted in the beginning becomes explicit in the third paragraph, the only place in the story where the author's voice may be detected. The man lacks the one asset that might equalize the odds against him—imagination: "He was quick and alert in the things of life, but only in the things, and not in the significances. . . . Fifty degrees below zero was to him just precisely fifty degrees below zero [actually it is seventy-five below]. That there should be anything more to it than that was a thought that never entered his head." The scope of his imagination is signified in his one stock comment: "It certainly was cold," a fatally inept response that recurs with increasing irony as the man's situation deteriorates. It is also in this paragraph that the theme of the story is subtly implanted in the reader's mind: "It [the extreme cold] did not lead him to meditate upon his frailty as a creature of temperature, and upon man's frailty in general . . . and from there on it did not lead him to the conjectural field of immortality and man's place in the universe." London drops the comment so deftly that it hardly ripples in the reader's consciousness, yet it is this idea precisely that gives the story its final impact: "unaccommodated man" is indeed a frail and pitiable figure when pitted against the awful majesty of cosmic force. London expressed the thought more elaborately in one of his earlier stories:

> Nature has many tricks wherewith she convinces man of his finity—the ceaseless flow of the tides, the fury of the storm, the shock of the earthquake, the long roll of heaven's artillery—but the most tremendous, the most stupefying of all, is the passive phase of the White Silence. All movement ceases, the sky clears, the heavens are as brass; the slightest whisper seems sacrilege, and man becomes timid, affrighted at the sound of his own voice. Sole speck of life journeying across the ghostly wastes of a dead world, he trembles at his audacity, realizes that his is a maggot's life, nothing more. Strange thoughts arise unsummoned, and the mystery of all things strives for utterance. And the fear of death, of God, of the universe, comes over him—the hope of the Resurrection and the Life, the yearning for immortality, the vain striving of the imprisoned essence—it is then, if ever, man walks alone with God.[13]

But the nameless protagonist of "To Build a Fire" is unaware of these deeper implications, as we learn not only from his own behavior but also through the only other animated character in the story, the dog. The inclusion of this *ficelle* or "reflector" is the masterstroke of London's revised version. By employing the dog as foil, the author has obviated the necessity for further editorial comment. Instead of being *told* that one needs a companion in the Northland, we are made to *see* dramatically through his relationship with the animal that the man is a "loner." Because he lacks imagination, he fails to see, until too late, that a companion—even a dog—might possibly save him in a crisis; more important, he is revealed as a man lacking in essential warmth. There is no place in his cold practical philosophy for affection or for what London called elsewhere "true comradeship." To this man the dog is only another of "the things" of life, an object to be spoken to with "the sound of whip lashes." From his relationship to the animal, we may infer a broader relationship—that to mankind. The protagonist is, in other words, a hollow man whose inner coldness correlates with the enveloping outer cold. And there is a grim but poetic justice in his fate.

The dog serves as a foil in the following manner also: his natural wisdom of conduct is juxtaposed against the foolish rationality of his master's behavior. By shifting point of view from man to dog, London provides a subtle counterpointing that enhances both theme and structural tension. For example,

> The animal [unlike the man] was depressed by the tremendous cold. It
> knew [without the convenience of a watch] that it was no time for
> traveling. . . . The dog did not know anything about thermometers [which
> are as useless as watches if one lacks the ability to interpret]. Possibly in
> its brain there was no sharp consciousness of a condition of very cold such
> as was in the man's brain [a consciousness vitiated in the latter by stock
> response]. But the brute had its instinct [a surer gauge than rationality]. It
> experienced a vague but menacing apprehension [absent in the man,
> because he is without imagination]. . . .

And, finally, by using the animal as objective correlative, London has managed
to give an extra twist of irony to the conclusion of his story. After the man's last
desperate attempt to save himself and after his dying vision of rescue, we shift
once more to the dog's point of view:

> The brief day drew to a close in a long, slow twilight. There were no signs
> of a fire to be made, and, besides, never in the dog's experience had it
> known a man to sit like that in the snow and make no fire. As the twilight
> drew on, its eager yearning for the fire mastered it, and with a great lifting
> and shifting of forefeet, it whined softly, then flattened its ears down in
> anticipation of being chidden by the man. But the man remained silent.
> Later the dog whined loudly. And still later it crept close to the man and
> caught the scent of death. This made the animal bristle and back away. A
> little longer it delayed, howling under the stars that leaped and danced and
> shone brightly in the cold sky. Then it turned and trotted up the trail in the
> direction of the camp it knew, where were the other food providers and
> fire providers.

Through its natural responses the dog conveys the finality of the man's death
more forcibly—and more artistically—than any overt statement by the author
might do. And in this concluding paragraph all the key elements of London's
story—the ironic polarity of life and death, the intransigence of Nature's laws,
the cosmic mockery of the White Silence—coalesce to produce a memorable
effect. As Frank O'Connor has written, a great story "must have the element of
immediacy, the theme must plummet to the bottom of the mind. . . . It must
have a coherent action. When the curtain falls everything must be changed. An
iron bar must have been bent and been seen to be bent."[14] Surely, with the firm
grasp of the master craftsman, London has "bent his bar" in this concluding
scene; and we must applaud his strength.

For more than a half-century now, men—as well as boys—have finished
reading "To Build a Fire" with the same profound satisfaction—and a shiver of
relief to be among the "food providers and fire providers." In view of the
story's durability, it should be evident that Jack London was thoroughly sensitive
to the meaning of the art of short fiction. He recognized moreover, as
comparison of the two versions of "To Build a Fire" reveals, the intricate

demands of the genre to which he committed most of his literary talent; and he knew the difference between juvenilia and adult fiction. Our critics would do well to exercise an equally fine discrimination in taking his measure as an artist.

NOTES

[1] The quotation is from Maxwell Geismar, *Rebels and Ancestors* (Boston: Houghton Mifflin, 1953), 189. According to our count, "To Build a Fire" has been reprinted in forty-nine anthologies since its publication in 1908; see *Jack London: A Bibliography*, Hensley C. Woodbridge, John London, and George H. Tweney, eds. (Georgetown, Calif.: Talisman Press, 1966), 143-149, 235-237. Despite its popularity, almost no serious critical attention has been given the story; a noteworthy exception is the commentary by Franklin Walker in *Jack London and the Klondike* (San Marino, CA: Huntington Library, 1966), 254-260.

[2] During his life London kept record books of his magazine sales in which he listed the title of the story or essay, the magazines to which the item was submitted, the date (if and when it was accepted), and the fee he received for it. Volumes I and II of the magazine sales record (1898 to early 1903) are now on file at the Utah State University Library; Vols. III and IV (1903 until his death) are in the Huntington Library. See King Hendricks, *Jack London: Master Craftsman of the Short Story* (Logan: Utah State UP, 1966), 3-9. This version of "To Build a Fire" was one of the few stories that was sold the first time it was submitted.

[3] *Letters from Jack London*, King Hendricks and Irving Shepard, eds. (New York: Odyssey, 1965), 273-274. London had been suffering from a combination of tropical diseases, including a strange skin disorder which the doctors could neither diagnose nor cure; the affliction, caused as he later discovered by over-exposure to ultraviolet rays, cleared up after he returned home—but his health was never again as good as before his *Snark* voyage.

[4] For the complete text of the *Youth's Companion* version of "To Build a Fire," see *Studies in Short Fiction* [*SSF*] 4 (1967), 342-347; or, *The Complete Short Stories of Jack London*,. Earle Labor, Robert C. Leitz, III, and I. Milo Shepard, eds. 3 vols. (Stanford: Stanford UP, 1993), I:698-704.

[5] In addition to the recent publication of London's letters and the London bibliography (perhaps the most extensive ever published on the works by and about an American author), five book-length studies of London's life, including two by Russian scholars, have been issued during the past six years. Also during this period the Bodley Head Press has published four volumes of London's works, under the editorship of Arthur Calder-Marshall, as a part of its series of modern classics; and Harper & Row has included *Great Short Works of Jack London* in its new Perennial Classics.

[6] See the perceptive essay by Thomas A. Gullason, "The Short Story: An Underrated Art," *SSF* 2 (1964), 13-31. We believe that the neglect of London's fiction is due, in part, to the more general critical neglect of the short story itself.

[7] See, for example, his correspondence with his first great love, Mabel Applegarth, in the *Letters*, 3-19 *passim*. Also, see his testimony in *Jack London's Tales of Adventure*, Irving Shepard, ed. (Garden City: Hanover House, 1956), 22-27, 35-39, 49-52.

[8] "Jack London in the Soviet Union," *The Book Club of California Quarterly News Letter*, 24 (1959), 55.

[9] See Margaret Schlauch, "English Short Fiction in the 15th and 16th Centuries," *SSF 3* (1966), 399-402; and Henry Seidel Canby, *A Study of the Short Story* (New York: Holt, 1913), 9-10, 22-26. Canby indicates that the *exemplum*, best known through Chaucer, was also a popular form for such later writers as Addison and Steele—and Dr. Johnson.

[10] To Cloudesley Johns, June 16, 1900, from the *Letters*, 108. Although London wrote few essays on the art of fiction, his letters to Johns reveal the essence of his theory.

[11] "The eternal silence of those infinite spaces terrifies me." See Frank O'Connor, *The Lonely Voice* (Cleveland: World, 1965), 19.

[12] *Rebels and Ancestors*, 144.

[13] "The White Silence," from *The Son of the Wolf* (Boston: Houghton Mifflin, 1900), 7.

[14] *The Lonely Voice*, 216.

Dramatic Mode and Tragic Structure in "To Build a Fire"

James M. Mellard

Jack London's "To Build a Fire" is a striking example of the way in which various fictional modes come together at a single point before diverging. The story is finally dramatic, but there are important residual effects from the pictorial and popular narrative modes. The pictorial element is seen very early in the story when London carefully locates his protagonist in a natural setting. London's method, if not his setting, is as conventional as Washington Irving's Hudson landscapes in "Rip Van Winkle" and "The Legend of Sleepy Hollow." In the omniscient comments about the opening pictorial scene's relation to far away places, north and south, London also betrays the urge to draw attention to himself we normally expect in the popular tradition of storytelling. Not content simply to locate his protagonist in an empty landscape, London feels compelled to shock us with the vastness of the distance between him and "civilization." It is in this role, as storyteller making mythic, didactic capital from virtually ritual acts, that London relates to the narrative mode, in which *mythos*, or story, is more important than the objective presentation of acts, the *dromenon*, or the thing-done. In this role, indeed, London becomes the creator of a new *mythos*—as popular novelist Kurt Vonnegut, Jr., calls such, "a beautiful new lie"—to justify, to rationalize, to the Naturalists their conviction of man's alienation from nature. This is the role most readers expect of London. It is this London, the philosopher, who has come to know that there is more to existence than the man realizes. But it is also London who tries carefully to treat the man as just as much an object as the hostile universe itself, and *this* London has the instinct of a dramatist who can tell a tragic story objectively through act, gesture, and event.

"To Build a Fire," combining as it does the pragmatic and the objective, operates at a point where the myth of oral tradition and the ritual of drama come together. Not mutually exclusive, of course, myth and ritual simply have different areas of activity: myth has to do with thought and meaning, verbal articulation; ritual has to do with act prior to its explanation in words. But, as anthropologist Clyde Kluckhohn says, both "myth and ritual have a common psychological basis. Ritual is an obsessive repetitive activity—often a symbolic dramatization of the fundamental needs of the society, whether economic, biological, social, or sexual. Mythology is the rationalization of the same needs—whether they are all expressed in overt ceremonial or not."[1] In "To Build a Fire" then, London employs the action of his protagonist in attempting to fulfill a very real need to develop a naturalistic myth. But the story, when it gets down to the stark facts of the protagonist's actions, is ultimately more concerned with the "obsessive repetitive activity" of ritual than with the narrator's explanations. And when it gets to this point, the story begins to take the shape of tragic drama.

London's title suggests the central dramatic ritual that provides the main action for the story. In *The Idea of a Theater*, Francis Fergusson employs a notion of the Moscow Art Theater to define the essence of the dramatic plot or character: "They say that the action of a character or play must be indicated by an infinitive phrase, e.g., in the play Oedipus, 'to find the culprit.'"[2] London's infinitive phrase, "to build a fire," thus radically compresses the relation between drama and ritual, for it is the rehearsal and the climactic failure to perform the life-death "ceremony" that provides the most important and most objectively presented content of the story. Just because the inability to perform the rite of fire-making may literally result in death, the successful performance of it is no less symbolic and dramatic. London insists a number of times upon the importance of a fire. Early in the story, he offers the man's thoughts on three primal values of the wilderness: food, fire, and companionship. "He would be in to camp by six o'clock; a bit after dark, it was true, but the boys would be there, a fire would be going, and a hot supper would be ready." London even presents the man's dog's "thoughts" as he expects, in the extreme cold, that the man will seek shelter and build a fire: "The dog had learned fire, and it wanted fire, or else to burrow under the snow and cuddle its warmth away from the air." But as the instincts of the dog suggest something of the man's limitations, London also suggests that he is not really equipped to cope with the death-dealing cold, as he ominously forgets "to build a fire and thaw out" when he tries to eat his bacon and biscuit lunch and only chuckles "at his foolishness." Beginning to realize now how extreme the cold has become, the man is forced to perform the story's major action for the first time: "he got out matches and proceeded to make a fire. From the undergrowth, where high water of the previous spring had lodged a supply of seasoned twigs, he got his firewood. Working carefully from a small beginning, he soon had a roaring fire, over which he thawed the ice from his face and in the protection of which he ate his biscuits. For the moment the cold of space was outwitted."

The infinitive phrase, "to build a fire," clearly suggests the crucial action of London's story. But in the man's lapses London also suggests that the performance of this act cannot be taken for granted. Hence, London prepares for the two subsequent repetitions of the performance, both of which are treated in greater detail than this summary presentation. These last two efforts to build a fire are, in every sense, obsessive repetitions. Having fallen through the snow's crust into water from a free-flowing spring, the man no longer chuckles, but curses his luck as his legs are wet halfway to the knee: "he would have to build a fire and dry out his footgear. This was imperative at that low temperature." Because he knows that with his feet wet "a man must not fail in his first attempt to build a fire," London's protagonist very meticulously goes about that crucial rite: "tangled in the underbrush about the trunks of several small spruce trees, was a high-water deposit of dry firewood—sticks and twigs, principally, but also larger portions of seasoned branches and fine, dry, last year's grasses. He threw down several large pieces on top of the snow. This served for a foundation and prevented the young flame from drowning itself in the snow it otherwise would melt. The flame he got by touching a match to a small shred of birch bark that he took from his pocket. . . . Placing it on the foundation, he fed the young flame with wisps of dry grass and with the tiniest dry twigs." Thus, while London the myth-maker can treat the rite as merely symbolic, the man himself can think of nothing but the literal meaning—the fire means life and safety. And in the process of building the fire he is as absolutely absorbed in the rite as man can be, his life, like that of ritual itself, proceeding "before all predication" as Fergusson says of dramatic actions[3] before thought, rationalization, explanation.

Despite his departures into *mythos*, into entertaining and/or didactic story, London creates a dramatic form in "To Build a Fire" simply by focusing upon the primary, unadorned, crucial action, the efforts of the man to build a lifesaving fire. By virtue of the trajectory, the direction of that action, moreover, London develops not just an illustrative naturalistic episode, but a truly noble tragic plot. Though focus on the objective action, the rite, ritual, or ceremony, is important, alone it is not enough to create a tragic structure. For such a structure a story must have a unified series of actions of the sort London provides in "To Build a Fire," where the minimal number of events (three) shows a rising and falling pattern in the fortune of the hero and culminates in the severest reversal of all, death itself. It is around the three fire-building scenes, then, that London develops the remaining elements of tragedy, elements that according to Aristotle are subordinate to action.

One of these is theme. London's thematic focus is upon the traditionally tragic distance between man and nature, the distance signified by man's mortality—the death toward which tragedy moves—and the distance that is not merely the province of naturalistic writers like London. Aside from the man's death, however, which necessarily comes at the end, this distance is suggested by London in the vastness of the natural setting and the man's being placed, as it were, at the apex between the natural environment and outer space itself, the point at which "The cold of space smote the unprotected tip of the planet; and he, being on that unprotected tip, received the full force of the blow."

But another tragic element is character. In tragedy, the conventional flaw of the hero is *hubris*, or pride, a mistaken conviction that one is capable of handling destructive situations more easily than he has a right to believe. London's hero, unnamed and perhaps standing for "everyman," all who must live in nature, manifests such a tragic, ultimately fatal, flaw. He flies in the face of the conventional wisdom offered by the "old-timer on Sulphur Creek," thus going against the life-preserving knowledge painfully acquired through longer, more cautious experience. After successfully making the first fire, London's hero, having thought before of the old-timer's warning about the deadly cold, thinks, "For the moment the cold of space was outwitted." And after successfully making a second fire to dry out his leggings and socks, he thinks again, even more pridefully: "The fire was a success. He was safe. He remembered the advice of the old-timer on Sulphur Creek, and smiled. The old-timer had been very serious in laying down the law that no man must travel alone in the Klondike after fifty below. Well, here he was; he had had the accident; he was alone; and he had saved himself. Those old-timers were rather womanish, some of them, he thought. All a man had to do was to keep his head, and he was all right. Any man who was a man could travel alone." But as must inevitably happen in tragedy at his moment of greatest pride he is struck down—and through his own actions. At seventy-five below zero his feet wet and hands freezing the man is forced once more to build his fire, buried now under a tree's snow avalanche, a result of his mistake in building the fire under a snow-laden spruce.

The conclusion of "To Build a Fire" now seems inevitable, the sequence of actions allowing no other end than the one London's hero senses: "The man was shocked. It was as though he had just heard his own sentence of death." Now the man knows "the old-timer on Sulphur Creek was right. If he had only had a trail mate he would have been in no danger now. The trail mate could have built the fire. Well, it was up to him to build the fire over again. . . ." But London has crafted his plot well, and we know, as well as the man, that his effort is doomed. And though London devotes several pages to the obsessive attempt to repeat the earlier performances and shows the man absolutely absorbed in his actions, all thought driven out of his mind, "devoting his whole soul to the matches," the important tragic theme that develops from the man's failure is his stoic, resolute facing of death. He has a "certain fear of death, dull and oppressive," but after manfully struggling against a force simply too powerful for his human weakness and suffering one last moment of panic, "he sat up and entertained in his mind the conception of meeting death with dignity. . . . He was bound to freeze anyway, and he might as well take it decently." He has broken a "law," he has recognized his error, and he meets his self-created fate nobly. And London leaves us at the end with death; the penalty exacted by nature; the dog, a symbol of the still mortal organism in that indifferent nature; and the natural order itself, imaged in "the stars that leaped and danced and shone brightly in the cold sky."

"To Build a Fire" recapitulates the events, if not the verbalized meaning, of a familiar *mythos,* the bringing of fire into an alien universe, the Promethean exploit that would modify nature but that would also bring death or extreme suffering to the hero himself. London touches upon this motif a number of times in the story when he reports the thoughts of the rather humanized husky—in his "instincts" he knows the man as a "fire-provider," and it is off in search of other "fire-providers" he goes at the story's end. Though there are other men who can provide fire, they are all mortal, as London's protagonist is, and they, no more than he, can ever win that battle with nature, the "god" that perpetually torments Prometheus for the theft of the symbolic flame. But these are "meanings" we must extract from London's objective presentation of acts, for these acts are depicted without much of the interpretive aid of the teller himself.

NOTES

[1] "Myth and Rituals: A General Theory," in *Myth and Literature: Contemporary Theory and Practice,* ed. by B. Vickery (Lincoln: U of Nebraska P, 1966), 44.

[2] (Princeton, N.J.: Princeton U P, 1949), 230.

[3] Ibid., 240.

"To Build a Fire": Physical Fiction and Metaphysical Critics

Charles E. May

Ten years ago Earle Labor and King Hendricks, perhaps the most avid partisans of Jack London, reproved critics for not giving London's fiction its "proper critical assessment" and urged that a "fine discrimination," equal to London's own, be exercised in taking his measure as an artist.[1] Labor's new book in the Twayne American Author Series and a recent *Modern Fiction Studies* special issue devoted to London may then be seen as steps toward reevaluating and rescuing a writer who has been considered too minor to merit serious attention. I have no major contribution to make toward this reassessment of London's fiction, but I do wish to express some reservations about the "discrimination" made in the last ten years in regard to London's best-known piece of short fiction, which Labor calls "a masterpiece" and says is one of the most widely anthologized works ever written by an American author.[2]

A common method of critics who wish to rescue a work that has not been highly valued is to subject it to a critical category that is highly valued. If the work "fits," even in the coarsest fashion, with physiognomy effaced and limbs lopped off, it is declared to have value because the category does. In especially difficult cases, not only must the work be reduced to an indistinguishable torso, but the Procrustean bed itself must be altered. Because the categorical bed of "naturalism" on which London has previously been laid seems to have laid him permanently to rest, more fashionable categories have been applied to disinter him. However, in applying universal terms to "To Build a Fire," the critics have so ignored Wittgenstein's exhortation to "look and see" that they have not only failed to tell us anything helpful about the story, they have applied the terms so uncritically that the categories themselves are in danger of losing their heuristic value in telling us anything helpful about literature at all. Three such categories that have been applied to London's story to claim it is both thematically and structurally more significant than heretofore realized are: the short story as a generic form, the archetypal theme of rebirth, and the structure and theme of classical tragedy.

Labor and Hendricks' argument that "To Build a Fire" is a "masterpiece of short fiction" is based primarily on a comparison of the story with an earlier juvenile version by the same name. The superiority of the adult story over the juvenile one is a result of three basic artistic improvements. First of all, London adds "atmosphere" to adumbrate the story's dominant symbolism of "the polarity of heat (sun-fire-life) and cold (darkness-depression-death)." Consequently, we are "subtly oppressed by that 'intense awareness of human loneliness' that Frank O'Connor has identified with the short story." Secondly, the protagonist in the juvenile story, a likeable and sympathetically identifiable young man named Tom Vincent has been changed to a nameless "naturalistic version of Everyman," representative of "unaccommodated man . . . pitted against the awful majesty of cosmic forces." Finally, the "masterstroke" of the adult version is the addition of the dog as a *ficelle*, an addition that not only makes us see dramatically by the man's harsh treatment of the animal that the protagonist is a "hollow man whose inner coldness correlates with the enveloping outer cold," but that also creates by "subtle counterpointing" the structural and thematic tension between the dog's "natural wisdom" and the man's "foolish rationality."[3]

The archetypal rebirth category applied to the story by Clell T. Peterson can be summarized quickly. The man's journey is that well-known symbolic movement into the unknown, first downward toward death and then upward toward a more enriched life; his physical and spiritual survival depends on his growing awareness of the metaphysical significance of his experience. Built on a contrast between the inadequacy of reason and the superiority of primal instincts, the story "implies that man may have gone too far to save himself; and, yet, if escape is possible it may lie in surrendering upon occasion belief in reason and falling back upon the ancient, inarticulate guidance of instinct. The man does not comprehend this, but the reader does when he sees the dog's instincts save it."[4]

The claim that "To Build a Fire" is a tragedy in the Aristotelian sense has been made both by James M. Mellard and by Earle Labor in his recent book-length study of London. Mellard uses Clyde Kluckhohn's definition of ritual—"a symbolic dramatization of the fundamental needs of society, whether economic, biological, social, or sexual"—to suggest that the story is primarily concerned with just such an "obsessive repetitive activity," and thus it takes on the "shape of tragic drama." He also uses Francis Fergusson's borrowing of the Moscow Art Theater's concept of the infinitive phrase to sum up the action of a dramatic plot. The action of "to build a fire" is similar to the action of "to find the culprit" in *Oedipus*. Mellard also urges that we see the traditional tragic structure in the three fire-building scenes until the final effort which results in the "severest reversal of all, death itself." He says the theme of the story focuses on the "traditionally tragic distance between man and nature," and the protagonist is guilty of the flaw of pride or *hubris* in his "mistaken conviction that one is capable of handling destructive situations more easily than he has a right to believe." Finally, Mellard says that the most important tragic theme to emerge from the story develops from the protagonist's stoic, resolute facing of death.[5] Earle Labor also uses Aristotle's *Poetics* to note the parallels between the story and Greek tragedy and suggests that the story is great because it articulates the mystery that animates the plays of Sophocles, Aeschylus, and all the great tragedians; that is, the common mystery of that "simple fact"—man must die.

I suspect that most, if not all, of these grandiose claims are based on this "simple fact" which is the central fact of the story—the protagonist dies. The basic critical fallacy of the various interpretations of the story is that the critics insist that the man's death has significance not because of any significance attributed to that death within the story, but rather because of the significance of death in the critical categories they have applied to the story. The man's death is significant because it symbolizes the frailty of unaccommodated man against cosmic forces, because it leads to psychic rebirth, because it is the tragic result of a tragic flaw and is confronted with "dignity." It should not have to be pointed out that the "significance" of a death in a piece of fiction depends not upon the imagination of the critics of that fiction, but rather upon the imagination of the author. And the "simple fact" of death is nothing but a simple fact if nothing is at stake but the "mere" loss of biological life, if the character who dies is nothing but a physical body killed to illustrate this "simple fact."

Labor and Hendricks inadvertently suggest the nature of the critical problem by calling the protagonist in the adult story a "naturalistic version of Everyman." The convention of the Everyman character in the sixteenth-century morality play from which the term comes, as well as in other allegories such as *The Faerie Queene* and *Pilgrim's Progress*, depends on the Everyman figure representing the soul, or, more narrowly, some specific moral or psychological aspect of man. The assumption of Naturalism, however, is that man is primarily a biological living body in a natural world of objects and forces. Thus, it follows that a naturalistic version of Everyman is simply Everyman as a body. And this is precisely what the protagonist is in London's story, and it is why the story has physical significance only, not the metaphysical significance the critics have attributed to it.

For Jack London, and consequently for the reader, the man in the story is simply a living body and the cold is simply a physical fact. To insist that the story is a symbolic dramatization adumbrated in a symbolic polarity between fire as life and cold as death is to run the risk of saying that the protagonist's symbolic failure to build the symbolic fire results in his symbolic death. Of course, such a statement is true in the sense that every art work can be said to "symbolize" or "mediate" a reality that is not identical with the verbal construct of the work itself. But such a statement tells us nothing about Jack London's story. Surely Labor and Hendricks realize that both Frank O'Connor and Pascal in their references to human loneliness and the terror of infinite spaces meant something more than the simple fear of being physical alone or losing physical life. Moreover, Labor and Hendricks' reaching for the inference that the man's treatment of the dog is an indication of his hollowness confuses the man's "inhumanity" as a naturalistic given of the story with a symbolic character flaw that leads to the "poetic justice" of his death.

London's central comment about the protagonist in the story itself clearly indicates the "naturalistic" nature of his Everyman: "The trouble with him was that he was without imagination. He was quick and alert in the things of life, but only in the things, and not in the significances." London says that the cold was a simple fact for the man. "It did not lead him to meditate upon his frailty as a creature of temperature, and upon man's frailty in general, able only to live within certain narrow limits of heat and cold; and from there it did not lead him to the conjectural field of immortality and man's place in the universe." If this comment "hardly ripples in the reader's consciousness," as Labor and Hendricks suggest, it is not because it is dropped so "deftly," but rather because London, like his protagonist, is without imagination in this story, because he too is concerned here only with the things of life and not with their significance. The reader may be led to meditate upon the physical limits of man's ability to live in extreme cold, but nothing in the story leads him to the metaphysical conjectural field of immortality and man's place in the universe.

James Mellard's claim that the obsessive repetitive activity in the story makes it a symbolic ritual assumes that the man's repetitive activity "to build a fire" in order to preserve bodily life is equivalent to Oedipus's repetitive activity to "find the culprit" in order to find his very identity. An activity that dramatizes a biological need should not be confused with an activity that dramatizes a psychological need. And to equate the physical limitations of being unable to survive a temperature of 75 degrees below zero with the psychic limitations suggested by the Greek *hamartia* is to confuse physics with metaphysics. Moreover, to call the man's final attitude toward death, which he himself thinks of as no longer "running around like a chicken with its head cut off," an heroic facing of his fate similar to the recognition and dignity of Oedipus's final gesture is to equate heroic resolution with a simple acceptance of the inevitable.

A close look at the story itself without the lenses of *a priori* categories reveals that the most significant repetitive motif London uses to chart the man's progressive movement toward death is the gradual loss of contact between the life force of the body and the parts of the body: "The cold of space smote the unprotected tip of the planet, and he, being on that unprotected tip, received the full force of the blow. The blood of his body recoiled before it. The blood was alive, like the dog, and like the dog it wanted to hide away and cover itself up from the fearful cold. . . . The extremities were the first to feel its absence." The man realizes this more forcibly when he finds it difficult to use his fingers: "they seemed remote from his body and from him. When he touched a twig, he had to look and see whether or not he had hold of it." The separation is further emphasized when he burns the flesh of his hands without feeling the pain and when he stands and must look down to see if he is really standing. When he realizes that he is physically unable to kill the dog, he is surprised to find that he must use his eyes to find out where his hands are.

Finally, realizing that the frozen portions of his body are extending, he has a vision of himself that the story has been moving toward, a vision of the self as totally frozen body, not only without psychic life, but without physical life as well. Picturing the boys finding his body the next day, "he found himself with them, coming along the trail and looking for himself. And, still with them, he came around a turn in the trail and found himself lying in the snow. He did not belong with himself any more, for even then he was out of himself, standing with the boys and looking at himself in the snow." The discovery of self in

London's story is not the significant psychic discovery of Oedipus or the Ancient Mariner, but rather the simple physical discovery that the self is body only.

Anyone who sees this purely physical fiction as a story with metaphysical significance does so not as a result of the imagination of Jack London, but as a result of the imagination of his critics. One can grant that the bare situation of the story has metaphysical potential without granting that London actualizes it, gives it validity. It is possible that the great white silence in the story could have had the significance it has in *Moby Dick,* that the cold of space could have had the significance it has in Crane's "The Blue Hotel," that the "nothingness" that kills the man could have had the significance it has in "Bartleby the Scrivner" or Hemingway's "A Clean, Well-Lighted Place." It is even possible that the obsessive concern with immediate detail could have had the significance it has in "Big Two-Hearted River." But without going into what makes such elements metaphysically significant in these true "masterpieces," it is sufficient to say that there is more in the context of these works to encourage such symbolic readings than in London's "To Build a Fire."

NOTES

[1] "Jack London's Twice-Told Tale," *Studies in Short Fiction,* 4 (1967), 334-341.

[2] *Jack London* (New York: Twayne, 1974), 63, 150. Labor neglects to mention that the story is most often anthologized in high school and junior high school textbooks.

[3] The logical fallacy of the argument is obvious. The fact that London's adult story is more carefully crafted than the juvenile version does not automatically mean that London understands the "intricate demands" of the short story genre, or that this particular story is a "masterpiece." Furthermore, an analysis of the craftsmanship of the work alone will do nothing either to enhance London's reputation or "sharpen our own insights into the ontological qualities of the short story as an art form." Anyone familiar with the history of short story criticism in America knows the kind of damage done to the reputation of the form by just this kind of craftsmanship criticism that proliferated in the handbooks and manuals during the very period when London was writing.

[4] "The Theme of Jack London's 'To Build a Fire,'" *American Book Collector,* 17 (1966), 15-18. See also James K. Bowen, "Jack London's 'To Build a Fire': Epistemology and the White Wilderness," *Western American Literature,* 5 (1971), 287-289, who argues that Peterson's exegesis is an oversimplification of London's more complex epistemological position. As is often the case, one critic's claim for metaphysical significance in a work leads another critic to try to do him one better.

[5] *Four Modes: A Rhetoric of Modern Fiction* (New York: Macmillan, 1973), 260-264.

Why the Man Dies in "To Build a Fire"

George R. Adams

During a discussion of "To Build a Fire" a student asked me, "Why was the man in the Yukon?" I answered that he was probably a prospector, since the "camp" in the story is an "old claim." But only the earliest version of the story tells us explicitly that men are in the Yukon "prospecting and hunting moose." I began thinking about that difference and other differences between the various versions of the story, especially major differences like the dog and the man's death, and it seemed to me that there was a general pattern to the changes London made. What was explicit and in the foreground of the first version became implicit or in the background of the later versions. This suggested to me that the foregrounded additions, the dog and the death, were thematically linked, and that in a special way the man dies because of the dog.

In the plot of the later versions of the story the man does of course die because of the dog; more precisely, he dies because he cannot kill the dog in order to warm his hands enough to build a fire.[1] This foregrounded and explicit plot detail is in accord with what can be called "the standard reading" of the story. In the standard reading the man dies because he is not biologically fit to live.[2] This Darwinian theme (actually a "moral") is foregrounded by the explicit comparison of the dog's innate characteristics to the man's. Because he is not the dog and because of a conjunction of arrogance, inexperience, and bad luck, the man learns the hardest way a bitter "law" of the Yukon, that no human goes out alone on the trail when the temperature is lower than fifty degrees below zero. This law is also a moral, and so the Yukon moral merges with the Darwinian moral to form the standard reading. And this reading easily accommodates a typical "moral" of Naturalist narrative: humans are cast into an existence over which they have no control, and their inherent failings and a disinterested but "implacable" Nature will always conjoin to produce disaster. For most admirers of "To Build a Fire" these interlocked morals of the standard reading combined with London's skilled storytelling produce a powerful examination of "the human condition." Unfortunately, there are ambiguities in the story which not only make the standard reading problematic but also suggest that another reading is required.

One set of ambiguities has to do with the distinction between evolution and inheritance. For example, are we to understand from the story that when in their evolutionary history humans lost the resources of fur and instinct they also lost the resources of intelligence, but developed the characteristic of arrogance? And what exactly is the range of the man's arrogance and lack of "imagination?" Is his attitude toward the "old timer" and his advice an aspect of this lack and inevitable and predictable because it is an evolutionary characteristic? Or is it genetic? Or is his arrogance a product neither of history nor of inheritance but the result of factors outside biology, for example experience? The story implies that had he been in the Yukon longer the man's experience would have been different and hence his attitude, behavior, and fate would have been different. If Yukon survival is a matter of experience, then any innate evolutionary or genetic weaknesses are irrelevant. Or is London's point that men like the one in the story are so biologically handicapped by evolution or genetics that they never live long enough to get the experience that could keep them alive?

These ambiguities about the importance of the man's biological makeup are compounded by an ambiguity about the events over which the man has no control. A significant foregrounded event in the plot, as the man himself recognizes, is bad luck.[3] As in many Naturalist narratives luck is the "laboratory" in which characters are tested, where the interaction of biology and circumstances is manifested as success or failure. But is the man's luck linked to his experience or to his biology? The man knows for example, that he must avoid the concealed water and what to do if he steps in it (466). Were he more experienced or more "imaginative" (or for that matter, if he had more fur) the man would be no better off if luck was against him. And what are we to make of the incident of the spruce tree which dumps the snow on his fire? Is it the result of inherited obtuseness? Or the result of inexperience? Or the predictable result of haste and fear, as the story seems to suggest? Or is it simply more bad luck? In short, does the story say that a man with his weaknesses will always have bad luck, or does it suggest that if his luck had been good, then any inherited or learned behavior would be irrelevant?

London thus seems indecisive about what the standard reading takes to be the theme of the story. But perhaps the problem is that London is less interested in the thematic elements of the story than in the narrative presentation, the "literary" aspects of the story, for example its irony.

For most of us, I suspect, the important result of evolution is that we humans, including the man in London's story, have become in significant ways superior to dogs and even to the environment. The man in the story obviously can do many things the dog cannot do: he can plan ahead ("He would be in camp by six o'clock," 463), he can apply the past to the present ("He remembered the tale of a man, caught in a blizzard," 474), he can carry prepared food with him, he can choose warm clothing, he can make fires, he can tame animals, and he can use tools such as matches, watches, thermometers, and knives. If suddenly transported to the Equator, he probably could survive (barring bad luck) but the Yukon husky might not. The fundamental irony in the story, as David Hamilton points out,[4] is that a creature endowed by evolution with the power to think, choose, and create, chose, without thinking, to create serious trouble for itself and the more it tries to demonstrate its superiority to circumstances the more it shows that only a more "primitive" and "inferior" creature could get itself out of the trouble. With the irony of the story we are again brought back to the biological questions raised by the story. Considering that most of the man's characteristics are those of other humans, are we to see the irony of the story as a "universalizing" aspect of the man's fate, telling us that it is the case for all humans that not only do our evolutionary characteristics of mental and technological superiority not guarantee us against disasters, in some cases they might actually get us into trouble, that in those cases we might be better off if we were more primitive? But what if our technology always works or our luck always holds? Certainly we could imagine a story where that would be the case. Possibly London is implying in his story that such will never be the case for humans, that either luck or matches will always fail. Or is he only warning us as a general principle not to be complacent about human superiority?

Perhaps I am wrong in seeing a universalizing motive for London. Perhaps he is saying that the man in the story is not a "representative" human but only an individual with specific characteristics in specific circumstances such that he will die, but because most of us do not correspond to the man's model we should not worry about a similar fate. The story can be read that way (the man does have specific characteristics—red hair, lack of imagination, inexperience) and such a reading greatly reduces both the story's ambiguities and its moralism. But even that reductive reading will not eliminate all the ambiguities and moralism in the story.

It may be, as modern literary theory holds, that the kinds of ambiguities I have been pointing out are the inevitable by-product of any fictional narrative and are not specific to London's story. Or they may be specific if they are the result of London's having to revise the story without the original version at hand.[5] I will argue that the ambiguities are not only specific to the story but also are the result of an intrusion during revision of an ideology which London was only partly conscious of, an ideology which generally went into the background of the revised versions but which is important in determining why the man dies.

In the first version of the story, printed in *Youth's Companion* in 1902, the protagonist survives his ordeal and learns his lesson: "'*Never travel alone!* . . . the precept of the North"[6] (343). In the second version the dog and the man's death were added, along with an epigraph when the story was printed in *Century Magazine* in 1908: "He travels fastest who travels alone . . . but not after the frost has dropped below fifty degrees or more. — Yukon code."[7] The epigraph was dropped when the story was printed in the collection *Lost Face* (1910), in effect creating a third version. The first version of the story is clearly what I suggested that we could imagine, an account in which the man's luck and technology do not fail. In that version we are told up front not only the moral of the story but also that one can live after having learned it, as "Tom Vincent found out" through "bitter experience" (342). The phrase "found out" and the symbolic name "Vincent" ("conquering") tell us that while reading the story we can relax and concentrate on the details of the lesson; we will feel no anxiety about the human condition from Tom's fate. He is young, "big boned and big muscled, with faith in himself" (342). He seems to have no more insight into human existence than the anonymous man of the revised versions and he is just as arrogant; because he is young and strong and arrogant he will not wear a nose-strap (a "feminine contraption") and exults in "mastering the elements" (343). Animals hole up in bad weather, but not a man (343). And though he will soon be "fighting for his life against those same elements" he thought he was master of, his arrogance is ultimately justified. If he runs in panic, he has the strength to run, and if he burns his flesh in kindling the crucial fire, he has the stoicism to endure it (346-347). What could be a typical Yukon disaster turns out to be only a learning experience, one which Tom passes on to others; he has become the old timer.

Obviously the 1902 version is aimed at young readers and does not raise the kind of questions that the revised versions do. The loss of the epigraph in the 1910 version suggests that London was no longer certain that the law of the Yukon is the point of the story; the removal of the epigraph emphasizes the focus on the laws of evolution. Linked to that shift in focus is a change in the overt motivation for being in the Yukon: in the early version Tom is a member of one of many groups hunting and prospecting, and he is prospecting successfully, for they had "struck 'pay' up there on Cherry Creek Divide" (342). This motivation is only implicit in the revised version, appearing as the "old claim" where "the boys" are waiting (463). But the most significant differences between the three versions are of course the foregrounded additions of the dog and the death of the man.

The presentation of the dog is generally read as the chief means of presenting the Darwinian moral, but London shows us not so much what the dog *is* as what it has been forced to *become*, an adjunct to the man. It is as though London was deliberately denying the cliché, "A man's best friend is his dog." In its original, evolved form, in the state of nature, the dog is protected by a heavy coat of fur (464) which suggests but contrasts with the man's "red beard and moustache" (464). The dog is the perfect Darwinian exemplar, capable of surviving if it and its environment are not interfered with. But London tells us that both have been interfered with.

When we first see the dog it is primarily in its altered role. No longer an autonomous entity, a "wolf-dog" adapted to its surroundings, it has been reduced to an object owned by the man and slinks along at the man's heels (464) expecting the man "to go into the camp and to seek shelter somewhere and build a fire" (464). It has been conditioned by humans to respond to an environment created by humans: it "had learned fire, and it wanted fire" (464); at the man's death it trots up the trail "to the other food providers and fire providers" (478). And the conditioning has been brutal. In what amounts to a capsule history of the relationship between the "superior" and "inferior" species we see the dog first as "native husky" trotting after the man (464), then it slinks along (464), then it is used as a means of detecting traps (466), then it is characterized as "the toil slave" of the man, trained by "whip lash" and "menacing sounds" (468), and finally it is to be sacrificed to save the man's life (474). The progression (or rather regression) is from the dog's function as companion to its function as disposable object; thus the dog is always "it," not "he" or "she."

The dog's dependent and objectified status and its partial assimilation to the man's environment makes ambiguous the implied physical resemblance of the two. The moisture of its breathing has caused the dog's "jowls, muzzle, and eyelashes" to be "whitened" by "a fine powder of frost" (464). The man's corresponding beard and moustache are also frosted with a "muzzle" of ice (464).[8] This coincidence can be seen as reinforcing the Darwinian theme, as suggesting that the man will be (or ought to be) reduced to the animal state. He does, after all, shy "like a horse" (466) and he does step into a "trap" and he must, exactly like the dog, immediately deal with the consequences of that mishap. Or the similarity can be seen as another aspect of the dominant irony of the story: the superior being, placed in primitive conditions which he long since evolved out of, can no longer function, even if he superficially resembles a primitive species. But the resemblance also suggests an entirely opposite reading: the dog, in the process of his assimilation to the life of the man, is being placed in the same peril as the man. As a "wolf-dog," half wolf and half dog, he cannot survive if he becomes dependent on human shelter, human food, human fire. Neither can he survive if he undergoes the final reduction to merely an object useful for the preservation of human life. By the resemblance between the two, London suggests a kind of perverse and ironic evolutionary process: humans will finally produce a dog so dependent and so objectified that it can no longer survive in its environment and hence will no longer be available to serve or save humans in that environment.

The essentially adversarial relationship between the dog and the man is the foregrounded version of the adversarial relationship between the larger environment and the man. Part of human evolution (at least social evolution) is the invention of the adversarial metaphor "hostile environment." The metaphor has a purpose: if anything in the environment is to be subjected to a superior species it has to be seen as an inferior, as an object, or as an adversary. In the first version of "To Build a Fire" the adversarial relationship is foregrounded; Tom the conqueror enjoys "mastering the elements" and "defying the frost." The cold "could not stop him." "Strong as were the elements, he was stronger." "He was a man, a master of things" (343). And though he limps "pitifully" into camp and bears the "scars on his hands" (347) of the battle he has won he is still master.

It seems at first that in the revised versions London abandoned the metaphor of battle and conquest, but in fact he only changed the implicit language defining the relationship. By a typical feat of "double speak" humans can redefine their adversarial relationship with nature so that "attack" or "conquest" becomes "defense." This redefinition is implied by the technology the man carries. To humans threatened by a hostile environment, clothes, food, matches, thermometer, knife and dog are merely "weapons of defense." And the Yukon is hostile and dangerous: it sets "traps" (466). But if we consider the

source of the man's weapons, the technology which manifests the human superiority to nature and the assumed right to defend against it (that is, the right to
master it), we can see technology as part of the redefinition of our relationship
to our environment. For the man to have a thermometer, watch, and knife the
earth had to be mined; for him to have a handkerchief and clothes the earth had
to be plowed; and for him to have lunch animals had to die. Thus the
foregrounded relationship between the man and the dog extends to every aspect
of the man and his history and to the Yukon environment in which the events
of the story take place.

        The bitter cold of the Yukon is in the foreground of the man's
consciousness and hence in the foreground of the story, but the emptiness and
"pure" whiteness (462) are not. A corollary question to the one asked by my
student is, "Why are there no native inhabitants of the Yukon in the story?" To
the obvious answer that the story is not about them I would respond that the
story is implicitly about them, just as the story is implicitly about the dog.
Northern working dogs like the "husky" in the story are after all an innovation
of those original inhabitants who were displaced by white intruders, whom we
call "Eskimos," and whose name the dog bears as a reminder.[9] In all that vast
whiteness surrounding the man the Eskimos occupy no physical or mental space.
But to us they are conspicuous by their absence, not only because of the Eskimo
dog but because of the man's attitude toward other humans. His companions at
the camp are "boys" (463), the Yukon shrubbery is "nigger heads" (465), and
the old timer on Sulphur Creek is both a horse ("hoss," 477) and too
"womanish" (470) to appreciate what a younger man can accomplish. When he
feels contempt for himself he is "a chicken with its head cut off" (478).
Obviously anyone or anything defined as inferior does not register in any
significant way on the man's consciousness; we are not surprised then when
without reflection he intends to slaughter the dog.

        Less shocking but just as significant is his lighting a fire. It is a simple
act and burns up only twigs and flotsam. But the burning wood was once part
of the timber resources of the Yukon and links the simple act to man's reason
for being in the Yukon: he has come "the roundabout way to look at the spring
from the islands in the Yukon" (463). Earlier we glimpse the "fat spruce
timberland" (462) and a "spruce-covered island" (462) and later the "big spruce
trees" (463) and the "small spruce trees" under which he builds the fatal fire
(469). Presumably the reason the man notices the "changes in the creek, the
curves and bends and timber jams" (465) is that successfully getting logs out in
the spring requires avoiding such timber jams. Thus dog and trees are
interchangeable, only two of the "things of life" which catch the man's
attention.

        Labor and Hendricks comment on this "coldness" and emptiness of the
man and suggest that it reflects and acts upon his environment;[10] but his coldness
is more than a matter of the "personality" or "attitude" of a single man
experiencing an event of significance only to. him, or even to other men like

him. Another aspect of the emptiness in the story is that everyone is unnamed, including the dog, who is also neuter in gender. Paradoxically, this anonymity is a kind of "fullness." In the sequence of revisions London changed the protagonist from "Tom Vincent" to "John Collins"[12] and then abandoned names entirely. When he changed from the personalized "Tom" to the anonymous "man" he allows us, almost forces us, to read the man not as individual or even as generic male but as species, with species-specific behavior. And that specific behavior is destructive. The expansion of the man's role from person to species alters the Darwinian moral of the story: the evolutionary point is now not the arrogance and failings of a single individual but the arrogance and failings of a species, the assumption that since it is a superior species it has the right to consume everything on the planet. The man's decision to kill the dog is only the foregrounded version of his decision to come to the Yukon in the first place.

If in fact this implied social critique, which is also an ideology, is in the story, it can reasonably be asked, "Why is that ideology not in the foreground of London's consciousness and hence foregrounded in the story?" I suggest as answer a paradox: London did not foreground the social critique because he was a Socialist. Our contemporary concern about the exploitation and destruction of the "biosphere," a concern which we call "environmentalism," is of course dependent upon earlier critiques of exploitation and earlier concern for "Nature." As David Morris points out in "The four stages of environmentalism" we are in the fourth stage; the modern environmentalist sees the destruction of the biosphere as the predictable result of the exploitation of natural and human resources begun in the Industrial Revolution.[13] But London wrote "To Build a Fire" during the first stage of environmentalism, when the concern was only to set aside and maintain "unspoiled" a part of the natural landscape, to symbolically "conserve" the American Eden. And though like socialism this concern for nature carries the seed of a larger ecological consciousness and critique, there was not in 1908 a widespread feeling of our moral duty to save the world but rather a sense of our duty to leave something of a pristine and primitive environment to posterity. It is not probable, therefore, that modern environmental concerns would be in the foreground of London's consciousness. As a Socialist his attention was focussed on the exploitation of the "wage slave." Nevertheless, we can see in London's story the shape of a larger critique in the attitude of the man toward animals and other humans. His refusal to take a companion on the trail suggests more than simply arrogance or inexperience; it suggests an ideology, a belief that going it alone is preferable to communal or cooperative action.[14] That London was subconsciously dealing with a clash of ideologies, one espousing cooperative action and one espousing individualism, is implicit in the man's attitude toward the womanish old timers and in the definition of the dog's function as "toil slave" of the man. The verbal echo in "toil slave," however faint, of London's socialist ideology suggests a source and meaning for the ambiguities in the story and a proper reading.

In the model I have been developing London rethought two or three times the moral he wished to convey in "To Build a Fire." He moved from a focus on the laws of the Yukon as the point of the story (1902 version) through a version emphasizing the Yukon code within a Darwinian framework (1908 version) to the 1910 version in which both the Yukon code and evolution become ambiguous. The cause of the ambiguity, I argued, was an intrusion into London's consciousness of a social critique linked to his socialist views; but it is a critique which was at the time too rudimentary to be manifested as a systematic denunciation of the human consumption of the planet. Hence we get only hints of the critique in the background of the story. But with the focus first on the dog and then on the final cause of the man's death we are drawn through the foregrounded events in the plot to the implied critique in the background. The man's final and desperate attempts to reduce the dog to disposable object and to build a fire of and under the spruce tree are the conjunction of acts which let us correctly read the story. The quenching of the fire emphasizes the reason why he came to the Yukon, to empty it of fur, gold, and timber. It is fitting that a dog and a spruce tree take away his last chance of survival.

Such a judgement of the man of course imposes another moral on a story already moralistic and emphasizes the irony of the story; in short, as Labor and Hendricks point out,[15] it imposes "poetic justice" on the man. It also moves the story away from realistic to fabular narrative. The man's death is no longer simply a plot device to convey a Darwinian-Naturalist moral about the human condition; it is a commentary on the man's motivation for being in the Yukon. The attempt to kill the dog is no longer simply "proof" of Darwinian laws; it is also an example of the arrogance of a self-styled dominant species. Nor is the incident simply an objective correlative incapsulating for us the emotions inherent in such a moment; it is a clue to how to read the story. At the risk of sounding like Polonius I could categorize "To Build a Fire" as a "proto-environmentalist fable," for there is indeed something fable-like in the anonymous man's being destroyed by what he intended to destroy.[16] The fable says that the man dies not because of an inheritance of bad genes, about which we can make no moral judgement, but because of an inheritance of bad ideology, which we, and London, can judge. For those of us who share London's moral concern about the world, however tentatively it is presented in the story, the judgement delivered by nature on a would-be violator is in fact a judgement, it is exactly what he deserves, and for us, as for London, that judgement is why the man dies.[17]

NOTES

[1] All references to the final version of "To Build a Fire" are to the *Lost Face* version in Donald Pizer, ed. *Jack London: Novels and Stories* (New York: Library of America, 1982), 462-478.

² This reading is summarily stated in *The Spectator* by Tony Tanner: the story is "simply about a man fighting a losing battle with frost" reprinted in *Twentieth Century Literary Criticism* 15 (Detroit: Gale Research, 1985), 270. The standard reading is vigorously espoused by Charles E. May, "'To Build a Fire': Physical Fiction and Metaphysical Critics," *Studies in Short Fiction* [*SSF*] 15 (1978), 19-24. But in *Jack London* (New York: Twayne, 1974) Earle Labor argues that the story follows the model of classical tragedy.

³ "He was angry and cursed his luck aloud" (469).

⁴ In *Critical Survey of Short Fiction* 5 (Englewood Cliffs, New Jersey: Salem, 1981), 1811.

⁵ Or perhaps they are the characteristic difficulties of London's work. Labor summarizes some of them in *Jack London*, 148-150. See also Charles N. Watson, Jr., *The Novels of Jack London: A Reappraisal* (Madison: U of Wisconsin P, 1983), 235-244. Labor and King Hendricks reprint the letter in which London says he is revising from memory in "Jack London's Twice-Told Tale," *SSF* 4 (1967), 334-347.

⁶ I am citing this version as reprinted in "Twice-Told Tale," 342-347.

⁷ The epigraph is in Pizer, *Jack London*, 997.

⁸ Labor and Hendricks point out in "Twice-Told Tale," 340. that the dog is just one of the "things of life" for the man. The muzzle metaphor does not appear in the 1902 version of the story.

⁹ This assuming the common etymology of "husky" from "Eskimo."

¹⁰ "Twice-Told Tale," 335.

¹¹ A curious exception is "Bud," who devised the nose-strap. But perhaps because the name is a diminutive/nickname it suggests the man's attitude toward Bud.

¹² Pointed out in Labor, *Jack London*, 155.

¹³ In *Utne Reader* 50 (1992), 157-159.

¹⁴ This was pointed out to me by two colleagues, Rebecca Hogan and Nancy Lewis. Labor and Hendricks see the man as a "loner" but do not connect that characteristic with an implicit socialist critique.

¹⁵ "Twice-Told Tale," 340.

¹⁶ In "Twice-Told Tale" Labor and Hendricks categorize the 1902 version as an "exemplum," but the category applies equally well to the later versions.

¹⁷ Perhaps London is making a distinction between those members of the species who exploit the planet ("the man") and those who oppose the exploitation (socialists). But how that distinction can be fitted into the evolutionary theme is not clear, unless he is suggesting that while exploitation is an innate characteristic of humans only some humans manifest that characteristic in behavior because of circumstances, "personality," etc. and others do not for the same reasons.

◄ 2 ►

A Daughter of the Snows

Early Reviews

Books of the Week and Literary Chat

B. G. Lathrop

Those readers of fiction who enjoyed *The Son of the Wolf* and *The God of His Fathers*—those two capital books of short stories from the pen of Jack London—will welcome *A Daughter of the Snows*. This is the first novel that London has written—all of his other literary work having been limited to magazine articles, some mediocre newspaper work, and a number of good short stories. It is in the short story that Mr. London is at his best; particularly in those that take for a theme the tribes of the frozen north.

This is not saying that the present novel is not most commendable. It is far and away ahead of the average fiction of the day, but it shows the hand of a writer trained rather in the art of short story writing than in conceiving and carrying out the more elaborate construction of the novel.

A Daughter of the Snows is rather a collection of connected sketches with the same persons playing a part in all of them than a novel according to the generally accepted idea of that class of fiction.

As the title suggests, this is a story of the north, Mr. London's chosen field. The great interest of the book lies first in the characters and then in the descriptions of different phases of life in the land of ice, snow and gold, and on the trail.

The heroine, the "Daughter" of the [title, is Frona Welse. She is the type of young] woman, strong, courageous, and beautiful, that Mr. London so delights in making the center figure. The first four chapters of the book concern themselves with the trip of Frona from the sea over the Chilcoot to Dawson. This is supposed to be at the time of the great Klondike boom and this part of the story is particularly interesting for the pictures, vivid and strong, which it offers of life on the trail—its tragic and bright sides. Here Frona meets Vance Corliss, a mining engineer, young, good looking and the right sort—as after events are to show.

Frona has been away from the land of her birth, this frozen land of ice and snow, and in the sunny lands of the temperate zone that she might acquire the education and cultivation requisite for the daughter of so important a man as Jacob Welse—the great man of the Klondike, whose hand appears in every investment or industry of note in the land.

The cleverest parts of the story are those in which the author works out the problem of a suitable mate for this daughter of the north. Frona has not had the sterling worth of the ice-zone thawed out of her veins by her southern education, nor has she lost any of her heritage of moral and physical courage from that pioneer of pioneer stock—Jacob Welse, her father.

She likes Vance Corliss; and as the author develops his character through various adventures peculiar to so rough and new a country, the reader comes to like him too and to wonder if really in the end he will lose Frona to the dashing, handsome braggart, St. Vincent.

That is one point in which Mr. London cannot be too highly complimented—his art in keeping the reader on the needle-point of uncertainty about the final outcome of the love story until practically the last paragraph.

It is easy to see for our own satisfaction that St. Vincent is a coward, but it is hard to tell whether Frona sees it or not. The author makes this contrast of bravery and cowardice the keynote and motif of his story. A man in a new country where it is the survival of the fittest may be a fool or a knave and command some respect somewhere from somebody, but he cannot be a coward—and Mr. London makes this specially evident in this story of the Klondike.

One of the strongest scenes in the book is where St. Vincent is accused by an old miner, now a Klondike king, and also the early and lasting friend of Frona. Matt McCarthy knows that St. Vincent has won the love of Frona under false pretenses and he knows the man to be a faint-heart. He goes to his cabin and accuses him to his face—the denouement is startling, to say the least.

This trial of St. Vincent later in the story is also worthy of notice and is really a short story in itself.

Another section of the book deserving of special mention is the account of the bravery of Frona and Corliss in striving to rescue a courier from the ice in the river. One of the pictures on this page shows them in the boat and fighting with the breaking ice of the Yukon. "Del" is another character of the story quite unique in its way and a most finished production in the art of character drawing. He is the typical pocket miner, who mines as much for the excitement as for the money he may find; a man who would rather fight than eat, straight as a string, and every inch a man, but absolutely without refinement or any of the graces of civilization.

A Daughter of the Snows gives the reader a fine idea of life among the early pioneers of the north during the first fever of the gold rush, and, moreover, is a good story. It is well worth reading.

San Francisco Sunday Call November 9, 1902, Magazine Section, 12.

An Unconventional Heroine

Such a wild and unconventional heroine! Frona Welse, the daughter of old Jacob Welse, the great dignity of Alaska, swings clubs and boxes and fences and swims, and can make high dives, chins a bar twenty times, and can walk on her hands. These are accomplishments indeed! Frona has been East at school, and has just landed on the Pacific Coast, and she hopes to reach Dawson in a few days.

A young woman on a journey in Alaska must be fully prepared for many hardships. Certainly she is placed in many peculiar positions. We are not prudish, for there may be certain accidents which might happen. Her meeting with Vance Corliss, a mining engineer, and the night spent by her in the young man's company, is a fairly risqué business. Anyhow Corliss is the soul of honor. Arriving at Dawson Corliss pays his respects to Frona. No wonder the young man who was really well brought up and used to the elegancies of life, was taken aback when he entered the Welse salon. There must be first-class decorators in Alaska. On the walls of the room there hung a Turner sunrise "and things in bronze." There were people present who talked quite glibly of French symbolism.

Frona goes out walking one day and comes across a woman of doubtful character and the two quote Browning. Frona falls in love with Corliss. The girl's happy-go-lucky ways rather disconcert the young man. There are differences of opinion between the two.

Then comes a queer man, who calls himself Gregory St. Vincent. He represents himself to be a newspaper personage. We find out shortly that he is a bad man. What is essentially clever in the romance is the part played by the Indians. Finally Corliss and Frona come to an understanding and are supposably married. The author of *A Daughter of the Snows* has great ability, and his ways of writing differ from the ways of most makers of fiction, only there have been stories written by Jack London which we like better than the one under notice. Nevertheless, as a study of a region as yet barely known, what he writes mainly about contains much that is novel. Everybody knows how they carry on in London or Paris or New York, but not in Dawson.

New York Times Saturday Review of Books and Art November 22, 1902, 806.

Telling What He Has Seen

Charles A. Moody

All the qualities which have given Jack London's short stories their compelling grip are well in evidence in his first novel, *A Daughter of the Snows*, with proof besides that his art is equal to the larger canvas. Yet the real secret of his power lies just in the fact that he is no mere spinner of tales—indeed, this broad-shouldered, square-set, firm-lipped, merry-eyed young man seems hardly of a piece with "the literary world" at all. But he is a man who has Done Things—things far outside the routine of ordinary lives. And in doing them, he has made them a part of himself. Outside this field of his own experience he does not go for material. Each of his stories, therefore, has a part of *himself* in it—and he is a Man of Power. Small wonder that they hold attention with a firm clinch. I do not know from which of the younger writers we may expect more important work as his field enlarges and his powers ripen.

Out West 17 (December 1902), 746.

An Elemental Maid

This novel of Jack London's shows more power than anything he has done. The book throughout is splendidly virile, and glowing passages illumine the narrative. He has created a new woman, something elemental, physically almost savage, but with touches of the eternal feminine that prevent her being a man in petticoats—*A Daughter of the Snows*, in truth, and a credit and embellishment of that wonderful region, Alaska. She must be an ideal of Mr. London's aggressive cerebrality, but she rings true and would not be herself in any other setting than that in which he places her. Frona Welse is a magnificent Amazon of the snowy Edge of Things, and if she ever seems escaping from the hold of her creator, Mr. London, it is when he lets her grow young-ladyish. She is a woman, clean-souled, strong-thewed, and with an essential touch of deep underlying sympathy. It is an achievement to have drawn a girl who has such a number of strictly masculine qualities and yet appeals to the best in a man keenly susceptible to womanly influence and charm.

    A Daughter of the Snows is the most vital presentation of Alaska that literature has yet known. The bitter cold, the wearying trails, the tremendous spring break-up of the ice-bound Yukon, the rough atmosphere of mining life, the biting color of social intercourse in Dawson and in the mining-camps, together with sharp-cut, forceful human beings, are all powerfully depicted. The reader is there and sees things pass before his eyes.

Mr. London could not handle his theme with such thorough assertiveness were he not strong and frank. He treats an episode, necessarily suggestive, in the wholesomest fashion, and with breezy purity. Frona Welse, the heroine, returns to Alaska after having been "on the outside" since she was a girl, getting cultured. She is twenty, and that the States and London have not enervated her is shown by the plucky and enduring way she treads the bitter trail which puts strong men on their mettle. She is separated from her outfit through some casualty, and arrives at a tent on a dismal night, wet and weary. An engaging young man is the sole occupant. She explains her plight and asks hospitality. He accords it willingly, and magnanimously says he will "sit up and watch the fire." "Fiddlesticks!" she cried. "As tho your foolish little code were saved in the least! We are not in civilization. This is the trail to the Pole. Go to bed." So they sleep like tired children, their blanket couches on either side of the stove. It is only allowing her a proper share of feminine inconsistency, that she falls in love, not with this fine Vance Corliss, but a specious adventurer named St. Vincent.

The book is open to some criticism on the ground of technique. Mr. London's craftsmanship is faulty. The narrative lacks perfect cohesion and unity. He dispenses his tale in sections which stand too much apart, and greater clearness as to place and date would help the novel materially. The language of two or three of the characters is absurdly polished. But it is a vigorous work, and Frona Welse is, as a whole, a wonderful and quite new phase of womanhood.

Literary Digest 26 (January 10, 1903), 60.

Fiction: *A Daughter of the Snows*

There is nothing quite so destructive of dramatic utterance as the pulpit tone; and it is especially prejudicial to dramatic art when an author is dealing with elemental qualities. In *The Call of the Wild* Mr. London, with a thoroughness suggestive of Mr. Kipling, felt for the brute force behind the actions of men and of other animals; and his knowledge of the unharvested North gave him a real and an unspoilt stage for exhibiting the attributes. A daughter of the snows, whom we first see on her return after a short lapse into New York education, passes across the same stage, and Mr. London would make her stand as type of the triumphant courage of her race in grip with the forces of nature. *A Daughter of the Snows* (Isbister, 6s.) is impelled by the same power as his other Klondike tales. We have fine pictures of those elemental forces in nature and in man—in the break-up of a frozen river, in the passions and the justice of decivilized miners fighting and condemning each other. In the attempt at a sort of Aeschylean grandeur, the language sometimes escapes from the grandeur into affectation; and the heroine is endowed with Amazonian virtues that slightly diminish her humanity. But carried on the flood of a strong romance in a virgin country these excesses are pardonable, the defects of virtues, the riot of virile imagination. What is difficult to pardon is the interspersed sermon on the strenuous life, a theme better in action than in speech. The heroine begins almost, as it were, a Pilgrim's Progress, and each person she meets, some of whom are dragged in with small dramatic excuse, is labelled with texts and preached from. The Teuton or Anglo-Saxon race is applauded with a fulsome insistence that should be distasteful to every quality in the elemental man. Mr. Winston Churchill made an attempt—and he was justified—to write an epic on his branch of the race; but to take himself seriously enough to write a homily is to exceed the privilege of an author. The self-consciousness appears in the tissue of the language as in the inserted exhortations. The heroine and one of lighter virtue at a psychological crisis, in a scene of lonely splendor, cap each other from Browning—and "Paracelsus" at that; and a lecture in moral philosophy breaks the tumult of a drinking saloon. It is a pity. The story would have been fresh, vigorous, and manly, but for this sort of Teuton priggishness—to adopt Mr. London's ethnology—this air of inheriting the earth by virtue of superior strenuousness. For the exhibiting of this courage the incidents are built up on too colossal a scale for physical probability to endure; and, in spite of much force of imagination and language, and a real knowledge of his place and people Mr. London must be judged to collapse beneath the weight of his own seriousness.

Times Literary Supplement July 22, 1904, 229.

New Books: *A Daughter of the Snows*

Julian Hawthorne

We are so much under the influence of mere external nature, that when we find ourselves in a place where civilization has not yet set its metes and bounds, and where the pressure of the social atmosphere (unknown millions of moral pounds to the square inch) is relieved, we swell up into our natural savage proportions. Unexpected sights are seen, in consequence. A man's real self is commonly so unlike the self which his fears, traditions and prudences cause him to show to his similarly intimidated friends—which is not, of course, his self at all, or even a self of any sort, but a ghastly puppet and simulacrum which his notion of what is becoming and expedient and expected prompts him to fashion out of who can say what odds and ends and rags and tatters of time-serving and hypocrisy—as to be utterly unrecognizable for the most part; even the physical man often undergoes transformation, and there appear a strange beard, long hair, loose hat, shirt and boots, such as would raise a mob about his ears if displayed in his own birthplace.

The rapid development, so-called, of this country of ours has made this spectacle so common that we have almost ceased to notice it; and our writers, beginning with Bret Harte, have so assiduously painted the portrait of it that it has entered into our literature, and we have come to regard these transmogrified persons, these renegades from the orthodox, these failures and waifs and revealed blackguards, as, somehow, a new race of men, who first began to exist as we now find them. These writers, and their readers too often, go so far as to make heroes and figures of romance out of the tatterdemalions; they give them the one quality which only by the rarest chance do they ever possess in reality—distinction. They render their vices and crimes dark and splendid and desperate—instead of painting them in their native baseness and vulgarity; and they arbitrarily and against nature combine them in unholy and impossible marriage with beautiful virtues, delicacies and self-abnegations, such as would be looked on with suspicion even in a convent, but which, on the frontier, are positively ludicrous. The real frontiersman is not the dregs of the human race, for at least he had gumption enough to get out on the frontier, instead of remaining to pick pockets or keep white slaves in the cities; but he comes from a very low stratum as a rule; he sometimes possesses animal courage, sometimes persistence and a certain measure of intelligence; but all his finer virtues could easily be written out on his unmanicured thumb-nail, and leave room and to spare. It is true that the man who flees to the wilderness generally "finds himself," as the phrase is; but the self that he finds has only one advantage over the self that he leaves behind him in civilization—it is the real thing, and therefore it is in most cases a thing one would prefer to turn one's eyes away from. This is an indictment of civilization itself. For if civilization were a wholesome and desirable thing, as at present administered, then its subjects would appear to better and better advantage the more they uncovered themselves. But inasmuch as, when the fine trappings and liveries are taken off, the thing underneath appears diseased and malfavored, the meaning is that civilization and not the wilderness is to blame. Civilization is a broadcloth coat, a silk dress, a lying tongue, and hands that shed innocent blood by stealth and carry round the contribution plate in churches in public. The wilderness simply brings the facts to light, and is deserving of our hearty encomiums for that service. But we do not care to contemplate the facts, unless we are psychologists or reformers, or cynics who deny the possibility of good in man. For others, the deception is preferable; for we have learned to make it very smooth, flattering and plausible: and if shocking things do not improve us, we would better ignore them, and continue to be deceived.

But this is an apologue. It was suggested by a novel written by Mr. Jack London, who is a young writer only lately heard of, but already achieving, in the enormous competition of modern literature, a measure of favorable reputation. Mr. London is obviously young; and he still wears upon him the marks of the newspaper reporter; and of by no means one of the most skilful newspaper reporters, either. But he is also more than a newspaper reporter, in that he is beginning to have ideas of his own, and ambitions, and, perhaps, hopes of reconstituting society and mankind. These aspirations still welter unformed and dim in his mind; but there is the promise of growth and sanity in them, by the aid of experience, self-control, and commonsense—of that loyalty to simple nature and truth, too, which, in the end, are found to be so much better than the fine writing and highfalutin in which at present he so frequently indulges. The fact is, Mr. London has not yet digested himself. Hitherto he has restricted himself to short tales, in which he has described with vigor and with a good eye for scenery and the rough outlines of character, the sort of renegade life to which I have referred; taking his cue, one would suppose, from Bret Harte, Owen Wister, and even from Kipling, though at some distance behind the least of these worthies. But, meanwhile, he has been having thoughts of higher things; he has been scrutinizing the foundations of human society and character, has found them not all they should be, and has been inspired by an impulse to indicate what, in his opinion, they ought to be. It is a generous impulse, and it may lead to great things; but at first, the result of his cogitations, as illustrated in this novel or romance, must be pronounced crude and incoherent. The only cure for these shortcomings is to keep on thinking, and observing; and not to make up dialogues and characters from the resources of one's notion-counter, but to trust exclusively to adaptations of what he has heard and seen. It will be a long time, perhaps, before he becomes competent to write such a story as *A Daughter of the Snows* as it ought be written; but he can always be attempting something towards that end—working systematically up from the less to the more difficult. The time will undoubtedly come when Mr. London will be very sorry he did not wait before doing what he has here done; and he will criticize it far more severely than I care to criticize it; but, after all there is no better teacher than failure, if only we do not allow ourselves to be discouraged by it. Mr. London, I think, has too much vitality and good sense in him to make twice the mistake he makes in this first long story of his; so that, in the long run, he may be said to gain as much as to lose by having perpetrated it.

His object in the story is clear enough; he wanted to draw a woman unhampered by the absurdities of modern conventions; one who had the courage to think and act according to her own views of what was right; who should dare to break with all manner of traditions and orthodoxy and proprieties, and yet should remain pure, clean and lovable. The thing has often been attempted before; Mr. London's attempt differs from most others in his having made his girl the possessor of a thorough education on orthodox lines; having got that, she then goes back to the home of her childhood (which happens to be Alaska), and there conducts herself by the light of nature and healthy impulse—as we are asked to believe. She is beautiful, athletic, and morally as well as physically brave; and she has at her fingers' ends all modern and classic literature and philosophy. Her father, an industrial and commercial power in the raw country, had fears that she would be "spoiled" by her long educational experience in Eastern schools and colleges; but she soon shows him that she is as primitive as ever, in spite of her learning. This is something, by the way, that would not occur in real life; a person, and especially a girl, cannot be subjected during the most impressionable period of her life to years of contact with the machine of civilization, without showing the effects of it in every manifestation of her existence. Mr. London tries to account for her by insisting at great length upon the power of "race"; she has the Scandinavian blood in her; is a sort of Brunhilda brought down to our times; but the explanation does not convince. In spite of all that her creator can do, the young lady betrays at every step the most wearisome self-consciousness and affectation; I cannot recall a single act or word of hers that has a genuine ring to it. She is, indeed, as much a monster—a thing contrary to nature—as the phenomenon constructed by the philosopher Frankenstein. After all the labor lavished upon her, she remains at the end of the story utterly incredible and even inconceivable; she never materializes—or precipitates, as the Theosophists say. Though she is talking all the time, we never hear her voice; or so much as see her face, though she is always before us. And it must be confessed that the things she is said to do and say are unpleasant, and actually vulgar. Mr. London probably thought to help the matter by adducing the Alaskan background; but this was a misconception on his part; it is in a sense a primitive background, but it is very far from being an ideal one. The only primitiveness is that of nature; the men, as I said before, are degenerates or renegades. It is true that the father of the girl is represented as being by nature a king of men; but in so far as he is this, he is unnatural; we cannot believe in him. There is a whole chapter of dialogue between him and his daughter which is entirely preposterous. It might pass in a book all conceived in the same highfalutin, transcendental key; but it is sandwiched in between passages of the most uncompromising realism. This incongruity is fatal to the book as a work of art; it is weaving cobwebs and tow in the same fabric. The fabric looks absurd, and the value of both its constituent parts is lost.

Frona Welse—such is the simple every-day name of the heroine—is placed between two men, one a villain, the other a hero, who are in love with her; and she is in company with other men who admire her, but do not quite pretend to be suitors. There is also a prostitute who is sought after by Frona, with altruistic and humane views, of course, but with an utter absence of reason and motive. The two women embrace each other, and talk much nonsense; and the upshot is that the prostitute marries an American army officer. Frona herself is much freer in her manner than the prostitute; she handles every man she comes across, and kisses many of the "on the mouth" as Mr. London is careful to mention. When she cùts her foot on the ice one of her lovers strips off his shirt to make footwear for her; and in that condition occupies the thwart in front of hers in the canoe; and she rejoices to see the sun making his back red. When her other lover, the villain, is arrested and tried for murder, she forces herself into the room where Judge Lynch is holding his court, undertakes the defence of the prisoner, cross-examines witnesses, listens complacently to stories of his amatory exploits among Indian squaws, and kisses him good-bye at the foot of the gallows. She thinks nothing of sleeping all night alone with a man in a hut. She grasps a French Baron by the hair, exclaims, "What a ridiculous, foolish, lovable fellow it is!" turns his face up and kisses him on the lips—though the baron was not in the least expecting it. One of her lovers kisses one of her bare toes; she tells him, that if he cares for her in a big-brotherly way, he may kiss "all my toes." "He grunted, but did not deign to reply." This is a virtuous, pure-minded American girl with an Eastern college education! If she is like this in her virgin condition, what will she be when she has been admitted to the free-masonry of married life? Which would you prefer to be:—her husband, or her lover? Or would you not rather give her a wide berth, and avoid nausea altogether? There is not an atom of femininity in her; and if she were physically ugly, nothing could prevent anyone from regarding her as an impudent trollop.

But when Mr. London turns aside from the hopeless enterprise of rendering this phenomenon amenable to human proportions and comprehension, his work is forcible, picturesque and interesting. He knows his scenery well, and can draw it vigorously; he understands his frontiersmen, and can make them credible. He is still inclined to extravagance and caricature; and does not know that a thing which might actually occur in real life is not therefore necessarily possible in fiction, which should be true in a manner and degree which nature often fails to compass. Again, he lacks the judgement or intuition which should tell him when to leave off; he fatigues us with too much of a good thing—as in the prolonged description of the canoe trip across the half-frozen river. Instead of grasping the essential elements of the adventure, and grouping them succinctly, once for all, he strings the story out till it expires for absolute lack of further material. The story of the murder is another instance of prolixity; it is pulled over and over like a mass of tangled string; there is no imagination shown in the treatment. One of the best, and best told episodes in the book is the interview between St. Vincent (the villain) and the old Irishman, McCarthy. It is a little extravagant and sentimental, but not beyond the bounds of possibility; and the point made is a good and new one. Such collisions of inner character are among the best material of novelists; they are seldom improved, because failure is so much easier than success in the handling of them; but Mr. London may be said to have succeeded, in this instance.

Upon the whole, this writer is to be welcomed; for it is much better to fail in doing a difficult thing than to succeed in doing a trifle. There is bone, fibre and sinew in Mr. London. If his good angels screen him from popular success, during the next few formative years of his career, he may do something well worth the doing, and do it well. But if he is satisfied with his present level of performance, there is little hope for him.

Wilshire's Magazine 62 (February 1903), 84-87.

Jack London: Blond Beasts and Supermen

Charles Child Walcutt

It has been said that a writer puts most of himself into his early work, a statement that is strikingly true of London's first novel, *A Daughter of the Snows* (1902). He subsequently lamented that he had squandered in it material for a dozen novels,[1] and he is lavishly prodigal of ideas. Beginning, then, with the ideas, we find a wealth of exposition that sets forth most of the beliefs which have been discussed earlier in this chapter.

The operation of determinism is presented in the clearest terms, with rather pompous pedantry:

> These be the ways of men, each as the sun shines upon him and the wind blows against him, according to his kind, and the seed of his father, and the milk of his mother. Each is the resultant of many forces which should go to make a pressure mightier than he, and which moulds him in the predestined shape. But, with sound legs under him, he may run away, and meet with a new pressure. He may continue running, each new pressure prodding him as he goes, until he dies, and his final form will be that predestined of the many pressures.[2]

But hard on the heels of this exposition comes a belief in primordialism. "Thus, in the young Northland," he writes, "frosty and grim and menacing, men stripped off the sloth of the south and gave battle greatly. And they stripped likewise much of the veneer of civilization—all of its follies, most of its foibles, and perhaps a few of its virtues. Maybe so; but they reserved the great traditions and at least lived frankly, laughed honestly, and looked one another in the eyes." Elsewhere this creed is expanded in a defense of atavism, of the notion that one's adaptability (and therefore one's likelihood of survival) depends upon one's nearness to a primitive state. The hero's greatest virtue lay in his not having become hardened in the mold formed by his several forbears:

> Some atavism had been at work in the making of him, and he had reverted to that ancestor who sturdily uplifted. But so far this portion of his heritage had lain dormant. He had simply remained adjusted to a stable environment. There had been no call upon the adaptability which was his. But whensoever the call came, being so constituted, it was manifest that he should adapt, should adjust himself to the unwonted pressure of new conditions. The maxim of the rolling stone may be all true; but notwithstanding, in the scheme of life, the inability to become fixed is an excellence par excellence.

With such an outlook it is not surprising that London sets forth as "survival values" the cruder kinds of physical might and brute courage; but he presents them with the self-consciousness and muscle-flexing self-idolatry of one who attaches spiritual values to brute force. The emphasis in the following passage upon body, body, body, upon those muscles of which your true primitive man is wholly unconscious, is typical of this attitude toward the struggle for existence and toward the kind of beings he would like to see prevail.

> Thus Frona, the heroine and superwoman, liked the man because he was a man. In her wildest flights she could never imagine linking herself with any man, no matter how exalted spiritually, who was not a man physically. It was a delight to her and a joy to look upon the strong males of her kind, with bodies comely in the sight of God and muscles swelling with the promise of deeds and work. Man, to her, was pre-eminently a fighter. She believed in natural selection and in sexual selection, and was certain that if man had thereby become possessed of faculties and functions, they were for him to use and could but tend to his good. And likewise with instincts. If she felt drawn to any person or thing, it was good for her to be so drawn, good for herself. If she felt impelled to joy in a well-built frame and well-shaped muscle, why should she restrain? Why should she not love the body, and without shame? The history of the race, and of all races, sealed her choice with approval. Down all time, the weak and effeminate males had vanished from the world-stage. Only the strong could inherit the earth. She had been born of the strong, and she chose to cast her lot with the strong.

The reader must not think for an instant that this passage authorizes any sort of sexual freedom. The heroine is unwaveringly chaste because, the tone of the book would seem to say, so fine a creature could be nothing else but chaste. A woman of question-able virtue in the story is scarcely allowed to speak to the heroine. In other words, the atavism is safely mixed with the sexual ethics of civilization—a concession partly, perhaps, to be traced to London's concern for the prejudices of his readers.

This affection for atavism merges, elsewhere, into a definition of "the will to power" that is strikingly close to the Nietzschean conception. Frona's love of bodily strength—a strength which is accompanied by a higher moral nature that shines through its splendid physical container—is presented as an ethical choice, a choice involving distinction between good and evil, rather than a choice which represents only the force of animal impulse. Her father, mighty trader of the North, expresses a higher, Nietzschean concept of will in describing the code of the strong:

> Conventions are worthless for such as we. They are for the swine who without them would wallow deeper. The weak must obey or be crushed; not so with the strong. The mass is nothing; the individual everything; and it is the individual, always, that rules the mass and gives the law. A fig for what the world says! If the Welse should procreate a bastard line this day,

it would be the way of the Welse, and you would be a daughter of the
Welse, and in the face of hell and heaven, of God himself, we would stand
together, we of the one blood, Frona, you and I.

These lines almost define the master-morality of self-assertion that Nietzsche
opposed to the miserable slave-morality by which the weak sought to protect
themselves from the strong. Frona Welse, likewise, combines beautiful physique
and hardihood with intellectual subtlety. Bred in the North, educated in the
United States, she is an ideal example, London seems to say, of the higher
woman, with perfect body and piercing intellect. In the treatment of the hero the
notion of the superman draws markedly away from the Nietzschean concept, the
difference being measured by the hero's atavism: as he works into the spirit of
the Northland his manhood waxes. "Gambling without stakes is an insipid
amusement, and Corliss discovered, likewise, that the warm blood which rises
from hygienic gymnasium work is something quite different from that which
pounds hotly along when thew matches thew and flesh impacts on flesh and the
stake is life and limb." And in a later conflict, "The din of twenty centuries of
battle was roaring in his ear, and the clamor for return to type strong upon
him."[3]

It would be impossible to show a logical connection between these ideas
which are brought forth throughout *A Daughter of the Snows*. A satisfactory
classification of them is to consider the determinism to be the conclusion of the
calm philosopher who contemplates the flow of life from without; whereas the
atavism, the "will to power" creed, and the glorying in physical prowess and
valiant struggle represent the attitude toward the same set of facts that the
intelligent and unscrupulous strong man would take when he found himself
embroiled in the conflict. Caught up in the struggle for existence and hence
unable to view it philosophically, he devises a plan of action that will enable him
to thrive and to develop those instincts by which he is guided. It is the
philosophy of a fighter, celebrating will (as vital force, which is thus
subjectively identified with ethical rightness) diametrically opposed to the
"experimental" calm of a Zola, and yet depending upon the same basic
assumptions.

Mixed with this glowing individualism is a good deal of conventional
and high-flown moral idealism; this latter element is woven into the structural
pattern of the novel even more closely than the idea of ruthless self-assertion.
The central complication of the story consists of a triangle: Frona Welse,
superwoman, is strongly attracted to Vance Corliss, the newcomer to the North
who is responding so atavistically to its challenge; but Frona's heart is ensnared
by Gregory St. Vincent. Since Corliss is the hero, St. Vincent must be the
villain. His villainy consists primarily in cowardice and secondarily in his lying
to conceal it. The main action of the story is a series of events in which St.
Vincent's cowardice is exposed to Frona while Corliss's rugged virtues are
given ideal opportunities to display themselves.

The reader will doubtless recognize the fictional device by which a fine woman's heart is won by an oily-tongued rascal, while the hero, suffering but inarticulate, is recognized only after he has helped expose the baseness of his rival. In so important a situation, odd though it may seem to the realistic reader, this convention permits the superwoman to err in judgment without any shadow being cast upon her perfection. This convention, it would seem, rests upon the assumption that wrong will be punished and that a just Providence will always reward patient virtue, the assumption of a moral order, a universe properly controlled by justice and right. It is diametrically opposed to the materialism which admits no possibility of moral control of the universe. Now, although atavism and self-assertion are constantly invoked in *A Daughter of the Snows*, the reader knows that he is reading steadily toward the final triumph of the moral order through the exposure of St. Vincent and the rewarding of Corliss's love, and he is not disappointed. Thus we see that the structural pattern of the novel is woven upon a framework of ethical thought, the Moral Principle displayed in operation. Frona's purity is providentially saved from too intimate contact with the baseness of St. Vincent; and just as her goodness is manifested in a truly heroic devotion—in the face of terrible doubts—to the man to whom she has pledged her heart, so Providence rises to the occasion with a magnificent exposure that resolves all her doubts.

Even though the belief in this moral order may have come to London as a bit of story-writing technique, as a pattern, that is, which had been employed in countless earlier novels, it is used in a way that makes the writer's acceptance of it unquestionable. It is the mainspring of the action; its presence indicates London's inability to make his determinism carry the burden of his plot.

Further evidence of the idealism which is mixed with London's materialism lies in the fact that Frona and Corliss are sexually chaste, whereas St. Vincent is not. The thoroughgoing materialist would not blame a man for acting upon his natural impulses; rather he would applaud him. London was writing books to sell, and he always worked to please his readers; but it is nevertheless significant that he should slide so easily into conventional thinking. The story makes the most of the moral ardor which is kindled by its situations; the final scene is devoted to the heroine's icy denunciation of the coward:

> "Shall I tell you why, Gregory St. Vincent?" she said again. "Tell you why your kisses have cheapened me? Because you broke the faith of food and blanket. Because you broke salt with a man, and then watched that man fight unequally for life without lifting your hand. Why, I had rather you had died in defending him; the memory of you would have been good. Yes, I had rather you had killed him yourself. At least it would have shown there was blood in your body." The novel is built around acts of free will and based upon an implicit faith in a moral order. In these respects London's determinism has not penetrated to its structure. In two

other respects, however, it has done so. In the first place, the action as
described above takes up only a small part of the novel. In the rest of it,
accompanying the digressive exposition of philosophical materialism, is
scene after scene in which the conditions of Alaskan life are depicted.
Gold-hunting, starvation, the rigors of the trail, the spectacle of an ice-pack
breaking up—these are some of the many sequences which make up the
background of the story. In this picturesque presentation of the frozen
North one sees the conditions under which the struggle for existence, as
naively conceived by London, is carried on, conditions which challenge
man's strength and courage. Although they are not part of the plot proper
of *A Daughter of the Snows,* they nevertheless account for a large part of
its content.

The other point at which London's "naturalism" enters is in his choice of
cowardice as the hallmark of villainy. Cowardice argues unfitness in the struggle
for existence more directly than dishonesty, deceit, or any of the "moral"
failings which would impair a man's status in a more civilized community. But
London brings what can only be called "moral" ardor to his championship of the
clean, rugged, he-man virtues he prizes so highly. Cowardice in this story is
regarded as the most loathsome of sins, so loathsome that the reader is indignant
at the thought of a coward's marrying Frona Welse. In this way the moral and
the amoral are intertwined.

NOTES

[1] London, Charmian. *The Book of Jack London*, 2 Vols. (New York: Century,
1921) I, 384.
[2] London, Jack. *A Daughter of the Snows* (ed. London, 1908), 201-202. There
is no complete edition of London's works.
[3] Ibid., 148. Later Corliss explicitly states the materialistic philosophy of living
life for the sake of what can be enjoyed on earth, since nothing afterwards is certain; see
220-221.

Beneficial Atavism in Frank Norris and Jack London

James R. Giles

In an 1899 letter to Cloudesley Johns, a literary associate, London wrote about his fellow California writer: "See Frank Norris has been taken up by *McClures*. Have you read his *Moran of the Lady Letty*? It's well done."[1] This bit of praise for Norris' *Moran*, understated though it is, has relevance to London's first novel and his earliest stories; for it often seems in these works as if Norris' Wilbur and Moran have been resurrected and transported to the far north. Indeed, the whole concept of beneficial atavism, which Norris outlined in his first *published* novel, is utilized by London in these early stories and developed in a much more detailed fashion. London's spiritual brothers of Ross Wilbur, the manly Anglo-Saxons battling for survival in an alien environment surrounded by "lesser breeds," are even given a label—they are the "sons of the wolf."

Jack London was in the perfect position to develop the pattern laid down by Norris in *Moran*; for he had just returned from a life of lusty adventure in the last American frontier—Alaska's Yukon. Thus, he had seen with his own eyes men from an urban civilization suddenly faced with the necessity of surviving, often through brutality and force, in a wilderness environment; indeed, he had been such a man. Of course, the extent to which London derived the idea of beneficial atavism from Norris is debatable. However, since the patterns of reversal are highly similar in the works of both men and since it is certain that London had read and admired *Moran* shortly before he published his first stories, some influence seems possible.

The concept of beneficial atavism seen in London's early Yukon tales is made up of the same basic ingredients which Norris used in *Moran*—belief in the healthful influence of a life of violence, emphasis on the idea of an individual becoming a man by struggling with a hostile environment, and a complete acceptance of Anglo-Saxon racism. There are, of course, superficial differences—the environment here is the frozen waste of the far north; and the "lesser breeds" are Indians and Eskimos, rather than Orientals. Indeed, one early volume of stories *(Children of the Frost*, 1902) reveals a degree of sympathy with the northern Indian which Norris (or London, for that matter) never felt for the Oriental. However, in London's first two volumes of short stories *The Son of the Wolf* (1900) and *The God of His Fathers* (1901) and in his first novel *A Daughter of the Snows* (1902), these differences are superficial.

Perhaps the character of Vance Corliss in *A Daughter of the Snows* best reveals the kinship of these early works to Norris' *Moran*. Corliss, like Ross Wilbur, is a city-bred sophisticate who attains manhood in his new environment. At one point, Corliss gets into a barroom brawl and experiences this moment of self-revelation:

He had found that he was very much like other men after all, and the imminent loss of part of his anatomy (a man was biting his ear) had scraped off twenty years of culture. Gambling without stakes is an insipid amusement, and Corliss discovered, likewise, that the warm blood which rises from hygienic gymnasium work is something quite different from that which pounds hotly along when thew matches thew and flesh impacts on flesh and the stake is life and limb. As he dragged himself to his feet by means of the bar-rail, he saw a man in a squirrel-skin *parka* lift a beer-mug to hurl at Trethaway [a friend], a couple of paces off. And the fingers, which were more used to test-tubes and water-colors, doubled into a hard fist which smote the mug-thrower cleanly on the point of the jaw. The man merely dropped the glass and himself on the floor. Vance was dazed for the moment, then he realized that he had knocked the man unconscious,—the first in his life,—and a pang of delight thrilled through him.[2]

The similarity of this scene to Wilbur's moment of triumph over the corpse of the knifed Chinaman is obvious—manly exultation is achieved in both cases through acts of violence which remove years of artificial culture and civilization. It is significant that, at one point in the novel, London uses the word "atavism" to refer to the mysterious element in Corliss' nature which makes him flee the sheltered life and pursue romance and adventure (76).

Moreover, the novel has a counterpart to that awesome female, Moran, as well. Frona Welse is not quite the Viking that Moran was; but she is a "new woman" with a highly individualistic code of conduct which stresses manliness and physical strength. For instance, she gives the following list of her physical accomplishments: "'Oh, I can swing clubs, and box and fence' . . . and swim and make high dives, chin a bar twenty times, and—walk on my hands. There!'" (21) Later, she takes part in an arduous march across the Yukon wastes and comes upon a weakling male, who has collapsed in the snow in tears because he is tired and sore from carrying his pack and because his partners have deserted him. Frona has no sympathy for him:

"My friend," and Frona knew she was speaking for the race, "you are strong as they. You can work just as hard as they; pack as much. But you are weak of heart. This is no place for the weak of heart. You cannot work like a horse because you will not. Therefore the country has no use for you. The north wants strong men,—strong of soul, not body. The body does not count. So go back to the States. We do not want you here. . ." (38).

The contradiction between this statement and Frona's earlier speech stressing physical accomplishment is only superficial—what she really says is that, if one's soul is strong, his body will automatically be strong as well.

In case there is any doubt as to which race has a monopoly on "soul strength," London makes Frona a spokesman for the idea of Anglo-Saxon superiority: one of her more pointed statements of this concept reads like this:

> "We [Anglo-Saxons] are a race of doers and fighters, of globe-encirclers and zone-conquerors. We toil and struggle, and stand by the toil and struggle no matter how hopeless it may be. While we are persistent and resistant, we are so made that we fit ourselves to the most diverse conditions. Will the Indian, the Negro, or the Mongol ever conquer the Teuton? Surely not! The Indian has persistence, without variability; if he does not modify he dies, if he does try to modify he dies anyway. The Negro has adaptability, but he is senile and must be led. As for the Chinese, they are permanent. All that the other races are not, the Anglo-Saxon, or Teuton if you please, is. All that the other races have not, the Teuton has. What race is to rise up and overwhelm us?" (83)

All in all, Frona seems to be a somewhat refined Moran with more "book learning" and more structured rhetoric (Moran's speech is quite blunt and earthy). That London meant for her to symbolize all the best traditions of the Anglo-Saxon race, just as Norris meant for Moran to do, is clear. At one point, he even refers to her as a "Valkyrie" (147), which is the same word Norris used to refer to his imposing heroine.

This concept of Anglo-Saxon racism is even more central to London's beneficial atavism than it is to Norris'; for, at least in these early stories, London believed just as strongly as Frona Welse that "the Teuton" was the only individual who could adapt to a hostile environment. Not all Anglo-Saxons were so adaptable; but, as a race, they had a greater potential for making adjustments to strange environments than did the "lesser breeds." Moreover, this ability to adjust was the source of the "white man's" superior strength and power.

NOTES

[1] *Letters from Jack London.* Eds., King Hendricks and Irving Shepard (New York, 1965), 36.

[2] London, Jack. *A Daughter of the Snows* (Philadelphia: 1902), 120-121. Further references in text.

London's Concept of New Womanhood

Susan M. Nuernberg

A Daughter of the Snows showcases London's concept of "new womanhood." Frona Welse, the heroine, is the prototype of London's ideal sex comrade in that she is both sexual and civilized at the same time. London writes that Frona Welse offers Vance Corliss "the culture he could not do without, and the clean sharp tang of the earth he needed."[1]

Welse is a twenty-year-old woman of Celtic and Saxon extraction who was born in the Northland and educated in the States. Her "fair and flaxen-haired" mother died when Frona was a young girl. Her only playmates as a child were Indian children. She is the prodigy of her father, Jacob Welse, a great man who "bore the country on his shoulders; saw to its needs; [and] did its work" (60).

At the opening of the novel, Frona returns to the Northland after three years of higher education in the States. Not only does she return "simple, and clean, and wholesome," London writes, but as a result of her advanced, continental education she interprets Darwin to explain and justify her own sexual drive. London writes:

> She believed in natural selection and in sexual selection, and was certain that if man had thereby become possessed of faculties and functions, they were for him to use and could but tend to his good. And likewise with instincts. If she felt drawn to any person or thing, it was good for her to be so drawn, good for herself. If she felt impelled to joy in a well-built frame and well-shaped muscle, why should she restrain? Why should she not love the body, and without shame? (86-87)

London portrays Frona as unconventional in that she is very highly spirited and intelligent. She discovers and questions with an irrefutable logic society's view of a "true woman" as pious, pure, submissive and especially as having no sexual drive of her own at all. Frona uses all the intelligence and logic that she gained from her education to question and demolish society's definition of woman as mother whose place is in the home.

Frona's sexual drive is depicted by London as entirely natural. Frona never learned to repress her sexual desires as young women are taught to do by their mothers in civilized society. Instead, as London writes, Frona "had nursed at the breast of nature . . ." (24). Frona has natural sexual drives which she seeks to express rather than repress and she is aware that civilized society does not permit woman to affirm her sexual being. Frona is strong in that she is aspiring to a world where she could assume her own destiny; she does not want men to determine the bad or the good conduct for her to follow. She wants to live according to her own code of right and wrong.

Frona's unconventionality manifests itself in the sympathy and sorority with which she treats Lucile, a whore, at a chance meeting on a trail. Frona is reminded that her comportment is socially unwise by the arrival of Vance Corliss who, after cordially greeting Frona, "deliberately" turns his back on her companion, Lucile. His behavior angers Frona, because, as she tells him:

> "I came upon her, alone, by the trail, her face softened, and tears in her eyes. And I believe, with a woman's ken, that I saw a side of her to which you are blind. And so strongly did I see it, that when you appeared my mind was blank to all save the solitary wail, *Oh, the pity of it! The pity of it!* And she is a woman, even as I, and I doubt not that we are very much alike." (107)

The only difference that Frona recognizes between herself and Lucile is not that Lucile has sexual drive but that Lucile, by being a prostitute, misuses hers and in so doing, hurts only herself. To make Vance understand, Frona deliberately burns her finger in the flame of a candle saying, "And so I point the parable. The fire is very good, but I misuse it, and I am punished" (107).

After accusing Corliss of behaving "as narrow-mindedly" as would have the society he represents, Frona says, "I want to see what I can see, so tell me about this woman" (107). Corliss does not want Frona to show interest in Lucile because, as he tells Frona, "I cannot bear to see taint approach you. . . . There are some things which it were not well for a good woman to understand. One cannot dabble with mud and remain spotless" (108).

Frona then demands why it is that Corliss, a man, "may court contamination," while she, a woman, may not. Is it that "only the men are . . . as gods, knowing good and evil?" (110) she asks him. "That is new-womanish talk . . . equal rights, the ballot, and all that," Corliss retorts (111). Frona then declares that she stands not for the "new woman," but for the "new womanhood."

London clearly assumes the existence of a distinction between his notion of "new womanhood" and that of the "new woman," i.e. the single working girl, who was emerging as a type around the turn of the century, but he does not clarify for his reader exactly what that distinction was. Perhaps London was influenced in his thinking about the liberated woman by British socialist and eugenicist, Karl Pearson, who in a lecture on "The Woman's Question," (1885) had defined the woman's "problem" not as a matter of rights but in terms of "the effect of [woman's] emancipation on her function of race-reproduction."[2] While London's language is somewhat elusive, it does suggest that he valued "a strongly developed sexual instinct" in a woman and like Pearson saw it as a "condition for race permanence" (373).

Frona's strong sense of self derives from her father, Jacob Welse, who is inordinately proud of being a white man and a "sturdy" Welse. She shares his sense of Welsh racial pride and accepts his notions of blood, kinship and family honor. Furthermore, Frona is self-reliant and spirited like her father who cares "a fig for what the world says!" (184) And precisely because she is strong willed and does think for herself, Jacob offers her his unconditional support:

> "If the Welse should procreate a bastard line this day, it would be the way of the Welse, and you would be a daughter of the Welse, and in the face of hell and heaven, of God himself, we would stand together, we of the one blood, Frona, you and I." (184)

This incredible father-daughter talk strikes a jarring note especially since there is no suggestion whatsoever within the novel that Frona is other than virginal. What did London have in mind when he wrote the above passage? One can only speculate but, recalling that Jack London was himself a "bastard," it seems possible that this father-daughter chat represents a wish-fulfilling fantasy of his. London's mother's name, Flora Wellman, is very similar to the heroine's name, Frona Welse. Frona is described as having lost her mother when a little girl just as Flora did. Flora was Welsh, like Frona, and Flora's father, Marshall Wellman, was a prosperous businessman as was Frona's father, Jacob Welse. A key difference is that Flora was abandoned by her parents and by her common-law husband William H. Chaney when she discovered that she was pregnant. She had to be taken in by friends. London never knew his grandparents and, even though he passed through Massillon, Ohio on his tramp East, he had no contact with Flora's family. Perhaps London imagined that he and Flora would have been spared much misery and want if her father, Marshall Wellman, had only put the concept of "one blood" above all else and stood by her, as Jacob Welse offers to do for his daughter in the novel. Perhaps on a personal level, London invested in the idea of "blood" and "race" because it offered (vaguely) to connect him to something larger than himself and his immediate family which was all he had upon which to base an identity.

London's ideas and attitudes on race in general and on the superiority of the English-speaking branch of the Teutonic "race" in particular as expressed through Frona in this novel mirror those held by the majority of well-educated and prominent Americans at the turn of the century. London gives expression to the spirit of the civilized (white) world through Frona as she explains to Corliss,

> "We are a race of doers and fighters, of globe-encirclers and zone-conquerors. We toil and struggle, and stand by the toil and struggle no matter how hopeless it may be. While we are persistent and resistant, we are so made that we fit ourselves to the most diverse conditions. Will the Indian, the Negro, or the Mongol ever conquer the Teuton? Surely not! The Indian has persistence without variability; if he does not modify he dies, if he does try to modify he dies anyway. The Negro has adaptability, but he is servile and must be led. As for the Chinese, they are permanent." (83)

Although Corliss initially protests that her race egotism is "manifestly untrue," he does begin to imagine, like her, that "the dominant races have come down out of the north to empire," and that there must be "a reason for the dead-status of the black, [and] a reason for the Teuton spreading over the earth as no other race has ever spread" (146). Corliss attributes the empire-building feats of the Teutons, finally, to "race heredity." Corliss confesses to Frona, just before proposing marriage to her, that "there must be something in race heredity, else I would not leap at the summons" (146).

Through Frona, Corliss atavistically reclaims his sense of racial heritage. Ultimately the function of London's "new womanhood" is to awaken in the Anglo-Saxon male a sense of his racial mission in the world. London describes his vision of the "new womanhood" through the eyes of Vance Corliss as he gazes at Frona:

> Outlined against the blazing air, her brows and lashes white with frost, the jewel-dust striking and flashing against hair and face, and the south-sun lighting her with a great redness, the man saw her as *The Genius of the Race*. (emphasis added, 147)

London characterizes Frona as an inspiration to man in racial terms. This racist vision of "new womanhood" is both flawed and confused. It is best understood as London's imaginative response to what Karl Pearson had defined as the real problem with the emancipated woman.

London's vision of the emancipated woman did not threaten the welfare of the "race." Rather, she offered to serve as its guardian spirit. Frona is depicted as accomplishing this by inspiring great race pride in a man. London describes Corliss under her influence:

> The traditions of the blood laid hold of him, and he felt strangely at one with the white-skinned, yellow-haired giants of the younger world. And as he looked upon her the mighty past rose before him, and the caverns of his being resounded with the shock and tumult of forgotten battles. With bellowing of storm-winds and crash of smoking North Sea waves, he saw the sharp-beaked fighting galleys, and the sea-flung Northmen, great-muscled, deep-chested, sprung from the elements, men of sword and sweep, marauders and scourgers of the warm southlands! The din of twenty centuries of battle was roaring in his ear, and the clamor for return to type strong upon him. He seized her hands passionately. (148)

Fantastic and incredible as this transformation sounds, atavism and racial memory were pet theories of London's and London was a very popular writer during his lifetime. He mistakenly believed that memories of the so-called youth of the white man's "race" were stored in the germ plasm of each of its members and passed on from one generation to the next through inheritance.

For London, racial memory in human beings was analogous to instinct in animals; he portrayed it time and again in his writing as a positive life force. Although he was unable to explain just how one entered or exited the grip of a racial memory, he clearly imagined that almost any strong feeling could trigger such a coarse and pretentious vision. Such visions of crude, physical power, however, could be conjured up on any occasion when physical strength, which had become unnecessary for survival within civilization, was needed. And this was, of course, its attraction to the (over) civilized man or woman. It served to affirm the belief that the white man was biologically superior to all others and pre-determined to inherit and possess the world to the exclusion of the "lower races." The emancipated woman, of course, had not only to sound the call of kind, she had also to procreate and perpetuate her and his kind.

London's synthesis of the civilized and the natural expressions of the love instinct, however, failed to rise above the level of male sexual fantasy. He never was able imaginatively to transcend the sex comrade versus asexual mother dichotomy. The sex comrade remains a sex comrade within his fiction only by *not* becoming a mother. It is ironic, of course, that Frona defines herself as "natural and strong" and as fit to "mother the natural and strong" because she does not become a mother.

NOTES

[1] London, Jack. *A Daughter of the Snows*. (Philadelphia: Lippincott, 1902), 90. Further references in text.

[2] Pearson, Karl. "The Woman's Question," in *The Ethic of Freethought*. London: T. Fisher Unwin, 1901. Reprinted in Bernard Semmel, *Imperialism and Social Reform*. Cambridge: Harvard UP, 1960. Further references in text.

The Call of the Wild

Early Reviews

Literary Notes: Jack London at His Best

Rudyard Kipling is preeminently the poet of steam and the machine.

Before him there was no "ship that found herself." Before him no poet wove the cable, the telegraph, the locomotive into a love-poem of power and beauty, nor before him did levers and cranks, cogs and wheels, figure in the vocabulary of romance. Kipling is the most modern of literary moderns. He is in harmony with the spirit of the age.

And if steam and the machine have worked a tremendous revolution in material things during the half-century past, the doctrine of evolution has worked a greater one in traditions and beliefs. Kipling is the poet of the one, and—without flattery we say it—Jack London has irrefragably established his title as the prose poet of the other. In his former stories of the North, in the *Kempton-Wace Letters*, but more than all, in his last and best book, *The Call of the Wild*, he has touched the dry bones of a scientific theory with imagination and made them live. Romance? Here is the new romance. William Morris sought romance in mediaevalism. Many another has sought it there. In the background of their books loomed vague and misty the Olympian gods. Romance bore upon its shoulders the burden of dead beliefs and outworn creeds. But the *Call of the Wild* belongs to a new dispensation. The poetry that is in it is the poetry of the living world's real, not its imagined, history. To Mr. London the Trojan War, the wanderings of Ulysses, the westward journeyings of Aeneas are not half so stirring, so epic, as primitive man's struggle for existence against huge and hairy mammals in an age of ice.

That evolution plays such a part in the *Call of the Wild* does not mean that the theory has run away with the story. The tale of a noble dog, bred to a lazy life under sunny California skies, sold into service on an Alaskan sledge, forced to labor, his ancient instincts quickened into a new life, his pride in his strength aroused, and finally his spirit dominated by the forest where he comes to roam masterless and free at the head of a wolf-pack, the sire of a stronger and swifter race—all this is told with fine imagination and poetic power. Like Kipling's stories, again, it will appeal alike to those who read merely "for the story," and to those whose interest is in its broader aspects. This is Mr. London's strongest and most virile work—thus far.

Argonaut 53 (August 3, 1903), 72.

Novels: *The Call of the Wild*

Animals have long played an important and honored part in the region of the fairy-tale, while in poetic narrative they have figured prominently from the days of Homer downward. But the substitution of animals for men and women in the *dramatis personae* of novels is an essentially modern development, and it is still a somewhat strange experience to find the usual so far inverted that the chief rôles are assigned to inarticulate and four-legged characters. Up to a certain point the innovation is deserving of a welcome. With the advance of realistic methods in literature it has become so increasingly fashionable to select for delineation characters of a disagreeable or degraded type that the substitution of an animal cannot make much difference. As an alternative to the sophisticated vulgarities of the "smart set," the squalor of the submerged classes, or the unscrupulous individualism of filibustering financiers, the portrait of a faithful dog, a high-spirited horse, or even a patient donkey may be quite refreshing. But as the tendency develops, and the conscientious novelist begins to apply the same methods to animals as to men, we are by no means sure that the result in the long run will prove any more delectable. Canine fiction already shows symptoms of differentiation into the romantic and the realistic schools, and once the main principle of cleavage is established we may expect to see a variety of subdivisions appearing on either hand, according as show dogs, pet dogs, sporting dogs, fighting dogs, or mongrels are selected for treatment. Nor is the movement likely to confine itself within the boundaries of dog-land. The Kailyard school of the future may be expected to devote its energies to the composition of idylls of the poultry-run or the pig-stye, while the taste for full-blooded adventure will be catered for by romances of big game. It requires only a little effort of imagination to forecast the time when the columns of literary gossip will contain such entries as the following:—"Mr. Blank has started for Colorado in order to accumulate local color for his new beetle story." Or: "Mrs. Jones, the serpentine novelist, is spending the winter in India in order to study the manners and customs of the *Thanatophidia* on the spot. We understand that she has finally determined on the title of *The Cobra's Bride* for her next novel." Or, once more: "Mr. James Henry, the celebrated simian psychologist, has completed his arrangements for a prolonged tour in the Abyssinian highlands in order to obtain first-hand confirmation for some of the incidents in his forthcoming romance, *The Tragedy of a Sacred Baboon*. The heroine of the story, a hamadryad of great beauty and accomplishments, falls a victim to the drink habit and dies of spontaneous combustion."

Admirers of the spirited dog novels of Mr. Ollivant may protest against the exaggeration and burlesque of the foregoing remarks; but we are prepared to rest a plea of extenuation on the remarkable story which Mr. Jack London has given us under the title of *The Call of the Wild*. We do not deny its vivid and engrossing quality, due chiefly to the author's intimate acquaintance with the Wild West and the Yukon territory. But we contend that a great many of its incidents and its *dénouement* will not appeal to the dog-lover in the truest sense of the word, in that they emphasize the qualities which distinguish our four-footed friends from ourselves rather than those which endear them to us. 'Buck,' the dog-hero of the story, is a splendid half-breed, son of a St. Bernard father and Scotch sheep-dog mother, living at the opening of the tale on a luxuriously appointed country estate in the Santa Clara Valley. A rascally under-gardener kidnaps and sells him to a dog-dealer at the time of the Klondyke boom, and 'Buck' is ignominiously deported to Seattle, clubbed into submission by a brutal dog-breaker, sold to the Canadian Government, shipped off to Dyea, and embodied in the mixed team—mostly "huskies"—employed to carry despatches on the Klondyke trail under the charge of Perrault, a French-Canadian, and François, a French-Canadian half-breed. The succeeding chapters deal with 'Buck's' experiences under his new masters and amongst his new companions. They describe with a wealth of circumstantial and realistic detail how he adapts himself to his new environment in regard to climate and food; how he learns his place and duties as one of the team; how he simultaneously is trained to the habitual exercise of a high degree of intelligence and cunning, and decivilized by contact and conflict with his savage companions and rivals. He fights his way to the leadership of the team, in which he is finally installed after a battle to the death with his relentless enemy 'Spitz,' and justifies his promotion by his endurance, his strength, and his sagacity. But after a long bout of hard work the team is disbanded and sold; 'Buck' falls on evil days, but is rescued from a cruel and inexperienced master by a prospector named John Thornton, repaying his rescuer by prodigies of devotion and courage. All the time, however, and this seems to us the weak point in the story, though his affection for Thornton exceeds that felt by him for any of his previous masters, "the call of the wild"—the desire, that is, to hark back to the untrammelled life of his primitive ancestors—appeals to him with greater insistence, and when Thornton and his comrades are surprised and annihilated by a party of Indians, 'Buck,' after avenging his master's death in a truly Homeric onslaught on the Indians, feels that man has no longer any claim upon him, and joins his cousins the wolves as their accepted leader and lord.

The book, as we have already noted, has that compelling quality which attaches to the work of a man who writes of that which he has seen and known, and has the power to describe. But as from first to last it is a story of the survival of the fittest under conditions which give free play to primordial instincts, it is seldom pleasant, and often positively gruesome, reading. That, it may be urged, is inherent in the nature of the theme, but the fact none the less remains. Again, though the successive incidents are each handled in a way that carries conviction, we find it difficult to reconcile ourselves to the suddenness with which 'Buck' completes his decivilization immediately after a period in which his friendship for man had reached its culminating point. There is, however, considerable imaginative power in the conception of the dog's dim consciousness of his remote ancestry, and the final scenes in which his metamorphosis is consummated are treated with a good deal of rude poetic power.

We must not conclude this notice without a word of high praise for the illustrations and designs for the inner cover by Messrs. Goodwin and Bull, which, whether dealing with dogs, men, or landscape, are extremely picturesque and impressive, and reproduced, alike in color or monochrome, by the Norwood (Massachusetts) Press with an artistic finish far in advance of that to which we are accustomed in works of fiction produced in this country.

Spectator August 22, 1903, 283.

Reviews: *The Call of the Wild*

J. Stewart Doubleday

The power of Jack London lies not alone in his clear-sighted depiction of life, but in his suggestion of the eternal principles that underlie it. The writer who can suggest these principles forcibly and well, though he may not be actually great, has something in him closely allied to greatness. Mr. London is one of the most original and impressive authors this country has known. His voice is large and vibrant, his manner straightforward and free, and we predict for him a success in Western narrative equalled only by that of Mr. Stewart Edward White.

The Call of the Wild is the story of a dog, reared in comfort in Southern California, but afterwards broken to the sled on the desolate Alaskan trail, where his experiences are related with a candor and ring of genuineness, exciting yet ofttimes heartrending in the extreme. The philosophy of the survival of the fittest runs through every page of Mr. London's book; the call of the wild evidently signifies the appeal (and in Buck's case, the triumph) of barbarian life over civilized life; in fact, this dog becomes, after a series of bloodcurdling incidents ending at the murder of a beloved master, the eventual leader of a pack of timber wolves, in whom, following a fang fight for individual supremacy, he recognizes the "wild brother," and joins the savage horde. The book, very brief, is filled from cover to cover with thrilling scenes; the Northern Territory is brought home to us with convincing vividness; every sentence is pregnant with original life; probably no such sympathetic, yet wholly unsentimental, story of a dog has ever found print before; the achievement may, without exaggeration, be termed "wonderful."

Yet it is cruel reading—often relentless reading; we feel at times the blood lashing in our faces at what seems the continual maltreatment of a dumb animal; we can scarce endure the naked brutality of the thing; our sense of the creature's perplexity in suffering is almost absolutely unrelieved; we sicken of the analysis of the separate tortures of this dog's Arctic Inferno. Not seldom we incline to remonstrate, "Hang it, Jack London, what the deuce do you mean by 'drawing' on us so?" But we forgive the writer at last because he is true! He is not sentimental, tricky; he is at harmony with himself and nature. He gives an irresistible groan sometimes—like Gorky; but this is only because he does, after all, feel for humanity—yes, down to the bottom of his big California heart.

It must be patent to all, we think, that the man who can, through the simple story of a dog set us thought-wandering over illimitable ways, is a man of language to be respectfully classed and reckoned with. There is nothing local or narrow about Jack London. Sectionalism is smaller than he. His voice is the voice of a man in the presence of the multitude, and he utters the word that is as bread to him. He has not, to say truly, much humor; the theme of necessary toil and suffering overburdens and drowns the casual note of laughter—he is buoyant rather than bright. Sometimes we are wearied by his too ecstatic hymning of the primitive, the rude, the elemental in spirit and nature—we begin to desire a little more mildness and beauty, a possible mercy and femininity, a hope; but these we must look for in other writers than the stalwart youthful leader of the promising Far West. In his own field he is master; and more than this we ought not to exact of any man. The book is profusely and excellently illustrated.

Reader: An Illustrated Monthly Magazine 2 (September 1903), 408-09.

Reviews: *The Call of the Wild*

Kate Blackiston Stillé

A clear, strong picture of the battlefield of life with the colors laid on in a way that brings to the strong and thoughtful the consciousness of the spiritual and material conflict that rages between civilization and savagery. A dog, not a man, is the hero of the story which is less fiction than a serious problem, that reaches down into the heart of life, with an anguish that throbs and cries aloud on every page. Buck, the master-spirit, is a dog, well-born and well-bred; all that is interesting in the men comes out through their intercourse with this splendid dog. A cross between the St. Bernard and the Shepherd, gives the size, the endurance, the placidity, the intelligence, the gentleness and faithfulness that count in civilization and in the struggles of life.

The Call of the Wild is the heart laid bare in that forcible, thrilling way that makes one groan in desperate resistance to the savage that is not worlds away, nor in ancestors dead and buried centuries ago, but within us. The truths of life under the skillful handling of Jack London take possession and press themselves into the soul in such a way that we seem in the horrors of a nightmare powerless to resist, unnerved and helpless under "the law of club and fang." All phases of life are touched with the unerring skill of the true artist.

The brush brings out softly the sensuous captivating life in Southern California.

Civilization is both beautiful and capable, is at home on Judge Miller's place. Buck is "neither house-dog nor kennel-dog. The whole realm was his," but he was saved from being the pampered house-dog by hunting and outdoor sports, which the author cleverly shows is the type of the country gentleman who is ease-taking and at the same time has the careful oversight of the details which makes his estate great. Buck was kidnapped and sold into the Klondyke by the gardener's helper, whose character and needs are graphically told in that he was a gambler, had faith in it, "which made his damnation certain." He required money for his sin, and "the wages of the gardener's helper do not lap-over the needs of a wife and numerous progeny." The result of the passion and the necessity bring to us such suffering on the part of the dog, and such brutality from men that we comprehend as never before, that there is a devil in man and that the savage is not on the frontier, but at our door.

Buck knew not fear until he was beaten; he was of gentle blood and understood that he stood no chance against the man with the club, but his splendid lineage saved him from cowardice and stood the test of starvation and merciless toil. He was put to work to draw sledges, subjected to cruelty and toil, but when he learned "the law of club and fang" he won the leadership of the team. We see the passiveness drop and watch until the toil of the traces becomes the best expression of life. Then comes the transformation, necessitated by the ruthless struggle for existence. How swift and terrible the going to pieces of the moral nature, which is a vain thing and a heavy handicap under strenuous circumstances. This is the primitive code for man and beast—not to rob openly, but cunningly, "out of respect for club and fang," not to steal for joy; "but because of the clamor of an empty stomach."

This going down of the true man, this awakening of the primeval man, is desperately real. Sight and sense grow keen, instincts long dead are alive, the savage nature is quickened, and the old tricks come back without effort. Buck came to his own again "when on the still cold nights he pointed his nose at a star and howled long and wolf-like, it was his ancestors, dead and dust, pointing nose at star and howling down through the centuries and through him. And his cadences were their cadences, and the cadences, which voiced their woe, and what to them was the meaning of the stillness and the cold and dark."

Through starvation and abuse Buck grew responsive to the call of the wild, and this he obeyed when Thornton, his only friend, was killed by the Indians.

Through the "comprehensive relation of things" Jack London shows that the heights and depths of the universe are within the soul, and no one has put it with such force and feeling, though all have known it.

How splendidly civilization brings out the fine steely strength that endures and triumphs; and how squarely the conditions of life are met. The thriftless, complaining go down! The strong and brutal overcome.

The telling thing in the book is its deep underlying truth. The call of the wild is no fiction. The things pointed out are the nameless things we feel, and the author shows clearly, unobtrusively that it is "the old instincts which at stated periods drive men out from the sounding cities to forest and plain to kill things." That man and dog alike are mastered by the wolf-cry, striving after things alive, as it flees before them. Both sounding the deeps of his nature and of the parts of his nature that were deeper than he, "going back into the womb of Time."

The Call of the Wild penetrates to the very marrow and flows in the blood of the veins. Its manifestations are everywhere.

When the society girl "camps out for fun" and tyrannizes over and neglects her pets, ignores and treats the old with scant courtesy, she as surely obeys "the law of the club and fang" as Buck, when he relentlessly pursued the "foe he had started on the way to death."

This is true of soldiers, of university men, who enter mining camps and take to ranching, of men who leave their wives and firesides to sleep on the bare ground, of the nation's Chief, whose delight is in pursuing and killing big game, and who devotes the Cabinet room to sport, filling it with boxing gloves, swords and foils.

These may all be taken as the legitimate guides to the trend of the times, which muzzles and massacres the individual, that touches society with decay, and drags men back to the primeval forest where their hairy ancestors clung with long arms to the trees.

The unknown self stands out on the pages of this thrilling romance, and from the depths of his heart the author says, Behold, you are no better than the—

"New caught peoples,
    Half devil, half child."

To bring us to our waking life, more literature like *The Call of the Wild* is needed, and more men like Herbert Welsh, these the benefactors of humanity, teach us to lift men rather than club them. True leadership always is in humanity, and it is not enough to possess pity and mercy, but we must be possessed by them. These give real authority and go to the heart, moves and persuades it, though this is not the language of greed and blood, but that of the Divine will.

There is sublime and pathetic beauty in the way the brute comes out in this noble dog. Driven to his own by man's cruelty and yet triumphing over the brute, becoming the master and leader of the pack, outdoing them in cunning, defying the bravest hunter, like man, and yet unlike him, always surrounded with mystery, through the touch of the human. Alone every year the dog goes down to the spot where his master was killed, and with one long mournful howl, stands motionless as a statue, the wolfish nature dead before the unforgettable Love that drew him there.

In this little drama we are brought face to face with that which we refuse to confess to ourselves, and are chilled by the realism of *The Call of the Wild*, and bidden by it to listen to the Voice of the Divine, which also is a part of our being.

Book News Monthly 22 (September 1903), 7-10.

Jack London's Book *The Call of the Wild*: It is More Than a Rattling Good Dog Story—It Is an Allegory of Human Struggles and Aspirations

Johannes Reimers

It is not simply a dog story, this story of Buck. It is not a story of the hunter or of the hunted, and no zoological sweet-coated pill to make little children acquire natural history in play. Jack London's narrative of the life of Buck is a story—I should call it a symphony—inspired by the most fundamental consciousness, which lives far back in—yes, beyond—man's civilization. For far back in man's soul—if he be developed or undeveloped enough in his association with primordial nature to have reached above human expression of song, of speech, above human endeavor of hand in molding, in picturing, in building—sounds the voice of the universe, becomes feelable an existence which walks behind him with barely audible steps, breaking twigs and touching fallen leaves in the vast loneliness of the woodlands.

As one opens *The Call of the Wild* and begins reading, one feels anxious. Will the author redeem the splendid title of the book? One's anxiety rises a bit as one reads on, for it is often hard to accept that it needs common experience to reach the uncommon, and that it needs the uncommon to picture, to make feelable, the mystery of the primordial, which is to make audible the call of the wild. For Jack London's latest book is not merely a story of an interesting dog; as such it would be an exaggeration. Neither is it a story of some gold-seeking adventurers, for of such he has written far better. Nor is it a description of the land of "the white silence" merely as voyagers describe it, interesting enough, of sufficient color and sufficient lack thereof. The author has taken upon himself the difficult task to lead struggle-blinded men through transmigration into a yellow cur, face to face, or ear to lips, with that which is the all-saving call from the fundamental to human souls.

The story of Buck, the St. Bernard-shepherd dog from Santa Clara valley, is an allegory. The human figures in the book are simply the fatalistic forces in society, born, bred and reared in our kind of civilization. They represent the force of dishonesty, of club, or simple half-civilization, of selfishness (and the author has clothed it in a woman's shape), of littleness coupled with over-beastly cruelty, of kindness building love, of grief as a last solace following the call of the wild.

And Buck? He is you and I. And the other dogs? They are the other fellows such as we meet them in homes, at play, at work, such as we pass them on the street, such as we rub against them in the struggle for supremacy. Man is a beast of prey. Civilization has refined his method. His left hand pats while his right hand reaches with a sharpened steel for the jugular vein. The downfall of one is the pedestal of the other. He is schooled thereby; it has become a part of his instinct—the desire to become a leader and not remain forever a wheeler in the dog-team. He fights for that position, attacking, receding, attacking. And, when he has won the position, he throws himself struggle-calloused into the traces, a conqueror, yet a dog under the whip of the driver. He forges ahead blindly with a nervous thirst for exertion; he strains every nerve, every muscle, and he overstrains them and is gladdened thereby. And he does it half to still a voice far back in his inner life, half for the compensation in gold and in vanity.

The dog-fight in the first part of the book is a fine picture of social struggle for supremacy—a strengthener of will power, yet a breaker thereof. Have you not seen men with the character of Spitz—such as "reach out their tongue and laugh when others go down?" It is such as he that strong men and women hate, "and Buck hated him with bitter, deathless hatred," with a righteous contempt for such soul-killed brutes who gloat and laugh over the one fallen, who feast their eyes on the blood which the dust drinks. Buck's sorely hurt dignity at being made a draft-animal is akin to human shame of labor, and Spitz' turning on the inoffensive Billy, driving him to the confines of the camp because Spitz could not master Joe, is the truest picture of his kind of dog and his kind of men.

One admires the author's conscientious and painstaking study of dog-nature and dog-action. Buck's way of fast learning is but an illustration of the human school of life—to deal with men and remain unhurt, to get advantageously out of everyday's occurrence; and when Buck stole the bacon it "made him fit to survive in the hostile Northland," as man can be too particular about his honor to succeed, for a "moral nature" became to Buck, as to civilized man, "a vain thing and a handicap in the ruthless struggle for existence."

We meet in life men of duty to whom duty has become an official habit, who must be in the harness or die. When worn and sick they stagger out of bed before healed to return to work. Theirs is a haunting fear of loss of position, and such a dog was Dave, "For the pride of trace and trail was his, and sick unto death, he could not bear that another dog should do his work." The description of his struggle again to get into the traces; his floundering alongside the sled the deep snow "where the going was most difficult, till exhausted;" his biting through Sollek's traces to put himself in front of the sled in his old place, and the pleading with his dim, sick eyes to remain there—all this is masterly told, an allegory of striking directness.

An Eastern critic has said that *The Call of the Wild* is purely materialistic, and a well-known San Francisco critic has answered him: "What of it? It is a rattling good story, and we live in a materialistic time, when the writer who will succeed financially must cater to the public taste." Both the gentlemen are far underestimating the story. Why, there is a fine spirituality standing back of the story, the cosmical atmosphere of it, which is its highest charm and its deepest value. Throughout the book winds "an old song, as old as the breed itself—one of the first songs of the younger world in a day when song was sad." And when man heard that song "it marked the completeness with which he harked back through the ages of fire and roof to the raw beginning of life in the howling ages," and he who has not the power to thus harken finds in *The Call of the Wild* simply a rattling good story. I only wish that space permitted me to quote the author in some of his most spiritual passages—simple, unsentimental, strong and high, high above everyday consideration. Have you ever read anything more poetically simple and beautifully than Buck's dream? If that does not show the author's ability to hark back beyond the limits! Surely, he is here "sounding the deep of his nature and the parts of his nature that were deeper than he, going back into the womb of Time."

The book does not lack in masterly description either. On page 148 begins a delicate, spiritual and fragrant description of the mystic awakening of spring in the far Northlands. It proves the author's immediate closeness to nature—how he has laid his ear to the soil and listened for "the music of unseen fountains . . . the bursting, rending, throbbing of awakening life."

It is this which is the highest in literary art, as it is in music, in picturing and in molding, to give the work the character, the superhuman strength and the delicacy of the indefinable something which stands far back in the highest human consciousness. Jack London's book, as it lies before me, seems audibly to breathe therewith, stirring the deepest longings for the lonely places where sounds the call of the wild.

Stockton Evening Mail September 30, 1903, 4.

Books New and Old

The Call of the Wild is a story altogether untouched by bookishness. A bookish writer might, beginning with the title, have called it An Instance of Atavism, or A Reversion to Type. A bookish reader might conceivably read it as a sort of allegory with a broad human application; but its face value as a single-minded study of animal nature really seems to be sufficiently considerable. The author, too, must be allowed to stand upon his own feet, though one understands why he should have been called the American Kipling. His work has dealt hitherto with primitive human nature; this is a study of primitive dog nature. No modern writer of fiction, unless it be Kipling, has preserved so clearly the distinction between animal virtue and human virtue. The farther Buck reverts from the artificial status of a man-bounded domestic creature to the natural condition of the "dominant primordial beast," the more strongly (if unwillingly) we admire him. There is something magnificent in the spectacle of his gradual detachment from the tame, beaten-in virtues of uncounted forefathers, his increasing ability to hold his own among unwonted conditions, and his final triumph over the most dreaded powers of the wilderness. . . . The making and the achievement of such a hero constitute, not a pretty story at all, but a very powerful one.

Atlantic Monthly 92 (November 19, 1903), 695-96.

To the Editor of The *Independent*

Jack London

In reply to yours of January 16. By all means go ahead and publish that article that accuses me of plagiarism of many passages in *The Call of the Wild*. So far as concerns the source of much of my material in *The Call of the Wild* being Egerton R. Young's *My Dogs in the Northland*, I plead guilty. A couple of years ago, in the course of writing to Mr. Young, I mentioned the same fact, and thanked him for the use his book had been to me.

I wish, however, that you would get the writer of the said article to include in it a definition of what constitutes plagiarism.

Mr. Young's book, *My Dogs in the Northland*, was a narrative of fact, giving many interesting true details of his experiences with dogs in the Northland. Fiction-writers have always considered actual experiences of life to be a lawful field for exploitation—in fact, every historical novel is a sample of fictional exploitation of published narratives of fact.

Take an instance from the article accusing me of plagiarism, now in your hands—that of the dog that lay down on its back with its paws in the air and begged for moccasins. This happened to one of Mr. Young's dogs, and I exploited it in my story. But suppose that I am in the Klondike. Suppose this incident occurs with one of my dogs. I can utilize this material in a story, can I not? Agreed. Now suppose it doesn't happen with my dog, but with some one else's dog, but that I happen to see the incident. May I use it? Again agreed. Now, however, I do not see the incident, but the man with whose dog it occurred tells me about it. May I sue it? Again agreed. A step further, instead of telling about it, a man writes the incident, not in a story, but in a plain narrative of incidents. May I use it in my story? And if not, why not?

Another instance. In the course of writing my *Sea-Wolf*, I wanted to exploit a tumor and its ravages on the brain of a man. I asked my family physician for data. It happened that he was the author of a brochure upon tumors on the brain. He turned this brochure over to me. In it was everything all written out. I used the material. Was it plagiarism? His brochure was not fiction. It was a compilation of facts and real happenings in a non-fiction form.

And so it was with Mr. Young's *My Dogs in the Northland*. Really, to charge plagiarism in such a case is to misuse the English language. To be correct, "sources of materials used in *The Call of the Wild*" should be substituted for "Plagiarism."

The *Independent* 62 (February 14, 1906), 375-76.

Jack London's One Great Contribution to American Literature

One book among the many written by Jack London in his literary career, now closed, of less than twenty years strikes the majority of American newspapers as his chief claim to immortality. That book is *The Call of the Wild*, published near the outset of his career. With this story of an animal spirit, "pathetically high, pathetically brave and pathetically dumb," to quote the N.Y. *World*, Jack London took his place among the greatest American story-tellers of his time. Along with his earlier short stories, it formed the basis of his European reputation. It made him, in a sense, a world-figure, and, in the opinion of most of the editors who venture to estimate his place in our literature, is the one work of the Californian which will live.

Popular opinion, the N.Y. *Evening Post* asserts, is justified in regarding this book, published thirteen years ago quite early in his literary career, as the best of his tales. "While the zest of life, the love of adventure in the open, remained with him to the end, the original impulse became in later years too much overlaid with generalization and formula drawn out of books. His brief and sporadic studies at college and his reading in economics and popular sociology tended towards a self-conscious primitiveness." With this book, declares the N.Y. *Globe*, Jack London founded a school. After his *Call of the Wild*, dozens of writers began to hear the same call. The *Rocky Mountain News* of Denver discerns merit of scarcely lower rank in his earlier stories, *The God of His Fathers*, and *A Daughter of the Snows*. With all these stories the "red-blooded" note, says the Chicago *Herald*, entered American fiction and gave a new orientation to the American novel:

> In sincerity and courage no less than power lay the secret of this writer's appeal to humanity. With the era of flub-dub fiction at climax, London dared to write of life in the raw, life as he had seen and lived it. His success was brilliant, instantaneous and productive of a new and still flourishing school.
>
> Before Beach, Bindloss, Curwood et al. began publishing 'red-blooded' stories, London produced pictures of man's struggle with primitive conditions and the elements that thrilled and stirred like a trumpet blast through a languid ballroom. Who can forget his early narratives of the Pacific coast, before-the-mast sailing or Alaska? No Seton or Roberts animal study yet has superseded London's *Call of the Wild* in effect or popular favor. Superlatively terse, virile in the extreme, strong almost to brutality, the London stories, whether dealing with love or lust, prize fights or the gold fever, prison abuses or ranch life in California, had the gripping quality, born of first-hand experience honestly, sympathetically reported, that invariably sets the world talking, that invariably brings followers and imitators in its wake.

A more critical note is voiced in the conservative and authoritative New York *Nation*. Jack London, it thinks, was interested in action rather than in character, and, despite his untrammeled freshness, the direct appeal of his storytelling art, he was not a creative artist. "In the long list of his books he has not added a living character to our literature." A writer of the N.Y. *Times* declares that London is entitled to be called a "creator:"

> He photographed, but he also created, and he somehow managed to do the two things at the same time. There are passages in not a few of his books that reveal truly amazing powers of observation and interpretation, and tho he often dealt with the impossible, he rarely, if ever, missed what in art is far more important than possibility—plausibility. His reader could believe, and did, in all the adventures and adventurers he described.
>
> Strength was the obvious quality of his writing, but it was far from the only or chief one, and those who call him 'rough' are strangely mistaken. He had convictions and he had knowledge. That is, he wrote what he knew.

If Jack London wrote far more than is good for his future reputation, if he failed to make the best of his reputation and the opportunities, says the N.Y. *Tribune*, we must at least credit him with extending the geographical frontiers of American literature. "He was the first to turn the Klondyke into literary material. . . . Wherever men stripped themselves of all the trappings, all the conventions and safeguards of civilization he was in his element."

Jack London, as several writers note, was swept to literary success on the crest of the Kipling wave. Thus the *Rocky Mountain News* says:

> As Kipling sat at the feet of Bret Harte in his 'prentice years, so did London fall under the Anglo-Indian's spell. But in each case the apprenticeship, while the most useful, was brief. Kipling found himself and forgot the mannerisms of the author of 'The Luck of Roaring Camp.' London, the young, untutored genius, was not long in breaking new trails and discovering his metier. *The Call of the Wild* is doubtless the most artistic of London's writings; but all of the work of that day, *The God of His Fathers* and *A Daughter of the Snows* are of lasting worth.

The same paper adds that "all that he has written since those impressionistic days would be lost and still London's name would live in American literature. There was no padding in his writing of that period and his inexperiences in the art gave them added zest."

According to an interview published several years ago in the *Western Comrade* by Emanuel Julius, Jack London never strove for literary immortality. He objected to being called an artist. "I am nothing more than a fairly good artisan," said London. "You may think that I am not telling the truth, but I hate my profession. I detest the profession I have chosen. I hate it, I tell you, I hate it!" He continued in the same strain:

> "I assure you that I do not write because I love the game. I loathe it. I cannot find words to express my disgust. The only reason I write is because I am well paid for my labor—that's what I call it—labor. I get lots of money for my books and stories. I tell you I would be glad to dig ditches for twice as many hours as I devote to writing if only I could get as much money. To me, writing is an easy way to make a fine living. Unless I meant it, I wouldn't think of saying a thing like this, for I am speaking for publication. I am sincere when I say that my profession sickens me. Every story that I write is for the money that will come to me. I always write what the editors want, not what I'd like to write. I grind out what the capitalist editors want, and the editors buy only what the business and editorial departments permit. . . .
>
> The editors are not interested in the truth; they don't want writers to tell the truth. A writer can't sell a story when it tells the truth, so why should he batter his head against a stone wall? He gives the editors what they want, for he knows that the stuff he believes in and loves to write will never be purchased."

This grim pessimism of Jack London's toward the latter part of his life concerned not only his writing but his spiritual outlook as well. He was, says Mr. Julius, a confessed pessimist. He admitted it in this fashion:

> "I am weary of everything. I no longer think of the world or the movement (the social revolution) or of writing as an art. I am a great dreamer, but I dream of my ranch, of my wife. I dream of beautiful horses and fine soil. I dream of the beautiful things I own up in Sonoma County. And I write for no other purpose than to add to the beauty that now belongs to me. I write a book for no other reason than to add three or four hundred acres to my magnificent estate. I write a story with no other purpose than to buy a stallion. To me, my cattle are more interesting than my profession. My friends don't believe me when I say this, but I am absolutely sincere."

How the hungry lad who had earned his own living since the age of nine, whose schooling was of the shortest and most intermittent type, acquired the ambition to become a great writer was once recounted by London himself. At the time of his death, November 22, the N.Y. *Times* reprinted this memoir:

> In my fitful school days I had written the usual compositions, which had been praised in the usual way, and while working in the jute mills I still made an occasional try. The factory occupied thirteen hours of my day, and being young and husky, I wanted a little for myself, so there was not much left for composition. The San Francisco *Call* offered a prize for a

descriptive article. My mother urged me to try for it, and I did, taking for my subject, 'Typhoon Off the Coast of Japan.'

Very tired and sleepy and knowing I had to be up at 5:30, I began the article at midnight and worked straight on until I had written 2,000 rds, the limit of the article, but with my idea only half worked out. I continued adding another 2,000 words before I had finished, and the third night I spent in cutting out the excess, so as to bring the article within the conditions of the contest. The first prize came to me, and my success seriously turned my thoughts to writing, but my blood was still too hot for a settled routine.

Current Opinion 62 (January 1917), 46-47.

Books: *The Call of the Wild*

Tony Tanner

Two of Jack London's most famous novels are about dogs: taken together they reveal a great deal about the author. In *The Call of the Wild* [Panther Books] we see Buck, snatched from the security of his master's home, adjusting to the brutal conditions of the northern wastes, and gradually responding to a lurking instinct for wildness which, dormant at the start, finally commands his whole being and obliterates the last traces of civilized training. Buck's story is a release, a sloughing off of bonds: it starts in the sobriety of the judge's house and ends with Buck running wild, "his great throat a-bellow as he sings a song of the younger world, which is the song of the pack."

The other dog, *White Fang* [Panther Books], reverses the process. He starts life in the heart of the wilds and ends up in a judge's home (i.e., claimed and tamed by "law"). Where Buck used to dream of a world of prehistoric violence and woke to answer the primordial call of the wolf-howl, White Fang dreams of camp fires and the communities of man, and although he is "ferocious, indomitable, and solitary," he hears a different call, an instinct to submit to man in exchange for food and companionship. Freedom is fine—but it involves great loneliness: the camp is constricting—but it means warmth and rewards. White Fang ends like an Horatio Alger hero. Transported from the wilds to civilization, he saves the judge's life, and though he does not quite marry the judge's daughter, he mates with the judge's dog—a snooty collie who fits the usual stereotype. He is now called "Blessed Wolf" and we last see him dozing in the sun with his progeny climbing all over him—the very image of domesticity, all wildness gone. Take the two books together and I think you get a very clear indication of Jack London's own deeply ambivalent attitudes towards the call of the camp and the call of the wild. When the man who tames White Fang starts to stroke him fondly for the first time, it causes the dog great confusion. "White Fang was torn by conflicting feelings, impulses. It seemed he would fly to pieces, so terrible was the control he was exerting, holding together by an unwonted indecision the counter forces that struggled within him for mastery." And so it was with Jack London.

This is clear from the story of his life—recounted so readably and fairly and with a wealth of interesting detail by Richard O'Connor in his excellent biography [*Jack London* (Gollancz)]—which was surely one of the most exciting, incredible and crowded lives ever lived by a writer. Between the ages of fifteen and twenty-three he was "Prince of the oyster pirates," seal hunter, hobo, socialist agitator, sailor, prisoner, and miner in the Klondike gold rush. And the energy he brought to the painful process of turning himself into a writer is truly staggering. But success never meant rest. He left a stable wife for a restless woman with more animal vitality: when things were going well he decided to embark on a round-the-world trip in a special boat called The Snark—it ended in sickness and near-disaster.

Yet as well as responding to the lure of adventure, he was always trying to find a fixed place, a secure abode. Just as he drank to fabulous excess and ate inordinate quantities of meat, so he developed an unappeasable hunger for land, buying up acres in the Valley of the Moon as fast as he could. As he was an illegitimate child, forever uncertain as to his father, unloved and hungry throughout his youth, these various appetites are fairly understandable. Above all, he hoped to found something of a dynasty in his magnificent home called "Wolf House," and so he longed for a male heir. Somehow it all went wrong. He only had daughters and these were estranged from him: his house burnt down just as his special ship had foundered; his friends drifted away. By the end he was spoiled for the wild, and his camp was in ruins. It is hard not to feel that those counter forces which harassed White Fang also undermined that prodigy of lonely energy, Jack London—or "Wolf" as he insisted his wife should call him.

These twin pulls—towards culture and social achievement, and again to the savage freedom of the wild—are blatantly apparent in some of his stories. Whichever world Jack London was in, he was drawn to the other. This is very clear in *Martin Eden*, in the latest *Bodley Head Jack London* [volume III], a distorted and selective account of his struggle up from brutalizing poverty to successful authorship, and his first love affair, with Mabel Applegarth. Despite some execrable writing, it does convey with genuine power the emotional and intellectual turmoil of a young struggling writer. But more revealing, to me, is London's practice of constantly juxtaposing the worlds of gentility and savagery by what he calls "memory pictures." The book opens with Martin's stumbling, awed entry into a cultured middle-class home—he longs to find a place in this world. But whenever he is at some cultured social gathering we read that "Martin kept seeing himself down all his past"—a past of fighting, drinking, and generally roughing it. At elegant dinners he dreams of brawls. Although he enjoys the struggle to break into cultured society, once he gets there he finds he has lost reality somewhere along the way. He is a genuine case of alienation. His vitality ebbs, a great torpor settles over him, and he commits suicide.

I have not mentioned the oft-remarked paradox of London's avowed socialism and his strenuous temperamental individualism ("The ultimate word is I LIKE") or the contrast between his humanitarian democratic feelings (see his warning against totalitarianism in *The Iron Heel*) and his shameless racism ("I am first of all a white man and only then a socialist,") because it seems to me that the most important struggle in his work is not between Superman and the mob, but between energy and inertia. His best stories are set in the frozen north, because there the battle between organic life and inorganic non-life was pursued with elemental simplicity. This is Buck, pulling a sledge: "he was mastered by the sheer surging of life, flying exultantly under the stars and over the face of dead matter that did not move." Thus it is that his greatest single piece of writing, "To Build a Fire," is simply about a man fighting a losing battle with the frost. For a man to succumb to the glacial immobility of "the white silence" was to "sleep off to death." Martin Eden thrives on the struggle for accomplishment and recognition, but when he has achieved it, he, too, sleeps off to death. Indeed, his last delight is to swim vigorously *downwards* to a deep-sea death, just as he had relished the struggle to climb *upwards* to a successful literary life. London seems to have sensed that at the heart of any great energy for life there is a reversible quantity—an energy for death, and that these twin hankerings somehow provided the most elemental struggle of all.

Although London exalted physical vitality to an abnormal degree ("I'd rather win a water-fight in a swimming pool . . . than write the great American novel,") he was deeply preoccupied with suicide and what he called "the instinct for death . . . the will to die when the time to die is at hand." The phrase comes from *John Barleycorn* [*The Bodley Head Jack London*, Volume II], to my mind one of London's two great books. In describing with unforgettable vividness his gradual involvement with alcohol past the point of no return, London gives an almost archetypal clarity to a tragically familiar pattern in the lives of many American writers. His realization that the attractions of drink and death are subtly intermingled is graphically revealed in his account of a night when he gets drunk, falls into the water and decides to swim out to sea and death—until he sobers up and directs his energy to a desperate and barely successful fight for life. As he says, this incident showed him "abysses of intoxication hitherto undreamed;" abysses to which he finally returned at the age of forty. I think he comes close to the secret when he says that he found drink often appealed, not to the mediocre and timid, but to those people of "superabundant vitality," for as he demonstrated by his own life, an excess of life-hunger often contains its own principle of self-destruction.

It was from another abyss that he drew his other great book—the East End of London in 1902, which became *The People of the Abyss* [Panther Books]. He found, indeed, that "all human potentialities are in it," but "the Abyss is literally a huge man-killing machine," "a vast shambles." The book is not merely an assemblage of appalling facts (though the facts are shocking enough to silence critics of the welfare state): what gives it its force is the way Jack London acquaints himself with "the ferocious facts of life," exposing his superb health and resilience to routines which thousands of homeless unemployed people went through daily—and finding he cannot take it. Because he has not slipped or been pushed to the bottom of the abyss, he does not have to take it. But as he says, "what is not good enough for you is not good enough for other men, and there's no more to be said." If this is progress, then something has gone terribly wrong. "There can be no mistake. Civilization has increased man's producing power an hundredfold, and through mismanagement the men of Civilization live worse than the beasts, and have less to eat and wear and protect them from the elements than the savage Innuit in a frigid climate who lives today as he lived in the stone age ten thousand years ago." The book is accurate and unanswerable. That civilization could produce societies which were worse to live in than any of nature's wildnesses was not only a sociological truth but, for Jack London, a lived truth.

Perhaps he was not a great writer (though he is underrated), perhaps, like Martin Eden, he suffered from "the clumsiness of too great strength." But much of what he called his "impassioned realism" still has an amazing power, and there are moments when he seems to have a hold on profound elemental issues. I see him as he saw White Fang, poised unhappily between civilization and wildness: "He could not immediately forgo all his wild heritage and his memories of the Wild. There were days when he crept to the edge of the forest and stood and listened to something calling him far and away. And always he returned, restless and uncomfortable. . . ."

Jack London's Buck

Primo Levi [Translated from the Italian by Raymond Rosenthal]

Einaudi's prestigious Writers Translated by Writers series reached its nineteenth volume with an unexpected gift: a new edition of *The Call of the Wild* by Jack London in the beautiful, rigorous translation by Gianni Celati. The book is very well known, and precisely because of this it has many surprises in store for the reader, or rather, for the rereader, no matter what generation he belongs to. A book one knows is read in a different way from a new book: one already knows "how it ends," and so one is more critical of its events and more attentive to the details.

Its authenticity immediately leaps to the eye. The *très curieux* London—a writer long considered marginal, popular, in short, a stray dog within the illustrious American literary tradition—has drawn from his brief adventure as a prospector for gold in Alaska a fabulous wealth of storytelling experiences, and he is a great storyteller. Nothing of what he relates smacks of the trite, of something written at the desk by borrowing from books or by thinking things out. The savage world in which he found himself immersed is decanted into his best books with the powerful immediacy of lived experience: here we have no Verne, no Salgari, but rather a man who has fought the struggle for life and for survival to the bitter end and has taken from this struggle a reason for writing.

With unerring intuition he poured this experience of his into a dog, and I believe that this dog has no rivals in world literature, precisely because he is not a literary dog. Buck, a well-to-do dog, master at home on a splendid California estate, is at once canine and human, as are all dogs whom fate and their owners have treated neither too badly nor too well. He emanates dignity and respectability: more than a subject of Judge Miller, he is his peer, companion; he has an instinctive knowledge of his rights and his duties. But at the turn of the century, at the time of the gold fever, all robust dogs are threatened: they have an incredible commercial value, they can be stolen, traded, and carried off up there, where it is no longer civil law that counts but, rather, the law of the cudgel and of the fang. They must become sled dogs or perish.

Thanks to his physical and moral vigor, Buck passes the first test, that of the deportation, an interminable journey by train and then by boat, and he arrives in a hostile new country: no longer the sun of California but snow on the ground and in the air. He is tamed: he learns that a man armed with a cudgel is invincible. His dignity is not extinguished but is transformed: he learns that he must adjust, learn new and terrible things, that he must distrust everyone, but especially his companions, who are already experienced sled dogs—if he is not as fast as they are, his daily ration will be instantly stolen from him; that at night the fire and the tent are not for him: he must learn, and he does learn, to dig himself a hole in the snow, where his animal warmth will allow him to endure the freezing arctic.

He must learn his job, and here London strikes masterful tones. Each of these dogs is of a hundred different breeds, and each, yoked every day to the sled, has a surprisingly credible personality of his own. An ethologist ahead of his time, London has penetrated canine psychology with a completely modern profundity. Rivals among themselves and yet gregarious, the sled dogs "elect" a chief, the leader of the pack, the dog at the head of the team. He must be the strongest but also the most experienced: the job of pulling the sled is a job that must be accepted, and Spitz, the head dog, enforces and speeds up this acceptance. He punishes anyone who hinders the work, bites the stragglers, breaks up the fights with his undisputed authority.

Buck understands, he learns, but he does not accept Spitz's authority: he feels within himself not only the perpetual hunger for food but also the hunger for primacy. But he does accept pulling the sled: "And though the work was hard he found he did not particularly despise it. He was surprised at the eagerness which animated the whole team, and which was communicated to him." This is work as the last refuge and as the alternative to servitude. How can one not remember Solzhenitsyn's story *One Day in the Life of Ivan Denisovich* and that wall that prisoners gladly build, struggling against the freezing cold of another arctic? Dave and Sol-leks, old sled dogs, are passive and indifferent, but when they are harnessed to the sled they become "alert and active, anxious that the work should go well, and fiercely irritable with whatever, by delay or confusion, retarded that work. The toil of the traces seemed the supreme expression of their being, and all that they lived for and the only thing in which they took delight." Work is a form of intoxication: they feel heartbroken when they are excluded from it. Here in germ is the intuition of the human pathology of early retirement.

Buck is different, he feels being reborn within him "the dominant primordial beast," he subtly provokes the leader of the pack, encourages disorder, until he openly challenges Spitz. This is the master page of the short book, and it is the fiercest: during a freezing night, surrounded by the starved but neutral pack, Spitz and Buck confront each other and Buck gets the better of him, thanks to his cleverness as a fighter: the loser is devoured on the spot by his former underlings. The next morning, Buck forces acceptance on his human masters: he has killed the leader of the team, he is the new team leader. He will be a chief (a *Kapo?*) even more efficient than Spitz, better at keeping order and discovering dangers along the track.

Then the team changes owners, and in spring, when the ice is most treacherous, they end up in the hands of three inexperienced men. Hunger, weariness, whippings: Buck's dignity rebels, the dog mutinies, he "knows" whom he must and whom he mustn't obey. Subjected to a deadly beating, he is saved by Thornton, the good prospector, and grows attached to him with total, exclusive love, the love of which only dogs are capable: and it's precisely here that, in my opinion, the book becomes weak. This devotion is excessive: where did the "dominant beast" go?

Nor are other pages convincing into which are filtered ill-digested Darwinian reminiscences. Thornton dies, pierced by Indian arrows, and Buck, his last link with the civilization of men broken, harkens to the call of the wild, that is, the howl of the wolves: within him, as an evolutionary force, he senses the wolf's blood. Despite his so very different life story, he runs with the pack until he becomes part of it, indeed becomes its leader. California, the sled, Thornton—all are forgotten, and Buck's story, as Celati remarks, becomes (though only, I believe, after this turn of the plot) myth. Buck's blood has prevailed over the blood of the wolves, to the point of modifying their appearance: a new generation of wolves with canine hair is born. Buck has become the Phantom Dog, ferocious, nocturnal savager of prey and men: but every summer he goes in pilgrimage to the spot where Thornton is buried, the only creature whom the dog-turned-wolf ever loved. Come now: this is a bit too human.

Answering the Call of the Wild

Daniel Dyer

I wouldn't read the classics, so my mother bought me comic books—not *Superman* or *Archie* (those I had to purchase with my own piddling allowance), but *Classics Illustrated,* a periodical which offered comic-book versions of major literary works. (This was, in fact, a public-relations coup by comics publishers, who were in those days viewed by responsible parents, like mine, as the "corrupters of youth," an unsavory reputation from which producers of Saturday morning television programs now suffer. *Classics Illustrated* helped sanitize the image of comic books just as *Sesame Street* has helped legitimize television viewing.)

Embracing the principle that any comic book was better than none, I accepted *Classics Illustrated* into my literary world (as did many of my coevals), thereby allowing myself to be coerced into a close encounter with "serious literature." The experience was not all that unpleasant. Urged along by simplified dialogue, full-color illustrations, and (I discovered much later) bowdlerized texts, I read—and enjoyed!—such acclaimed works as *Ivanhoe, Les Misérables,* and *Romeo and Juliet.* (The editors of *Classics Illustrated* were somewhat liberal and eclectic in their tastes: listed with works of Shakespeare, Dumas, and Homer were other "masterpieces" like *Tom Brown's Schooldays, The Adventures of Kit Carson,* and *Wild Animals I Have Known.)*

Seeing me sprawled in a chair in contented company with *Hamlet*—never mind that it *looked* as if I were reading a comic book—my parents must have felt that curious glow of pleasure I now feel whenever I entice my own fourteen-year-old son into doing something which has even the most nebulous intellectual content. Of course, parents were just beginning to become sneaky in the 1950s. Responding to child psychologists who urged understanding and restraint, enlightened parents employed guile rather than violence with their offspring. Manufacturers and advertisers were quick to cooperate, and it was during my boyhood that such products as sweetened toothpaste and children's orange-flavored aspirin began to appear—medicine-chest analogues of *Classics Illustrated.*

To this day I vividly remember my comic book *Call of the Wild*—from the front cover (Buck barks in the foreground, the frozen Yukon wilderness behind him), to the opening panel (Buck, blood dripping from his jaws, lunges at a wounded stag), to the final, mournful portrait of broken-hearted Buck—no longer a pet, but a beast, a creature of the wild—baying at the full moon.

As I look at that comic book now, I am certain that I did not accept the gracious invitation printed at the bottom of the final page: "Now that you've read the 'Classics Illustrated' edition, don't miss the added enjoyment of reading the original obtainable at your school or public library." Nor, I am sure, did I read the subsequent full-page biography of Jack London, which features such florid distortions as "He died a martyr to his craft and to truth as he knew it"—hyperbole acceptable in a comic book, I guess.

But I *did* read the *Classics Illustrated* versions of two of London's other novels, *The Sea-Wolf* and *White Fang,* never realizing at the time that this inchoate interest in Jack London would one day lead me on a transcontinental quest, from Harvard University's Widener Library (to locate long out-of-print works by London) to Dawson City, Yukon Territory, one of the principal settings of *The Call of the Wild.* And I would have been astounded had I known that this search would lead me directly to the roots of my family tree.

I don't like teaching what I don't know.

My distaste for doing so began the first days of my career in September 1966 when I discovered that I was not *exactly* a seventh-grade English teacher; I was, more precisely, a "core" teacher. Translation: I would teach English *and* American history.

In 1966, the dimensions of my knowledge of American history were not impressive. Oh, I knew a few things about the *Mayflower* and the Alamo. Pearl Harbor. That was about it. Nevertheless, I managed to fool my students for, oh, a week or so before their feral instinct informed them that I was a fake. (Once we passed the Pilgrims I was in serious trouble.)

Later in my career—especially in the heyday of elective English courses—I made an art of teaching subjects and topics about which I knew next to nothing. Could I teach a mini-course in filmmaking? Radio drama? Science fiction and fantasy? You bet.

In those days I was also an inveterate romantic; if called upon to defend myself ("How can you teach what you don't know?"), I had a knapsack stuffed with nifty replies: I was "learning along with the kids," "modeling effective strategies and behaviors," "demonstrating the rewards of lifelong learning." But in realistic moments (i.e., on Friday afternoons) I was agonizingly aware I was a fraud, terrified to admit my ignorance with the frequency that truth demanded.

And so it was that I developed one principle that has impelled my career in its recent stages: Know everything you conceivably can about the subject at hand. Become a fanatic. A freak.

Accordingly, when our board of education recently adopted Ginn's *Exploring Literature* as the eighth-grade literature text, I promptly scanned the table of contents for potential problems. There were many (alas), the most serious being the novel which consumes the final eighty pages of the volume; it was *The Call of the Wild,* which I'd read only in its *Classics Illustrated* version. Twenty-five years earlier.

I should note that I was not *completely* ignorant of London: in high school I'd read *Martin Eden* (a book report); in college, *The Sea-Wolf* (for a course). And my memory of the comic-book *White Fang* remained unaccountably acute and complete. On the diskette of my brain I also found partial sectors of biographical information that I'd once "written to file" in high school English classes during sessions devoted to "To Build a Fire" or "All-

Gold Canyon." I knew I had much to do before acquiring even marginal competence with Jack London and his work.

I began my study in the same manner as a kid assigned an odious social studies report: I looked in the *World Book* encyclopedia. But I quickly progressed to more respectable publications (like *Cliff's Notes* and *MasterPlots*). After reading the popular biographies *(Sailor on Horseback, Jack: A Biography of Jack London,* and *A Pictorial Life of Jack London),* I finally opened *The Call of the Wild.*

As I read, insights banged against my windowpane brain: The vocabulary was extremely difficult. (In the short, four-line epigraph, I was brought up short by "brumal" [wintry]. The kids, I knew, would have problems with "nomadic," "chafing," and "ferine.") And beyond the epigraph, reading becomes no easier: on the first three pages alone appear such words as "veranda," "artesian well," "demesne," "imperiously," "kindred," "unwonted," "intimated," and "conveyance"—words not littering the tongues of most junior-high schoolers.

London was fond of complex locutions which are unfamiliar to today's generation bred on television's pidgin English: "Buck multiplied himself, attacking from all sides, enveloping the herd in a whirlwind of menace, cutting out his victim as fast as it could rejoin its mates, wearing out the patience of creatures preyed Upon, which is a lesser patience than that of the creatures preying." Yow! An impressive string of participial phrases, each trailing a prepositional phrase or two, or an adverb clause, or another participle, the whole thing finished off with a wham-bang adjective clause, slightly misplaced.

The settings were completely foreign to me. I knew nothing about the geography of the "sunkissed Santa Clara Valley," even less about the Yukon wilderness. A confession: I thought the Yukon was part of Alaska, not a Canadian territory!

I had only vague notions about the historical context of the novel—the Klondike Gold Rush. I was certain only of this: lots of people wanted gold, so they rushed to the Klondike to get it.

The kids would need a lot of help with this novel. So would I.

A wisp of a memory: my father had known something—done something?—about the Gold Rush.

A phone call home revealed an unlikely coincidence: my great-grandfather, Addison Clark Dyer, had joined the stampede to the Klondike in 1898. Better yet: he'd kept a diary of his experiences, a diary my father had transcribed and photocopied ten years earlier. He'd sent me a copy—didn't I remember? (Oops.)

A frantic search through file drawers rescued the document from the clutter, and I eagerly read the words of my gold-seeking ancestor. The entries were, understandably, brief—after all, he was traveling one thousand miles by horseback through dense forests (from Spokane to Wrangell, Alaska); he was struggling across brutal mountain passes; he was shooting the Whitehorse Rapids on the Yukon River; he was laboring on his claim in frigid temperatures that sometimes dropped to sixty below. He was, in a word, busy.

Addison Clark Dyer spent a year working a claim on Bonanza Creek then returned to Walla Walla, Washington, where he used his modest "poke" to purchase the farm that only the Depression could wrest from the family.

Great-grandfather died before my father was born, so neither of us knew him, except through one faded photograph . . . and through his diary, which he scrawled with the stub of a pencil over campfires and woodstoves in the very country Jack London describes in *The Call of the Wild*.

I spent a year squirreling money away, then applied for a sabbatical leave (request granted!), thereby equipping myself with the time and money I would need to re-trace my great-grandfather's journey—and, coincidentally, to walk in the footsteps of Jack London.

My son and I substituted Alaska Airlines for horseback (a decision we did not ponder long) and arrived in Skagway, Alaska, not far from Dyea where Buck first hit the beach.

In 1898, Skagway was the busy seaport where the gold-seekers began their overland journey; now it's a tourist attraction and center for the Klondike Gold Rush National Historical Park. We rented a car (Avis had two on the lot, a dirty red one and a dirtier red one), and we set out to cross the White Pass on the Klondike Highway.

During Jack London's day the White Pass was a heartbreakingly difficult, barely passable way over the mountains. Klondike historian Pierre Berton asserts that no horse made it across alive, and it soon became known as the Dead Horse Trail.

In "Which Make Men Remember" (a story contained in *The God of His Fathers,* 1901) London describes the brutal conditions confronting those who crossed the White Pass:

> The horses died like mosquitoes in the first frost, and from Skagway to [Lake] Bennett they rotted in heaps. They died at the Rocks, they were poisoned at the Summit, and they starved at the Lakes; they fell off the trail, what there was of it, or they went through it; in the river they drowned under their loads, or were smashed to pieces against the boulders; they snapped their legs in the crevices and broke their backs falling backwards with their packs; in the sloughs they sank from sight or smothered in the slime, and they were disembowelled in the bogs where the corduroy logs turned end up in the mud; men shot them, worked them to death, and when they were gone, went back to the beach and bought more. Some did not bother to shoot them—stripping their saddles off and the shoes and leaving them where they fell. Their hearts turned to stone—those which did not break—and they became beasts, these men on Dead Horse Trail.

Several years later the White Pass and Yukon Railroad traversed that rugged terrain, and now an asphalt highway provides glorious vistas to travelers who enjoy aesthetic pleasures that would have been inconceivable to my great-grandfather.

Just over the mountains is a string of lakes where the stampeders stopped to build boats to float the remaining 350 miles down the Yukon River to the goldfields. Most boats were of the homemade variety—equal in quality to what a random group of English teachers might construct—so quite a few were destroyed in one of three perilous places along the river: Box Canyon, the Whitehorse Rapids, or Five Finger Rapids. Fortunately, the Mounties quickly took control of the river and required that all craft be piloted through the rapids by experienced whitewater men; a year after the rush began, there was regular steamboat service on the river.

At the confluence of the Klondike and Yukon rivers stands the little town of Dawson City, Yukon Territory, about one hundred miles east of the Alaska border and two hundred miles south of the Arctic Circle. It was here that most of the gold was dredged from two rich, gold-bearing tributaries of the Klondike, the Bonanza and El Dorado creeks. At the height of the rush in 1898, there were 30,000 people in Dawson. There was an opera house, newspaper, church, post office, bank, and an entire street known as Paradise Alley where lonely miners could purchase female "companionship." Dawson was called the Paris of the North.

Once the stampeders reached Dawson, they quickly found out the bad news: all the prime sites had been staked and claimed nearly a year before (poor communications and transportation prevented news from reaching the outside until it was too late), so there was nothing for most of them to do but work the claims of others to earn enough for a steamboat ticket home. About thirty miners became millionaires from the rush; the other 29,970 had a "learning experience."

The streets of Dawson City today (population 700) are dirt; many of the buildings—some crumbling, others in the process of restoration by Parks Canada—date to the early twentieth century. Across the Yukon River are the deteriorating remains of a few of the two hundred or so sternwheelers which once chugged up and down the river, sometimes consuming as much as a cord of wood per hour. Only three remain intact, all in dry dock. The only craft now operating on the river are the canoes and outboards of the Yukon denizens and a couple of launches which transport tourists to various historical spots along the river.

In the short Yukon summer, Dawson survives on a tourist economy. During our week there we saw many tour buses and countless RVs, many of which had been disgorged by the enormous cruise ships which call every day at Skagway. Dawson offers Gold Rush museums, old-time dance-hall entertainment in the restored opera house, tours of the gold-fields, gambling at Diamond-Tooth Gertie's (the only legal gambling spot in all of Canada), readings from the works of Klondike poet Robert W. Service . . . and from Jack London . . . and opportunities to pan for gold along the very creeks the stampeders worked in 1898.

We were surprised to see that gold mining continues unabated throughout the Dawson City area. Although most of the creeks have been dredged down to bedrock (the landscape appears to have been gouged by a giant claw), claims are still bought and sold, and *No Trespassing* signs are still enforced, if necessary, with firearms.

In the Mining Recorder's Office in Dawson, my son and I were able to identify the site of the claim once worked by my great-grandfather, and later, following a surveyor's map, we drove along a dusty mining road a few miles up Bonanza Creek and found the spot, which is now labeled 49 Gulch. Grandpa's claim. Heavy machinery was still working there, and visitors were clearly not welcome, so we did little more than walk around, pick up a few rocks, take a few photographs . . . and imagine.

During his short time in the Yukon, the young Jack London (he was in his early twenties) did not do much "mucking for gold," although he did file a claim on the nearby Henderson Creek and did live for awhile in a remote cabin which was recently found and verified to have been his. (The "Jack London cabin," as it's known, has been divided in two: the lower half is in Dawson City, the upper in Oakland; at each location new "halves" have been combined with the old to give both Dawson and Oakland an entire cabin—the Wisdom of Solomon!)

Even though London did not find mining a lucrative endeavor, his experiences with miners, Indians, Mounties, and the vast Yukon wilderness would nourish his prolific and highly profitable literary career. It is said that Jack London extracted more wealth from the Klondike than any miner.

My journey to Dawson took me to many of the locations London describes in *The Call of the Wild*. Readers of the novel will recall that the dog Buck, stolen from sunny California where he lived a life of ease, is taken to Dyea, Alaska (Dyea, now abandoned, is nine miles from Skagway; we drove to the site along the unimproved road which still connects the two). In Dyea, Buck becomes a sled dog, owned first by a couple of couriers who haul mail from Skagway to Dawson, then by a group of slovenly novices to the North (who, ignoring warnings that the spring thaw has begun, die under the Yukon River ice), and finally by John Thornton, for whom Buck finally feels "love" and to whom he manifests unquestioning devotion and obedience.

When Thornton is killed by Indians in the MacKenzie Mountains (east of Dawson; no public roads go there), Buck joins a wolf pack, returning to life in the wilderness where the instincts of his ancestors emerge from their long period of dormancy.

London never realized much profit from *The Call of the Wild;* in 1903, he sold it to the *Saturday Evening Post* for $750, then released all book rights to Macmillan for $2000. These figures must have seemed immense to a struggling writer in those days—but, in hindsight, London made one of literary history's great miscalculations: his heavily anthologized novel still can be found on the shelves of just about every bookstore in America and has never been out of print.

Publication of *The Call of the Wild* made London a celebrity; from then on he published anything he wanted *wherever* he wanted. His output was astonishing (fifty books in fifteen years), and he soon became the most popular and highest-paid author in the world. He built an ocean-going yacht and set out to circumnavigate the globe (he made it no farther than the Solomon Islands where illnesses forced him home). He designed and constructed a dream house in the Valley of the Moon near Glen Ellen, California (it burned to the ground the day before he was to occupy it). He supported Socialist causes (primarily the abolition of child labor, conservation of natural resources, and the establishment of old-age pensions). But mostly he wrote, averaging more than three volumes a year.

His work varied enormously in genre (and quality!). Between 1901 and 1916 he published volumes of short stories, memoirs, essays and monographs, allegories, plays, and, of course, novels. His long works of fiction displayed tremendous energy and a desire to experiment with subject and form: he wrote on such topics as the Klondike Gold Rush *(A Daughter of the Snows)*, boxing *(The Game)*, pre-historic man *(Before Adam)*, marital relationships *(The Little Lady of the Big House)*, out-of-body experiences *(The Star Rover)*, and dystopian futures *(The Scarlet Plague* and *The Iron Heel)*; he collaborated with Anna Strunsky on an exchange of letters dealing with the subject of love *(The Kempton-Wace Letters);* he wrote an autobiographical novel *(Martin Eden)*, traditional yarns set on the high seas *(The Mutiny of the Elsinore)*, a novelization of a screenplay *(Hearts of Three)*, adventures in the South Seas *(Adventure* and *Jerry of the Islands)*, children's stories *(Tales of the Fish Patrol* and *The Cruise of the Dazzler);* he wrote stories which urged wise use of the land *(The Valley of the Moon)*, which excoriated unscrupulous businessmen *(Burning Daylight)*, and which exposed corruption in athletics *(The Abysmal Brute)*. And, of course, he wrote about dogs *(White Fang, Jerry of the Islands,* and *Michael, Brother of Jerry)*.

I have read every one of his books.

Before my sabbatical year, I'd read only those works still easily available *(The Sea-Wolf, Martin Eden, White Fang,* and *The Call of the Wild)*. Most of the others are now out of print—deservedly so, in many cases, I fear.

I found most of the volumes at nearby Kent State University library; others I ordered through my local public library's interlibrary loan. But the final seven I could find nowhere in the area.

During a trip to Boston to visit my brothers I located five of the seven in Harvard's Widener library. (The remaining two were in special collections, unavailable to me.)

Desperate to read the last two (*Scorn of Women*, 1906, and *The Acorn-Planter*, 1916—both were plays originally published in very small runs), I phoned Russ Kingman, a London biographer who operates the Jack London Bookstore (Glen Ellen, California), which specializes in first editions of London's works and other London memorabilia. He did not have either of the two in stock, but, aware of my unfulfilled passion (he'd once experienced it himself), he graciously provided me with copies of both plays to read. Within hours of their arrival in the mail I'd finished them both.

They were dreadful—almost laughably bad—but I'd read them!

Generally speaking, London's best-known works are also his best. *The Sea-Wolf, Martin Eden, The Call of the Wild,* and *White Fang* deserve the continuing attention and admiration they've received over the years. Of the lesser known novels, *The Star Rover,* one of his last (1915), should take its place alongside *The Sea-Wolf* as his greatest effort. *John Barleycorn* and *The Road* are interesting for the biographical bounties they yield. A handful of short stories are among the best written by an American realist.

Unfortunately, most of the rest of the London canon is embarrassing to read nowadays. In his later work especially, he expresses white supremacist and macho sentiments which modern readers would find repugnant. His social idealism seems naive and simple-minded. Moreover, throughout his career he wrote about the same sorts of people (strong men of action; weak men who redeem themselves through physical exertion; women who share his passions for horseback riding, hiking, boxing, and intellectual debate); his characters are interchangeable—only the names are different. Finally, nearly all his work bears the mark of haste—not surprising, for he was, in fact, forced to write rapidly to keep up with the debts which troubled him throughout his life. Always eager to move on to the next project, he revised his work in a cursory manner, but editors and publishers didn't care: readers were hungry for anything by London.

Chronic ill health in his later years worsened the situation and must have made concentration difficult. Years of alcohol abuse, debilitating illnesses acquired in his trips to the tropics (yaws, dysentery, pellagra), and bizarre eating habits (he went through a period when he would consume only partially cooked or raw duck)—all combined to make miserable his waking hours. At night he slept very little, preferring to use his bed as an extension of his study (much of the night he read, edited manuscripts, and maintained his wide correspondence). He rose before dawn each morning and wrote fifteen hundred words before he would emerge from his study to begin another long day of strenuous mental and physical activity.

To relieve his agony, he began injecting himself with morphine. Finally, on November 22, 1916, following an attack of uremia and a final injection, his poor body could stand no more. Jack London was dead at 40. Official cause of death was kidney failure, but, in fact, his lifestyle had been a form of slow suicide.

So now, I guess, I'm ready to do a better job with *The Call of the Wild*. I can show my slides of Skagway, Dyea, Dawson City, and London's home in Glen Ellen (now a California state park); I can describe my cruise on the Yukon River, summarize all of London's published work, read relevant passages from my great-grandfather's diary, display my growing collection of first editions of London's work (and *Classics Illustrated*).

I can share with my students other Londoniana I've acquired over the past year: an authentic London autograph, a mint sheet of the 25-cent postage stamp issued in his honor, videotapes of *The Call of the Wild* and *Jack London* (an awful film made during World War II displaying London's vile anti-Japanese sentiments, which were, at the time, shared by many Americans), tape recordings of 1940s radio broadcasts of *The Sea-Wolf* and *The Scarlet Plague*, a numbered reproduction of a watercolor of the Jack London Cabin (painted by Yukon artist, Jim Robb), a German translation of *The Cruise of the Snark (Die Fahrt der Snark)*.

I can bake sourdough biscuits prepared from the authentic starter I bought in Whitehorse, Yukon; I can . . . well, I could continue for quite awhile, far beyond the limits of space and reader patience. But the point is made: I think I'm ready.

Now just watch what will happen: the school board will adopt a new literature text. Nothing by London will be included. Featured instead will be works by authors whom I know only from *Classics Illustrated*. And I'll be forced by conscience and insecurity to embark on yet another crazed quest. To tell you the truth, I can hardly wait.

Call **Forwarding—The Adventure Continues**. The school board did, indeed, adopt new literature texts in 1991. But because I participated in the selection, I was able to make certain that *The Call of the Wild* was included.

Well . . . sort of. When I first used the volumes, I was alarmed to discover that Scott, Foresman had heavily edited London's text (to protect the delicate sensibilities of the Beavis and Butthead generation?): Individual words were different; sentences and entire paragraphs were missing; and although the editors generally employed ellipses to indicate cuts, at other times there was no sign at all that the words on the page were not London's.

Most prominent among the missing passages were Buck's ancestral memories of the hairy man (to appease Creationists?); missing, too, were London's characterizations of Perrault and François as "swarthy" and "black-faced." Gone, as well, were the descriptions of Curly's face being "ripped open from eye to jaw," of her "screaming with agony" as the "onlooking huskies" literally tore her to pieces, and of Buck's desire "to kill with his own teeth and wash his muzzle to the eyes in warm blood." *The Call of the Mild* would be a better title for this particular edition. Jack London would not be pleased.

When my article, "Answering the Call of the Wild," appeared in April 1988, I was fairly confident that the end of my obsession with London and the novel was imminent. After all, I had by that time read all fifty of London's works, had visited many of the relevant London shrines in California and the Klondike, had reached the point at which my eighth graders were wondering if there were any other novels ever written in America.

Two years later, however, I was once again in California, this time at Sonoma State University attending a summer seminar in "London's Major Works" sponsored by the National Endowment for the Humanities and conducted by the principal London scholar in the world, Prof. Earle Labor. For five wonderful weeks we seminarians read and discussed London's tales, hiked the grounds of the Jack London State Park in Glen Ellen, haunted the Oakland waterfront, met other London enthusiasts from all walks of life, and searched the local antiquarian book shops for first editions of London's works.

Among the requirements for participants was an individual project of some sort. Because I had for some years been dissatisfied with the amount (and accuracy) of information provided in the few scholarly editions of *The Call of the Wild* (the Library of America edition has only fifteen endnotes, three of which are in error), I decided that summer to prepare a thorough annotation. I could not have imagined at the time that this proposal would be so immodest as to result in a two-year search for material, leading me to libraries and museums and historical societies all over the country.

Again, the NEH helped in a significant way by selecting me for the Teacher-Scholar Award, a generous stipend to support elementary and secondary school teachers in year-long sabbatical projects. With the assistance of other London scholars and enthusiasts (including Prof. Labor, the late Sal Noto, Russ Kingman, and Milo Shepard) I spent the entire 1992-1993 academic year chasing down every allusion in the novel—historical, linguistic, geographical, and autobiographical.

Although a complete account of my research is beyond the scope of this article, I will nonetheless summarize some of my principal activities and findings:

● I read all published criticism of *The Call of the Wild*, including the introductions and afterwords to every edition of the novel I could find. I confess I was surprised by the dearth of criticism on this, London's best-known work. Has its deceptive simplicity and reputation as a book for children dissuaded scholars from giving it more serious attention?

● My search for information about John Myers O'Hara, the minor poet who composed the epigraph, took me to the Newberry Library and to the Library of Congress, where O'Hara had deposited many of his papers and unpublished manuscripts. O'Hara, who was a law-school graduate, a polyglot, and a self-characterized "genius" on Wall Street, occasionally corresponded with Jack and Charmian London after publication of *The Call of the Wild*—and on one occasion in 1912 the Londons dined with O'Hara in New York City. Ruined by the Crash of 1929, the poet died in miserable poverty in a New York hotel in 1944, forced by sad circumstance to sell at auction his priceless collections of antiques, works of art, and books—including all of his many inscribed editions of London's works, Jack's own desk copy of *Wild* among them.

   • From the Library of Congress I acquired copies of nineteenth-century maps of all the settings for the novel. (A map of downtown San Francisco, 1897, cleared up what I had always found confusing: Buck's journey through the city after the train arrived from Santa Clara.) From the United States Geological Survey and the Canada Map Office I acquired topographical maps, enabling me to pinpoint Yukon locations like Cassiar Bar and the mouth of the Tahkini River.

   • From the University of Washington, the Newberry Library, the California State Library, the San Jose Historical Museum, the Santa Clara Historical and Genealogical Society, the California State Railroad Museum, the Library of Congress, and elsewhere I obtained late nineteenth-century photographs of virtually every place and item London mentions in the novel—from the Seattle waterfront to the Yukon River islands near the mouth of the Pelly where a rabies-maddened Dolly chases Buck in a scene both terrifying and comic.

   • By reading London's letters and biographies I was able to determine that many of the names of the people and dogs in the novel were names significant to London. For example, John Thornton, the most admirable human in the book, may have been based upon John Thorson, London's companion on his voyage out of the Yukon in the spring of 1898. And Skeet (one of Thornton's dogs) was the name of a dog owned by one of London's close friends back in the Bay Area, the poet George Sterling.

   • Visits to the Bancroft Library (Berkeley), the Oakland History Room at the Oakland Public Library, the Martin Luther King Library (San Jose), and the San Francisco Public Library provided additional information about the Bay Area aspects of the novel.

   • "Judge Miller's place," the Santa Clara County ranch which London selected for the initial setting of his novel, was based upon the ranch of an actual Judge, Hiram G. Bond, whose sons (Marshall and Louis) London had met in the Klondike in 1897-1898.

   Back in Oakland after the Gold Rush, London began to have his initial successes in publishing and lecturing. Following one of his lectures in San Jose in mid-October, 1901, London stayed with the Bonds at "New Park," the ranch, which, like "Judge Miller's place," featured orchards, artesian wells, a cement swimming tank, and a house with a wide veranda and a library with fireplace.

   In 1913, the Carmelites purchased some of the ranch property (including the house, which they razed in 1917) for use as a monastery. During a visit to the site in the summer of 1992, I met Sister Emmanuel, the unofficial historian for the monastery, who provided me with a copy of a wonderful drawing of the property as it appeared in a local newspaper in the 1890s. Anyone who looks at that drawing can have no doubt that New Park was in

London's memory and imagination as he composed the opening paragraphs of *The Call of the Wild*.

Following another tip from Sister Emmanuel, I discovered at the Huntington Library a collection of spectacular photographs of the Bond property taken sometime during the late 1890s.

• From the California State Railroad Museum I acquired train schedules that enabled me to establish the actual times that Buck would have been on the train between College Park and San Francisco and between Oakland and Seattle. I learned as well the names of Bay ferries operating at the time and acquired from the San Francisco Maritime National Historical Park photographs of the sort of vessel which would have carried Buck to Oakland the morning after his abduction.

• From the Puget Sound Maritime Historical Society I learned that no vessel named *Narwhal* had departed from Seattle during the Gold Rush years. Subsequent research informed me that during the Rush there were two vessels named *Narwhal* in U. S. waters. One, a steam-whaler, was hunting in the Arctic throughout the Rush (I read the captain's log, obtained on microfilm from the Old Dartmouth Historical Society Whaling Museum); the other, an East-coast luxury steam-yacht, did not participate in the Rush, either. However, London may have seen both vessels: Home port for the steam-whaler was San Francisco, and the steam-yacht was in New York harbor that summer day in 1902 when London sailed from New York to England to begin the research that would lead to *The People of the Abyss*.

• After reading every book ever published about the Gold Rush (including many first-hand accounts), I verified virtually every historical detail of the novel. I also learned that the "log store" where Curly is killed by the pack of huskies was an actual business in Dyea owned by John J. Healy and Edgar Wilson—a structure so important in the Northland's early days that "Healy's Store" appeared instead of "Dyea" on some maps.

• At the Leddy Library, University of Windsor, I read the official reports of the North-west Mounted Police for the Gold Rush years. Among the documents I discovered descriptions of impoverished American Indians camped near Lake Laberge—just where London said they were in the novel.

• Among the Bond family papers (housed in the Beinecke Rare Book and Manuscript Library at Yale University) I read Marshall Bond's diary for the Gold Rush years and discovered that the Bond brothers' dog, "Jack" (the original for Buck), one day pulled a 1000-pound load, an event which occurred on a day that London had visited the Bond cabin.

• From the Hudson's Bay Company archives in Winnipeg, I received information about the sorts of trade muskets which John Thornton and his partners discovered in the "ramshackle cabin" in the Mackenzie Mountains near the end of the novel. And I learned that London's assertion that such a weapon had once been "worth its height in beaver skins packed flat" was a Northland canard: The guns were worth about 1/25 as much.

• At the Anthropological Archives in the Smithsonian's Museum of Natural History I found century-old photographs of the Chilkat-Tlingit Indians, possible models for London's fictional Yeehats. The National Archives of Canada sent additional photographs and information.

• Using dictionaries of Chinook Jargon (the Northland *lingua franca*), I was able to determine that "Sol-leks" did, indeed, mean "angry" or "angry one," and "Chook!" (which François shouts at Buck at the beginning of Chapter Four) meant "go away" or "hurry up."

• From the Yukon Archives in Whitehorse I learned that the Eldorado Saloon (where John Thornton's wager on Buck's pulling prowess was laid) was an actual structure in Klondike City (across the Klondike River from Dawson). No photograph has emerged as yet, but the Archives did send me a photocopy of the liquor license for the establishment.

Not all my year was spent in peripatetic pursuits through the aisles and electronic catalogs of libraries and historical societies. On two memorable occasions I was able to visit principal settings of the novel and actually walk in Buck's footsteps on his trip to the Klondike.

• In June 1993, I re-traced the initial stage of Buck's journey: I walked the three miles from the old Bond Ranch in Santa Clara to the College Park depot (still standing), boarded Caltrain for a ninety-minute ride to San Francisco, walked to the Blue and Gold Ferry depot (another couple of miles), caught a ferry to Oakland (another thirty minutes)—then stood in Oakland's Jack London Square and felt the enormous irony of the old socialist's being remembered with this impressive array of up-scale boutiques and restaurants.

• In August 1993, I slung a fifty-pound pack on my back and began the final phase of my research—a four-day hike over the Chilkoot Trail between the old Dyea, Alaska, townsite and Lake Lindeman in British Columbia. Maintained jointly by the U.S. National Park Service and Parks Canada, the trail continues to demand much of the traveller—especially the daunting final quarter-mile to the Chilkoot summit, looming ahead at a forty-five degree incline and littered with enormous rocks and boulders. At the summit I stood in bright sunlight (a rarity), ignoring the strained ligaments in my left knee, looked back into Alaska, then turned to gaze at the Canadian interior, whose arid, rocky terrain would look positively lunar were it not for the deep azure of the pristine waters of Crater and Deep Lakes. I confess that at that moment I bellowed in truly intemperate celebration, reached to remove my hat to wave or toss it, and discovered to my surprise that it was frozen solid.

The next day, at Lake Lindeman a pregnant Canadian warden (ranger) drove me and my throbbing knee across the lake in a speedboat; another mile-long hike then brought me to Lake Bennett, where I took the White Pass and Yukon Railroad back over the spectacularly beautiful Coastal Mountains to Skagway—a journey my own great-grandfather had taken in a boxcar on 16 October 1899 as he returned to his family after a year in the Klondike.

Back in Ohio, I began the long and frustrating process of trying to find a publisher for a new, annotated-illustrated edition of the novel. Many were reluctant because of a simple fact: There are now more than twenty editions of the novel in print. Why add yet another?

But one September evening . . . success. I received a phone call from the University of Oklahoma Press—an offer to publish a complete scholarly edition of the novel (with maps, photographs, illustrations, and full annotations). Moreover, Oklahoma wanted to publish a new student edition (with somewhat simpler notes and illustrations) and an accompanying teacher's guide.

And so my long association with *The Call of the Wild* finally nears an end. As I prepare the manuscript to send off to Oklahoma, I am overwhelmed with gratitude for the countless librarians, archivists, London scholars (and fans and fanatics), historians, park rangers, family members, and others who were so helpful in my two-year quest to answer so many questions, some of which must have seemed awfully insignificant to those who answered them nonetheless.

The research, however, has enabled me to enter the mind of Jack London, to glimpse the world of the novel through his eyes, to hear the howls of wolves and the jingling bells of the teams of dogs on the Long Trail, to feel the bite of the wind at the Chilkoot summit. Best of all, I know the exhilaration that comes to all who hear the call. And are willing to answer.

4

The Sea-Wolf

Early Reviews

The Sea-Wolf

For the protagonist of his new and powerfully told story, *The Sea-Wolf*, Mr. Jack London seems to have deliberately taken Milton's Satan, demeaning him to a modern, unpoetical environment. That, we fancy, is the worst that can be said of *The Sea-Wolf*. The best that can be said of it is that it is a stirring and unhackneyed tale of life on the high seas, full of the seafaring spirit, in its most violent manifestations, picturing vividly the conflict of man with the elements.

While its central figure is actually impressive, (until the closing chapters,) the minor characters, seal hunters and sailors and a cockney sea cook of the lowest type, are wonderfully lifelike. We mean that they are made to seem real and living, not that we have met such persons and recognize their portraits.

The controlling idea, the adaptation of Milton's Satan, is a purely "literary" idea. The conventional romance of the book, the meeting on the high seas of an ineffably beautiful young "authoress" and the literary critic who has deliberately called her "The American Mrs. Meynell" has its value, both artistic and commercial. In its development it recalls Charles Reade's "Foul Play" and Clark Russell's "Marooned." The heroine is a really attractive young woman, though we could have spared the literary side of her and her views on literature. The hero is a literary critic only in certain moods; the reader of the story is not bothered much by his literary criticism. He is a man of wealth, used to luxury and sedentary habits, suddenly put in the power of a brute of the seas, forced to eat the food and do the labor of an incompetent seaman and to endure his share of ill-treatment. Drowning, starvation, strangulation, and synovitis threaten him. He is transformed for a time into an enslaved, abject creature. But his muscles harden, the salt air invigorates him, and he triumphs. He also wins the girl.

On the whole, therefore, the love story, the purely romantic element, in Mr. London's book is very good, though his descriptions of his hero and heroine and the development of their passion for each other are not nearly so coherent and convincing as his descriptions of the seal hunters and sailors and the detestable cook already mentioned.

The central personage is Captain Larsen, called "Wolf" Larsen, the skipper of a sealing schooner, a tightly built, finely modeled craft called the Ghost. Larsen was born of poor, unlettered Danish parents on "a bleak bight of land on the west coast of Norway;" suffered privation and injustice in his boyhood, and was sent to sea early. He is endowed with a splendid body and an ample mind; he has read much (having taught himself to read) and mastered the principles of navigation; he is in his way a thinker, but his good mind is wholly undisciplined. He is utterly evil. He is courageous, hopeless, shameless, brutal. Not only the conventions of good people, but their principles, are to him alike absurd.

We need not dwell upon his doctrines. There can be nothing new in the literary representation of evil. But Mr. London manages to endow this cynical demon, this cold-hearted monster, with a certain majesty, which is not dispelled till the story is nearly finished. The Wolf's doings toward the close of his life are too grotesquely extravagant. The manner of his taking off seems inconsistent. If he has been a victim of brain disease all along—a tumor or a cancer—then there is nothing but insanity in his brutality and devilishness. It seems a pity that the author did not make Larsen die battling with the storm.

From first to last there is a great deal of vitality in the book. Some of the chapters have an excess of detail which somewhat injures their effect, as that devoted to the adventure of the hero and heroine in the "rookery" when it becomes necessary to club a few seals in order to roof the house on the island with their skins, and that describing the painfully laborious effort to restore the masts to the Ghost after the schooner has been wrecked. But there are some excellent word pictures of storm and calm at sea; the reader feels sure of the reality of many things Mr. London writes about.

Like some of London's other stories, this has an excess of brutality. London delights in pictures of cruelty and in studies of monsters. But he gives them appreciable literary value. *The Sea-Wolf* has caused a great deal of discussion as a serial in *The Century*. Now that the Macmillan Company has published it in book form it will be talked about still more. We shall hear a great deal about "red blood." There is plenty of blood in *The Sea-Wolf*, and the color of it is red. We do not see our way clear to herald the book as an epoch-maker. But it is an ingenious and powerful story, with some obvious faults and some striking merits. It is above the average alike in plan and execution.

New York Times Saturday Review of Books and Art November 12, 1904, 768-69.

Literary Notes: Jack London's Remarkable Book

Perhaps no work of fiction has in late years attracted so much attention during its publication in serial form as Jack London's *The Sea-Wolf*, which began in the January number of the *Century Magazine*, and ends with the issue for November.

The most various criticisms have been passed upon it: some seem to have thought the story great; some perniciously immoral; some have simply choked at "the brutality," and refused to read further. All of which stimulates interest in the volume which is now from the press.

The scene, when the story opens, is a ferry-boat of San Francisco Bay, running from Sausalito to the city, on a January Monday morning. One of our characteristic heavy fogs blankets the bay, and there is a collision with another ferry-boat. Humphrey Van Weyden, artist and *dilettante*, rich, idle, feminine of manner, is one of those on board. He leaps into the water and is swept by the tide out to sea. Off the Heads he is picked up by the schooner *Ghost*, Wolf Larsen master, bound to Bering Sea to hunt seals. Larsen is short-handed, takes a fancy to the idea of compelling this soft-palmed rich man's son to work—work hard—and therefore refuses all offers to put him on shore. The book is the story of the voyage, of the ultimate escape of Weyden and a girl (who is rescued from a wrecked ship by the *Ghost*) in a small boat, their landing after many days on an island inhabited only by seals, the arrival at the island of the wreck of the *Ghost*, her sole passenger Wolf Larsen, and the final escape on the *Ghost* of the three persons.

This is the bare skeleton of the tale. But all its interest lies in a single character, that of the master, Larsen, well called of his men "Wolf"—an epic figure; an amazing personality; a unique character in literature[. . . .]

Life is piggishness; piggishness is life, says Larsen, in another place; he denies immortality; he denies that life has sacredness; he denies that life has value:

> "Why, if there is anything in supply and demand, life is the cheapest thing in the world. There is only so much water, so much earth, so much air; but the life that is demanding to be born is limitless. Nature is a spendthrift. Look at the fish and their millions of eggs. For that matter, look at you and me. In our loins are the possibilities of millions of lives. Could we but find time and opportunity and utilize the last bit and every bit of the unborn life that is in us, we could become the fathers of nations

and populate continents. Life? Bah! It has no value. Of cheap things it is
the cheapest. Everywhere it goes begging. Nature spills it out with a lavish
hand. Where there is room for one life, she sows a thousand lives, and it's
life eat life till the strongest and most piggish life is left. . . . Why should
I be parsimonious with this life that is cheap and without value? There are
more sailors than there are ships on the sea for them, more workers than
there are factories or machines for them. . . . The only value life has is the
value life puts upon itself. And it is of course over-estimated, since it is of
necessity prejudiced in its own favor. Take that man I had aloft. He held
on as if he were a precious thing, a treasure beyond diamonds or rubies.
To you? No. To me? Not at all. To himself? Yes. But I do not accept his
estimate. He sadly overrates himself. There is plenty more life demanding
to be born. Had he fallen and dripped his brains upon the deck like honey
from the comb, there would have been no loss to the world. He was worth
nothing to the world. The supply is too large. To himself only was he of
value, and to show how fictitious even this value was, being dead he is
unconscious that he has lost himself."

With such argument, Larsen beats down the arguments of Van Weyden wherein
he talks of ideals, of altruism, of unselfishness, of aspirations. The reader feels
that Van Weyden ought to be right; the ethical basis from which argues is the
ethical basis upon which we all of us stand; but still Larsen, by sheer logic,
argues him down, leaves him floundering in a sea of words and phrases, vapid,
meaningless.

Where is the flaw in Larsen's logic? The answer is, There is
none—*from Larsen's point of view.* Larsen's philosophy is the true philosophy
for the Superior Man. His scheme of society is a scheme of society that would
originate among a score of men, cast upon an island, where there was
insufficient food and water. The strong man would inevitably prevail—not
necessarily the physically strong—he would have to have brains, too. But the
ethics of our society are not the ethics of the Superior Man; they are the ethics
of the Under Man, who is in a numerical majority. Laws, conventions, ideals,
are the buffers that the many little men—the Thomas Mugridges, the Humps, the
Johnsons—have erected to protect themselves from the strong man—the Wolf
Larsen. Strong men are proud; the ethics of the dominant theology condemn
pride and laud humility. The Superior Man is strong and rudely exercises his
strength; the morality of the weak many praises gentleness. The strong man
robustly joys in life, and violently lays hold upon its good; the current ethical
system honors asceticism and self-sacrifice. Larsen denies the utility of
sympathy. "Sympathy," said a certain man, "preserves what is ripe for
extinction. . . it is the conservator of all misery. . . chief instrument for the
promotion of decadence."

Who said that? Friedrich Nietzsche, the Mad Philosopher. And what is
The Sea-Wolf? A vivid illustration of the philosophy of Nietzsche; a keen,
subtle, brilliant satire.

Indeed, it is amazing the cleverness with which London has clothed the philosopher's skeletal idea in flesh and blood in the person of Wolf Larsen, has opposed to him exponents of "slave morals" in the persons of Van Weyden, Thomas Mugridge, and the delicate poetess, Maud Brewster, and has set the contestants in the most vital of all discussions apart from the world where debate and illustration of it go hand in hand. If he did it consciously, London must wake up at night and laugh to himself to think how he has "shoved off" on an innocent, unsuspecting world, under the guise of "a good story," the most damnably heretical of all philosophy.

This explains "the brutality" of the story. All this exhibition of tigerish instincts in the men of the *Ghost* is not mere wantonness on London's part. There's method in it. He is illustrating a theory. He is making real a vague philosophy.

And who is the hero of the book?

Larsen!—Larsen, undoubtedly. Despite all seeming reason we dislike Van Weyden (such is London's art), and the deep, true-running instinct is to side with the strong man. When he steps from the pages the book grows dull; when he returns—solitary, blind, head "bloody yet unbowed"—interest wakes and quickens; the book again thrills us. There are few figures in modern literature more greatly stirring to the imagination than the great, blind, brutal hero of the last few chapters.

In style, the book is even an improvement over the style of *The Call of the Wild*. Phrases are tense. They seem to crack like whips. The movement of the story is irresistible; it goes forward like fighting men in line. There is nothing sinuous about London's style. He does not cajole the reader into being interested, as does Stevenson, for example. He compels.

As usual, Mr. London's work is weak where women are concerned. We suppose it could not have been avoided, but a young man and a young woman—lovers—in a boat together—many days—alone—is a crassly indelicate situation. Much of the "love talk" is infantile. As some French critic has said of Victor Hugo's Marius and Cosette, one sees the lovers, but not the man and woman. The washing out of all human characteristics in Maud and Humphrey while they are alone together is, we suppose, a concession *virginibus puerisque*; but they are too virtuous.

As a whole, *The Sea-Wolf* is a remarkable achievement. It is the strongest book London has yet given us.

Argonaut (San Francisco) 55 (November 14, 1904), 311.

New Novels: *The Sea-Wolf*

This is easily the best piece of work which Mr. London has done. Its faults are robust faults; its merits are positive, generous, outstanding. It is an adventurous tale, full of incident and movement, compact of ingeniously contrived situations, and containing much first-hand knowledge of the sea. Withal, it is throughout an almost entirely consistent study of character, and of notable character. Its opening suggests *Captains Courageous*, and Mr. London owes a good deal to the writer of *McAndrew's Hymn* in most of his work. But it need not be supposed that this story is imitative. It is not. It deals with the lives of those who hunt the seal in the forbidden waters—men who rate but one thing lighter than their own lives, and that, the lives of others. Among such fellows as these, an American man of letters finds himself suddenly flung by the merest chance. They pick him up at sea, utterly exhausted, one of the victims of a collision between two steamers near San Francisco. The captain of the seal-hunters, Wolf Larsen, is the central figure of the tale: a man of extraordinary strength, physical and mental, and of remorseless, unmitigated ferocity. To the last page, his character is unfolded with admirable consistency. His figure is a credit to the author. One fears a softening toward the close of the book, when a feminine element is introduced, but it does not come. The author is tempted at times to air scholarly attainments, and then he is mischievously misled. But in dealing with rough men and their rough work he is admirable. His chief fault is a tendency to exaggeration, a sort of riotous rejoicing in his own virility and enthusiasm. Then his central figure makes one think of Bret Harte's Rawjester.

Athenaeum 4024 (December 10, 1904), 801.

Recent Fiction: *The Sea-Wolf*

Whenever a new volume by Jack London comes out, we anticipate vigorous writing, brilliant descriptions, and a surfeit of horrors. The fulfillment was seldom as complete as in this instance, but it is the third item that compels our chief attention. Never has sickening brutality been more gloatingly described than in this story of life on a sealing schooner, under a captain of whom the hero says: "This man is a monster. He is without conscience. Nothing is sacred to him, nothing is too terrible for him to do." Whether this is a probable or even possible evolution for a Norwegian sailor-boy, is, of course, an open question. To most readers the man who strikes and tortures and kills as his daily occupation, while for his pastime he reads Herbert Spencer and Browning, or talks philosophy, will seem no less grotesquely fictitious than the Caliban to whom he is compared. Yet the conception is at least novel and powerful, and the breath of the sea is almost painfully perceptible throughout. Indeed, the book might have compelled admiration, if not belief or liking, but for two grave faults—first, a strained exaggeration, which makes the scenes of horror nauseating rather than thrilling, and the love-passages distressingly mawkish; and, secondly, a long-windedness, perhaps to be explained by the original serial form. In a volume of 366 pages we have only the following main incidents: the rescue from the sea, *à la* Kipling, of a man-writer and a woman-writer successively (their meeting being brought about as violently as in a game of "Consequences"); their life on and escape from the sealing schooner, their life on and rescue from a desert island, and the death by paralysis of the Sea-Wolf himself. All the rest is padding of the most tedious kind, with exasperating tricks of speech, such as "what of" for "what with." We are left regretting that Mr. London should ever have abandoned the short stories that he told so well. But perhaps the whole book is to be regarded as a parody, in which case 'Captain Outrageous' would be a more fitting title.

Nation 79 (December 22, 1904), 507.

Recent Fiction: *The Sea-Wolf*

William Morton Payne

A fastidious man of letters, whose life has never been ruffled by anything more serious than the clash of conversational wits or the controversies of the critical pen, is one day crossing the Bay of San Francisco on a ferry-boat. The Bay is foggy, but he has no thought of danger until the ferry is suddenly struck amidships and speedily sunk. The cause of the mishap is an outward-bound sealer, and upon this craft the victim of the collision finds himself after he is restored to consciousness. He then discovers to his consternation that he is in for a voyage of several months to the coast of Japan and Kamschatka, and that he has ceased to be even a free agent. The captain of the sealer, it appears, is a brute of violent disposition who is a law unto himself, and this autocrat decrees that the new passenger shall sign as cabin-boy, 'for the good of his soul,' as the Sea-Wolf grimly remarks. Since this person has a rough and ready way of enforcing his arguments by a free use of his fists, and since the newly-rescued man has then and there a convincing object-lesson of the validity of this method of reasoning, the views are perforce accepted, and he faces for the first time in his career the realities of life. From this point on, the book becomes a tale of the sea, and of the daily routine of a floating hell. The Sea-Wolf is the incarnation of sheer animalism, the vigor of his physical frame matched by the strength of his will, and capable of every sort of brutality. He is also—and this is the curious thing about him—by way of being a philosopher; he reads Spencer and Browning, and interprets them by the light of a vigorous and unsophisticated intellect. Of ethical obligations he has no notion whatever, being a very startling embodiment of Nietzsche's ideal of the *Uebermensch*. Nothing like a scruple is ever known to him, and he is in equal measure hated and feared by his men. Under this rough tutelage the man of letters turned ship's drudge learns many things not set down in the books, and develops a strength and a resourcefulness that he would otherwise never have known. Thus the story becomes essentially an account of the development of character under extraordinary conditions, and its aspect as a narrative of adventure is obscured by its aspect as a psychological study. It is not a pleasant tale to read—it is too strongly seasoned to be that,—but it acquires a certain fascination in the course of its telling, and fairly grips the attention in its culminating passages.

Dial 38 (January 1, 1905), 16.

Literature: A Nietzsche Novel

The chief interest of Jack London's latest novel, *The Sea-Wolf*, lies in the admirable way in which he has made use of a fictional form to work out an ethical problem without making puppets of his people or losing the story in the lesson. Notwithstanding that Wolf Larsen is a typical Superman, the great blond beast of Nietzsche, and is altogether too consistent in his selfishness to be quite human, yet he is no mere symbol, but very much alive. He remains with us a real acquaintance, however glad we would be to forget him. And, altho thousands read in *The Sea-Wolf* nothing but an exciting tale, yet the ethical theorem is developed by argument and illustration with a symmetry and completeness rare even in a serious treatise.

In form *The Sea-Wolf* is very similar to the author's first success, *The Call of the Wild*. In place of the high-bred and pampered pet dog "Buck," plunged into hardships, treated with brutality, forced into servitude, compelled to stand abuse and to fight for his life, we now have Mr. Humphrey Van Weyden, *litterateur* and dilettante, who thinks he is doing his share of the world's work and earning his luxurious living by writing essays on the position of Poe in American literature. He, shanghaied on a sealing schooner, tyrannized over by its crew of brutal men from captain to cook, finds it possible to live in the new environment and even so to adapt himself to it as to rise to a position of power.

But this is not accomplished as it usually is in romances, by his nobility of character or goodness of heart arousing the admiration and love of his associates. He has to fight for his place like "Buck" with the dogs of his pack. He is no hero. He is denuded of the last shred of his personal dignity and forced to play the part of a coward and a slave. The modern cultured woman also has not, according to Mr. London, lost her power to reacquire the primeval virtues and to become a fitting mate for a man of the Stone Age. The description of the life on the island, the building of the hut and the raising of the mast is as fascinating as a chapter from *Robinson Crusoe*.

In his arguments with Wolf Larsen Van Weyden is always beaten, or, rather, is never able to prove to him that altruism is advantageous. Or, to put it more succinctly, it is impossible to derive from selfishness a sufficient motive for unselfishness. And in this matter none of our ethical teachers has succeeded much better than Van Weyden. No one has yet been able to frame an argument sufficiently strong to convince an individual that it is for his interest in this life always to "do right." In other words, ecclesiastic and agnostic are alike agreed that there must be a superhuman sanction for altruism. The religious man believes that a supernatural motive is essential to morality. The positivist finds it in idealization of the race as a conscious object of self-sacrifice. The evolutionist considers it as a blind instinct developed by the necessities of interracial struggle.

Apparently Mr. London holds the last view, for Van Weyden, in saving the life of Larsen and tending him on his deathbed, is acting not from reason, but from motives which, whatever their origin, have become an essential part of his moral constitution. Van Weyden, with his finger on the trigger, but unable to shoot the man whom he knows ought to die, is a graphic picture of modern humanity, which cannot use the harsh measures necessary to rid the world of the human brutes who thrive and multiply under its care and protection, because by such action it would destroy in itself those sentiments which make humanity great. As men become more merciful and tender-hearted they apparently become more powerless against the cruel and hard-hearted. Apparently, we say, for we believe that Jack London is right in the thesis of his novel: that altruism must conquer egoism in the end; that no Superman, however strong, can ultimately prevail against the combined forces of men bound together by the law of love and using only the weapons it allows. The ethics of Nietzsche must on the deathbed say, like Julian the Apostate, "Thou hast conquered," to the ethics of the Galilean. It is fitting and logical that Wolf Larsen should die like the philosopher whose teachings he exemplified, in a second childhood, for he had forgotten the lesson of his first, and cared for by the virtues he had scorned and derided.

Independent 58 (January 5, 1905), 39.

Yes, you sent me *The Sea-Wolf*

Ambrose Bierce

Yes, you sent me *The Sea-Wolf*. My opinion of it? Certainly—or a part of it. It is a most disagreeable book, as a whole. London has a pretty bad style and no sense of proportion. The story is a perfect welter of disagreeable incidents. Two or three (of the kind) would have sufficed to show the character of the man Larsen; and his own self-revelings by word of mouth would have "done the rest." Many of these incidents, too, are impossible—such as that of a man mounting a ladder with a dozen other men—more or less—hanging to his leg, and the hero's work of rerigging a wreck and getting it off a beach where it had stuck for weeks, and so forth. The "love" element, with its absurd suppressions and impossible proprieties, is awful. I confess to an overwhelming contempt for both sexless lovers.

Now as to the merits. It is a rattling good story in one way; something is "going on" all the time—not always what one would wish, but something. One does not go to sleep over the book. But the great thing—and it is among the greatest of things—is that tremendous creation, Wolf Larsen. If that is not a permanent addition to literature, it is at least a permanent figure in the memory of the reader. You "can't lose" Wolf Larsen. He will be with you to the end. So it does not really matter how London has hammered him into you. You may quarrel with the methods, but the result is almost incomparable. The hewing out and setting up of such a figure is enough for a man to do in one life-time. I have hardly words to impart my good judgment of that work.

Letter to George Sterling dated February 18, 1905.

Jack London's Code of Primitivism

Robert H. Woodward

One of the greatest misfortunes of Jack London's literary life, it would seem, was his concession to popular taste in the latter half of *The Sea-Wolf*. The obvious hero of the first half of the novel is Wolf Larsen, a powerfully-built, unscrupulous sea-captain whose will is law aboard the schooner *Ghost*. He is an example of the superman-type popular even in serious literature at the turn of the century, an embodiment of Nietzsche's *Will zur Macht*. Recording Larsen's words and deeds is Humphrey Van Weyden, a literary dilettante who, after a shipwreck, has been rescued by the *Ghost* and forced into its service as a cabin-boy. Van Weyden represents a philosophy of moral idealism, as opposed to Larsen's primitive materialism. The conflict between the two men—or, allegorically, between the two philosophies—rises toward a climax. But this conflict is never resolved. Instead, another castaway, Maud Brewster, a young poetess, is brought aboard the *Ghost*. Van Weyden, falling in love with Maud, concerns himself after her arrival with escaping from the boat with her rather than with bringing his ideological feud with Larsen to a climax. After Maud's introduction into the plot, the novel deteriorates into a melodramatic romance, interesting to a point, but certainly devoid of the philosophical ramifications promised by the early chapters.

Even with this deficiency in structure and plot, however, *The Sea-Wolf* clearly points up London's naturalistic tendencies and hints that the author, at this very early stage, was leaning toward a philosophy of pure naturalism. The novel illustrates several aspects of that type of naturalism which was begun by Frank Norris. A deterministic philosophy is evident throughout the story; and, while it plays only a minor role concerning the plot, it is pedantically stated by several of the characters. The jungle spirit is a prominent feature of the novel, and atavism and primordialism are seen in the characters of Van Weyden and Maud as well as in the more clearly brutish and primitive sailors of the *Ghost*. A study of these naturalistic elements will illustrate, in some measure, the latent naturalism in Jack London's philosophy.

Determinism is especially evident in three of the prominent characters of the book. Van Weyden, for instance, who has spent his thirty-five years primarily with books and has seen little of life for himself, is unable at first to adapt himself to the violence and brutality of the conditions on the *Ghost*. His character has been shaped by his past environment, and he is not responsible for his inability to stand up against the attack of Larsen. There is something in Larsen's personality—a primitive violence, a completely amoral view of life, which is so foreign to Van Weyden's previous experience that he is unable even to argue with him, much less to pit his physical forces against him. But even the character of Larsen has been determined by his environment. Born of penniless Danish parents on a bleak Norwegian coast, he had been reared in an atmosphere of deprivation and hardship. Going to sea as a cabin-boy at the age of ten, he endured the rough fare and rougher usage: "kicks and blows were bed and breakfast and took the place of speech, and fear and hatred and pain were my only soul-experiences," he said.[1] He had taught himself to read and to write, had studied Spencer and Darwin, and had evolved his own philosophy that the only positive value is life itself—and that only to the individual. What promotes the comfort of the individual—be it money or even the servitude and death of others—is good; all else is evil. No opportunity had come to him to elevate himself above the brutish level of existence that he had always known. He had aspired to a level of life where *ethics* was more than a word; he had prepared himself. But, a pawn in the hands of inexorable destiny, he had been unable to rise. "No man makes opportunity," he said. "All the great men ever did was to know it when it came to them. The Corsican knew. I have dreamed as greatly as the Corsican. I should have known the opportunity, but it never came. The thorns sprung up and choked me" (102). And, too, the hateful little Cockney cook, Thomas Mugridge, is also a product of his environment. "Life had been unfair to him. It had played him a scurvy trick when it fashioned him into the thing he was, and it had played him scurvy tricks ever since. What chance had he to be anything else than he was?" Van Weyden asked himself (123). And, after cataloguing his early and late misfortunes, the Cockney himself concluded: "'Ow Gawd must 'ave 'ated me w'en 'e signed me on for a voyage in this bloomin' world of 'is!" (124)

These examples of determinism in *The Sea-Wolf* are concerned with environment as a factor in shaping the present conditions of men. But, as past environment has shaped men to be what they now are, present environment must be able to re-shape men. This aspect of determinism is also evidenced in several characters of the book. Under the tyrannical rule of Larsen, some of the sailors assume new personalities. Johnson, an honest, idealistic man, is broken physically and mentally by Larsen. He changes from a firm-willed, upright character to one melancholy, moody, and pessimistic. Reacting in another way to Larsen's brutality, the young George Leach becomes a virtual animal, with a perpetual snarl at the lips and guttural noises in the throat at the sight of the hated captain. More importantly, the ethereal and spiritual Maud adapts herself to the rugged nature of the life and even finds in herself a latent, primitive strength. She is in striking contrast to some of the earlier heroines of American fiction—to Hawthorne's Lilias Fay or Sylph Etherege, for instance, who are unable to cope with their environment and fade away like roses in a shadowed forest. And the scholarly Van Weyden, pressed by circumstances, uncovers hidden resources in his character.

Specifically, however, the changes effected in Maud and Van Weyden are manifestations of atavism rather than of determinism. These two characters, forced from a highly intellectual and cultural society into one where conventional laws do not operate, find that they must take recourse to the more elemental levels of existence if they wish to survive. Van Weyden, helplessly caught in a feud with the treacherous Mugridge, finds that he can win only if he retaliates in kind, with an animal-like ferocity and violence. Looking back at his experience, he was unable to visualize how he could have effected the pose of courage which he did not feel. Later on, compelled to meet the primitive conditions on an uninhabited, uncharted seal island, he felt strange instincts rising within him. "The youth of the race seemed burgeoning in me, over-civilized man that I was," he wrote of his battle with the seals, "and I lived for myself the old hunting days and forest nights of my remote and forgotten ancestry" (291).

Part of his atavism, then, was a result of racial memory. But another factor, and one which London stresses strongly, was the fact that upon Van Weyden's shoulders fell the responsibility for another person. Because the other person was a woman, Van Weyden became highly conscious of his own manhood. "The primitive deeps of my nature stirred," he reflected. "I felt myself masculine, the protector of the weak, the fighting male" (291). He secretly called Maud "my woman, my mate," exulting in this primitive attachment. Even so, Van Weyden's atavism is a higher level than that of the brutish sailors. What helped to recall the primitive impulses in Van Weyden—the feeling that a loved one must be protected—explains the failure of the sailors ever to raise themselves above bestiality. They had never experienced an elevating type of feminine companionship; not for years had they known a good woman. As a result, the balance in their lives had been destroyed. "Their masculinity," observed Van Weyden, "which in itself is of the brute, has been overdeveloped. The other and spiritual side of their natures has been dwarfed—atrophied, in fact" (129). Like Van Weyden, Maud was also able to adapt herself to primitive conditions. Forgetful of her culture, she shared with her companion the hardships of the lonely island and, when he was attacked by Larsen, came to his aid fighting like a savage or an animal that had been trapped.

The novel deals, too, with the primordial in man, that in him which is neither determined nor arrived at atavistically. Larsen, a superman-type, is the chief embodiment of this aspect of naturalism in the novel. His was an elemental strength, such as is associated with "things primitive, with wild animals, and the creatures we imagine our tree-dwelling prototypes to have been" (19). He is spoken of as an anachronism, "born a thousand years or generations too late" (75). Perhaps the epithet *superman* is wrongly applied to Larsen. He is more exactly a brute with a materialistic philosophy—a brute with the ability to reason intelligently. He is a superman in the same sense that Milton's Satan is a superman: strong, selfish, vengeful, referring all values to his own security. But he is not the Nietzschean superman. True, he has energy, intellect, and pride—the requisites; but he lacks the discipline of self which is the harmonizing element, the catalyst in Nietzsche's formula. Without this requisite discipline he is but a highly-developed brute, an embodiment of the gross materialism which results from naturalism.

Certain other obvious sidelights of naturalism might be mentioned, such as the attention to violence, description of brutality and death, and general interest in the sensational, exclusive of sex. London's interest in these aspects of naturalism is akin to Norris's, and certain definite parallels in plot could be drawn, for instance, between *The Sea-Wolf* and Norris's earlier *Moran of the Lady Letty*.

Several of the naturalistic elements in *The Sea-Wolf* have been discussed at some length in this paper; yet, despite their presence, the final impression of the novel is that it is romantic rather than naturalistic. The misfortune mentioned in the first paragraph of this paper accounts for the inconsistency. The introduction of Maud brings an element of romance and a new hero. Attention is diverted from Larsen to Van Weyden, and, while the latter character is an interesting one, he possesses none of the dramatic potentiality of Wolf Larsen. The conflict between Larsen and Van Weyden is never resolved. When Van Weyden flees, Larsen follows accidentally, and the end of Larsen is by a paralytic stroke—perhaps poetic retribution, but not of the nature which the reader had been led to anticipate. Determinism is no factor in the denouement of the plot. As a result, *The Sea-Wolf* is really two books—the first an incomplete, naturalistic study of character, and the second a popular sea romance carried to its inevitable happy ending. If London had refrained from ending *The Sea-Wolf* as a romance and had made at least an attempt to come to a philosophical conclusion, the novel might stand today as a statement of his naturalism or his idealism, dependent on which philosophy or character was triumphant. Instead, it is remembered as a red-blooded adventure of sea life and as sentimental melodrama. Such a classification takes no cognizance of the serious aspects of the book. The dynamic strength of Larsen's character and philosophy, which could have elevated the novel above romance into a serious study of an important level of human experience, was sacrificed to the demands of popular taste.

NOTE

[1] Jack London, *The Sea-Wolf* (New York: Macmillan, 1904), 101. Page references to further quotations from this book will follow, in parentheses, the quoted material.

Jack London in the Tradition of American Sea Fiction

Bert Bender

> And at last my dream would be realized: I would sleep upon the
> water. And next morning I would wake upon the water; and
> thereafter all my days and nights would be on the water.
> —Jack London, *John Barleycorn*

During the last two decades, Jack London has emerged as a much more
significant American writer than critics were prepared to admit during the half-
century following his death.[1] But it is a strange and unfortunate oversight that
the author of *The Sea-Wolf* has never been fully recognized as a major writer in
the tradition of American sea fiction. The most obvious reason for this oversight
is the mistaken assumption that the tradition virtually ended with the publication
of *Moby-Dick*. Also, like Cooper, who came to be identified with but one part
of his work (the Leatherstocking series), London has become known mainly for
his Alaskan stories, particularly *The Call of the Wild*. Furthermore, the sheer
volume and range of London's work has confused many of his critics, leaving
his own figure as an important sea writer enshrouded, like the sealing schooner
Ghost in one of the great fogbanks of the Bering-Sea. In his meteoric sixteen-
year career, this most energetic writer of the "Strenuous Age" produced over
fifty books, Earle Labor reminds us, "with an astonishing range of subjects:
agronomy, architecture, astral projection, boating, ecology, gold-hunting,
hoboing, loving, penal reform, prize-fighting, Socialism, warfare" (viii). Labor
presents this impressive list in alphabetical order, but it should be rearranged
and the subject "boating" replaced at the head of the list with The Sea. For like
Dana, Melville, and others who are now unknown, London entered the literary
world by way of the sea, and he remained until his death a more potent force
in perpetuating the tradition of American sea fiction than we have yet
recognized. From his seventeenth year, when he published his first story,
"Typhoon Off the Coast of Japan," until he wrote his last story, "The Water
Baby," he turned repeatedly to the sea in his efforts to grasp the essential reality
of our existence.

Like the other great figures in our tradition of sea literature—Philip
Freneau, Cooper, Dana, Melville, Crane, Joshua Slocum, O'Neill, Hemingway,
and Peter Matthiessen—London wrote from direct experience of the sea and was
inspired by other writers in the tradition who had sailed before him. But
excepting only Freneau and Slocum, none of these writers can claim to have
drawn on so broad and varied a basis of firsthand sea experience. As a boy
London was an estimable small boat sailor in San Francisco Bay, where he won
local fame as "prince of the oyster pirates" and served on the California Fish
Patrol. At seventeen he sailed before the mast as an able seaman on the sealing
schooner *Sophia Sutherland*, and at twenty-one he steamed and, on the last leg,

reportedly sailed in an Indian dugout canoe from San Francisco to Dyea, Alaska.[2] Following a two thousand-mile journey in a hand-hewn boat down the Yukon River from Dawson to St. Michael, he worked his way back to British Columbia passing coal on an ocean steamer. Later he would sail as a passenger on innumerable coastal and transoceanic voyages by steamer and would continue until the end of his life to sail his own small boats in the waters of San Francisco Bay. Finally, in addition to the famous eighteen-month cruise that he logged in *The Cruise* of *the Snark,* he fulfilled a lifelong dream in 1912 by sailing from Baltimore to Seattle on a five-month voyage around Cape Horn. He was our last major writer to make the passage and tell the story before steam power and the Panama Canal left buried at sea one of our literature's earliest and most compelling tales of mythic proportions.

In addition to this impressive firsthand sea experience, London drew heavily on his experience with sea literature. In the first place he read Melville. In fact, as Charles N. Watson, Jr., has emphasized, London should be credited with having read *Moby-Dick* "more creatively than any novelist" before him and "at a time when few readers remembered Melville at all" (61, ix). But he also read widely and deeply in Cooper, Dana, Frederick Marryat, Algernon Swinburne, John Masefield, Robert Louis Stevenson, Rudyard Kipling, and his contemporaries, Crane, Norris, Slocum, Morgan Robertson, and Conrad. Of these, he was most inspired and influenced by Melville, Dana, Slocum, and Conrad. But London's sea fiction bears the unique stamp of his own genius, and his notable work in the field includes not only his masterpiece, *The Sea-Wolf,* but the neglected novel, *The Mutiny of the Elsinore* (1912), and such memorable stories as "The Seed of McCoy," "Make Westing," "The Heathen," "The 'Francis Spaight,'" "The Sea-Farmer," "Samuel," and "The Water Baby." In addition to a number of other good but less notable sea stories, including "Under the Deck Awnings" and "The Pearls of Parlay," he produced a fine boys' book in *The Cruise of the Dazzler* and the collections of boys' stories of his own boyhood contained in *Tales of the Fish Patrol* and *Dutch Courage and Other Stories.* Finally, he produced several stories and books that are shaped significantly by the sea even though they cannot he described as pure sea fiction; the most important of these are *The Cruise of the Snark* and *Martin Eden,* but there are as well *John Barleycorn,* "An Odyssey of the North," *Jerry of the Islands* and *Michael, Brother of Jerry.*[3]

Clearly, Jack London had more to say about the sea than can be fully represented in a single chapter, but perhaps a brief examination of four of his sea pieces—*The Sea-Wolf, The Mutiny of the Elsinore, Michael, Brother of Jerry,* and "The Water Baby"—will reveal what he saw in the sea that drew him so constantly to it and what he contributed to the tradition of American sea fiction.

Like so many memorable American novels *The Sea-Wolf* is great but flawed. Its estimable energies, like those of *Huckleberry Finn,* for example, are sadly dissipated in the closing chapters. One of London's disciples, Jan de

Hartog, put it distinctively. Remarking that "the best reading matter at sea is Jack London," he explained the circumstances under which he first read *The Sea-Wolf.* "In sharp competition with the cook's digestion; owing to the fact that he tore out about fifty pages per book, I rarely managed to catch up with their endings. I was thus spared Jack London's women who come in at the end of his books and spoil them" (351-52). But most readers can agree with Ambrose Bierce's remark that the novel's "great thing—and it is among the greatest of things—is that tremendous creation, Wolf Larsen. . . . The hewing out and setting up of such a figure is enough for a man to do in a life-time" (quoted in Foner 61- 62).

Wolf Larsen is certainly London's greatest creation of the sea, and the purpose of my limited remarks about him here is to emphasize his uniqueness among sea captains as a creature of the water. Despite his many resemblances to Captain Ahab and the influence of *Moby-Dick* on *The Sea-Wolf*, Larsen is certainly more than a mere copy of Ahab or even "the Captain Ahab of literary Naturalism."[4] With Ahab and a more recent American sea captain, Captain Raib in *Far Tortuga*, Wolf Larsen stands on his own legs (as he would have put it) as one of America's great characters in literature. He is, admittedly, a descendant of Ahab, but Jack London is his father, and he was shaped by London's own times and preoccupations as surely as Ahab was shaped by Melville's. Larsen's unique watery nature is a reflection of London's effort to represent concretely in his character the essential biological reality of all life as it had come to be understood forty-three years after the appearance of the *Origin of Species*. Darwin had first appeared in the tradition of American sea fiction in the "Extracts" of *Moby-Dick,* where (eight years before the *Origin of Species)* Melville quotes briefly from "Darwin's Voyage of a Naturalist;" but Darwin's profound influence on the tradition begins in *The Sea-Wolf.* Henceforward in the tradition, the sea as the source of all life on earth would often influence the portraits of seamen by revealing—as in Wolf Larsen—the primordial sea—animalness of man. Such would be the case in Hemingway's portrait in *To Have and Have Not* of Harry Morgan, whose prodigious lovemaking is compared to that of a loggerhead turtle; or, more subtly, in later Peter Matthiessen's portrayal of his fishermen in *Far Tortuga*. In *Moby-Dick,* Melville had emphasized the bloody sharkishness of life, but he could not see, as London could in 1904, how the salt sea reflects the harsh reality of biological time rather than an ambiguous promise of eternity.[5] Melville's wonderful sensitivity to the water finds expression not through Ahab, who is maddened by the ambiguity of life, but rather through Ishmael in his sense of the "sweet mystery about this sea, whose gently awful stirrings seem to speak of some hidden soul beneath" ("The Pacific"). And whereas Ishmael is *drawn* to the water, where he sees reflected the "image of the ungraspable phantom of life" ("Loomings"), Wolf Larsen is *of* the sea.

Larsen's entry into our literature is significant. We see him first as he glances "out over the water" (9). There is "life and death" in his "gaze," and "deep thought;" and when his "gaze [strikes] the water," he finds there the shipwrecked Humphrey Van Weyden, afloat "in the midst of a gray primordial vastness." Thus Wolf literally saves Humphrey from drowning in San Francisco Bay, but London's figurative meaning is that Wolf will save Humphrey by causing him to go through the process of evolution aboard the "miniature floating world" of the sealing schooner *Ghost*, the actual process of life that Van Weyden, a "romantic," sophisticated "landsman," has somehow escaped (25). As Humphrey Van Weyden begins to regain consciousness aboard the *Ghost*, he will awaken to what is for him a new reality. In his first dreamy sense of "swinging in a mighty rhythm through orbit vastness," of being "lapped in the rippling of placid centuries," we can see London's first attempts to breathe new life into him (10). Moments before the collision, Humphrey had imagined that he rode "through the gray shadow of infinite mystery" (i.e., the fog) on a "steed of wood and steel" like a man, a "mere mote of light and sparkle" (5). Now he will awaken to the twentieth century, when men would be depicted as Stephen Crane had depicted them in "The Blue Hotel," for example, as so many "lice" clinging to a "whirling, fire-smote, ice-locked, disease-stricken, space-lost bulb" (*Tales*, 165). (Crane's sense of the species' origin was not as acutely biological as London's, nor is it reflected at all in "The Open Boat;" but he saw that the "black riders came from the sea.") And because London's sense of the new reality—the flux, the biological strife and instability—was always most intensely clear to him at sea, Humphrey Van Weyden opens his eyes to see that "his mighty rhythm was the lift and forward plunge of a ship on the sea" (10).

Humphrey has embarked on a traditional sea journey to knowledge, and his course is charted in the "life and death" he first sees in Wolf's gaze. But before London allows Humphrey to look more deeply into Wolf's eyes, he forces him to witness a reenactment in flesh and blood of the eternal drama, *life* in Wolf's flesh confronting *death* in the "diabolical grin" of the dead mate. Humphrey's first impression of Wolf's "strength" is that it is "the essence of life. . . the potency of motion, the elemental stuff. . . of life," that "which lingers in a shapeless lump of turtle meat and recoils and quivers from the prod of a finger" (14). But despite Wolf's Mesozoic vitality and even the "thunderclap" and "electric sparks" in his oaths, the dead mate's grin of "cynical mockery and defiance" makes *him* "master of the situation" (15-16). The great sea captain is a mere survivor, left to create order in his "miniature floating world" and to instruct his new cabin boy. And Humphrey certainly has much to learn from Wolf, something that he first senses is beyond "sounding," something asleep "in the deeps of [Wolf's] being" and that is reflected in his eyes: "a baffling protean gray which is never twice the same. . . gray, dark and light, and greenish-gray, and sometimes of the clear azure of the deep sea" (18-19). When Humphrey does first look "steadily" into Wolf's "cruel gray eyes," he sees no sign of the "light and warmth of a human soul," only the "cold" and "gray" of "the sea itself" (24). Thus it is that London ends his introduction to this allegorical voyage, before the *Ghost* enters the "lonely Pacific expanse," by arranging for Wolf to express the sum of his wisdom and sea experience—all that was contained in his first gaze of "life and death" and all that he can ever teach Humphrey about reality. Presiding over the sacred ceremony, while "the wind shriek[s] a wild song through the rigging" and the men sway "in unison to the heave and lunge of the deck," Wolf says it all: "And the body shall be cast into the sea" (25-26).[6]

By the end of chapter 12, a "carnival of brutality," Humphrey has begun to learn about the "realities of life;" he sees himself now as "Hump, cabin boy on the schooner *Ghost*," and affirms, "Wolf Larsen [is] my Captain" (79, 86). Then, by the beginning of chapter 16, having evolved far enough for Wolf to congratulate him for having discovered his own legs, Hump is the *Ghost*'s mate. The crucial steps in his development were his descent into "the inferno of passion" and violence in the forecastle and his being "deluged" by Wolf's arguments that "might is right." Also, he had heard Wolf speak of his own death, which, inevitably, would be "at sea:" then he would "cease crawling" and "be acrawl with the corruption of the sea," the "strength and movement of [his] muscles" then only "strength and movement in fin and scale and the guts of fishes" (94, 77, 54). And Humphrey had viewed and touched the "terrible beauty" of Wolf's naked body, the supreme "mechanism of the primitive fighting beast" (102). His physical evolution now complete, Hump is aware that he will never be the "same man," and he is grateful to Wolf for opening up for him the "world of the real" (109). Soon, of course, Maud enters the novel, but before London subjects Hump (and his readers) to her disappointing spiritual influence (she is the permanent "etherealized essence of life. . . in the changing order of the universe"[190]), he celebrates Hump's new manhood in a ceremonial storm scene that illuminates Wolf Larsen's watery powers.

Wolf's stormy nature is repeatedly emphasized in the prophecies of the character Louis: "Look out for squalls," he warns Hump (74). So it is appropriate that in the great storm scene of chapter 17 we see Wolf as he is most fully himself; here also we see London most fully himself as a sea-writer. At once "joyous" and "ferocious," Wolf is "thrilled and upborne with knowledge that one of the great moments of living, when the tide of life surges up in flood, was upon him" (111). In the "purplish light" of the coming storm, "Wolf Larsen's face glowed and glowed" as if "encircled by a halo" (112). The ensuing storm scene is one of the most memorable in literature, but my point is that it is more than an exciting true picture of a storm, drawn from the author's own sea experience: it is a celebration of the ultimate experience that London could imagine in life. Knowing that the sardonic grin of death is the final master of man, London celebrates not resurrection but survival—the *Ghost*'s repeated "miracle" of being "buried beneath the sea" and then righting herself and breaking, "like a whale's back, through the ocean surface" (114, 117).[7] From his lofty perch in the crosstrees, Hump sees the *Ghost* "against the foaming sea as she [tears] along instinct with life" (113). When a huge wave overtops the schooner, he gazes "sheer up into it. . . . a rushing green backed by a milky smother of foam" (115). Then "under water," he fears the "terrible thing. . . being swept in the trough of the sea;" but he is "pounded," "dashed," "turned over and over," and he breathes "the stinging salt water into [his] lungs" before finally envisioning Wolf "standing at the wheel in the midst of the wild welter" (115). By taking the salt water into his lungs, by clinging to the image of Wolf, and by struggling to fulfill his order—"get the jib backed over to windward"—Hump survives this deluge (115). And when the *Ghost* is repeatedly submerged, he

> felt strangely alone with God, alone with him and watching the chaos of his wrath. And then the wheel would reappear, and Wolf Larsen's broad shoulders, his hands gripping the spokes and holding the schooner to the course of his will, himself an earth god, dominating the storm, flinging its descending waters from him and riding it to his own ends. And oh, the marvel of it! That tiny men should live and breathe and work, and drive so frail a contrivance of wood and cloth through so tremendous an elemental strife! (117-18)

It is a mistake to see such storm scenes and feats of seamanship in London's fiction as mere romantic adventure, the boy's way to manhood, even though we know how thrilled the seventeen-year-old Jack had been in proving himself an "able-bodied seaman" by steering the *Sophie Sutherland* through a night of storm. In fact, such scenes and the logic underlying them provide a clear view of London's deepest understanding of the sea and a clear measure of the distance between himself and Melville as sea writers of different times. Great storm scenes make up a very small part of *Moby-Dick*, and serve (as in "The Candles") to highlight the spiritual struggle between Ahab's doubt and Ishmael's faith, a struggle that is subsumed in Ishmael's meditative wonder, his sense of the sea's "sweet mystery" ("The Pacific"). Ahab's death and Ishmael's survival constitute a spiritual affirmation that London could not accept. Despite his acknowledged love for Melville and the apparent influence of *Moby-Dick* on *The Sea-Wolf,* London's only explicit reference to *Moby-Dick* registers his objection to its "imaginative orgies."[8]

London always strove to dispel the sea mysteries that he felt were embodied in the traditional romantic sea stories. In his autobiographical story "That Dead Men Rise Up Never," for example, he confesses that he had felt the "fibre-instinct of ten thousand generations of superstitious forebears" and imagined that he saw the ghost of a shipmate (the *bricklayer*) whom he had helped bury at sea and whose bunk he had taken over despite the superstitious warnings of the other sailors (*Human Drift*, 46). The "ghost" proved to be only the play of moonlight in the *Sophia*'s rigging. Similarly, *The Cruise of the Snark* dispels Melville's dream of the paradise of Typee and the fabled "horrors" of the leper colony at Molokai; and the name he chose for his famous boat, *Snark,* constitutes a grand, good-natured sneer at all who would romanticize the sea. The constant process of evolution was for him the essential reality in which he could express a kind of "faith." Its machinelike laws caused him to compare "the mechanism of the primitive fighting beast" he saw in Wolf's body to "the engines of a great battleship or Atlantic liner" (102). And the same biological laws drove the engines of evolution that would perpetuate the race through the love of Maud and Humphrey, sentimental and comic as it is. As he later wrote in *Martin Eden*, it had at first "struck him as ridiculous and impossible" that "in the fabric of knowledge there should be any connection whatever between a woman with hysterics and a schooner carrying a weather-helm or heaving to in a gale." But "Herbert Spencer had shown him, not only that it was not ridiculous, but that it was impossible for there to be no connection. All things were related to all other things, from the farthermost star in the wastes of space to the myriad atoms in the grain of sand under one's foot" (121).

The *Mutiny of the Elsinore* (1914, written ten years after he had finished *The Sea-Wolf* and four years after he had abandoned the cruise of the *Snark*) is a far better sea novel than is generally recognized. Only Grant C. Knight, in a very brief footnote, has found it to be "one of the best sea stories in our literature" (132). It is seldom read today, and when it is, it is usually dismissed as an example of London's racism and his willingness late in his career to write anything that would sell. The novel does reflect the glare of Darwinian race theory that troubled the time, but the glare would soon lose its scientific luster and appear to be a "ghastly mistake," as Richard Hofstadter has explained (202). There is no need to apologize for London's having fallen for the idea of the "Yellow Peril." Although for a time it was widely accepted as part of the new theories of evolution, it seems likely that London would have come to deny it altogether. It is certain, at least, that in *The Mutiny of the Elsinore* he came to express a very jaded view of the biological destiny that such theories projected for his race. Whereas in 1904 he had smiled at the love of Maud and Humphrey, in 1913 he would deride it in a mood of black comedy, even if he could not deny it. By this time, his faith in love as the mechanism of evolution, as well as his faith in the working class, had darkened. He had produced no son to carry on his line, and he could imagine a victory for the working class only in the distant future, after it had been ground under the totalitarian iron heel and roused to resistance.

London always knew that mutiny is a natural state, as it is, for example, among the sled dogs in *The Call of the Wild* (*GSW*, 42). And he was well aware of the history of mutiny among men at sea. His point in *The Mutiny of the Elsinore* is that the real mutiny in nature is not at all like that depicted in traditional sea fiction. Thus his view of this modern mutiny of 1913 emphasizes both the degenerated state of the once great sailing ships and their sailors, and the brutal but regenerative forces of evolution.[9] The *Elsinore* is among the last of the old ships, and its officers, Captain West (accompanied by his daughter Margaret), and the mates, Mr. Pike and Mr. Mellaire, represent the old order.

But the ramshackle crew is made up of "gangsters," "broken men and lunatics" (51). London's narrator, Pathurst, another gentlemanly writer like Humphrey Van Weyden, has gone to sea as a passenger because he has lost his "taste for [his] fellow man," for his career as an artist, and for women, whose "almost ferocious devotion to the destiny of sex" had become disenchanting (9). He is outraged that Captain West's daughter is aboard, and he wonders, with the reader, "was there ever such a freight of human souls on the sea?" (98).

Captain West is an old aristocrat, cool and detached, who reminds Pathurst of a "plantation" owner, a "samurai," or a "king;" he believes in God and is willfully blind to his mates' brutal exercise of authority (118, 77, 178). But this is his last voyage, for he dies before the *Elsinore* rounds the Cape, his death brought on by his awareness that he had committed a blunder in navigation. Both of the mates are old and both had served under a Captain Somers. London emphasizes the name, for he was aware of the alleged mutiny in the famous Somers affair of 1842, even though he could not have known that Melville, too, had worked with the idea in *Billy Budd*.[10] According to London's plot, Pike had been a favorite of Captain Somers, who had given him license to exercise severe discipline. But the mutinies Somers had suppressed inevitably overtook him; he was murdered, and Mr. Pike had vowed to spend the rest of his days at sea searching for the murderer. As it turns out, the *Elsinore*'s second mate, with the suggestive name of Mellaire, was the murderer, and before he is found out, he warns Pike that the men "won't stand for this driving. . . . Times have changed. . . and laws have changed, and men have changed" (272). Of course, the mutiny must come, and when it does, Pathurst repeatedly remarks that this modern mutiny is "ridiculous and grotesque" (335). Eventually Pike and Mellaire disappear, apparently having killed each other in a death struggle that took them overboard. With all the members of the old order now buried at sea, the grotesque mutiny becomes even more ridiculous. For Pathurst ascends to the "high place," and with the help of Margaret—the "blind-instinctive race-mother"—he masters the mongrel crew in one darkly comic scene after another (100). At one point, Pathurst can "scarcely keep from laughing" at his own "ludicrous" exercise of brute authority, even as he relishes it under the "cool, measuring eye" of Margaret; and another scene is an obvious parody of the "crucifixion" and "resurrection" (325-26, 359-60). Finally, it is clear that Margaret and Pathurst will see the *Elsinore* safely in to Valparaíso, where "the law and order that men institute" is sure to provide a happy ending; and as the book closes, we see Margaret and Pathurst "hidden in the darkness, clasped in each other's arms [talking] love and love plans" (369, 379). They will be married in Seattle, to which port the grotesque machinery of biology—"the destiny of sex"—will surely drive them. Pathurst, like many a good early twentieth-century hero, is happily caught by Margaret, one of the "instinctive huntresses of men" who hunt "with quite the same blind tropism that marks the pursuit of the Sun by the sunflower" (52). Pathurst's last remarks, uttered between loving kisses, reveal London's ironic view of it all: "But I was stupid," he remarks; "'Oh, the weary, weary months' [he] complained;" "I am a fool. . . I am aware of only one thing: I want you. I want you;" "I stammered;" "she confirmed;" "I rattled on" (378).

The one minor character aboard the *Elsinore* whose point of view is reliable and with whom London is clearly sympathetic is Mulligan Jacobs, a pathetic creature of the abyss who "might have been an artist, a philosophic poet, had he not been born crooked with a crooked back" (372). Jacobs is well-read and he is particularly fond of Shakespeare (to whose Edmund the Bastard he seems related), Émile Zola, and Maxim Gorky. And he has the authority even to judge that "Joseph Conrad was living too fat to turn out the stuff he first turned out" (96). In short, he is London's ideal representative of the proletariat who *would* resist and eventually overturn the reigning order. "He was a direct actionist. The mass strike was the thing. Sabotage, not merely as a withdrawal of efficiency, but as a keen destruction-of-profits policy, was the weapon" (96). Drawing on such powers of bitter defiance, Jacobs successfully resists even Mr. Pike, and he stands in stark contrast to another of the *Elsinore's* crew, the type of modern sailor with whom London had no sympathy, the "sea lawyer." Pathurst can see Jacobs only as a "filthy, malignant rat" and wonder at his powers of defiance: "How dare he—with no hope of any profit, not a hero, not a leader of a forlorn hope nor a martyr to God. . . how dare he. . . be so defiant?" (98). London's personal commitment to Jacobs is evident in Pathurst's description of his face, its "concentrated rage. . . on the verge of bursting into incandescence" (98). In all of London's sea fiction, only Wolf Larsen's face glows with such promise, and in the flesh of these two beings—one, the supreme product of physical evolution; the other, the combustive source of an inevitable social revolution—we see reflected all that remains for London of the mystic powers that Melville had seen in St. Elmo's fire—St. Elmo, the patron saint of sailors.

Thus it is that Mulligan Jacobs survives the *Elsinore's* modern mutiny and puts the new Captain Pathurst in his place: "An' who in hell are you an' your fathers? Robbers of the toil of men. I like them little. I like you and your fathers not at all. . . . To hell with you" (371). There is no question that London shares the "actionist" Jacobs's view of Pathurst, whose rise to brutal dominance parallels London's 1908 fable of the "cosmic process and purpose" of social evolution in *The Iron Heel* (Watson 121). Like Wickson in that novel, Pathurst gloats in his superiority over the "weaklings and the rejected" aboard the *Elsinore:* "My heels were iron as I gazed on them in their peril and weakness" (197-98). Thrilled to have found that "culture has not emasculated [him]," Pathurst envisions himself and his "royal woman" holding "the high place of government and command until our kind perishes from the earth." But Jacobs's vision of him is prophetic: "You'll end in the darkness," he tells Pathurst, "And your darkness'll be as dark as mine" (336-37). It is a fitting end to the *Elsinore* affair that both Pathurst and Margaret remain "hidden by the darkness" as they rattle on to Seattle.

Despite the grotesque and comic allegory that thickens almost un-
bearably toward the end of *The Mutiny of the Elsinore,* it is a very readable
book with many of London's characteristically fine and authentic scenes of
sailing in stormy seas and rounding the Horn. And, as an individual work in the
tradition of American sea fiction, it is a landmark, rich with London's
meaningful references to those who had sailed before him. Even Pathurst, the
new American captain whose course toward the obscure ends of biological
regeneration and race destiny was only recently charted, has a possible forebear
within the tradition in Melville's Captain Amasa Delano, whose dubious heroics
in preserving white supremacy were also performed with his eyes closed.
Following Pathurst, later sea captains in American literature would reveal their
authors' changing views of the Darwinian reality as it centers in sexual
regeneration. The veil of Victorian tastes and editorial judgments that influenced
London's presentation of the sex drama would be lifted, as theories of the
aggressive race mother gave way to theories of the dominant, virile male; and
the sea captain's authority would be associated, as it is in *To Have and Have
Not* and *Far Tortuga,* not only with his seamanship but with his ability to
survive in the elemental sexual competition of life.[11]

If *Michael, Brother of Jerry,* (completed a year before, and published
a year after London's death) is remembered at all, it is dismissed as a "mere
dog story" or as London's exposé of the cruelty of trained animal shows.[12] But
it is also the last novel in which London drew on the tradition of sea fiction to
define man and his true place in nature. Following in the wake of *The Sea-Wolf*
and the *Elsinore* mutiny, the first half of *Michael* projects London's ever-
darkening allegory based on the "ship of fools" idea. As in *The Mutiny of the
Elsinore,* he intensifies the allegory by centering it on critical references to the
masterworks of nineteenth-century British and American sea literature, his
constant purpose being, as it had been since *The Sea-Wolf,* to burn off the fog
of romanticism that he felt had blinded the earlier writers. Here, in the dark
months following the *Lusitania* incident, London wrote his versions of *Moby-
Dick* and "The Rime of the Ancient Mariner."

He first signals his allegorical intent in chapter 9, where he introduces
both the "Albatross" and "The Ancient Mariner." But the "Albatross" appears
only briefly, as a warship—a "British cruiser of the second class;" what had
been the romantic symbol of nature's inviolable mystic order is now for London
a symbol of its actual order (59).[13] And London's twentieth-century "Ancient
Mariner" is no wretched sinner but an ingenious survivor. He presents himself
under the false name of Charles Stough Greenleaf, a name he compounded from
"the pages of the history of the United States" (103). As we learn later, the
Ancient Mariner had actually been born into a wealthy family and had "trod the
quarterdeck" as a junior officer before he left the sea, squandered his wealth,
and was eventually disowned by his wealthy family. He then spent six months
in the poor-house, where he learned his formative lesson—what it means to he
"shut out from life" (103-6). Renewed by this descent into the abyss, he reen-

tered society as a common laborer until he devised the confidence game of leading wealthy investors on long, futile sea searches for buried treasure he claims to have left on an uncharted island in the Pacific after being ship-wrecked on the vessel *Wide Awake* in 1852. He tells his tale convincingly, making it as "literary" as possible. In this way, he makes a good living and does his money-hungry victims a favor: the long sea voyages are good for their health. This incredible Ancient Mariner, a benevolent confidence man who embodies the full range of American economic experience, is clearly "the finest man on board" London's "ship of fools" (90).

The ship's name, *Wide Awake*, is another of London's devices—as in the "white logic" or the character called "Burning Daylight"—to illuminate his fiction with the harsh reality of early twentieth-century thought and thereby to dispel the "imaginative orgies" he saw, for example, in *Moby-Dick*. Thus it is that in 1915 this "ship of fools" has its own encounter with a whale, and London's rendering of its disastrous end is both realistic and darkly comic. The catastrophe is brought on by one of the wealthy treasure hunters, who becomes frustrated in his efforts to paint the sea. When he fails to reproduce the "color-delicacies" of "seminary maidens," he bursts into a "violent rage." Repeatedly on such occasions, he would tear up the attempted painting, "stamp it into the deck, then get out his large-calibred automatic rifle, perch himself on the forecastle head, and try to shoot any stray porpoise, albacore, or dolphin. It seemed to give him great relief to send a bullet home into the body of some surging, gorgeous-hued fish, and turn it on its side slowly to sink down into the death and depth of the sea" (94). Sometimes he would shoot at whales, despite the Ancient Mariner's grave warnings that whales have been known to sink such "full-rigged ship[s]" as the "whaler *Essex*" (95; again and again, as in this repeated reference to the *Essex* incident, London emphasizes his awareness of the tradition and his intention to extend it). But the frustrated painter will not believe such tales; he persists, eventually killing a helpless calf whose "grief-stricken" mother turns on the ship.

London's description of the calf's death, the cow's ramming and final sinking of the ship, and the crew's escape in the lifeboats is in stark contrast with Melville's melodramatic sinking of the *Pequod,* for the authors' purposes are different. Whereas Melville's whale, with all its power of divine retribution, sinks the *Pequod* in an instant, London's eighty-foot cow whale is only an eighty-foot cow whale: she finally succeeds in sinking the ship, but she is badly wounded herself, as in the actual *Essex* incident. And she takes no notice of the lifeboats: "It was from the huge thing, the schooner, that death had been wreaked upon her calf; and it was upon the schooner that she vented the wrath of her grief" (138). In contrast to *Moby-Dick*, there is no cosmic justice here: the whale's tormentor escapes with the rest of the crew. London's description of the scene is flatly realistic, but though his sympathy for the whale is clear, he portrays the crew's escape in black comic tones. In their panic, they argue over the limited space and overload the boats with a "clutter. . . of men, provisions, and property" (133). When the first sailor ignores the captain's orders and, "sea-bag in hand," prepares to escape, another calls him "a rat leaving the ship." But the Ancient Mariner voices London's judgment of the incident: "We're all rats. . . . I learned just that when I was a rat among the mangy rats of the poor farm" (123-24). When the ship sinks, "only the whale" remains, "floating and floundering, on the surface of the sea" (138). The survivors are picked up two days later by the passing steamer *Mariposa*, none the worse for their adventure. And when they arrive in San Francisco, no one believes their tale: "Sunk by a whale?. . .   Nonsense," exclaim the cub reporters and moviegoers, for whom "the real world and all its spaciousness does not exist" (143).

The constant lure of "the real world and all its spaciousness" that first drew the young Jack London to experience the sea for himself and to publish his story "Typhoon Off the Coast of Japan" took him to sea once again in the last story he wrote. "The Water Baby," which he finished the month before he died, has been cited as evidence of London's "rebirth" in 1916, his envisioning of a "saving illumination" in the "powerful energies" of the "Jungian subconscious" that could "triumph over the death-dealing wasteland" (McClintock 72-73). There is no question that London had become interested in Jung, that he was among the first American writers to be influenced by both Freud and Jung; but what he saw in Jung, as reflected in "The Water Baby," seems mainly to have corroborated the sense of reality he had already projected in *The Sea-Wolf*. The story brings together an old Hawaiian fisherman and a white narrator named Lakana (Hawaiian for London), who converse in the old man's canoe as he tends to his fishing lines. The story presents the vital old fisherman's songs of the Creation as being more believable than the account given in Genesis, and London admits that they are as reasonable as his own version based on early twentieth-century science. It is "funny," he remarks, that the Hawaiian myth is true to what he knows of "evolution," "astronomy," and "seismology," which teach "that man did run on all fours ere he came to walk upright, that. . . the speed of the revolution of the earth on its axis has diminished steadily, thus increasing the length of day, and that. . . all the islands of Hawaii were elevated from the ocean floor by volcanic action" (*Makaloa Mat*, 144-45).

But the energy of this story does not derive simply from London's sense that ancient myth and modern science point in the same direction. It is true that London senses a profound general wisdom in the old fisherman's humble sense that he is "of little worth, and. . . not wise," and in his Jungian mythic sense that the sea is his mother, "the milk giver, the life source" (144). But the old fisherman's long tale of the Water Baby is baffling and comically unverifiable, despite his claim—to "know for a fact." The story's undeniable "facts" and its most intensely memorable imagery derive from direct observation, after Lakana bares his "eyes to the stab of the sun['s]" "glare on the water." Then he watches the vital old fisherman dive for a large squid:

I saw him steady himself with his right hand on the coral lump, and thrust his left arm into the hole to the shoulder. Half a minute elapsed, during which time he seemed to be groping and rooting around with his left hand. Then tentacle after tentacle, myriad-suckered and wildly waving, emerged. Laying hold of his arm, they writhed and coiled about his flesh like so many snakes. With a heave and a jerk appeared the entire squid, a proper devilfish or octopus.

But the old man was in no hurry for his natural element, the air above the water. There, forty feet beneath, wrapped about by an octopus that measured nine feet across from tentacle tip to tentacle tip and that could well drown the stoutest swimmer, he coolly and casually did the one thing that gave him his empery over the monster. He shoved his lean, hawklike face into the very center of the slimy, squirming mass, and with his several ancient fangs bit into the heart and the life of the matter. (147-48)

This compelling scene (he had created a similar one in the story "Yah! Yah! Yah!") is one of the "great moments of living" in Jack London's sea fiction and, indeed, in the tradition of American sea fiction. It depicts the essential biological struggle that London had always recognized, and not at all a "struggle between the most fundamentally human desire for salvation and the most fundamentally human fear of damnation" (McClintock 174). The myths of "rebirth," "salvation," and "damnation" can never survive the harsh light of London's "white logic." For London, there is only the "elemental stuff itself," the vital life strength like that embodied in Wolf Larsen's flesh. And even if it "lingers" as in a "shapeless lump of turtle meat and recoils and quivers from the prod of a finger," it will very quickly be "acrawl" and give up even its final shapeless identity to "the corruption of the sea."

Through Jack London, the tradition of American sea fiction survived the passing of the great sailing ships. Sensing and responding to the sea's timeless influence on our lives, he was certainly ahead of his own time in retrieving for the tradition and our culture in general a sense of Melville's permanent value. And like his fellow writers before and after him in the tradition, he was of his own time in celebrating the ecstasy of survival, "the great moments of living" that he had known personally at sea and that revealed to him the essential reality: for the species, the constant lift and forward plunge of evolution; for the individual, only that "the body shall be cast into the sea." To Maud Brewster's question, "And immortality?" he would answer, with Wolf Larsen, "Bosh!" But it is revealing of London's feeling for the sea and for his great sea captain that Wolf Larsen's last word is not actually "bosh," as Humphrey reports it to be. A full week later, in response to the question, "Are you all there?" Wolf uttered his actual last word: "Yes" *(Sea-Wolf,* 248-50). Always, even at the moment of his own entry into "the vastness and profundity of the quiet and dark" that finally overtakes Wolf, Jack London affirmed his readiness to go to sea, to search for and perhaps grasp yet another of the "great moments of living" that he found at sea and in his fellow writers' tales of the sea: "The last work in which he read that night" he died, as Charmian London reported, "was 'Around Cape Horn, Maine to California in 1852, Ship *James W. Paige*'" (*Book of Jack London*, 2:385).

NOTES

[1] Important scholarly works on London since 1966 include those by Franklin Walker, *Jack London and the Klondike* (San Marino, CA: Huntington Library, 1966); Earle Labor, *Jack London* (New York: Twayne, 1974); James I. McClintock, *White Logic* (Cedar Springs, MI: Wolf House Books, 1975); Andrew Sinclair, *Jack* (New York: Harper, 1977); Joan D. Hedrick, *Solitary Comrade* (Chapel Hill: U of North Carolina P, 1982); and Charles N. Watson, Jr., *The Novels of Jack London* (Madison: U of Wisconsin P, 1983).

[2] Franklin Walker theorizes that London made the last leg of his journey from San Francisco to Dyea, Alaska, in an Indian canoe (52).

[3] For complete bibliographical information see Dale L. Walker and James G. Sisson III, *The Fiction of Jack London* (El Paso: Texas Western Press, 1972) and Hensley C. Woodbridge et al. *Jack London* (Georgetown, CA: Talisman, 1966).

[4] Labor 95. For a discussion of the influence of Melville, Shakespeare and Milton on *The Sea-Wolf*, see Watson 53-78.

[5] Similarly, no sea writer in the 1970s or 1980s could see what Hemingway saw in 1935 in his rhapsody of the garbage scows off Havana: "The stream. . . takes five loads. . . a day. . . and in ten miles along the coast it is as clear and blue and unimpressed as it was ever before the tug hauled out the scow; and the palm fronds of our victories, the worn light bulbs of our discoveries and the empty condoms of our great loves float with no significance against the one single, lasting thing—the stream" (*Green Hills,* New York: Scribner's, 1935, 148-50).

[6] This sea burial is based on London's experience aboard the *Sophia Sutherland*, when the "bricklayer" was hurried at sea. The extent to which London was affected by the scene is clear from his having recreated it in his story "That Dead Men Rise Up Never" and from the emphasis he gives it in his notes for the projected novel, "The Mercy of the Sea" (TS notes numbered 941 in London collection, Henry E. Huntington Library, San Marino, California).

[7] See also London's description of Wolf's wateriness and his power to survive when he climbs back aboard the *Ghost* after having been knocked overboard in the attempted mutiny: "A sinewy hand, dripping with water was clutching the rail. A second hand took form in the darkness beside it. . . . I saw a head, the hair wet and straight, shape itself and then the unmistakable eyes and face of Wolf Larsen. . . . The seawater was streaming from him. It made little audible gurgles that distracted me" (93).

[8] In his essay on *Two Years Before the Mast*, "A Classic of the Sea," in *The Human Drift* (New York: Macmillan, 1917), 102. London's remarks on Dana in this essay provide a clear view of his own understanding of the sea. Whereas D. H. Lawrence would credit Dana for "profound mystic vision" (125); London praises Dana for having provided "a document for the future centuries"—"the photograph detail of life before the mast and hide-droghing on the coast of California. . . of the unvarnished simple psychology and ethics of the forecastle hands who droghed the hides, stood at the

wheel, made and took sail, tarred down the rigging, holystoned the decks, turned in all-standing, grumbled as they cut about the kid, [and] criticized the seamanship of their officers" (101, 108).

[9] London was not the first to lament the passing of the great sailing ships; Melville did so in *John Marr and Other Poems* (Princeton, NJ: Princeton UP, 1922). But he was the first major writer to emphasize the theme that would soon dominate American sea literature, as in O'Neill. See, for example, his remark in "A Classic of the Sea:" "The life and conditions described in Dana's book have passed utterly away. Gone are the crack clippers, the driving captains, the hard-bitten but efficient foremast hands. Remain only crawling cargo tanks, dirty tramps, greyhound liners, and a somber, sordid type of sailing ship. The only records broken today by sailing vessels are those for slowness. They are no longer built for speed, nor are they manned before the mast by as sturdy a sailor stock nor aft are they officered by sail-carrying captains and driving mates" (*Human Drift*, 102-3).

[10] The commander of the U.S. brig *Somers* was, of course, Captain Alexander Slidell Mackenzie; Melville's cousin Guert Gansevoort was a lieutenant aboard her.

[11] In *Far Tortuga*, Captain Raib's authority as a sea captain is associated with his virility: he has fathered eighteen children.

[12] Watson, xiii.

[13] London might have known of the famous British torpedo-boat destroyer, HMS *Albatross*, one of the new powerful warships like those that had impressed Stephen Crane. See Crane, *War Dispatches* (New York, New York UP, 1964), 114.

◄ 5 ►

The Iron Heel

Early Reviews

Review of *The Iron Heel*

Jack London has developed his Socialist ideas and gratified his hatred of the capitalist class in his new story, *The Iron Heel*, which is brought out by The Macmillan Company. London refers in this book in very complimentary terms to H.G. Wells, and the framework of his story owes much to several of Wells' romances of the future, notably "When the Sleeper Wakes." London presents his story in the guise of the diary of Avis Everhard, who wrote in 1912 the history of the great Socialist revolution of that year which was stamped out by the iron heel of the Oligarchs or capitalists. This diary was discovered in 2632 A.D., or 419 years after the Socialist millennium began. Jack London handles the story with a fine regard for the dramatic effects, and he indulges his passion for blood and carnage in the chapters that deal with the failure of the great Socialist revolt in Chicago. Horrors are piled on horrors in this fierce street fighting between the desperate revolutionists and the mercenaries hired and armed by the capitalists. To give greater realism to his story London has inserted footnotes in which he describes, for the benefit of the reader of the future, many of the customs of our day. It is in these notes that London has distilled the bitterest essence of the Socialism that he has absorbed from reading and from contact with the desperate men who preach this creed of destruction. And he puts this doctrine of fierce anger against all who have property and an equally mad desire to tear down all the framework of society in such powerful words that his book is a source of danger to impressionable minds. There is no question that London believes in this doctrine, just as there is no question that he has been profoundly stirred by the misery of the poor who live in the big cities and who cannot be induced to accept employment in the country. And when he thoroughly believes in anything he has the faculty of putting it in such form that it stamps itself upon the memory.

As a young woman's story of her gradual love for a Socialist, who flouts all the accepted doctrines of her class and station, London tells a very dramatic tale of the fight waged by the Socialists against the huge trusts, which he calls the Oligarchs. London uses the case of several big corporations that fight all claims for damages by their employees who are injured, but he doesn't speak of the hundreds of manufacturing concerns throughout this country that run full time even in dull seasons in order to furnish work to their employees, nor of the other hundreds that spend large sums for sanitary dwellings for their workmen. He gives the instance of a college professor who is cheated out of stock that he held in a big corporation, and whose very home is taken from him by means of a fictitious mortgage. London knows that such a case is absurd, yet he gravely sets it down here as a specimen of the iniquitous revenge of the Oligarchs upon one who refuses to bow to their will.

The same disregard of facts is shown throughout the book, and this is especially seen in the notes. Thus, on page 260, in a note he develops the proposition that most of the crimes committed by anarchists in our day were really the work of the big corporations. Thus he declares flatly that the railroad station at Independence, Colorado, was blown up by agents of capitalists, and he insinuates that Governor Steunenberg fell a victim to the same hired assassins of the capitalists. He extols Moyer and Haywood as "two strong, fearless leaders of labor," and he refers to "the ferocious and wanton judicial murder of the innocent and so-called Haymarket anarchists in Chicago."

London has drawn a number of ideas from H.G. Wells' dream of the future, in which the population of a whole country is gathered in one or two big cities and the great mass of the people are virtual slaves. He has not Wells' philosophical power, but what makes this book, *The Iron Heel*, dangerous is the emotional force that London puts into his description of the woes of the common people and of their terrible struggle to overthrow the huge money power that dominated and ground them down. And yet it is a pity as a mere story teller that London should have selected this theme for a romance, as he is as much out of place in it as Tolstoy is in the moral tales that have occupied his later years. *The Iron Heel* as a romance bears about the same relation to *The Call of the Wild* that *The Kreutzer Sonata* does to *Anna Karenina*.

San Francisco Chronicle, March 8, 1908, 10.

Current Literature: *The Iron Heel*

Joseph Wanhope

Beyond all question this volume must be considered as the high-water mark of Jack London's literary effort. There have been many stories and forecasts of the approaching social revolution, but none, we venture to say, that can for a moment compare in power and intensity with the terrific narrative of struggle and defeat which the virile London portrays in the pages of this work. And we further assert that the tremendous power displayed in *The Iron Heel* will render abortive any studied attempt to limit its circulation. This is not the sort of book that can be suppressed. It will go far to create its own circle of readers, a circle which will not, by any means, be confined to Socialists. It can be and will be read by both socialists and non-Socialists with much profit to their souls, and we may add, their bodies also.

The narrative is supposedly the work of the wife of a revolutionist, one Ernest Everhard, who took part in the struggle between labor and capital, between the years 1912 and 1932, and lost his life in the latter year. Avis Everhard, wife of the revolutionist, details the part her husband took in the conflict, and concealed the manuscript in a hollow oak tree, where it was discovered several hundred years later, after the revolution had been accomplished. Her story, however, is one of defeat and disaster. The revolt of 1912 and the succeeding years is crushed with terrible ferocity by the Oligarch of capitalism, who had prepared to meet the revolution with physical force. Several revolts are thus crushed, and the Oligarchy manages to maintain itself in power for three hundred years, until finally the revolution succeeds and wipes it out of existence.

Everhard, the strong man of the story, is a Socialist with most pronounced views on the struggle of the classes. He accepts literally and unreservedly the doctrine of power—of physical combat—as necessary to finally decide the conflict, and warns his fellow Socialists of the folly of imagining that the capitalists will surrender peaceably to the vote of the majority, while they have the entire military force of the nation at their command. His opinion proves correct, and after a long period of terrorism, murder and massacre on both sides, the Oligarchy firmly establishes itself, and reduces the entire population, with the exception of the most powerful and highly paid unions, who desert labor and make common cause with the capitalists, to a condition of slavery. These favored unions gradually crystallize into a caste, between whom and the mass of unskilled helots grows an ever increasing hostility and estrangement. The Oligarchy itself develops a new ethic, in which it sincerely believes. Into the minds of its succeeding generations is instilled the idea that they are the guardians of civilization who must be ever on the watch against the wild beasts below who would destroy it. Its powers of offense are continually increased and improved in organization. Revolt after revolt is put down in blood, and millions of lives are sacrificed in defense and attack. The narrative breaks off after a description of the Chicago Commune, an appalling slaughter of the working classes of that city, who fight with the utmost vindictiveness, but are destroyed in thousands by the machine guns and weapons of precision in the hands of the highly organized forces of the Oligarchy.

There is something in the book that reminds one of W. J. Ghent's well-known forecast of the possibility of "Benevolent Feudalism"— with the qualifying adjective omitted. The Socialists of Everhard's time did not believe an Oligarchy possible; it had no place in the evolution of things; Socialism was to succeed capitalism; theoretically there was no room for this period of autocracy, nevertheless it came. In the preface, London himself admits that there is no adequate theoretical explanation of this unlooked-for phenomenon, and it is probably fair to assume that his object in presenting to the Socialist reader this particular contingency, was that it might at least receive consideration, for even if one hundredth part of the terrors he depicts so vividly in this story, lie ahead of us, it is of the first importance that attention be given them as possibilities at least.

Probably there are few Socialists who believe that the social revolution can be consummated thru the ballot alone. In some countries we have little hesitation in declaring it impossible. Still the Socialist agitator cannot be fairly charged with concealment of his views, for he lets it be plainly understood that the ballot can accomplish the desired change, if—and there is no need to conceal the proviso—the capitalists will abide by the rules of the game—the will of the majority, legally, and peaceably expressed at the ballot box. And as no capitalist spokesman has as yet at least, unequivocally stated that capitalism will not do so, we are thoroughly consistent in our advocacy of the ballot to achieve Socialism. If the point is ever reached when the ruling class refuse to abide by this method, nothing remains for Socialists but armed revolution—conquest by physical force of the powers of government. But this simply means that the ruling class have the choice of determining what form the revolution shall take, and forcing it upon the workers.

In calling our attention to these contingencies, Jack London has performed a valuable service for the Socialist movement as well as producing the most powerful and absorbing piece of Socialist literature that has appeared in many years.

We strongly advise every Socialist to procure this striking volume and give it a careful perusal. As for non-Socialists, the book itself will take care of them. It will force itself upon them—a portent that no thinking man or woman can avoid of fail to see. We should not be surprised to see this work, despite its extreme revolutionary character, become the most widely read book of the year, and once read it will not be easily forgotten.

Worker March 14, 1908, and
Wilshire's April, 1908, 8.

Current Fiction: *The Iron Heel*

Of the recourse to violence Mr. London makes a much more distinct forecast. We have little more regard for him as a man of letters than for his "comrade" in Socialism, Mr. Sinclair; but his book, like the former's, is interesting as a sign of the times. In its character of tract, its force of assertion, and narrowness of generalization, it is strikingly similar. The events described are supposed to take place in the years 1912 and 1913. The narrative is written by the wife of a Socialist and leader of revolt, and the manuscript, hidden in a hollow oak, is discovered seven centuries later and edited, with introduction and notes, by one of the enlightened gentry of that day. "Too late," he comments, "did the socialist movement of the early twentieth century divine the coming of the Oligarchy. Even as it was divined, the Oligarchy was there—a fact established in blood, a stupendous and awful reality." The "Iron Heel" is, of course, the ruthless power of capitalism, or "the Oligarchy." What Mr. London wishes to give is not so much prophecy as warning of what might happen if, contrary to the hopes of Socialists, unprincipled capitalism were to get the upper hand and do its logical worst. He sees society in the grip of an oligarchy enforcing its will by mercenaries, annihilating the power of the middle class, and making serfs of the "people of the abyss." A series of bloody revolts follow, extending over some three centuries, upon which arrives at last the beneficent triumph of Socialism. Theoretically, Mr. London's role as a Socialist is that of apostle of peace, but his nature—his imagination, at least—is, one recalls, a trifle bloodthirsty. A future such as Socialism hopes for, of steady progress, of peaceful conquest by propagandism and the ballot, would afford small material for his talent. The gore through which, in the course of these pages, we are invited to wallow, is far more to his taste; three hundred years of it is not a day too much for him.

Nation 86 (March 19, 1908), 264.

New and Notable Novels: *The Iron Heel*

Sidney G. P. Coryn

As a teller of ingenious and unbelievable dog stories Mr. London attracted a certain amount of attention wholly incommensurate with his literary ability. His autobiography aroused a languid interest that rapidly changed to disgust, and now he dons the mantle of the prophet and under a thin veil of weak romance he predicts a class struggle that is to last for some three hundred years and in which blood is to flow like water. It is just such a book as the perpetrator of the autobiography would be likely to write, and if we knew of any form of censure stronger than this it would be cheerfully applied.

With a daring originality the story is introduced as a manuscript that has been hidden in an oak tree for seven centuries. If the author fails to use the other accessories of a sliding panel and a midnight ghost he has no doubt reserved them for future occasions. The manuscript is supposed to tell the story of the years 1912 and 1913. It is written by the wife of a Socialist leader, Ernest Everhard, who is eventually executed after an outbreak of what is practically civil war with the attendant horrors of general massacres and a reign of terror. Everhard is, of course, the hero, and if the ravings of this intolerable maniac represent any volume of sentiment now existing it is surely to be found only in the penitentiary. Here is a specimen of the hydrophobia that seems to be his chief natural endowment. He says: "Such an army of revolution twenty-five millions strong is a thing to make rulers and ruling classes pause and consider. The cry of this army is 'No quarter! We want all that you possess. We will be content with nothing less than all that you possess. We want in our hands the reins of power and the destiny of mankind," etc., and then we are told that he extended his arms and his hands "were clutching the air like eagle's talons." It was a very appropriate gesture, but the author makes Everhard talk a great deal too much. A more tiresome windbag never existed, but perhaps Mr. London is only adding another chapter to his autobiography.

We need not fear the result of *The Iron Heel*. If the "myrmidons of capital" knew their business they would subsidize Mr. London in the comfortable assurance that he could anaesthetize the average anarchist in half an hour.

Argonaut [San Francisco] 62 (April 18, 1908), 256.

In the Realm of Bookland: A New Novel by Jack London

The Iron Heel is Jack London's latest novel. It is socialistic, and is a prophecy of the outcome of the present struggle between capital and labor. The story is a transcript from a manuscript written by Avis Everhard, wife of Ernest Everhard, the hero of the story. The manuscript has been discovered by a critc of the twenty-eighth century, who annotates and explains various historical characters of the story. It is evident from the first that Ernest has been assassinated; and Avis lovingly recounts her life with her husband, beginning with the days when, a college girl, she first met Ernest, a hornyhanded son of labor; but withal, a quickwitted, keen thinker. The manuscript recounts scenes bloodier than the French Revolution—more terrible than deaths in Siberian prisons, and runs to a time when the power of wealth has reduced labor to abject slavery; and it ends abruptly at the end of the second revolt of labor against capital, leaving at last the secret of Ernest's death in doubt.

Many names familiar to us are written high on the walls of fame and notoriety: Henry Van Dyke, President David Starr Jordan, being among the number. Dr. Jordan is quoted as giving as the test of truth: "Will it work? Can you trust your life to it?"

The book is written in London's usual strong, virile style, and carries the reader along with it. We cannot, however, agree with the author that the country is coming to any such era of bloodshed as he so vividly describes. That we face serious problems there is no doubt, but that we will not be able to peacefully settle them is entirely another question. The end in America is to be reached by a process of peaceful evolution rather than by war.

Overland Monthly 52 (July 1908), 89.

Small Contributions

Ambrose Bierce

Jack London's titanic exaggerations may be obvious enough when he writes of social and industrial conditions, but mark his accuracy and moderation in relating (in *The Iron Heel*) the things that he knows about:

> The mob came on, but it could not advance. It piled up in a heap, a mound, a huge and growing wave of dead and dying. Those behind urged on, and the column, from gutter to gutter, telescoped upon itself. Wounded creatures, men and women, were vomited over the top of that awful wave and fell squirming down the face of it till they threshed about under the automobiles and against the legs of the soldiers.

As an authority on the effects of gun-fire Colonel London stands foremost among the military men of his period.

Colonel London's book is supposed to be written in the year 419 B. O. M. (Brotherhood of Man), and following the cheerful incident related above come three centuries of similar controversy between the people and their oppressors, the mound-builders and wave-makers. Then—a natural and inevitable result of tempers and dispositions softened by slaughter—behind this frowning providence the Brotherhood of Man reveals its smiling face and the book "ends happily," its gallant author in receipt of a comfortable pension.

Cosmopolitan 45 (July 1908), 220.

Review of *The Iron Heel*

The Iron Heel, by Jack London (Everett & Co.) purports to be the diary, found in the year 419 B.O.M. (Brotherhood of Man), of one Avis Everhard, wife of the great agitator Ernest Everhard, who was executed in 1932 A.D. As a forecast of the possibilities of the future it is sufficiently harrowing. It is an indictment of wealth which would be overpowering were it not for the fact that there are in the present day instances of such wealth being used for levelling up the many rather than adding to the aggrandizement of the few. Whether such a process will prevent the bloody revolutions here depicted many are seriously debating. Though the action is mostly transatlantic, we command the book to the attention of all who are troubled by the present inequalities of opportunity, work, and recompense for it.

Athenaeum 4233 (December 12, 1908), 757-58.

Critique of *The Iron Heel*

Leon Trotsky

The book produced upon me—I speak without exaggeration—a deep impression. Not because of its artistic qualities: the form of the novel here represents only an armor for social analysis and prognosis. The author is intentionally sparing in his use of artistic means. He is himself interested not so much in the individual fate of his heroes as in the fate of mankind. By this, however, I don't want at all to belittle the artistic value of the work, especially in its last chapters beginning with the Chicago commune. The pictures of civil war develop in powerful frescoes. Nevertheless, this is not the main feature. The book surprised me with the audacity and independence of its historical foresight.

The world workers' movement at the end of the last and the beginning of the present century stood under the sign of reformism. The perspective of peaceful and uninterrupted world progress, of the prosperity of democracy and social reforms, seemed to be assured once and for all. The first Russian revolution, it is true, revived the radical flank of the German social-democracy and gave for a certain time dynamic force to anarcho-syndicalism in France. *The Iron Heel* bears the undoubted imprint of the year 1905. But at the time when this remarkable book appeared, the domination of counter-revolution was already consolidating itself in Russia. In the world arena the defeat of the Russian proletariat gave to reformism the possibility not only of regaining its temporarily lost positions but also of subjecting to itself completely the organized workers' movement. It is sufficient to recall that precisely in the following seven years (1907-14) the international social-democracy ripened definitely for its base and shameful role during the World War.

Jack London not only absorbed creatively the impetus given by the first Russian revolution but also courageously thought over again in its light the fate of capitalist society as a whole. Precisely those problems which the official socialism of this time considered to be definitely buried: the growth of wealth and power at one pole, of misery and destitution at the other pole; the accumulation of social bitterness and hatred; the unalterable preparation of bloody cataclysms—all those questions Jack London felt with an intrepidity which forces one to ask himself again and again with astonishment: when was this written? really before the war?

One must accentuate especially the role which Jack London attributes to the labor bureaucracy and to the labor aristocracy in the further fate of mankind. Thanks to their support the American plutocracy not only succeeds in defeating the workers' insurrection but also in keeping its iron dictatorship during the following three centuries. We will not dispute with the poet the delay which can but seem to us too long. However, it is not a question of Jack London's pessimism, but of his passionate effort to shake those who are lulled by routine, to force them to open their eyes and to see what is and what approaches. The artist is audaciously utilizing the methods of hyperbole. He is bringing the tendencies rooted in capitalism: of oppression, cruelty, bestiality, betrayal, to their extreme expression. He is operating with centuries in order to measure the tyrannical will of the exploiters and the treacherous role of the labor bureaucracy. But his most "romantic" hyperboles are finally much more realistic than the bookkeeper-like calculations of the so-called "sober-politicians."

It is easy to imagine with what a condescending perplexity the official socialist thinking of that time met Jack London's menacing prophecies. If one took the trouble to look over the reviews of *The Iron Heel* at that time in the German *Neue Zeit* and *Vorwaerts*, in the Austrian *Kampf* and *Arbeiterzeitung*, as well as in the other Socialist publications of Europe and America, he could easily convince himself that the thirty-year-old "romanticist" saw incomparably more clearly and farther than all the social-democratic leaders of that time taken together. But Jack London bears comparison in this domain not only with the reformists. One can say with assurance that in 1907 not one of the revolutionary Marxists, not excluding Lenin and Rosa Luxemburg, imagined so fully the ominous perspective of the alliance between finance capital and labor aristocracy. This suffices in itself to determine the specific weight of the novel.

The chapter, "The Roaring Abysmal Beast," undoubtedly constitutes the focus of the book. At the time when the novel appeared this apocalyptical chapter must have seemed to be the boundary of hyperbolism. However, the consequent happenings have almost surpassed it. And the last word of class struggle has not yet been said by far! The "Abysmal Beast" is to the extreme degree oppressed, humiliated, and degenerated people. Who would now dare to speak for this reason about the artist's pessimism? No, London is an optimist, only a penetrating and far-sighted one. "Look into what kind of abyss the bourgeoisie will hurl you down, if you don't finish with them!" This is his thought. Today it sounds incomparably more real and sharp than thirty years ago. But still more astonishing is the genuinely prophetic vision of the methods by which the Iron Heel will sustain its domination over crushed mankind. London manifests remarkable freedom from reformistic pacifist illusions. In this picture of the future there remains not a trace of democracy and peaceful progress. Over the mass of the deprived rise the castes of labor aristocracy, of praetorian army, of an all-penetrating police, with the financial oligarchy at the top. In reading it, one does not believe his own eyes: it is precisely the picture of fascism, of its economy, of its governmental technique, its political psychology! The fact is incontestable: in 1907 Jack London already foresaw and described the fascist regime as the inevitable result of the defeat of the proletarian revolution. Whatever may be the single "errors" of the novel—and they exist—we cannot help inclining before the powerful intuition of the revolutionary artist.

Jack London's Dream at the Turn of the Century

Do Duc Duc [Translated from the Vietnamese by N. T. Ngoc-Phuong]

It is not a coincidence that Jack London is called the "Gorky of the United States." He was born in the same period as Gorky, a period in which capitalist ideology had reached its ultimate stage, a period of confusion and imperialism, the eve of the socialist revolution. Like Gorky, Jack London (1876-1916) experienced misery and suffering in his youth and was a victim of a cruel and unjust social regime.

Just like the young Alyosha Pescope in *My Children, In the World* and *My Universities*, Jack London had done all kinds of work: from farmhand, newsboy, sailor, dock worker, guard, factory worker. . . and with his cane and his bag, he had wandered all over the United States, from the immense virgin forest covered with snow all year around, right next to the North Pole to the vast and rough waters of the Pacific Ocean which is dotted by thousands of islands.

Besides leading a life full of adventures, the young Jack London loved to read, to learn, and to reflect; he felt very attached to the writing profession; he taught himself to be a writer and became famous both at home and abroad. He died at the early age of forty and left behind fifty books of short stories and novels and three plays. His works have been translated into many languages; his most important work is *The Iron Heel*.

As he had known a life full of hardship and as he had struggled with his social and natural environment, Jack London put into his works his most bitter cries of revolt and anger; sometimes he would describe the most fierce struggle of the classes in America, sometimes the fight to the death of the white men against the minority population such as the Eskimos, the Indians of the Northlands or of the Brown people of the South Sea Islands. He constantly insisted on the cruel aspect of life, on the law of the jungle in a society of men; the survival of the fittest, eat or be eaten. Alongside the conflict of men among themselves, he loved to illustrate the equally dramatic struggle of men against nature: death, disease, snowstorms, avalanches, typhoons. . . . With a sharp and fierce stroke of the pen he brought out the wild and inhuman forces of nature surrounding and oppressing man, thus underlining the tragedy of men against men.

Even though he emphasized the ruthless character in the conflict of men among themselves and that of men with nature Jack London was not pessimistic; on the contrary, his own life is an example of a striving force, a strong will, and that of a humble, illiterate child, abandoned by society; yet by sheer strength he became a famous writer. Like a young wolf, running straight against the "wall of the world,"[1] he found "the stir of life that was in him, the play of his muscles, was an unending happiness. To run down meat was to experience thrills and elations" (108). Or, as the Indian Keen had said:

"No man makes my kill. I make my own kill. I am glad to live when I make my own kill. When I creep through the snow upon the great moose, I am glad. And when I draw the bow, so, with my full strength, and drive the arrow fierce and swift and to the heart, I am glad. And the meat of no man's kill tastes as sweet as the meat of my kill. I am glad to live, glad in my own cunning and strength, glad that I am a doer of things, a doer of things for myself. Of what other reason to live than that?"[2]

And before the adverse force of nature, man is only a reed, but a thinking reed, an active reed. Thus Jack London wrote:

All around me Nature is unleashing its fantastic forces, its frightening oppression, its destructive giants, its cruel monsters; they value me as I would value the grains of sand I trample upon. Those monstrous giants are called storms and typhoons, they are lightenings and thunders, high waves and water spouts, they are earthquakes and volcanoes, they are foamy waters beating against the rugged rocks, they are the moving waves sweeping over the biggest ships, smashing all human lives, pulling them into the deep. . . . In this conflict those Giants, in this Hell that they are trapping me, I must find a way out. And this tiny seed of life that is in me will be delighted after mastering them.

So, is it right to conclude that Jack London worshipped "sheer strength," that "his characters are amoral? Stimulated only by their egotism, they find a way to satisfy their own desire without the least scruple; the strongest will win, that is the rule."

In reality, Jack London was only describing contemporary American society with its philosophy, its morality, its law, all of which were based on force. It is also true that in American capitalistic society, every individual, such as Jack London himself, who wants a place under the sun, who wants to elevate himself, must have personal strength, and that strength is brought about mainly by money. One other aspect that should not be forgotten is that Jack London carried in his bloodstream the undaunted determination of his European ancestors who were the pioneers of America. Therefore, it is not rare to find in his work a certain admiration for strength and for the individual hero. But basically if one wants to know if Jack London had sincerely approved of that philosophy of strength in the ruthless and inhuman world of the American capitalist system, then one should ask which side was taken by Jack London in these conflicts, who did he defend, who did he accuse?

Let us examine the so-called "tragic conflict between the white and the colored" which is no other than the racial struggle. Whether it be the war between the white man and the Indian in the North, or the fight between the white man and the brown people in the South Seas, the American capitalist system at the end of the 19th century and at the beginning of the 20th century was still in its powerful stage. The initial expansion, throughout Jack London's works, had two directions:

(1) It expanded toward the unexploited lands of the North, for example, the Alaskan Peninsula with its unexploited mineral resources still buried under the snow, such as gold mines and animal furs. Gold particularly attracted a lot of people who wanted to get rich in a hurry and thus contracted gold fever.

(2) It expanded into the multitude of islands in the South Seas which contain extremely precious products such as pearls, copra, corals. . . . The picture of the English-American capitalist, in particular, and white capitalists in general, men who conquered and exploited new lands, came vividly into life in Jack London's tales. In their march into these two areas, these white capitalists had to deal with the aborigines, colored people, hence "the racial conflict between the white and the colored."

In reference to these racial conflicts, which are framed by the fight of men against nature, Jack London was not aware of the true character of the problem, therefore, he had somewhat heightened what is called "the virtues" of the pioneers such as courage, boldness, astuteness, and the capability to overcome most mortal dangers. For that reason, when talking about the conflict between white men and the aborigines, who still lived in tribal societies, Jack London could not help but emphasize the primitive customs of the latter. But generally speaking, Jack London did not possess the capitalist view of Rudyard Kipling. On the contrary, throughout many of his stories, it is quite clear that he was on the side of the oppressed, the conquered, and the exploited. He denounced the capitalists for being greedy, cruel and more vicious than wild beasts. One thinks of such characters as John Saxtorph [in "The Inevitable White Man"], or MacBunster [in "Mauki"], or McAllister [in "Yah! Yah! Yah!"], who have used guns, liquor and the Bible in order to conquer, govern, oppress, harass primitive people; they killed the men, attacked the women, took over their land, maintained an abusive treatment towards the people who worked for them, poisoning their mind as well as their body, they went as far as annihilating entire populations, those who refused to submit to their will. Hence, the image of "the white man" symbolizes a terrifying force, the object of deep rooted vengeance for the Indians in the North as well as for the blacks in the South Seas.

Let us listen to the accusation of Imber, the old Indian, before the colonialist court:

> "I am Imber of the Whitefish people. . . . The land was warm with sunshine and gladness when I was a boy. The people did not hunger after strange things, nor hearken to new voices, and the ways of their fathers were their ways. . . . Men were men in those days. In peace and plenty, and in war and famine, they were men. . . .
>
> "And one day came the first white man. He dragged himself, so, on hand and knee, in the snow. And his skin was stretched tight, and his

bones were sharp beneath. . . . And he was weak, most weak, like a little child, so that we gave him a place by the fire, and warm furs to lie upon, and we gave him food as little children are given food.

"And with him was a dog, large as three of our dogs, and very weak. The hair of this dog was short, and not warm, and the tail was frozen so that the end fell off. And this strange dog we fed, and bedded by him, and fought from it our dogs, which else would have killed him. And what of the moose meat and the sun-dried salmon, the man and dog took strength to themselves; and what of the strength they became big and unafraid. And the an spoke loud words and laughed at the old men and young men, and looked boldly upon the maidens. And the dog fought with our dogs, and for all of his short hair and softness slew three of them in one day. . . .

"And that was the beginning. Came a second white man, with short-haired dogs, which he left behind him when he went. And with him went six of our strongest dogs, for which, in trade, he had given Koo-So-Tee, my mother's brother, a wonderful pistol that fired with great swiftness six times. And Koo-So-Tee was very big, what of the pistol, and laughed at our bows and arrows. . . and went forth against the bald-face grizzly, with the pistol in his hand. Now it be known that it is not good to hunt the bald-face with a pistol, but how were we to know. . . ? So he went against the bald-face, very brave, and fired the pistol with great swiftness six times; and the bald-face but grunted and broke in his breast like it were an egg, and like honey from a bee's nest dripped the brains of Koo-So-Tee upon the ground. . . . And we were bitter, and we said, 'That which for the white man is well, is for us not well.' And this be true. There be many white men and fat, but their ways have made us few and lean.

"Came the third white man, with great wealth of all manner of wonderful foods and things. And twenty of our strongest dogs he took from us in trade. Also, what of presents and great promises, ten of our young hunters did he take with him on a journey which fared no man knew where. It was said they died in the snow of the Ice Mountains where man has never been, or in the Hills of Silence which are beyond the edge of the earth. . . .

"And more white men came with the years, and ever, with pay and presents, they led thy young men away with them. And sometimes the young men came back with strange tales of dangers and toils in the lands beyond the Pellys, and sometimes they did not come back. . . .

"So we grew to hunger for the things the white men brought in trade. Trade! Trade! All the time it was trade! One winter we sold our meat for clocks that would not go, and watches with broken guts, and files worn smooth, and pistols without cartridges and worthless. And then came famine, and we were without meat, and twoscore died ere the break of spring. . . .

"The best of our young men and women had gone away with the white men to wonder on trail and river to far places. And the young women came back old and broken, as Nada had come, or they came not at all. And the young men came back to sit by our fires for a time, full of ill speech and rough ways, drinking evil drinks and gambling through long nights and days, with a great unrest always in their hearts, till the call of the white men came to them and they went away again to the unknown places. And they were without honor and respect, jeering the old-time customs and laughing in the faces of chief and shamans.

"As I say, we were become a weak breed, we Whitefish. We sold our warm skins and furs for tobacco and whiskey and thin cotton things that left us shivering in the cold. And the coughing sickness came upon us, and men and women coughed and sweated through the long nights, and the hunters on trail spat blood upon the snow. And now one and now another bled swiftly from the mouth and died. And the women bore few children, and those they bore were weak and given to sickness. And other sicknesses came to us from the white men, the like of which we had never known and could not understand. . . .

"And yet—and here be the strangeness of it—the white men come as the breath of death; all their ways lead to death, their nostrils are filled with it; and yet they do not die. . . . And yet they grow fat on their many ills, and prosper, and lay a heavy hand over all the world and tread mightily upon its peoples."[3]

Imber's story was a very tragic one indeed; it was a joint accusation of the white man by both the Indians and the blacks. According to a number of critics, it was not because Jack London had wanted to be the defender of the primitive people and their way of life, but most important of all he had uncovered all the crimes, especially that of genocide.

Particularly noteworthy was the fact that Jack London disapproved of the practice of racism as seen in the "colonialist" Captain Woodward or in Charley Roberts, the snack bar owner. They said: "The Black will never understand the white. . . the white man's mission is to farm the world. . . " and, "the white has to run the niggers whether he understands them or not."[4]

On the contrary in many of his stories, Jack London often heightened the noble traits of the colored man: for example, the courage of Lone Chief, the great understanding, boldness and calmness of the mulatto island chief McCoy, the frankness, patience and indomitable character of the black Mauki and the perseverance and courage of the sixty-year old Nauri [in "The House of Mapuhi"].

To prove wrong the belief that black and white would never understand each other, Jack London told us the story of the faithful and true friendship between a black and a white man in "The Heathen." The black heathen Otoo, from Tahiti, had met a white man after a shipwreck, while they were both drifting away. They shared the same piece of driftboard that saved their lives, and thus became the closest of friends. Praising his friend's noble character, the white man said:

"I never had a brother; but from what I have seen of other men's brothers, I doubt if any man ever had a brother that was to him what Otoo was to me. He was brother and father and mother as well. And this I know: I lived a straighter and better man because of Otoo."[5]

Indeed there are no words more eloquent than these to heighten the nobleness of a black man. It is clear that Jack London did not share the colonialists' condescension and cruelty; but that he sided with the oppressed and the enslaved.

So much for the question of race conflict. Now let us examine the class struggle in American society. (In fact the class struggle is at the very center of the race problem; that is the dilemma between the white capitalist and the colored slaves).

The class struggle in American society at the beginning of the century is the central point in Jack London's best known, most outstanding and most typical novel, *The Iron Heel* (1908).

It was a unique masterpiece of its time, well-known throughout the world, and comparable to Gorky's *The Mother* (1906), which was only published a year earlier. Both books, by two authors living thousands of miles apart, condemned capitalist ideology, and led the way toward a social revolution by the proletarian class.

This fact only shows that these two literary works had one and the same historical background, i.e. the vast society of men, when the evolution from capitalism to imperialism was taking place, had spread worldwide. At that particular moment the Czarist regime had reached its weakest point in what has become the revolution center of the world. It was the proletarian revolution of 1905, which was marked by bloodshed, that had moved both Maxim Gorky and Jack London and that had left its imprint on both *The Mother* and *The Iron Heel*.

Naturally *The Iron Heel* differs from *The Mother* in many basic ways because of different social situations in the two countries. As for personal influence, Gorky was more fortunate for having been near Lenin, the great master of the proletarian revolution, whom Jack London did not have the opportunity to meet, as one proletarian French writer, Vaillant-Couturier has often remarked.

At the time, when Russian capitalism, enclosed within the Czarist regime, had reached old age and decadence, American capitalism was still at its prosperous stage; it had not yet experienced the terrible destruction at Wall Street in 1929. In other words the Russian Revolution of 1905 had failed; American capitalism was going strong at the time. These are the two characteristics of the social situation that had great influence upon the thought of Jack London in *The Iron Heel*.

If *The Mother* had become an effective weapon for the Russian proletariat in their successful October Revolution, Jack London's *Iron Heel*, in spite of its accusation and condemnation of American capitalism, remains but a prediction, guess work, a dream of the socialist ideology, a very far-fetched dream that took three hundred years to materialize.

The above factors also explain the uniqueness of Jack London's novel's literary form: it was written in 1907, but was based on the author's optimistic and bold prediction. Through one of his characters he tells a story of what was to happen in the future; at the same time he placed himself seven centuries later looking back to comment on these events. Even though the story was framed within a very short time span (1912-1918), he is able with the use of footnotes to trace the progress throughout seven centuries beginning with the twentieth century and including the last three centuries under the domination of the Iron Heel, i.e. under the capitalist system, plus for centuries of the unification of the world.

Naturally, *The Iron Heel* was a futuristic story, but nevertheless it was based on contemporary U.S. society. The clearer the description the more convincing it appeared. The social picture of the United States was described by Jack London in an extremely realistic and complete manner; it is impressive and lively, complex and incessantly changing. At the same time it uncovered the human, ugly and disgusting character of the American capitalist system as well as its inevitable road to failure.

It was a reflection of all social classes, a most characteristic analysis. Of course, at the very top was the class of magnates in whose hands were centered all the trusts and business, the class to which belonged the seven major groups that desired to centralize and monopolize all capital and trades rapidly. The most representative of all was the Rockefeller group, which, drawn by the "wave of dividends," were striving to monopolize all commerce and every industry: oil, railroads, natural gas, electricity, even streetcar systems and mortgages on property. What can we say about the intelligence and morality of the "master class?" Ernest Everhard, the main character in *The Iron Heel*, observed: "And so it was, instead of paradise, that I found myself in the arid desert of commercialism. I found nothing but stupidity, except for business. . . . What I did find was monstrous selfishness and heartlessness, and a gross, gluttonous practiced, and practical materialism."[6] He had found these "masters, men and women" intellectually shallow, and morally they think they are superior, but if their money-bags were threatened then we could hear "the growl of the pack" (84). "That will shake them to the roots of their primitive natures. If you come you will see the cave-men, in evening dress, snarling and snapping over a bone" (74).

One step under that social ladder one would find a middle and a lower capitalist class that Ernest called the pitiful and "perishing middle class" (151). Faithful to the profit motive and "dog eat dog" (129), they "dealt" with one another, at the same time they themselves were slowly being swallowed alive by the big magnates on the unobstructed road to the development of a corrupted capitalism. But the big city "business man" or the country "farmers" do not want to admit that the "sun of the small capitalist is setting." They still believed in the illusion of free enterprise, thus they put forth this fantastic slogan "Bust the Trusts" (121). A group of farmers even wanted to "return to the ways of our fathers" (131).

To serve the capitalist class there were a whole group of men who worked at the very top of the social structure: politicians, educators, "independents," such as lawyers, doctors, journalists, artists and ministers. "One and all, the professors, preachers, and the editors held their jobs by serving the Plutocracy, and their service consists of propagating only such ideas as are either harmless to or commendatory of the Plutocracy," said Ernest (157). Lawyers such as Ingram or Col. Van Gilbert have a special "knowledge of the law, of how best to evade the law or make new law for the benefit of thieving corporations" (91-2).

If among these so-called "independents" there happens to be one who advocates anything that could be a threat to the power and privileges of these rich capitalists then he will suffer a most terrible fate. Such is the case of Prof. J. Cunningham, a famous scientist, who was stripped of all his property, and then made to disappear. Such also is the case of Bishop Morehouse, who was jailed and then placed in a mental hospital only because his humanitarian view was contrary to capitalist doctrine, in which "A rich man today who gives all he has to the poor is crazy" (203).

Naturally to oppose the capitalist class, there is the working class. Jack London's whole novel brings out the indomitable spirit of the working class in America whose most deserving representatives are the leaders of the American Socialist Party; the most typical and most clairvoyant of them all is Ernest Everhard. With all his enthusiasm, Jack London had truly carved out the greatest leader of the American working class! Avis Everhard, Ernest's wife, said this about her husband: "I think of what has been and is no more—my Eagle, beating with tireless wings the void, soaring towards what was ever his sun, the flaming ideal of human freedom" (2). About the members of the Socialist Party, she said: "Amongst the revolutionists I found, also warm faith in the human, ardent idealism, sweetness of unselfishness, renunciation, and martyrdom—all the splendid singing things of the spirit" (79).

The most outstanding trait about Ernest Everhard is that he had used the most concrete, the most powerful argument to condemn the capitalist ideology, to put down private property owners, clergymen who wanted to discuss humanism, or members of the middle class who want to "break the machines" (128). By analyses and demonstrations as strong and clear as a mathematical solution, he passionately predicts the inevitable breakdown of the capitalist ideology, and the sure victory of the proletariat. He shouted in the face of the capitalist: "If modern man's producing power is a thousand times greater than that of the cave-man, why then, in the United States to-day, are there fifteen million people who are not properly sheltered and properly fed? Why then, in the United States to-day, are there three million child laborers?" "The capitalist class has mismanaged. In face of the facts that modern man lives more wretchedly than the cave-man, and that his producing power is a thousand times greater than that of the cave-man, no other conclusion is possible than that the capitalist class has mismanaged, that you have mismanaged. . . " (86). Thus, based on that steel argument, Ernest Everhard had dreamed of the future of the socialist ideology. He said: "The United States, and the whole world for that matter, will enter upon a new and tremendous era. Instead of being crushed by the machines, life will be made fairer, and happier, and nobler by them" (152). That was the romantic dream, "the mathematics of my dream" (141) to quote Jack London himself.

Furthermore, the remarkable clairvoyance of Ernest Everhard, and of Jack London himself, is his prophecy of the long and difficult road of the revolution. Before his unbeatable argument capitalist masters had to remain tongue-tied. Here is the reply of the capitalist Wickson: "We will not reply to the bear in words. Our reply shall be couched in terms of lead. We are in power. Nobody will deny it. By virtue of that power we shall remain in power. . . . And in the dirt it shall remain as long as I and mine and those that come after us have the power" (97). And the genius of Jack London had foreseen right in the beginning of the century the inevitable road to Fascism on the part of Capitalism in general, and of American capitalism in particular. He said: "Then, you, and labor, and all of us, will be crushed under the iron heel of a despotism as relentless and terrible as any despotism that has blackened the pages of the history of man. That will be a good name for that despotism, the Iron Heel" (152). Thus, Jack London was able to predict the coming of Hitler, Mussolini, McCarthyism and the Taft-Hartley laws in America.

The novel seems to be about to explode in a terrifying and asphyxiating atmosphere created by the American leaders, who rely on a gigantic and oppressive machinery; the very atmosphere to-day still, that is constantly caused by the American security agencies, the psychological warfare agencies of the "free" United States! That oppressive machinery is composed of the courts of justice, prisons, camps, asylums, the IRS army, the militia, down right to the Gold Syndicate leaders and the aristocratic employees who have been bought. But the most dangerous of all are the secret agents, the informers, the "Black Hundreds," all kinds of agents provocateurs, who infiltrate everywhere in order to spy, arrest, destroy, kidnap, and particularly to provoke violence in order to give those in power the opportunity to severely repress the working class.

Indeed the revolutionary struggle of the American working class is extremely difficult and painful. It has met many obstacles and failures. Jack London had brilliantly foreseen that part; and his novel ended in a most devastating defeat, the defeat of the Chicago commune buried in flames and bloodshed.

However, American workers never gave up. If at first you don't succeed, then try again. After that defeat Ernest and the other socialist leaders kept right on reorganizing their revolutionary forces. Ernest Everhard calmly said: "Tomorrow the Cause will rise again, strong with wisdom and discipline"

(351). And Jack London had prophesied that three hundred years later the socialist ideology would appear in America; man will step into the era of world unification. That was Jack London's dream at the turn of the century.

At any event, *The Iron Heel* was but a dream of a democratic American, a member of the socialist party at the beginning of the twentieth century. To fully appreciate the value of *The Iron Heel* we must put ourselves in the time frame in which Jack London wrote the novel. Today living in a period of general crisis of world capitalism, and advancing into socialism, and especially finding ourselves in a country striving to build up socialism, we cannot help but find in Jack London's world quite a number of naive, unrealistic, and out-dated beliefs. However, even though he wrote this novel in 1907, basically he made a rather strong point, since he had a bold and far-sighted outlook. Principally it is because he was able to write on the reality of contemporary American society. He described and analyzed it with great insight. That is mainly why he condemned so harshly capitalist ideology. The remarkable thing is that he was never lured by the road to socialist revolution by way of Congress, through peaceful means. He traced back the final road to Fascism through Capitalism; he emphasized the awareness of the revolutionary spirit, on the long lasting, painful, and even bloody character of the socialist revolution. Jack London himself, nine years after having written *The Iron Heel*, resigned from the American Socialist Party "because," he said, "of fire and fight, and the loss of emphasis upon the class struggle." It was at that moment that the American Socialist Party began to decline and allowed itself to be divided.

Jack London's basic weakness was his severe view of the world, as we have already analyzed: he over-emphasized the cruel and barbaric aspects of life when he described the race as well as the class struggle, he could not abandon his tendency to look upon human society the same way he did the animal world, along with the law of the jungle. From that point of view he sometimes tended to emphasize brute strength, to heighten individual heroism; he even went so far as to hold the view that the best government is no government at all. For that reason he idealized, even deified, the individual in Ernest Everhard, hence he described the faith that socialists had in the revolution as though it were the faith of a religion. Meanwhile he saw in the working people whom he called "people of the abyss," an animal strength that was at the same time blinding, disorganized and even sanguinary. With such a view of life, Jack London, like most members of the socialist party of his time, put forth methods of struggle which are quite fantastically adventurous; his individual heroes, even his revolutionary leaders, all infiltrated the enemy spy ring; and what he highlighted was the means of "underground fighting," which produced a spy novel atmosphere in *The Iron Heel*.

Based on such views, Jack London's dream is nothing but a very limited dream, no matter how daring it may be; because in order to foretell the future of the revolution one has to believe in the unparalleled strength of the masses, in the boundless capability of the people. That is Jack London's weakness, which makes him see the future of the social revolution as too far off. Jack London did not suspect that it was not three hundred years later, but ten years after *The Iron Heel* was written, and only one year after his death, that the social revolution has become successful on one-sixth of the earth, after having gone through *Ten Days that Shook the World*, which has been described also by an American writer, John Reed in his most famous novel. And less than forty years later, a whole system of socialist countries was established, which includes up to one third of the human race.

In spite of everything Jack London's *The Iron Heel* has not lost its timely character, for the iron heel of American imperialism is still trampling, not only on American soil, but also on many other areas of the world, including our southern part of Vietnam. It is from this point that we can still draw some appreciable lessons from *The Iron Heel*, as well as from his over-all work, in both aspects: the national struggle and the class struggle, which are linked together in the social struggle of mankind today.

NOTES

[1] Jack London, *White Fang* (New York: Macmillan, 1906), 89. Further references in text.

[2] Jack London, "In the Forests of the North" in *Children of the Frost* (New York: Macmillan, 1902), 24-25.

[3] Jack London, "The League of The Old Men" in *Children of the Frost*, 248-55.

[4] Jack London, "The Inevitable White Man" in *South Sea Tales* (New York: Macmillan, 1911), 235, 239.

[5] Jack London, "The Heathen" in *South Sea Tales*, 173-4.

[6] Jack London, *The Iron Heel* (New York: Macmillan, 1908), 80, 82. Further references in text.

Looking Forward/Looking Backward: Romance and Utopia in *The Iron Heel*

Christopher Gair

> I see in the near future a crisis approaching that unnerves me and causes me to tremble for the safety of my country. . . . Corporations have been enthroned, an era of corruption in high places will follow, and the money-power of the country will endeavor to prolong its reign by working upon the prejudices of the people until the wealth is aggregated in a few hands and the Republic is destroyed.
>
> —Abraham Lincoln[1]

> There is no document of civilization which is not at one and the same time a document of barbarism.
>
> —Walter Benjamin[2]

> The leisure class lives by the industrial community rather than in it.
>
> —Thorstein Veblen[3]

The Iron Heel (1908) is a novel which, in its responses to both class conflict and, to a lesser degree, to the antimodern impulse prevalent in America at the turn-of-the-century, is centrally concerned with competing definitions of the term "America." Contrasting representations of civil war and urban degeneration with pictures of a future classless society and of urban and rural harmony, it anticipates a Utopian community whilst registering the horrors of the mob and the police state in graphic detail. The epigraphs to this essay—the words of Abraham Lincoln, Walter Benjamin, and Thorstein Veblen—each suggest that the acquisition of power by the corporations will result in precisely these battles over what "America" should mean: Lincoln, with his doctrine of class mobility, attempts to cling to a Jeffersonian Republican tradition in the face of a nascent corporate capitalism which established an impassable gulf between the classes. He talks of "working upon the prejudices of the people," that is, using hegemonic rhetoric to divide and conquer, until the "Republic is destroyed;" Benjamin argues that the "high" culture of any civilization depends on the toil of the masses and implies that the ruling class will, if its hegemony breaks down, impose itself via violent repression and exploitation. London's novel, and his extensive references to the Oligarchy's "wonder cities" (469) built by serfs, can be seen as an extended thesis on this point; perhaps most interestingly, Veblen produces a double meaning which simultaneously explains capitalist/proletariat relationships, the ability of the capitalists to live off their workforce, and the reasons why that workforce find it so difficult to alter the situation. As Richard Godden has pointed out in a detailed examination of the relationship between the leisure class and the industrial community:

> Veblen's "live by" in this instance means simultaneously "in proximity to" and "by means of," exemplifying how far the behavior of any leisure class is founded on the desire to control, and ideally to forget, the behavior of the laboring class.[4]

It is necessary to qualify Godden's emphasis on "control," by suggesting that the leisure class appear happy to allow the workers to spend their own (limited) leisure time as they like, at least in the pre-Fordist period when London was writing. As long as they perform their function as producers, and do not encroach onto that space "by" (within/without) the industrial community inhabited by the families of the capitalists, the proletariat—living at subsistence or starvation levels and thus unable to act as consumers—are forgotten, but not controlled.

In London's work, this gap between "control" and "forget" is repeatedly highlighted: for example, when he asks his friends for directions to the East End, in *The People of the Abyss* (1903), his autobiographical account of conditions in working class London, they suggest that he seeks guidance from the police, who act as border guards, forming an enclosure around the working class. The friends rely on hearsay to advise the would be investigator:

> "You don't want to *live* down there!. . . Why, it is said there are places where a man's life isn't worth tu'pence. . . ." "But we know nothing of the East End. It is over there, somewhere." And they waved their hands vaguely in the direction where the sun on rare occasions may be seen to rise.

This collective loss of class memory is reiterated when London, making no progress with his friends, approaches Thomas Cook & Son, "pathfinders and trail-clearers to all the world." He is told:

> "We are not accustomed to taking travellers to the East End; we receive no call to take them there, and we know nothing whatsoever about the place at all."

The only information that the travel agent can offer the "insane American who *would* see the East End," is the address of a detective, once more emphasizing the role of the police, whose presence allows the leisure class to forget the "abject poverty" which London discovers in the "unending slum" of the working class district.[5] However, Veblen's point remains important, to *The People of the Abyss*, and central to *The Iron Heel*, London's most famous revolutionary novel. I will use it as a focal point from which to examine London's narrative strategies—his twin focalizers, giving a local and a global/historical version of events—and to instigate a close look at the antagonistic class relations within the text.

The Iron Heel represents, in several ways, attempts to bridge the class gap as experienced in corporate America. First, Ernest is allowed to enter the homes of the leisure class, though this privilege is soon withdrawn. Later, Avis Everhard and her father, Professor John Cunningham, move from the world of bourgeois domesticity, where they remain oblivious to the realities of working class life, into the city slums. Finally, in the commentary provided by Anthony Meredith, a future is posited in which the class system has been abolished, and communal values have replaced individualism. The novel thus represents both the horrors of the industrial world and the leisure class space created "by" that world, as well as imagining an alternative to urban class conflict.

With its twin narratives, then, *The Iron Heel* provides a critique of corporate America and promises that revolutionary socialism will eventually triumph. In this, its literary antecedents can be traced back to the "pioneer labor activist," George Lippard, who "dramatized the dual vision of darkness and light within emergent industrialism"[6] in the 1830s and '40s. Lippard's novels, which portray increasingly bleak industrial landscapes and describe the betrayal of Republican ideals by an emergent capitalist class promise, like *The Iron Heel*, that socialism will provide a better life for the American masses, and create a truly democratic community. In addition, London's precursors certainly include Mark Twain's *A Connecticut Yankee at King Arthur's Court* (1889), Ignatius Donnelly's *Caesar's Column* (1890), and Edward Bellamy's *Looking Backward*[7] (1888), and the novel shares these books' simultaneous embrace and rejection of technology and capitalism. Like both *Connecticut Yankee*, and *Looking Backward, The Iron Heel* depends on the juxtaposition of alternative social structures, and relies on an intelligent and articulate guide to steer the reader through the events leading to transformation. However, this standard naturalist ploy, which is attained by Twain and Bellamy through the magical (non-naturalist) transplantation of their central characters into the past and the future respectively, is divided in two by London. On the one hand, he offers a localized picture of Ernest Everhard, via the memoirs of Ernest's wife, Avis, written in "1932" (or the near future); on the other, Anthony Meredith, historian of the "Brotherhood of Man," looks back seven hundred years to offer a Utopian socialist overview of events. It is the effects of this authorial doubling—from which it is possible to generate a third narrative—that I now wish to examine.

Critics of *The Iron Heel* have tended to overlook the results of this doubling process, and have thus equated London's own views with those expressed by Avis Everhard. Anthony Meredith's commentary has been largely ignored. For example, Ronald E. Martin calls Ernest Everhard one of "the infrequent unambiguously heroic characters in London's fiction," and suggests that he is "an idealized projection of. . . an individual response to the deterministic social forces." He goes on to call Everhard "too one-sidedly heroic," and subsequently dismisses *The Iron Heel* as "not a very effective novel."[8] However, this critique ignores the book's "Foreword," which points out "errors of interpretation" made by Avis, and suggests that she "lacked perspective" (319). When we look more closely at Avis' narrative, and the manner in which London modifies it via his footnotes, it becomes apparent that Ernest's "unambiguously heroic" characteristics are precisely what would be expected from a description made by the educated daughter of an academic father.

It is clear that Avis Everhard's narrative is shaped by her class background. Initially she appears to be a representation, par excellence, of the leisure class living "by" the industrial community, and she is ignorant of the oppression that exists. Before Ernest gives her "glimpses of reality" (368), Avis makes no connection between her fine clothes and the impoverished state of the working community. Furthermore, her account of the events leading to the formation of the Iron Heel, if taken without Meredith's commentary, closely resembles many naturalist texts: a member of the middle class, Avis experiences a political awakening as a result of her exposure to the literature of socialism, and the injustices she witnesses. However, because of her language and manners, Avis' participation is qualified by a strange ambivalence, and she is distanced from what she describes. In addition, she is prepared to exercise this class privilege to escape from the riots she encounters late in the book. (Avis takes a "calm interest in events," is an "interested spectator," and is rescued by a soldier) (536-548). As an outsider, Avis is best-placed to record events for a future readership presumed unfamiliar with the horrors she recounts. Like the naturalist narrators examined by June Howard in *Form and History in American Literary Naturalism* (1985), she "plays the role of the readers' guide and interpreter in an alien land, [although she] is not a native of that land either."[9] Despite adopting the cause of socialism, Avis never abandons the received pronunciation of her own class (except as a disguise), and the discourse of the working class, apart from Ernest, is differentiated by speech marks and idiosyncratic spelling. In addition, as I will demonstrate later, Avis' narrative contains many generic discontinuities and these discontinuities point to other class strategies.

Avis' opening chapter, revealingly entitled "My Eagle," commences with a representative selection of her linguistic and ideological assumptions:

> The soft summer wind stirs the redwoods, and Wild-Water ripples sweet cadences over its mossy stones. There are butterflies in the sunshine, and from everywhere arises the drowsy hum of bees. . . . (323)

If the passage is compared with the famous opening of Stephen Crane's "The Open Boat" (1897), Avis' position as participant observer is revealed to be problematic. Crane's story commences with a declaration of the split between the potential for sentimental or imaginative descriptions of reality that is available to spectators and the actual pragmatic observations of the men in the boat:

> None of them knew the color of the sky. Their eyes glanced level, and were fastened upon the waves that swept toward them. . . .
>
> Many a man ought to have a bathtub larger than the boat which here rode upon the sea. These waves were most wrongfully and barbarously abrupt and tall, and each froth-top was a problem in small-boat navigation. . . .
>
> Viewed from a balcony, the whole thing would doubtless have been weirdly picturesque. But the men in the boat had no time to see it, and if they had had leisure, there were other things to occupy their minds.[10]

Immediately, Crane uses several naturalistic tactics to set the scene for his reader, and to bring her or him up to date with an incident which appears to have been in progress for some time. As Jules Chametzky has succinctly observed:

> No time for innocent swoons of rapture at the conventional images of nature's grandeur—a level view of the waves is primary, essential to survival. . . . The picturesque did not exist for them—nor should it have. . . . As for sunrise, that bewitching staple occasion for an outmoded language and imagery of "beauty" . . . Crane's castaways "were only aware of [its] effect upon the color of the waves that rolled toward them." Again the question arises of perspective, purpose, function as determinants of appropriate perception and response—to the natural world and beyond that to individual and social experience.[11]

In contrast, the language of Avis' opening paragraph is sentimental and melodramatic, full of the "innocent swoons of rapture" which Crane avoids. It suggests that the writer has had much leisure time to observe nature, and to become familiar with pastoral conventions. London introduces his participant narrator in such a way as to immediately warn the reader that Avis' "perspective, purpose, function" may well be problematic. Her description of nature is out of place and picturesque in a novel of urban class struggle, and tells us that Avis' judgement is not to be trusted.

This view is reinforced on the following page when she introduces her husband in similarly sentimental and conventional terms:

> And so it is, in this anxious time of writing, that I shall write of my husband. There is much light that I alone of all persons living can throw upon his character, and so noble a character cannot be blazoned forth too brightly. He was a great soul, and, when my love grows unselfish, my chiefest regret is that he is not here to witness to-morrow's dawn. (324)

At once, the commentary points out that "With all respect to Avis Everhard,. . . Everhard was but one of many able leaders," and asserts that "even had he lived, the Second Revolt would not have been less calamitous in its outcome than it was" (324). Avis is exposed as having a definite preference for the individual over the collective, and her narrative is loaded with other signs of its focalizing position: she goes on to describe her husband in the language of the (courtly) romance (he is "a natural aristocrat"), and Ernest emerges as a combination of seemingly contradictory forces. He is "a superman, a blond beast such as Nietzsche has described, and in addition he [is] aflame with democracy" (326). (Meredith calls Nietzsche "the mad philosopher of the nineteenth century of the Christian era" in another statement designed to qualify Avis' assertions.)

Despite my outlining of the differences between Avis Everhard's narrative and Crane's "The Open Boat," many of her textual strategies can clearly be equated with "scientific" naturalism. In the same way in which her father uses his dining room as a "sociological laboratory" (338), in which he observes the interactions of his guests, Avis' narrative illustrates Ernest's strengths via a series of encounters with representatives of the Oligarchy, and its supporters, in every one of which Ernest skilfully deconstructs their arguments. In this way, Ernest confronts the "metaphysicians" of the Church, whom he describes as "anarchists in the realm of thought" (327), and agents of the capitalists; the ultra-rich "Philomaths," whose wealth runs "well into the hundreds of millions" (370); and the "truly representative middle class business men"—the "Machine Breakers," as Ernest calls them—who fail to follow through the implications of their own faith in laissez-faire economic conditions. In each of these instances, Avis' narrative allows socialism's enemies the chance to put forward their arguments, before Ernest responds with a point by point negation. The narrative is constructed so as to display Ernest's rhetorical abilities, in the fight against the Oligarchy. I will use Ernest's encounter with the Philomaths as representative of these encounters, to illustrate how Avis' narrative works towards "proving" the inevitability of socialist triumph, and elevating Ernest, the individualist hero. I will now pause to take a closer look at its structure and content, before completing my analysis of the other strands of Avis' narrative.

The Philomath Club, with its emphasis on a conspicuous knowledge denied to the general public (journalists are not admitted to its talks), is a representation of Veblen's leisure class at its most self-assured. Its members are the wealthiest families in San Francisco, and they congregate to listen to leading speakers from the arts, sciences, and politics. Each speaker is paid a "princely fee," and allowed "fully to speak their minds," since "it was the Philomath's policy to permit none of its discussions to get into the papers" (369). The members of the club mostly acquire their wealth from hereditary fortunes, or else by acting as corporate lawyers, who use their professional specialization to ensure that "law is one thing and right is another thing" (352). (The chapter on

"Jackson's Arm" illustrates the degree to which law is dependent on linguistic manipulation.) It is in front of this gathering that Colonel Van Gilbert, "subtly facetious," and with an "undertone of faint irony," invites Ernest to speak.

Clearly, the "social reformer and member of the working class" (371) is believed to have been led into a trap, and even Avis has a momentary suspicion that Ernest may be "overawed by this imposing array of power and brains" (371-72). However, he effortlessly responds by outlining his early knowledge of the upper classes, gained by reading Seaside Library novels, which, as the commentary points out, "served to make the working class utterly misapprehend the nature of the leisure class." Having recounted the myth, Ernest switches to the reality of life in the mills, to his early meetings with socialists, and to the punishments imposed on Churchmen and academics for straying from "subservience to the ruling class" (372). In turn, Ernest moves through the agents of hegemonic discourse—the Church, the universities, the press, etc.—and contrasts them with the "human, ardent idealism, sweetness of unselfishness, renunciation and martyrdom" (373) of the revolutionaries.

Everhard's remarks about revolution are aimed at the manner in which the leisure class live "by" the industrial community, as opposed to "in" it, and he points out to Avis that this appeal to the economics, rather that the morality of capitalism is what will provoke the true, atavistic colours of the Philomaths:

> "I'll make them snarl like wolves. You [Avis] merely questioned their morality. When their morality is questioned, they grow only the more complacent and superior. But I shall menace their money-bags. That will shake them to the roots of their primitive natures. If you can come, you will see the cave-man, in evening-dress, snarling and snapping over a bone. I promise you a great caterwauling and an illuminating insight into the nature of the beast." (370)

Of course, given the nature of Avis' narrative, Ernest's speech has the desired effect. When he concludes, a "throaty rumble" goes round the gathering, the "enormously wealthy old maid" (369) Miss Brentwood (the founder of the club) is "helped, weeping and laughing, out of the room," and, in a complete breakdown of hegemonic discourse, even Colonel Van Gilbert is rendered near-hysterical (378-79). The Colonel is reduced to "flinging his arms, his rhetoric, and his control to the winds," and then to silence (381-82), as Ernest unravels the split between intellect and emotion in his opponent. Ernest's use of the "rapier" and the "club," and his "encyclopaedic command of the field of knowledge" (382-83) enable him to defeat the lawyer at his own game, turning hegemonic discourse on its head to illustrate its weaknesses and its "inevitable" demise.

Only Mr. Wickson is unaffected by Ernest's onslaught, and he sneers "Utopian," a word which the commentary identifies as having "magic. . . greater than the conjurer's art," and the utterance of which "could damn any scheme, no matter how sanely conceived, of economic amelioration or regeneration" (373). Fredric Jameson equates anti-Utopianism with an "easily decodable and unambiguous political position:. . . [in which] Utopia is a transparent synonym for socialism itself, and the enemies of Utopia sooner or later turn out to be the enemies of socialism."[12] Clearly, this summary of anti-Utopian views is applicable to Wickson, who points out that Ernest's argument is lacking in one vital respect. In an implicit acknowledgement of the actions available to a dominant group when its hegemonic status is threatened, Wickson tells Ernest:

> "Our reply shall be couched in terms of lead. We are in power. Nobody will deny it. By virtue of that power we shall remain in power.
> "We have no words to waste on you. When you reach out your vaunted strong hands for our palaces and purpled ease, we will show you what strength is. In roar of shell and shrapnel and in whine of machine-guns will our answer be couched. . . . There is the word. It is the king of words—Power. Not God, not Mammon, but Power. Pour it over your tongue till it tingles with it. Power." (384)

Where hegemonic discourse breaks down, it is replaced by violent domination, and Ernest acknowledges that "Power" is "the only answer that could be given." The confrontation is the precursor of the violence which dominates the second half of the novel, in which the socialists are crushed after triumphing at the ballot box. That this power includes the right to control freedom of speech, and to censor accounts of history is illustrated later in the novel by the suppression of the *Appeal To Reason*. The volumes containing Avis' father's book are found, "by arbitrary ruling. . . to be not the regular circulation of the paper, and for that reason [are] denied admission to the mails." This ban is quickly extended to the paper as a whole, which is ruled to be "seditious" (431). The suppression is completed by a "patriotic" mob, which burns down the production plant.[13]

Before inspecting Anthony Meredith's commentary in more detail, and combining the two narratives to produce an overview of *The Iron Heel*, it is necessary to complete my examination of Avis' own version of events. So far, I have only briefly mentioned the generic discontinuities within the text, choosing to concentrate on the "scientific" naturalism which constructs a series of exchanges between labour and capital. However, the political is only one among several generic strains combined within the one text. Most notably, Avis' story is also a romance, but, in addition, it contains traces of religious allegory (Ernest reminds her of "Christ!. . . [and] his end upon the cross" [361]), the adventure story, and racist tracts. Each of these layers of narrative are united by Avis, but their union does raise issues of contradiction and discontinuity. For example, Avis' early sexual longing for Ernest, during which she "grew frightened at my thoughts . . . [he was] so alien and so strong" (339), sees a split within the narrator between her repressive class ethic and her desire for the "other." However, she is soon content to slip back into her class/gender role as comforter:

> And in that moment I knew that I loved him, and that I was melting with
> desire to comfort him. . . . All my heart seemed bursting with desire to
> fold my arms around him, and to rest his head on my breast—his head that
> must be weary with so many thoughts; and to give him rest—just rest and
> easement and forgetfulness for a tender space. (361)

Later in the novel, as the Oligarchy becomes progressively more assertive, Avis is still happy to regard her principal function as bringing "forgetfulness, or the light of gladness, into those poor tired eyes of his" (440). When Avis does work, it is in the standard female occupation of secretary (443) to her husband. Even when she steps out of received gender roles, Avis is unable to throw off all her old habits: she faints when a spy begs for mercy (509), and when she is confronted by the mob (537); she is struck by a "splitting headache" (545), when trying to escape; and she is twice rescued by soldiers (540-548). Neither Ernest's own socialism, nor the commentary seem to suggest that Avis' gender role is under threat: the revolution will be for the men, and the new hegemonic group is the Brotherhood of Man.

Likewise, Avis' narrative differentiates between native born, and immigrant Americans, and between whites and other races. June Howard argues that in London's work, "a naturalistic ideology of heredity combines smoothly with the "deeds of empire" in a profoundly racist image of Anglo-Saxon superiority. That superiority is most effectively embodied, of course, in the hero."[14] London's racism is much more complex and intermittent than Howard suggests, and at times he was extremely sympathetic to non-white individuals and cultures. Likewise, his fiction contains many villainous Anglo-Saxons. However, in *The Iron Heel*, it only needs a minor modification of Howard's assertion for Avis to stress that although Ernest is working class, "he was a descendant of the old line of Everhards that for over two hundred years had lived in America" (338). She also points out that her father is of "stout old "Mayflower" stock, and the blood was imperative in him" (437), thus echoing hegemonic use of Lamarckian notions of physical inheritance as a guide to "character." In these instances, Avis' racism is at least qualified by the commentary, which comments that the "distinction between being native born and foreign born was sharp and invidious in those days" (338), and thus implies that socialism has eliminated discrimination according to birthplace. With regards to the Japanese, no such qualifications are added. Avis notes that the Japanese Oligarchy was "Most savage of all," and Japan is depicted as "ever urging and aiding the yellow and brown races against the white" (473).[15]

The generic discontinuities which fragment Avis' story are more than simple fears of otherness, and sedimented traces of her leisure class background. In addition, they produce a fundamental split within her narrative. As a naturalist account of the "inevitable" battle between capitalism and socialism, the text follows its Social Darwinist impulse, in which it is "Power" that determines denouement. However, as a sentimental romance, Avis' story is transformed into a battle of good and evil. Whereas her generalizations about the Oligarchy state that they, "as a class, believed that they alone maintained civilization" (518)—that is, they act as a result of the highest ethical motivation—the individual Oligarchs, such as Wickson, are presented as cynical and vicious thugs. At the other end of the scale, Ernest is portrayed as a hopelessly idealized figure, whereas the working classes as a whole are depicted as an uncontrollable and drunken mob. It is precisely this "potentially disruptive fissure in the text"[16] (as Howard describes the generic discontinuity between naturalism and the domestic formula) that London's other narrative attempts to close, and I now wish to examine the ways in which Meredith's commentary modifies and resolves Avis' narrative.

In his review of Louis Marin's *Utopics: Spatial Play*[17], Fredric Jameson suggests that in later Utopias, the "phantom spatial superposition" of Utopia and the Real Place—which here includes turn-of-the-century America—is assisted by "the emergence of a wholly new element, namely history itself and the new bourgeois sense of historical change and evolution." Thus, for example, when Julian West (the narrator of *Looking Backward*) "finds a new and more perfect Boston on the site of the old noisy and dirty nineteenth-century industrial metropolis of the same name," Jameson points out that Bellamy is under an "obligation to provide a historical account of the transition from old to new, or rather from reality to Utopia."[18] In the same way, in *The Iron Heel*, Avis Everhard's narrative recounts the transformation of the "real" America of emergent corporate capitalism, into the fascistic regime of the Oligarchy. Her narrative is augmented and challenged by Anthony Meredith's commentary, which provides further documentation explaining the unexpected historical evolution of the Oligarchy, and its eventual destruction by the revolutionaries. Following Ernest's own insistence on the inevitability of socialist triumph (which in turn bears close resemblance to *The Communist Manifesto*,) Meredith details the events leading up to a change of mode of production, and explains how these events took "three centuries" (322) to be completed.

Equally importantly, in terms of London's own portrayal of urban existence, Meredith also provides occasional glimpses of the "Brotherhood of Man" city, and constantly glosses Avis' narrative with observations on the "irrational and anarchic" (343) behavior of early twentieth century humans. As in Utopian narratives, the new community is established as a kind of negation of the historical/geographical conditions it is supposed to have replaced, and serves to resolve the contradictions within Avis' version of events. This can be demonstrated by a comparison of Avis' anxieties about the city, with the manner in which Meredith treats communal life. Despite her conversion to socialism, Avis Everhard's narrative depicts bourgeois fears of the mob running amok in the city, and destroying the space of the individual. During the battle for Chicago, the stream of working class faces are described in apocalyptic terms:

> It was not a column but a mob, an awful river that filled the street, the people of the abyss, mad with drink and wrong, up at last and roaring for the blood of their masters. . . . Dumb apathy had vanished. It was now dynamic—a fascinating spectacle of dread. It surged past my vision in concrete waves of wrath, snarling and growling, carnivorous, drunk with whiskey from pillaged warehouses, drunk with hatred, drunk with lust for blood—. . . the refuse and the scum of life, a raging, screaming, screeching, demoniacal horde. (535)

The mob is described in terms of a collective beast, lacking self-control and any interest in the future. Avis' concern resides in her anxieties about what Jameson calls "sheer urban concentration," and her narrative suggests "the unconscious agoraphobia of contemporary bourgeois consciousness, with its monitory images of overpopulation and its clogged dystopias of all kinds." Of course, such anxieties are at one with the desire to preserve the earlier capitalist notion of the city, with its promises of individualism, and the "emergence of the bourgeois subject."[19] However, they are clearly incompatible with Avis' own hopes for a socialist, working class triumph.

The fear of the mob is a recurrent theme in London's work. It is central to *The People of the Abyss*, and surfaces in "South of the Slot" (1909). Likewise, in "The Dream of Debs" (1914), and his other (very different) dystopian vision of the future, *The Scarlet Plague* (1915), the breakdown of hegemonic order quickly results in the mob terrorizing the bourgeois community. In *The Valley of the Moon* (1913), London produces a fictional escape from urban tension, in which the protagonists abandon the city, and establish a Utopian community in the country. Building a new community is only achieved by running away from the problem. As a solution to the "individualistic terror about urban concentration," *The Valley of the Moon* is clearly unsatisfactory, since it cancels out "that other fundamental vocation of the city to stand as the locus and the figure of collective life."[20] In *The Iron Heel*, however, the escape is to be found in a new kind of city, where collectivity and "simplicity of living" (369) have replaced individualism. After the revolution, the Oligarchy's "wonder cities" (469), such as Ardis and Asgard are transformed to house communities which "know nothing of bloodshed" (484), and which have abolished private property (501). Thus, despite the increase in population (Meredith comments that twentieth century California was "sparsely populated") (547), class has been eradicated and even racism is not a problem (338-365).

Although it would be too much to claim that the limited information provided about Ardis and Asgard gives a comprehensive, point by point negation of the real industrial American city, enough detail is available to suggest that they represent a collective vision of the future, occupied communally by the Brotherhood of Man in opposition to the capitalist ideology of individualism. This observation is reinforced by remembering that the cities were constructed by the Oligarchs as a space "by"—that is "in proximity to" and "by means of"—the industrial community. Ardis and Asgard thus lack the slums and factories which defined the urban America of the turn-of-the-century. Furthermore, the Brotherhood of Man offers a fictional "perfected community," which does away with the "fundamental contradiction about capitalism. . . [i.e.](the paradox of a collective social form organized on the basis of individual profit)."[21] In this, the Utopian cities are beyond the imaginative limits of Avis Everhard's bourgeois ideology, since her fear of the mob represents an apparently unconquerable class position. Perhaps they are also beyond London's own historical imagination, considering the minimal detail he provides. If we accept the limits of Jameson's "closed system," it would take an "extreme gesture" to "eradicate the contradictions of the system."[22] However, the addition of the commentary is, at the very least, an attempt to deconstruct and supplement the narrative voice which Avis provides, and an outline of an economic system in which all individuals are equally within, rather than "by" the industrial community.

Until now, I have treated London's twin narratives in *The Iron Heel*, as being related, but separate. London's voices act in a dialogical relationship, in which each provides new insights into the other, filling in the absent spaces in the two texts. Although the division is clear, however, it now remains to reconstruct the versions of events presented by Avis Everhard and Anthony Meredith, and remember that they are both subsumed within that totality which is London's novel. This process can be regarded as a continuation (or inversion) of the earlier breakdown of Avis' narrative into a combination of fragmented layers, in which the commentary is now viewed as one more generic discontinuity among many. *The Iron Heel* can thus be seen as an amalgamation of (amongst others) naturalist novel, sentimental romance, and Utopian fiction, with each of these generic types progressing according to its own structural "logic," and reaching a meaningful conclusion in its own different way. Thus, the romance attains a generically satisfactory closure when Avis and Ernest are reunited in Chicago, after enforced separation. The plot sticks closely to London's own rules for popular romance, outlined in *Martin Eden* (1909), in which "marriage bells" act as the inescapable conclusion. However, the opening page of Avis' narrative tells us that Ernest is already dead (323), a fact uncomfortably at odds with the romance and its happy ending, and it would be hard to describe *The Iron Heel* as "light literature."

Likewise, the abrupt ending of Avis' record implicates her in events in a most non-naturalistic manner: her narrative is cut off in mid-sentence, in a dramatic example of a hegemonic group's ability to censor versions of "truth." Although this ending is clearly compatible with the naturalist strategy of "catastrophic closure,"[23] as identified by June Howard in Norris' *The Octopus* among others, the effect here is to deny Avis the control generally accorded to the "privileged" narrator, and to shatter the illusion that the narrator is somehow free in a deterministic universe. The commentary speculates that Avis "must have fled or was captured" (553), negating the usual naturalist expectation that, as Howard puts it:

> although the menacing and vulnerable Other is incapable of acting as a self-conscious, purposeful agent, he can only be observed and analyzed by such an agent. Sometimes this perspective is inscribed in the text through a character, sometimes it is embodied only by the narrator or implied author. But although we explore determinism, we are never submerged in it and ourselves become the brute.[24]

It is left to Meredith to complete Avis' task, and to illustrate how she eventually succumbed to that other naturalist peril, proletarianization, in which she becomes the silenced, hunted "brute." For Avis and her father, this process contains two distinct developments: initially, they regard proletarianization as a rejuvenating experience, which enables them to "unlearn" the habits of their class, and to acquire (some) of the collective actions of their new peers. However, as a result of the battles for power which ensue, her father is denied a voice via the suppression of his book, misrepresented as making a "howling anarchistic speech" (429), and later vanishes, presumed dead (503). Likewise, Avis welcomes her new environment, but is forced into silence and flight, and can only be judged by others. (Although it is common in naturalism for bourgeois characters to sink into otherness, as is the case with Magnus Derrick in *The Octopus*, and George Hurstwood in *Sister Carrie*, they are not primary focalizers. Norris uses Presley and a narrator as free agents, and Dreiser's narrator speculates on determinism without becoming implicated by its rules. Although Derrick and Hurstwood function, at times, as secondary focalizers, they do not act as the reader's guide in the same way as Avis Everhard.[25])

The historical, retrospective version of events, offered by Anthony Meredith from a Utopian future thus emerges as the privileged voice in the text. It, alone, is not undermined from within, and it is the voice which attains satisfactory generic closure. Meredith offers both a critique of twentieth century America, and an alternative, compensatory vision of a classless society. Although the transformation from one to the other is very different from Bellamy's bloodless transition, in *Looking Backward*, the change acts as a similar reassurance about the future. As in the earlier book, contemporary America is "a distant curiosity sealed safely and harmlessly in an attic of history,"[26] and the new America comes across as a "golden age."

However, this panaceaic vision of the future is simultaneously a review of the omnipresent class battles of London's own time. Although Meredith offers a fictional escape from conflict—Utopia being both *good* place and no place—he continually reminds his readers of that conflict. In addition, he suggests that the immediate future is bleak, since it will be three hundred years before the Brotherhood of Man triumphs. It is not until his later fiction that London seeks more immediate escapes from urban class wars, transplanting his characters into the country, the South Seas, and the past.[27]

NOTES

[1] Quoted in London, Jack: *The Iron Heel*, New York: Macmillan, 1908. Reprinted in London, Jack: *Novels and Social Writings*, Cambridge: Library of America, 1982, 315-553; Footnote, 389. Subsequent page numbers from this edition are referred to in parentheses in the text.

[2] Benjamin, Walter: "Theses on the Philosophy of History," in *Illuminations*, translated by Harry Zohn, New York: Schocken, 1969, 256.

[3] Veblen, Thorstein: *The Theory of the Leisure Class*, New York: Mentor, 1953, 164.

[4] Godden, Richard: Fictions of Capital: *The American Novel from James to Mailer*, Cambridge: Cambridge U P, 1990, 3. See Godden's "Introduction" and Chapter I for a more detailed investigation of this point.

[5] London, Jack: *The People of the Abyss*, New York: Macmillan, 1903. Reprinted in London: *Novels and Social Writings*, 1-184, 7-9.

[6] Buhle, Paul: *Marxism in the USA: From 1870 to the Present Day*, London: Verso, 1987, 64. See Chapter 2 of Buhle's book for an outline of the history of Utopian literature in the USA. See also, Michael Denning, *Mechanic Accents: Dime Novels and Working-Class Culture in America*, London: Verso, 1987, 85-117, for an exploration of the "paradoxical union of sensational fiction and radical politics" (87) manifested in the writing of George Lippard.

[7] Twain, Mark: *A Connecticut Yankee at King Arthur's Court*, Harmondsworth: Penguin, 1971 (1889). Donnelly, Ignatius: *Caesar's Column: A Story of the Twentieth Century*, Cambridge, Mass.: Belknap Press, 1960 (1890). Bellamy, Edward: *Looking Backward*, Harmondsworth: Penguin, 1986 (1888). For an account of London's reading as he prepared to write *The Iron Heel*, see Charles N. Watson, *The Novels of Jack London: A Reappraisal*, Madison: U of Wisconsin P, 1983, 99-112. Watson pays particular attention to *Caesar's Column*, and points out that the final third of *The Iron Heel* is closely influenced by Donnelly's novel. In 1902, London wrote to his publisher that he wished to write a book "with which I shall bid for a popularity such as Bellamy received," and *The Iron Heel* is his only book related to this statement. (See Susan Ward, "Ideology for the Masses: Jack London's *The Iron Heel*" in: Jacqueline Tavernier-Courbin (ed.), *Critical Essays on Jack London*, Boston, Mass.: G. K. Hall, 1983, 166-79, 167.)

[8] Martin, Ronald E.: *American Literature and the Universe of Force*, Durham, North Carolina: Duke U P, 1981, 193-94, 212.

[9] Howard, June: *Form and History in American Literary Naturalism*, Chapel Hill: U of North Carolina P, 1985, 159.

[10] Crane, Stephen: "The Open Boat," in Crane, Stephen: *Great Short Works*, New York: Harper & Row, 1968, 277-302, 277-79.

[11] Chametzky, Jules: "Realism, Cultural Politics, and Language as Mediation in Mark Twain and Others," in *Prospects* 8 (1983), 183-95, 192.

[12] Jameson, Fredric: "Of Islands and Trenches: Neutralization and the Production of Utopian Discourse," in Jameson, Fredric: *The Ideologies of Theory: Essays, 1971-1986.* 2 *Syntax of History*, 75-101, 76-77.

[13] The treatment of hegemonic control of the arts and media in *The Iron Heel* proved to be remarkably prophetic in many ways: For example, when the novel was published, it was "largely ignored by the same newspapers that had hailed [London's] earlier books, and had almost no sale." It was only with the onset of the First World War and the coming of Fascism that its prophetic nature led to renewed interest. See Max Lerner, Introduction to Jack London, *The Iron Heel*, New York: Sagamore Press, 1957, viii-ix.

During the War, the *Masses* was suppressed under the 1917 Espionage and Sedition Acts. See John Graham (ed.), *"Yours for the Revolution:"* The Appeal To Reason *1895-1922*, London: University of Nebraska Press, 1990, 283-88, for evidence of just how accurate London's other prophecies proved. For example, in 1918, striking steelworkers in Weirton, West Virginia, were forced to kiss the American flag by citizens. The 1918 Sedition Act "made it a crime to 'utter, print, write, or publish any disloyal, profane, scurrilous, or abusive language about the form of government of the United States,' [and] opened the way to stifle any criticism that remained." Postmaster Burleson rapidly implemented the Espionage Act of 1917 to censor fifteen major publications: Burleson decided (backed by the Supreme Court) "that once censored, a publication was no longer 'continuous,' and consequently no longer entitled to a second class permit." This repressive atmosphere made "anything less than absolute endorsement of the war grounds for intimidation and prosecution."

[14] Howard: *Form and History in American Literary Naturalism*, 173.

[15] This hegemonic fear of Japan has persisted throughout the century: A report commissioned by the CIA, entitled *Japan 2000*, "warned that Japan's 'world dominance appears inescapable and incontrovertible' in the absence of 'some dramatic unified reassertion of Western intent.' It warned. . . that Japan was a 'racist and non-democratic' culture whose values 'are unimpeded by any sense of international responsibility of global welfare.'" Quoted in Martin Walker, "America's Victory Dilemma," in The *Guardian*, September 20, 1991, 19.

[16] Howard: *Form and History in American Literary Naturalism*, 180.

[17] Marin, Louis: *Utopics: Spatial Play*, translated by Robert A. Vollrath, Atlantic Highlands, New Jersey: Humanities Press, 1984.

[18] Jameson: "Of Islands and Trenches," 84-85.

[19] Ibid., 89.

[20] Ibid., 90.

[21] Ibid., 89-90.

[22] Ibid., 91.

[23] Howard: *Form and History in American Literary Naturalism*, 142.

[24] Ibid., 104.

[25] See Norris, Frank: *The Octopus*, in Norris, Frank: *Novels and Essays*, Cambridge: Library of America, 1986, 573-1098 (1901), and Dreiser, Theodore: *Sister Carrie*, Harmondsworth: Penguin, 1986 (1900).

[26] Tichi, Cecelia: "Introduction" to Bellamy: *Looking Backward*, 7-27, 13.

[27] London's last four major novels all encapsulate this shift. *Burning Daylight* (1910) and *The Valley of the Moon* (1913) both involve movement from the city to the country; *The Star Rover* (1915) narrates a series of past lives of a condemned murderer;

and *The Little Lady of the Big House* (1916) is set on the estate of a wealthy farmer. *Adventure* (1911) takes place in the South Seas, with the substitution of racial for class tensions. *Martin Eden* (1909), London's next novel after *The Iron Heel*, envisages a similar shift to the South Seas. However, Eden commits suicide as a result of the overpowering ennui he contracts in bourgeois America, and his imperialist project is not put into operation.

◄ 6 ►

The Valley of the Moon

Early Reviews

Jack London's Latest Novel: In *The Valley of the Moon* He Writes of Love and Sociology

E. F. Edgett

Unrestrainedly lavish of himself is Jack London in *The Valley of the Moon*. A long novel, it is the epitome of his style, his theories and his genius. His fable is plausible, ingenious and entertaining, and woven into it are the many problems of society and industry that present themselves to the mind of a Socialist for solution. Mr. London, however, does not let his sociological beliefs run away with him to the disaster of his story. He has the shrewdness of the practiced novelist, and he knows that his characters and incidents must be a part of his presentation and argument of the status of modern society, and that they must be a part of his story.

Few phases of our present industrial turmoil are neglected by Mr. London in *The Valley of the Moon*. Strikes and other forms of labor unrest, with an eloquent statement of the problems peculiar to the invasion and usurpation of California by the Japanese, the Portuguese and other peoples, are constantly in the forefront of his novel, and he is never hesitant in his description of the brutal element of mankind. In fact, the first chapters of the story are scarcely anything more than a continuous "rough-house"—a picturesquely descriptive word that we use for want of a better, and because it frequently recurs in Mr. London's pages—and he gives us one scene after another in which more than one man is deliberately mauled to his death. "Beaten up" is a phrase that comes trippingly from Mr. London's pen, and he apparently takes no little delight in setting before his readers a minute description of a strike riot in the streets of Oakland, and a vivid account of a prizefight from the lips of its defeated participant who reached home late at night in such condition that he was unrecognizable to his wife.

> Though she had heard his voice and knew him to be Billy, for the instant she did not recognize him. His face was a face she had never known. Swollen, bruised, discolored, every feature had been beaten out of all semblance of familiarity, one eye was entirely closed, the other showed through a narrow slit of blood-congested flesh. One ear seemed to have lost most of its skin. The whole face was a swollen pulp. His right jaw, in particular, was twice the size of the left. No wonder his speech had been thick, was her thought, as she regarded the fearfully cut and swollen lips that still bled. She was sickened by the sight and her heart went out to him in a great wave of tenderness. She wanted to put her arms around him and cuddle and soothe him, but her practical judgment bade otherwise.

Let the reader not imagine that this short paragraph is the extent of Mr. London's description of physical violence. It is the least of many horrible scenes that fill the first half of the novel. In his plot Mr. London carries along, always directly in the eye of the reader, a man and a woman, both of downfallen American descent, both of the extreme lower classes, both illiterate, both slangy of speech, but both possessed of traits that lift them above the men and women among whom they live. Billy Roberts and Saxon Brown meet, they are mutually attracted, he by her feminine charm and delicacy, and she by his manly boyishness, his brawn and his protective attitude over all womankind. He is a teamster and an amateur prize-fighter of considerable local reputation, and she is a laundry washer. They marry, undergo numerous vicissitudes and periods of personal and marital depression until finally Saxon sees and leads the way out of their difficulties. They plan to leave the city with all its economic unrest and disturbances for the freedom of the country, and penniless though they are Saxon was sure that that was their only destiny.

More than a third of the story is given to their rambles through the country and to their search for a habitation, and it is there that Mr. London exploits his views regarding the occupancy of California by the shrewd and thrifty foreigners, and their driving out of the original settlers of English ancestry. The case is presented fairly and squarely, perhaps more eloquently than it has ever before been given in any conventional economic study, and in its appeal to the wisdom and common sense of the reader it has as effective a place in the story as have its romantic incidents. Although both Billy Roberts and Saxon are somewhat too fluent of speech—Mr. London even goes so far as to cause his heroine to speak of the "unspeakable color" of a sea-scene—and at times too much the novelist's own mouthpieces, it must be confessed that they are never otherwise than enlightening. "I should guess not," Billy Roberts remarks when his wife says that "Work isn't everything." And he continues:

> "Why, look here, Saxon, what'd it mean if I worked teamin' in Oakland for a million dollars a day for a million years and just had to go on stayin' there an' livin' the way we used to? It'd mean work all day, three squares, an' movin' pictures for recreation. Movin' pictures! Huh! We're livin' movin' pictures these days. I'd sooner have one year like what we're havin' here in Carmel and then die, than a thousan' million years like on Pine street."

Aside from the industrial problems that are so wisely and pleasurably considered by Mr. London, the story does not lack the graces of romantic fiction. Doubtless both the characters and the relations of Billy Roberts and Saxon Brown are highly idealized, both before and after marriage, and unquestionably too great stress is laid upon his physical prowess, and too much glory given to him for his ability to protect a woman from insult simply because the other man is afraid of him and trembles at his pugilistic reputation. But is must be confessed that the wooing of Saxon Brown is delicious in its restraint and commendation must be given to Mr. London for his thoroughly consistent account of pure love and personal adoration between man and woman. There is both the fleshly and the spiritual in the love of Billy Roberts and Saxon Brown, and Mr. London mingles them with a judicious skill that shows his absolute command of human nature.

We have to thank Mr. London for telling us the story of a marriage that turned out happily. Contrary to the impression given us by fiction, not only in this but in all other epochs, happy marriages are possible, and Mr. London's description of the love-life of Billy Roberts and Saxon Brown is singularly real. It contains no excessive sentimentality, and it brings before us the woman as she is, the man as he is, and the man and woman as they are. Both suffer on occasions, and both recover from their physical and their mental ills. Both are shrewd-minded observers, both of themselves and of the life about them, and we may forgive Mr. London readily when once in a while their philosophy seems somewhat beyond the reach of the intellect with which he endows them. Here, for instance, is a moment when their reasoning is perfectly plausible. Billy Roberts is answering Saxon's question as to whether other girls have not loved him, and he is obliged to confess that they have. "Well, it wasn't my fault," he said slowly.

> "If they wanted to look sideways at me it was up to them. And it was up to me to sidestep if I wanted to, wasn't it? You've no idea, Saxon, how a prize fighter is run after. Why, sometimes it's seemed to me that girls an' women ain't got an ounce of natural shame in their make-up. Oh, I was never afraid of them, believe me, but I didn't hanker after 'em. A man's a fool that'd let them kind get his goat."

By his wild chase through the highways and byways of literature during the past ten years, Mr. London has filled many of his readers with not a little apprehension. They recognized him as a man of genius, but they never knew into what his genius would take him. At times he seemed to be running amuck with it. In *The Valley of the Moon* are to be found certain tendencies of this. He gives us too much of himself, too much of everything under the literary sun. He is too liberal. He does not conserve his forces. Yet, in spite of all this, his latest novel is a novel for all thoughtful readers. It is filled with all the usual Jack London short-comings—the greatest being lack of restraint—but it is at the same time a notably faithful study of a variety of critical social conditions, and at the same time a significant story.

Boston Evening Transcript, November 8, 1913, Sec. 3, 8.

Jack London Writes Genial "Back to the Land" Book—Latest Fiction Crop

To begin with, Jack London's *The Valley of the Moon* (Macmillan) is unlike any book of his we have met before, an extremely pleasant and genial book, holding the reader's attention to the end, which means through 530 closely printed pages. In it he develops various theories, some of which he explains and demonstrates, while others must be taken on faith. For instance, his hero, his heroine and pretty nearly everyone who amounts to anything are of what he calls "Saxon" blood, the inference being that their descent is direct, with as little admixture as possible, from the energetic Teutons who conquered Britain, and whose descendants, he assumes, settled America and made their way across the continent to the Pacific coast. The enduring virtue and value of that stock he rates very high; the merits of Portuguese, Greeks, Chinese, Japanese, Dagoes and others which he has occasion to mention seem somehow of a much lower order. Mr. London seems as fully convinced as was the late lamented author of "Pinafore" that it is creditable to be an Englishman.

  As a work of art his story may be compared to the pride of the New England housewife, the patchwork quilt. Vivid blocks of realism, brilliant scraps of California scenery, sober bits of preaching, put together rather haphazard, wherever they will be effective. The background is solid and of one texture, the desirability for the man who would be free to turn from the city and toil on the land. If the reader is not thoroughly sure of this by the time he has finished the book Mr. London's effort has been vain.

  The heroine and the hero meet in the slums of Oakland. She is a working girl, employed in a laundry. Saxon by name and by ancestry, he is a teamster and prizefighter, likewise of pure breed, though his name is Bill. They fall in love at first sight and are soon married, but not before the reader has tasted the rude amusements of the poor, has seen the degrading life in workshop and tenement house and has watched several lively fights. He is also certain of the intrinsic nobility of each, and has heard each tell the other more than once how their immediate forbears crossed the plains as pioneers.

After a brief interval of domestic bliss there is a strike in Oakland in which Bill goes out. He takes to attacking strike breakers and also to drink; she takes to thinking. There is a lively description of a riot, there are accounts of brutality on both sides, there are bitter arraignments of industrial conditions and of the misuse of power by capital. The outcome is that Bill goes to jail for assault, that the two come near breaking apart, and that Saxon in destitution wanders by the waterside picking up driftwood and scraps and does more thinking. She meets a boy in a boat who puts the idea of getting away into her head. When Bill comes out, completely sobered, she makes him share the idea. They leave Oakland, nearly penniless, to seek a home where they may be free.

Here the romantic part begins. The two wander up and down California watching what people are doing with the land. Bill supports them by taking odd jobs when necessary, but both keep their eyes open and they move on when they have learned their lesson. They are treated with great kindness by many people, including that inevitable group of Bohemians. Saxon assimilates culture with amazing facility, Bill develops horse sense; the two investigate agricultural conditions, the training of the body and other matters with the eagerness of a Government report. Their long wanderings allow the author to expatiate on the geography and advantages of California. Finally they find the place they have been longing for in the Sonoma Valley, the difficulties in the way for their acquiring it are removed rapidly, they find inspiring neighbors, and prosperity as well as freedom and happiness in their grasp.

They are delightful young people whose adventures it is a pleasure to follow; but not withstanding Bill's picturesque and vigorous vocabulary and Saxon's weakness for dainty underwear and her mother's primitive poetry, both suffer a little from the author regarding them as types rather than individuals. We are glad that Mr. London has faith in the Saxon element in our population at least.

New York Sun November 8, 1913, 8.

Jack London: His *Valley of the Moon* a Pioneer Story

Helen Bullis

Perhaps every good press agent has something of the preacher in him, and perhaps every successful preacher has something of the press-agent. In his latest story Jack London is very much of both.

In Billy Roberts, prizefighter and teamster, and in Saxon, his wife, the author has typified the multitude of descendants of "the finest stock in the world"—that adventurous pioneering stock that poured over the Alleghanies and streamed in thin lines across the thirsty plains to fulfill the dream of the old discoverers and empire-planners of the Pacific Coast. But the old stock had the defects of its qualities. It derived from Saxon and Norman sea-rovers, from French *coureurs des bois*—all men of their hands, accustomed to act first and think afterward, men whose view was limited only by the horizon toward which they rode, to whom the little virtues of prudence and economy were meaner than vices. Their children inherited their point of view without their opportunities, perhaps without their sturdiness of soul, and according to a diatribe Mr. London puts into the mouth of one of his characters, the country became "a gambler's paradise."

To-day, the descendants of the Argonauts are herded in cities, working for masters, competing, struggling, striking, going under, while the land which their fathers won becomes the property of a horde of Asiatics and southern Europeans. And then—

> "But if this goes on, what is left for us?" asked Saxon.
> "What is happening. Those of us who haven't anything rot in the cities. Those of us who have land, sell it and go to the cities. Some become larger capitalists; some go into the professions; the rest spend their money and start rotting when it's gone, and if it lasts their lifetime their children do the rotting for them."

It is a gloomy picture, but we feel the too frequent truth of it. Mr. London has never done better work than in his description of the life of Billy Roberts and his wife in Oakland. The strike, in particular, with its culminating bloody scene which made a shambles of their front yard and cost Saxon her baby and almost her husband, stands up strongly and vividly in three dimensions:

> It was battle without quarter—a massacre. The scabs and their protectors, surrounded, backed against Saxon's fence fought like cornered rats, but could not withstand the rush of a hundred men. Clubs and pickhandles were swinging, revolvers were exploding, and cobblestones were flung with crushing effect at arm's distance. Saxon saw young Frank Davis, a friend of Bert's and a father of several month's standing, press the muzzle of his revolver against a scab's stomach and fire. There were curses and snarls of rage, wild cries of terror and pain. Mercedes was right. These things were not men. They were beasts, fighting over bones, destroying one another for bones.

At last, her husband in jail, herself almost starving, out of a sort of madness Saxon draws the inspiration that saves them both. On his release, they pack a roll of blankets, and with a capital of $30, start on a new Canterbury Pilgrimage. The object of their quest is the "Government Land" they have heard of, land that they can grow out of and into and raise a new generation upon—"a valley in the moon," they call it as the likelihood of reaching it grows more remote. But the dream finally comes true, and the story ends like the most orthodox of fairy tales, with a "and they lived happy forever after."

Some time before this satisfactory conclusion, Jack London, the preacher, has joined hands with Jack London, the press agent. California, the great, the glorious, the golden, is the burden of his song. Billy and Saxon stray the length and breadth of it, running across women intensive farmers who take them in and reveal the enormous profits that ten acres are capable of yielding; a colony of literary and artistic folk who go in for intensive athletics and intensive poetry, and entertain the wandering prizefighter and his pretty wife with intensive hospitality; more intensive farmers, and a philosopher who has never farmed but can tell anybody exactly how to do it, because "he is a student of good. He studies all good things done by good men under the sun."

Of course, everybody is strictly native—no effete first-generation trekker from the East among them, and to point the moral more pointedly, they are all of the same pure Saxon stock, and are engaged in the same struggle to hold their own against more efficient agriculturists—Chinese, Portuguese, and Dalmatian. Here and there the colors are laid on so lavishly that it occurs to the reader that he must be perusing a romance written by Miss Marie Coreill under the direction of the Department of Agriculture: but it is a proof of the immense vitality of Mr. London's book that it shoulders off, as it were, page after page of descriptive incubus, and emerges with "all its silk," to use Billy's favorite prizefighter's phrase.

If the author had only applied his own theories and adopted "intensive" methods in writing *The Valley of the Moon*, he might have produced not only a vastly interesting and suggestive book, but a great one. As it is, it spreads like a rich quarter section under partial cultivation. And if a quick rotation of crops gets good results in the Sonoma valley, why should not a reasonable rotation of synonyms improve the product of the literary field? As of old, when Mr. London finds a word or a phrase he likes, he works it to death. In *John Barleycorn* it was "jingled," which was at least good expressive slang. In *The Valley of the Moon* it is "pretties," which isn't anything, apparently, except a fool word, and the repetition of it becomes maddening.

Yet, when all is said and done, Mr. London has written a man's size book, containing a man's size idea. The land is still the ancient Mother, from whom we come, and to whom we go. On her breath is healing and in her lap is peace. We need sanguine, enthusiastic books to reminds us of her, to renew our faith in her, to inspire us to return to her.

If only Mr. London would not write (to use one of his own locutions) so much like Mr. Man-in-a-Hurry!

New York Times November 9, 1913, 607.

Fiction: *The Valley of the Moon*

A reasonable belief that the first novel received for 1914 was an average specimen of the coming output would enable us to wish our fellow-reviewers a "Happy New Year" with some hopefulness of fulfillment. The story is that of a working-class couple ideally mated. Before their marriage he is a prizefighter, and she is a laundry-hand. An appalling picture of the life she escapes by wedlock is given, as well as more than one vivid description of his competence in the ring. She is possessed of that marvelous strength of sacrifice on behalf of her man which can only be properly appreciated, perhaps, by those who have experienced it. He has the gentleness which goes with strength under control, though he all but loses it when his temper is upset by a strike of teamsters, his mates in a calling which he follows after his marriage. Their flight from the sordid struggle of the town to the open solves the struggle of existence for them, and, further, makes the opportunity somewhat too obviously for a display of much agricultural lore in an atmosphere the sweetness of which becomes cloying towards the end of the tale.

The narrative is written breezily throughout, though the author's handling of the bellows has not been sufficiently masked. He has, perhaps, more scorn for, than sympathy with, the pettiness with which he is obliged to endow many of his puppets in order that they may be true to life. The individualism of Socialists, and the trickery by which even the well-intentioned are content to earn a living, are, after all, but the natural concomitants of an environment in which the breadth of outlook is lacking to make "Waste not, want not," a world-maxim.

The tale, which is essentially American, may not appeal to all English readers, but, though the conditions vary in different lands, the author has grasped the essential traits of humanity in its present stage of development, and such understanding being a necessary preliminary to further advance, any one who helps us to it deserves our thanks.

Athenaeum 4497 (January 3, 1914), 4.

Our Booking-Office

Mr. Punch's Staff of Learned Clerks

If for nothing else, Mr. Jack London's latest story would deserve a welcome for its topicality. In these days of strikes and industrial conflict every one might be glad to know what a writer of his individuality has to say about unions and blacklegs and picketing. True, this is hardly the kind of thing that one has learnt to associate with his name; and for that reason perhaps I best liked *The Valley of the Moon* (Mills and Boon) after its hero and heroine had shaken the unsavory dust of the town from their feet and set them towards the open country. But much had to happen first. The hero was big Billy Roberts, a teamster with the heart of a child and the strength of a prize-fighter—which was in fact his alternative profession. He married Saxon Brown ("a scream of a name" her friend called it when introducing them to each other), and for a time their life together was as nearly idyllic as newly-wedded housekeeping in a mean street could permit it to be. Then came the lean years: strikes and strike-breaking, sabotage and rioting, prison for Billy, and all but starvation for Saxon. Perhaps you know already that peculiar gift of Mr. Jack London's that makes you not only see physical hardship but suffer it? I believe that after these chapters the reader of them will never again be able to regard a newspaper report of street-fighting with the same detachment as before, so vivid are they, so haunting. In the end, however, as I say, we find a happier atmosphere. The adventures of Billy and Saxon, tramping it in search of a home, soon make their urban terrors seem to them and the reader a kind of nightmare. Here Mr. London is at his delightful best, and his word-pictures of country scenes are as fresh and fine as anything he has yet done. *The Valley of the Moon*, in short, is really two stories—one grim, one pleasant, and both brilliantly successful.

Punch 146 (January 7, 1914), 19.

Recent Reflections of a Novel-Reader

I would not make oath that *The Valley of the Moon* is not something of a fairy-tale, yet if it is not true, it ought to be. Billy Roberts, a sweet-tempered teamster who occasionally works at prize-fighting, and his wife, a pretty girl who does "fancy starch" in an Oakland laundry, sicken of the town. The wife discovers that "poor people can't be happy in the city where they have labor-troubles all the time," so, being of sound country stock, the two set out with knapsacks on their backs to find their way home to the soil. They are not yet, you see, true city-dwellers, or they would throw stones, explode bombs, and demand that somebody better their condition. The book is a chapter from the pilgrimage of our nation back to the land, which it has so lately, yet already so disastrously, left. There are many thousand chapters to be written in that book. The more convincingly they are indited, the better for us all. Perhaps Jack London paints the blessings of ranching in California in high colors, but the subject is one that tempts to emphasis. The book is the most refreshing its author has written, and even if over-roseate, it is really practical. When Billy Roberts remarks, after sleeping a few nights in the open, "'Gee! I don't care if I never see a moving-picture show again!'" he puts his finger in one sentence upon the disease of our city-ridden age and its cure. Only as we escape the horrors that we ourselves have created in the towns can we free ourselves from need for the opiate we have devised to deaden them.

Atlantic Monthly 113 (April 1914), 494.

Introduction to *The Valley of the Moon*

Russ Kingman

The Valley of the Moon has been out of print in the United States for several years. This republication makes a truly unique book available again. The story carries on the American literary tradition advocating a life style based on a closeness to the soil, a rejection of urban values and problems, and an appreciation for the pleasures of "the road"—the theme which has appealed to American writers from Walt Whitman to Jack Kerouac. The story is set in Northern California, and the reader is treated to vivid descriptions of a California less crowded where the natural environment still makes the predominant impact on human senses.

    The Valley of the Moon is a proletarian novel portraying the point of view of the working class—a viewpoint seldom elucidated in American letters.

    Fiction at the turn of the century expressed primarily the genteel side of life. Stephen Crane, Frank Norris, and others had made great contributions to the school of realism, but it was Jack London's vigor and strength of narrative style that made realism a vital part of American literature. His writings are alive with virility, and his characters are exceedingly true to the lives of the people he used for models. The introduction to *Tales of Adventure* describes it perfectly:

> The world was still knee-deep in Victorian morals, traditions, and ideals when Jack London burst upon the literary scene. To the generations exposed to the sentimental pap of the popular writers of the day, his stories of savage realism and heroic conflict had the effect of a tidal wave, sweeping before them the false, romantic idealism that was the vogue. . . . He bridged the gap between the nineteenth and twentieth centuries and blazed the trail for a new, more realistic school of writing.

This is especially true of *The Valley of the Moon* which came right out of London's heart and his own experience. Saxon Brown and Billy Roberts, the central characters, are a composite drawn largely from Jack and Charmian London.

    The story is a California romance based on London's youth in Oakland, his experiences with the Bohemian artists in Carmel, his four-horse trip to Oregon in 1911, his many adventures on the delta waters off the Sacramento and San Joaquin Rivers, and his ranch in the actual Valley of the Moon, just sixty miles north of San Francisco. These experiences are mirrored in the lives of Billy and Saxon, who, leaving behind a miserable working class existence in Oakland, embark on an epic walking journey in search of prosperity, fulfillment, and a dream ranch they thought could only exist in "a valley on the moon."

Jack London arrived in Oakland in 1886 during an era when East Bay culture was just beginning to develop. Oakland's population mushroomed from 48,682 in 1890 to over 150,000 in 1910, with most of the growth due to the influx of people from San Francisco following the earthquake and fire of 1906. The rapid growth resulted in economic and social disorganization to which was added severe industrial turmoil as, nationwide, the old capitalistic system was wrecked by the early struggles of the fledgling labor movement during the early twentieth century. To help support his impoverished family during those years, Jack worked at a prodigious number of odd jobs. But his real introduction to the system which he was later to term the "economic trap," came in 1890 when, like Billy and Saxon, he graduated from grammar school right into a job working ten or more hours a day, six days a week, for wages averaging ten cents an hour.

> I was barely turned fifteen, and working long hours in a cannery. Month in and month out, the shortest day I ever worked was ten hours. When to ten hours of actual work at a machine is added the noon hour; the walking to work and walking home from work; the getting up in the morning, dressing, and eating; the eating at night, undressing, and going to bed, there remains no more than the nine hours out of the twenty-four required by a healthy youngster for sleep. . . . Many a night I did not knock off work until midnight. On occasion I worked eighteen and twenty hours on a stretch. Once I worked at my machine for thirty-six consecutive hours. And there were weeks on end when I never knocked off work earlier than eleven o'clock, got home and in bed at half after midnight, and was called at half-past five to dress, eat, walk to work, and be at my machine at seven o-clock whistle blow.

From this experience, Jack London developed a feeling of love and kinship for the exploited workers of the world and contempt of gigantic proportions for those who willingly exploited them. Strong seeds of rebellion were born and flourished in this work-beast environment. It was a world controlled by capitalism—rich versus poor, and the educated versus the ignorant. His feelings of kinship appear in *The Valley of the Moon* in his powerful description of Billy and Saxon's Oakland experiences.

But Jack yearned for something better, and the books he read awakened him to possibilities. In the novel, this awakening comes to Saxon through a young fisherman on the Bay, whose advice, "Oakland is just a place to start from," becomes her strength in leaving behind her miserable life there. The Bay fisherman is surely a personification of the obsession that fired Jack London to brief stints as an oyster pirate, fish patrolman, and able-bodied seaman. These periodic escapes from the city made apparent to him the folly of remaining caught in its urban industrial bondage.

Billy and Saxon express the same realization when Saxon comments, "All I do know is that poor people can't be happy in the city where they have labor troubles all the time. If they can't be happy in the country, then there's no happiness anywhere, and that doesn't seem fair, does it?"

With their bindles on their backs, Billy and Saxon begin a walking trip through Northern California—a journey which serves as their educational awakening and eventually leads them to their dream ranch in Sonoma Valley—the Valley of the Moon.

They first meet Mrs. Mortimer, a thriving gentlewoman farmer, formerly a head librarian, who has learned her skills from books. From her they learn that with a limited amount of land, money, and labor, it is possible to live comfortably and with style in the country. The characterization of Mrs. Mortimer is almost certainly drawn in part from Jack's mentor, Oakland city librarian Ina Coolbrith.

The walking journey continues south to Carmel, where the former teamster and fancy starch laundress encounter the playful Bohemian artists' colony. Prior to 1906, many of Jack London's artist friends had congregated in a Bohemian-like subculture which revolved around the famous Coppa's Restaurant in San Francisco. George Sterling, Xavier Martinez, Jimmy Hopper, Herman Whitaker, Edwin Emerson, Gelett Burgess, Porter Garnett, Will and Wallace Irwin, Bobby Aitken, Perry and "Buttsky" Newberry, Harry A. Lafler, Maynard Dixon, Arnold Genthe and others were among the group. After the earthquake and fire, many of the Coppa's group fled to Carmel and formed the nucleus of the Carmel art colony. They were joined there by Harry Leon Wilson, Ferdinand Burgdorff, Sinclair Lewis, Mary Austin, and others.

As Billy and Saxon join the tribe of abalone eaters at Bierce's Cove, London gives the reader an inside look at the Lotus-land antics of these famous personalities. Jimmy Hopper is met as Jim Hazard, George Sterling as Mark Hall, Herbert Bashford as the drama critic, and probably Harry Lafler, the poet, as Hafler. Jack and Charmian London appear later as Jack and Clara Hastings.

From the Bohemians, Billy and Saxon learn a principle very important to Jack London—that grownups, like children, can successfully mix work with play and be light spirited. This ideal becomes an essential ingredient of the life they are seeking.

After wintering in Carmel, the adventurers return to the road in the spring. Their wandering takes them north to the river lands of the Sacramento and San Joaquin deltas where they meet Jack and Charmian London as Jack and Clara Hastings on their yawl *Roamer*. Jack and Clara suggest that the sought-after dream ranch might be found in the Sonoma Valley.

But Billy and Saxon first turn north, in order to explore the country up to the Oregon border. On their return trip, they meet Jack and Clara again, on the 1350 mile four-horse wagon trip to Oregon upon which the Londons embarked in 1911.

And finally, Billy and Saxon turn their steps toward the valley where they will end their journey. Jack London loved adventure, but the adventure he loved most was "making two blades of grass grow where only one grew before." He had fallen in love with the Sonoma Valley at first sight in 1903, and in 1905 bought his first valley land. More and more acreage was added as opportunity arose until he owned over 1400 acres from the valley floor to the top of Sonoma Mountain. The ranch was near Wake Robin Lodge which becomes Trillium Covert to Billy and Saxon. In real life, Edmund and Annette Hale were Edward Biron Payne and Ninetta Payne. Ninetta was Charmian London's aunt who had raised her from the age of six. One day as Jack looked out over the ranch, he reportedly turned to Charmian and said, "When I look out over it all it kind of makes me ache in the throat with things in my heart I can't find words to say."

Billy and Saxon, upon entering the valley, find all the conditions and requirements to be right at last. Their education nearly complete, the wanderers are ready to settle and begin building in reality the life they have been building so long in their imaginations. As they enter the valley, Billy affirms, "I guess we won't winter in Carmel. This place was specially manufactured for us." And Saxon: "There isn't the slightest doubt. This is our place, I know it."

Jack London's New Woman in a New World: Saxon Brown Roberts' Journey into the Valley of the Moon

Jeanne Campbell Reesman

On November 9, 1913, a reviewer in the New York *Times* called Jack London's *The Valley of the Moon* a "man's size book, about a man's size idea." Yet the novel, first serialized in *Cosmopolitan*, is more its heroine's story that its hero's. In so many respects a literary descendant of the works of Emerson, Thoreau, Hawthorne, Melville, and Twain, *The Valley of the Moon* nevertheless offered something new in treatment of the theme of freedom in the American West. It enacts the traditional American themes of the search for a middle landscape of pastoral harmony and the urge for individual freedom within community, and it follows the wounded retreat from oppression with the re-discovery of the land. But *The Valley of the Moon* invokes these and other broad cultural concerns through London's expanded development of a feminist heroine instead of a traditional male hero.

London's heroine, Saxon Brown Roberts, may best be described a "dialogic" character, for she is the character London's narrator addresses, the character who addresses the other main character, and the character who speaks most to the reader.[1] As in "Samuel," "The Night Born," and "When Alice Told Her Soul," dialogue in this work is the primary vehicle for London's feminist values. As a novel, *The Valley of the Moon* allows London more expanded treatment of these dialogic, communal values than do the short stories.

The topic of feminism in London's work has often been touched on but seldom addressed in depth. One can sympathize with the reaction: "WHAT?! Jack *London* a *feminist*?!" But London's typecasting as a writer of boy's books and machismo survival epics severely curtails the intellectual and artistic richness of his canon, especially with regard to gender issues. Few critics today are familiar with the richly rewarding works of London's later period, and fewer still have recognized that a major portion of London's later work demonstrates his feminist values.

Teamster and sometime prizefighter Billy "Big Bill" Roberts is a man at whose name all others step aside (or on their own feet, as Billy is fond of challenging). When he and Saxon meet, he is a simple but intelligent, sensitive, and playful young man and Saxon is a diminutive, imaginative, and sturdy young woman of character and integrity. Despite their happy marriage and their attempt at a middle-class domesticity in the working world of early twentieth-century Oakland, the cruel war between unions and capitalists brings destruction upon them. During a riot, Saxon loses their baby. After Billy's desperate fighting for his union and his drunken frustrations land him in jail, Saxon determines that upon his release they will leave the city of horrors to find a place where they can live happily. She assumes responsibility and nurses Billy back to health for the journey. With Saxon as the guiding force, they make their journey and find their Valley of the Moon.

As a rich blend of realism and romance, *The Valley of the Moon* appealed strongly to an audience that responded to stories of an underdog succeeding in physical and spiritual odysseys in the American landscape and to portraits of the many types of human life trying to exist—often desperately—in the New World. It particularly appealed to a generation witnessing the closing of the American frontier. Certainly London's paeans to the struggles of Anglo-Saxon settlers can grate on modern ears, as presented in Saxon's notions of the struggle of her pioneer ancestors and ancestresses and in the couple's occasionally racist reactions to various communities of other American immigrants, Portuguese or Chinese people, for instance. The best way to understand these passages is to realize that London is constantly concerned with racial issues—that is, in this book as elsewhere, he didn't get it right, but he confronted and addressed racism throughout his career. He varies dramatically in his presentations of ethnic groups. In some works he is blatantly racist, while in others he develops minority or alien protagonists with whom the narrator clearly places his sympathies and sense of righteous indignation. In London's questioning of established gender roles he is more successful, but in both cases he meaningfully addresses problems of "otherness" in American culture in a manner that contrasts sharply with the lack of such engagement by the romanticized magazine fiction of his day.

London accomplishes racial and gender identifications largely through dialogue, and this tendency grows in the later works. Reading even a fraction of London's works beyond the dog stories that made his initial success reveals the dualism in his values that underlies the preponderance of dialogue in his stories and novels. In much of London's work, characters are allowed free verbal expression at the expense of narrative exposition, and the reader attains greater understanding of "the other"—the other as partner in dialogue instead of unaddressed and pre-judged entity. In the late South Seas tales of 1916 written only months before London's untimely death at the age of 40, one notes an almost total reliance on story-telling and dialogic characters of non-white races, especially the native Hawaiian women, who direct themes of community and openness. This is especially evident in the stories of *On the Makaloa Mat*, published posthumously in 1919. But several years before this burst of psychological and narrative complexity, which many scholars attribute in part to London's April, 1916, reading of Carl Jung's *Psychology of the Unconscious*, in *The Valley of the Moon* we find a highly critical portrait of the white male power structure coupled with a female protagonist whose values and strength allow her to triumph happily and healthily over the Establishment of her day.

The Valley of the Moon was one of London's longest and most successful books, featuring elements of his biography, marriage, socialism, bohemianism, and agrarianism—and inspiring the reader with love of adventure and promise of fulfillment in life for men and women. It also contains a striking portrait of San Francisco area labor unrest in the early twentieth century. In the Oakland that Saxon and Billy flee, there is only horror, misery, and bloodshed, an overwhelming poverty of spirit and flesh. On a different note, the novel offers an inside look at the artists' colony at Carmel-by-the-Sea, where Jack London, George Sterling, Mary Austin, Harry Leon Wilson, Jimmy Hopper, Sinclair Lewis, Grace MacGowan Cooke, Nora May French, and others of "the crowd" played and worked.[2] Various London personae appear throughout the story, including the little boy John on his bay boat the *Roamer* and Jack Hastings, a writer and adventurer. The Londons' 1911 four-horse wagon journey up the Pacific coast was also a resource; indeed, the novel was in progress during this trip.[3] But of all the influences, situations, and ideas that are reflected in *The Valley of the Moon*, none is more important to its thematic definition of the American spirit in the West than the role of the woman. Indeed, all of the ideas and episodes in this novel are contextualized and addressed by London's feminism as demonstrated in Saxon.

London defended the "spirituality" of *The Valley of the Moon* when it was attacked in a review as an example of "the Jack London school" that exalts the animal side of human nature.[4] He seemed to regard it as a statement of his dearest beliefs concerning human beings in their relationships to each other as they live and work in the American landscape. He knew the novel would be popular, but it was more to him than that: As he wrote to George Brett, his editor at Macmillan, in May, 1911, "It is a story of which I shall absolutely and passionately believe every word." He goes on to characterize the book as a traditional American call to move "back to the land," but he also emphasizes that in place of a visionary hero "the woman gets the vision. She is the guiding force."[5] Indeed, the focus throughout the novel is on Saxon Brown Roberts; we see through her eyes and hear through her ears. When the novel was in progress, London told Roland Phillips at *Cosmopolitan*, "I agree to eat my hat if it resembles any other book in the ruck of the books or in the exception of the books. It may be rotten—God knows; but at least it will be different. And I'm going to pick up some raw facts of life in it, and turn them over." He praised *Cosmopolitan* for its willingness to "enable one to handle sex frankly."[6] Much of this frankness in *The Valley of the Moon* lies in its straightforward detailing of the woman's consciousness of sexuality and a feminine sense of relationships in general.[7]

Clarice Stasz, whose most recent critical works focus on Charmian London's feminism and its influence on Jack, has identified Saxon Brown Roberts as an example of London's far-reaching redefinition of gender roles for American women and men, particularly in the context of the "New Woman" who appeared in popular fiction at the turn of the century. This is the woman to whom we are asked to listen and are invited to address in *The Valley of the Moon*. Stasz focuses on how London attacked the class system that locked lower and middle-class men and women into sharply defined sex roles; in this attack he evolved over the course of his career "a radical, even visionary conception of masculinity and femininity." New Women were proud of their independence and equality with men. Saxon's vitality and openness to development offer a refreshing contrast to the usual portraits of lower-class women. In connecting this to Billy's role as work-slave in the context of London's own political disenchantment, particularly as it was followed by the flight into the countryside, Stasz describes how both male and female characters such as Saxon and Billy struggle together for redefined sex roles within an exploitive and reifying economy. She concludes that both personally and publically, when male or female characters fail to achieve androgyny—that is, when men remain locked into traditional male stereotypes and when women restrain themselves from being creative, assertive, and competent to lead their own lives—true happiness is as impossible to achieve as is a just economy for humanity.[8]

Obviously, London's decision to replace the "classic" American hero in his novel of moving back to the land is an inversion of a deeply ingrained cultural myth. In a sense *The Valley of the Moon* is a *tour de force*—a "what if" featuring a dramatic sex role reversal. But London's innovation is more sharply defined when one examines some important sources for this novel, some two dozen articles he tore out and annotated in 1910 and 1911 from publications including *The Saturday Evening Post, The Pacific Rural Press, Pacific Monthly,* and *Country Life in America.* These articles, preserved with his own notes and his corrected manuscript in the vast London collection at the Huntington Library, offer facts and figures about farming and land values, and nearly all of them are first-person accounts of entering the wilderness to begin a new life. The articles feature titles such as "How I Learned to Farm" or "Cutting Loose from the City." The most striking thing about these articles is that with one exception (across the top of which London wrote, "San Jose Woman"), they are all narrated by men and focused on masculine achievements. Oftentimes the new farmer's wife is barely mentioned. London's annotations, however, refer to Saxon in a different light than that in which these nearly forgotten women are presented in the articles. In addition to his general notes for the "farm novel," as he called it, London sketches possible dialogues between his two main characters that clearly place Saxon in charge of leading the dialogue and working through dialogue toward important decisions. For example, London noted in one margin: "Billy: 'Here's where we can do it.' Saxon: 'No, no, no redwoods here.'"

The most telling source in London's file is one of the earliest. An article by Leroy Armstrong entitled "The Man Who Came Back: Two Twentieth Century Pilgrims and Where They Landed," published on November 12, 1911, in *The Saturday Evening Post,* tells from a husband's point of view how he and his wife, Mary, unable any longer to face the poverty of the city, leave Chicago at Mary's instigation and head west on foot to search for a special valley where they can settle and live as independent farmers. They find their valley in Colorado, which the narrator repeatedly calls "Mary's valley." He claims that she is also his inspiration to work hard, but he focuses throughout his lengthy narrative on *his* role as worker and hero; indeed, the pronoun "I" seems to be his favorite word. At the end, he tells us:

> I can make a living for myself and the family on a forty-acre farm, and raise the usual farm products too. I can make a fortune with twenty acres in fruit and nut trees, or in poultry. And the only thing I will have to give is just what I would have had to give if I had stuck to the trade back there in Chicago—work. The difference is now I work for myself. . . . I get the wages and the profits.[9]

Virtually no mention is made of what must have been a grueling life for Mary. London used several situations and events from this article in *The Valley of the Moon*; it is a key source, especially in its notion of "Mary's valley." The change from male to female narrator and focal character is a profound one. Saxon's valley and Mary's valley are two entirely different destinations for the two couples who journey into the western landscape.

Though London often portrayed strongly independent women—from the Indian women of the Klondike stories to the Hawaiian women of the late tales—perhaps nowhere does he offer so clear and spiritually complete a female protagonist as Saxon Brown Roberts. Though modeled on Charmian London and the New Woman image, Saxon goes beyond these contemporary models. And she is no superwoman—throughout the novel her ideas and actions, heroic as they are, are portrayed realistically, and though through dialogue she brings out what Stasz would call "androgyny" in herself and her husband, her peace even at the end is imperfect. This open-endedness makes Saxon even more a living symbol of the American idea of the West. Saxon's journey in the novel expresses London's continually evolving notion of the Self and of the American tradition of seeking freedom as well as community in the pastoral landscape. *The Valley of the Moon*'s challenge to traditional sex roles and its characterization of that freedom as an American freedom may be disguised as a traditional love story, but the novel's magnitude is great.[10]

The book is almost *all* dialogue. Saxon and Billy literally talk themselves into their new world, their Sonoma Eden.[11] In the second half of the book they wander from locale to locale, talking with each other about what they need and engaging in dialogue with the local inhabitants. Saxon is throughout more articulate than Billy, though his attraction to her lies in his awareness of how he is able to talk to her. In general, dialogue among women is more productive than among men in this novel. Male-only dialogue is quite limited—in a world in which a man's worth is based upon his physical strength and hence ability to earn a living, words seem unimportant. When talking with men Billy talks only about his job, or lack of one, the union and the strike, and his physical prowess as boxer, though usually the other men are the ones who focus on this last subject. His conversation, like that of the others, is most often overly idealistic or superficial, especially as times get harder. When he hurts from fighting in the ring or in the street, he preserves his macho appearance rather than talk about his pain. The male characters do not discuss emotions, a factor, perhaps, in their abuse of alcohol. Nevertheless, Billy manages to escape much of the male stereotyping because he is different in important ways from the other men, but also because he has been lucky enough to marry Saxon. In dialogue with her or with the many people she urges him to talk with, he moves toward androgyny and wholeness. Throughout *The Valley of the Moon*, it is Saxon's voice that is the voice of reason and reality; indeed, because she assists London in creating Billy as an integrated human being, she resembles an author herself. Metafictively, she too relies on creating speech.

Dialogue predominates in the book from the very first page. The opening scene is a dialogue among women working at a steam laundry in Oakland. Modern readers are struck, no doubt, by the awkwardness of much of the slang and working-class lingo of the novel, but this becomes more meaningful when located in the overall dialogic context, for London's adherence to dialect seems to argue for the humanizing function of words. A woman collapses in the heat, interrupting a lively discussion between Saxon and her friend Mary about the men who will be at the Bricklayer's dance the next day. Their quick glances at the sufferer, along with those of many of the other piece-work ironers of fancy starch, betray fears about losing money. Saxon and Mary sadly mention the woman's seven children and her current pregnancy, while another worker disgustedly declares she'll quit the job and go "that way," or into prostitution. We next learn that the orphaned Saxon, with her slender wages in hand, goes home to face the crude and vituperative attitudes of her brother and sister-in-law, Tom and Sarah, and their hungry children. In this house, slave labor has produced physical and spiritual ugliness. Saxon maintains personal dignity and kindness by remembering her pioneering ancestors, particularly her mother. Sarah's deadening harangues and shrieking fits demonstrate her agony as a desperately unhappy woman in a desperately unhappy world; London later calls it "soul-sickening hysteria and madness." It is a warning to Saxon.

Saxon meets Billy at the dance, and these scenes contain a very high proportion of dialogue important to establishing characters. Billy and Saxon, unlike the flirtatious Bert and Mary, speak to each other honestly and not "in the mode," a slangy style with much silly sexual innuendo and belittling of women. Saxon and Billy discussed their body weights measured stripped and clothed without embarrassment, and as Bert and Mary giggle, Saxon and Billy go on talking to discover their common heritage as pioneer children.

Saxon associates Billy with her exploring forbears, particularly with her "mother-myth," Daisy Brown, who "had been different from other women, too. This, forsooth, meant to [Saxon] what God meant to others. To this she strove to be true, and not to hurt or vex."[12] Saxon keeps the artifacts of her mother's independence and bravery in an old chest which she opens from time to time for inspiration. Her mother was a poet, widely known in her day, whose manuscripts Saxon often reads aloud when she is alone. Her mother's words enrapture and inspire Saxon; the line, "'I have stolen away from the crowd in the groves,'" occurs in a poem that is a tribute to the "nude statues" Aphrodite, Pandora, and Psyche, "'struck voiceless forever.'" Daisy Brown celebrates the

> "naiad that stands
> In the spray of a fountain, whose seed-amethysts
> Tremble lightly a moment on bosom and hands,
> Then drip in their basin from bosom and wrists."

Such erotic female poetry is "'beautiful, just beautiful,'" Saxon thinks, but she is at the same time "appalled at. . . the mystery" of life it touches on; she puts away the volume "among the cherished fragments of her mother's hidden soul" (48-49). One has to remind oneself that a man, London, wrote these intensely feminine verses, especially when one relates the imagery of the "voiceless" goddesses to the novel's overall quest for that intensely feminine archetype, a valley in the moon.

Unlike the abusive Charley Long, who forces his attentions upon Saxon, and unlike the other men in his crowd, Billy tries to resolve conflicts with dialogue, a characteristic which endears him to Saxon. In Chapter X of Book I, Billy and Saxon talk frankly about misconceptions they have held about men and women. On their day together in the countryside, they reveal themselves, this time without the reductive talk of their friends and the clichés of the fiction of the times to distract them. This setting occurs within a series of dichotomized values the novel has been building: city versus country, old versus young, rich versus poor, Saxon versus Sarah, men versus women, integrity versus destruction. As they talk they determine that neither their age difference (she is older) nor the usual "sex antagonism" come into play. He explains his joy in prizefighting, as well as his disillusionment, and he mourns the way men and women of his class are victimized into prostitutes or work slaves of one kind or another. He is amazed later in the day at his volubility:

> "I never talk this way to other girls. They'd think I'm workin' up to designs on 'em. They make me sick the way they're always lookin' for them designs. But you're different. I can talk to you that way. I know I've got to. It's the square thing." (83)

He welcomes Saxon's words: "'Go on,' he insisted. 'You can't say anything I won't like'" (95).

Chapter XIV shifts sharply back to a less happy world with a difficult conversation between Saxon and Sarah. Sarah "was conservative," London writes. "Worse, she had crystallized" into a bitter and spiritually abandoned woman. Sarah does have a certain turn of phrase, as when she calls Billy a "'prizefighter, a hoodlum, a plug-ugly'" (110), but she is mostly concerned that with Saxon's marriage she will lose Saxon's rent of $4.50 per week. The dialogue here is abortive, as is Saxon's later conversation with her brother. Book I closes with the wedding supper of Bert and Mary, and again Saxon's and Billy's language demonstrates their readiness for new worlds. Many scenes in this novel counterpoint each other the way these do—as though the scenes too are in dialogue with each other.

Book II begins with the happy newlyweds talking lovers' talk, playing word games, telling each other the news of the day, and sharing their aspirations. They praise and thank each other in frank, full and innocent conversation. Even their silences are "quick with unuttered love" (130). Simultaneously, difficulties as well as important new developments arise from Saxon's daytime talks with Mercedes Higgins, whose conversations with Saxon progress from hints, "dropped in casual conversation" about the life of a married woman, to dark mysteries: "She was destined to learn much from the strange woman" (132). Mercedes has the reputation, particularly among men, as "bughouse," but when Billy hears the things she tells Saxon, he is intrigued by her, though Saxon doesn't tell Billy all of what Mercedes says. Saxon's conversations with her neighbor begin with discussions of different nationalities—Mercedes is a much-traveled South American of Irish/Peruvian/Spanish descent, and she is as "voluble as a Greek." Interestingly, Mercedes has spent a great deal of time in the Klondike and the South Seas. Chapter III is a set-piece first-person narrative of Mercedes' life that begins,

> "Listen, my dear. I shall tell you about the world of men. Do not be stupid like all your people, who think me foolish and a witch with the evil eye. . . . Oh, I am wise, very wise, my dear. I shall tell you of women's ways with men, and of men's ways with women, the best of them and the worst of them. Of the brute that is in all men, of the queerness of them that breaks the hearts of stupid women who do not understand. And all woman are stupid. I am not stupid. La, la, listen." (139-40)

Mercedes narrates an intimate but broad-ranging story of a singular woman's life with many people in many lands. At Mercedes' bidding, Saxon begins to make and sell lace work for house money. Later, Saxon discovers that Mercedes is underpaying her when she resells the garments for Saxon to shops in town, and then Billy finds out and strongly objects to her labor. Though the work comes to an end, it is an important transition for Saxon toward a sense of independence.

Saxon confronts Mercedes when she discovers her friend's profit margin. Mercedes sounds rather like Wolf Larsen of London's *The Sea-Wolf* as she explains her view of "the way of the world." Her talk of the "salt vats" in which she has seen floating the pauper dead is the strongest image of her naturalism and materialism. Mercedes concludes: "Some time I shall talk to you about God. Never be afraid of him. Be afraid only of the salt vats and the things about God. Never be afraid of him. Be afraid only of the salt vats and the things men may do with your pretty flesh after you are dead" (164-65). This tone is also carried on in the subsequent conversations of Bert and Tom and Billy over their labor troubles and their determination to quash scabs in the coming teamster strike. Times are getting harder. In their conversations the men begin to object less strongly to Tom's socialism and the idea that capitalist America—their master—has betrayed their New World dreams. Another conversation between Mercedes and Saxon occurs after this episode and before the terrible riot and massacre that follow. Mercedes' cynicism and her terming democracy "the dream of the stupid peoples" form a fitting introduction to the gore that flows when the police attack (181).

Things collapse with the riot, Saxon's miscarriage, and Billy's slide into alcoholism and fighting in the street. He is jailed. Saxon holds dialogues with herself as she walks on the ocean rock wall, scavenging for mussels to eat. Her life seems life "bereft of its last reason and rhyme. It had become senseless, nightmarish. Anything irrational was possible." Billy "had been whirled away from her in the prevailing madness" of Oakland:

> So radical was the change in him that he seemed almost an intruder in the house. Spiritually he was such an intruder. Another man looked out of his eyes—a man whose thoughts were of violence and hatred; a man to whom there was no good in anything, and who had become an ardent protagonist of the evil that was rampant and universal. (224)

Even Charley Long makes a reappearance to harass Saxon. But it is a new character who seems to make the difference, a very dialogic one indeed. The little boy at the rock wall in his bay boat who takes Saxon for a ride and rattles on and on about the adventures he has had and will one day have is a Jack London persona who, "sweeping the circle of the world with a wave of his arm" (263), reiterates to Saxon, "*Oakland is just a place to start from.*" He causes her to view everything in a new light, or rather in new words: "A place to start from? Why not? Why not like a railroad station or ferry depot?" (268). Saxon's dialogue with him is healing. As with Mercedes, the author again addresses Saxon through a character with the sort of "dialogic advice" that urges her onward. Saxon's transformation helps transform Billy; when he is released from jail they decide to "chuck" Oakland. They pawn his boxing medals and go out "just travelers through this town" (278) for steaks, hash browns, oysters, and, for Saxon's sake, mussels. They even attended a movie about country life. After Billy is yet again beaten, this time by mistake as a scab, their decision is final.

In Book III, the final Book, Saxon and Billy first make their plans through talking with as many people as they can, starting with the doctor tending Billy's latest wounds. As they carefully deliberate, Saxon urges them on when they falter, just as she earlier talked Billy out of scabbing and fighting. They march out with backpacks through the streets of Oakland into the awaiting landscape. From this point on in the novel they spend their time working here and there and yet staying on the move; but mostly they talk to local people they encounter, first a single woman farmer, Mrs. Mortimer, on a farm near San Jose. She seems to be another Jack London persona, particularly in her careful and imaginative agrarianism. To her polite conversation and offer of shelter for the night, Saxon and Billy have many questions to ask about farming: "'Oh, all kinds. How does it pay? How did you manage it all? How much did the land cost? Did you build that beautiful house? How much do you pay the men? How did you learn all the different kinds of things, and which grew best and which paid best?,'" and so on (333). Billy and Saxon do well in the natural landscape; interestingly, their only sour episode in this section occurs with a constable in the stuffy enclosure of a barn in which they sleep.[13]

Conversing and learning as they go, Saxon and Billy stop at Carmel with the beach crowd of artists and writers there, mingling physical exercise with intellectual enjoyment, as well as participating in the singing, laughing, and literary jokes of the others. The group nature of this activity is expressed in the never-to-be-finished "Abalone Song" jointly composed by all the group members. They meet a poet and his wife, with whom Saxon shares her dream of a home place, describing it as a mystery like a valley in the moon—there, certainly, but seemingly unattainable. There is much talk of the boundlessness and the failure of the American experiment in the West. The poet, Mark Hall, sounds very much like London himself when he muses:

> "When you think of the glorious chance. . . . A new country, bounded by the oceans, situated just right in latitude, with the richest land and vastest natural resources of any country in the world, settled by immigrants who had thrown off all the leading strings of the Old World and were in the humor for democracy. There was only one thing to stop them from perfecting the democracy they started, and that thing was greediness. They started gobbling everything in sight like a lot of swine, and while they gobbled democracy went to smash. Gobbling became gambling. . . . They destroyed everything—the Indians, the soil, the forests, just as they destroyed the buffalo and the passenger pigeon. Their morality. . . was gambler morality. . . —how to play the game. . . . Nobody objected, because nobody was unable to play. . . . The losers went to work for the winners, and they've been working for them ever since, and democracy side-tracked up Salt Creek" (413-14).

Billy seems content to stay in Carmel and box and surf, but they move on from this idyllic spot. They next meet Jack and Clara Hastings in Sacramento, the firmest portrait yet of the Londons—even their dogs and boat bear the Londons' names for them. Their talk, like that of Mark, is of the "land-skimming" going on in the area.

Wintering in the grape country of Ukiah, Billy begins to practice horse-trading, and when he fights again he wins—at first. But, badly beaten in a rematch, he gives it up and vows that there will be nothing short of the Valley of the Moon: "'Easy money's hardest in the end. From now on it's horse-buyin' on commish, an' you and me on the road till we find that valley of the moon'" (455). From then on till the end of the book, they examine places even more closely, saying from time to time, "'This is wonderful and glorious,. . . but it is not the valley of the moon'" (465). They encounter Jack and Clara Hastings again on a road in Northern California, just before they circle back south and east toward their destined Sonoma.[14]

They finally find the canyon in Sonoma that meets all their requirements. At this dramatic moment the emphasis is again upon their speech: "'I've got a hunch,' said Billy. 'Let me say it first,' Saxon begged. He waited, his eyes on her face as she gazed about her in rapture. 'We've found our valley,' she whispered. 'Was that it?' He nodded, but checked speech at the sight of a small boy driving a cow up the road, a preposterously big shotgun in one hand, in the other as preposterously big a jackrabbit.'" This boy, seemingly a final incarnation of the London spirit, makes the place of maples, alders, madrones, manzanitas, laurel, wild grape, oaks, ferns, brakes, and Spanish moss, filled with "sunset fires, refracted from the cloud-driftage of the autumn sky, [bathing] the canyon in crimson" (481), absolutely the right place. Billy and Saxon settle in by learning from the locals and from the San Jose farmer Mrs. Mortimer, whom they invite as manager of the small farm they purchase.

Billy is excitedly voluble in the penultimate chapter, dreaming dreams of the speculative ventures he will make. As he has so often in the text, here he resembles an overenthusiastic puppy. Full of ideas and grand plans, he sees a farmer plowing and thinks that he can learn to plow immediately, simply by watching. By talking to the farmer, though, he learns that there is much more to plowing than meets his eye. Saxon is the one who initiates this practical and educational dialogue, and here as elsewhere Billy becomes more realistic by following her conversational lead. The novel's conclusion surprises with its lack of closure. As the story ends with Chapter XXII, things are still unresolved as to Billy's and Saxon's future values and life. Their wanderings conclude not so much with their talk of the farm but of Billy's talk having found a source of clay to sell to house-builders. "'But you'll spoil all the beautiful canyon hauling out the clay,'" Saxon responds in alarm. If not silenced, her doubts are momentarily sidetracked by his sudden but well-timed revelation that he has written Tom for Saxon's chest to be sent. Next, when she tells him of her pregnancy, they are sitting beside a still pool with a "spotted fawn [looking] down upon them from a tiny open space between the trees," and Billy's fingers are upon Saxon's lips. He is thanking her, perhaps, for not pointing out his mistake of planning his clay business any further, or perhaps he is just silencing her. London's idyllic yet disturbing open ending is typical of his later works. *Has* Billy been transformed? Despite the twist London gives the ending, Saxon's fertility represents a hopeful future for herself and her husband, brought to the Valley of the Moon through their transformative dialogue. It seems fitting, and supremely responsible, for London to project the need for future transformations through further dialogue.

The Valley of the Moon clearly displays a narrative structure that through dialogue with "the other" promotes a philosophy of community, even if that community has to be founded in a far-away "valley of the moon." This effort exists within a context of progressively open notions of knowledge within fiction, a hermeneutics of openness to the other, whomever or whatever that other might be. Feminism such as London's is naturally a part of such a hermeneutics, and his work should accordingly be addressed a great deal more than it is in relation to recent developments in opening up the canon of American literature for women and others. Though London's various philosophies frustrate one in their contradictions, there is a traceable movement in his thought towards rejection of closed epistemologies and towards a more complex hermeneutics, in both theme and style. *The Valley of the Moon*'s flowering of thought and style promotes freedom of speech for characters and freedom of imagination as addressed—particularly in its troubling conclusion—to readers. London speaks to his heroine; she speaks to Billy; and readers as well find themselves addressed in *The Valley of the Moon*. This novel dialogizes classes and continents and sexualities—in the end it provokes readers to continue to ask important questions.

NOTES

[1] The definition of "dialogism" in narrative used here arises from the theories of Mikhail Bakhtin and refers to the function of "addressed" language as a means of developing community among characters as well as readers. See Bakhtin, *The Dialogic Imagination: Four Essays*, ed. and introd. by Michael Holquist, trans. Caryl Emerson and Michael Holquist (Austin: U of Texas P, 1981); and Bakhtin, *Problems of Dostoevsky's Poetics*, trans. Caryl Emerson, introd. Wayne C. Booth, Theory and History of Literature Series Volume 8 (Minneapolis: U of Minnesota P, 1983).

[2] Russ Kingman, *A Pictorial Life of Jack London* (New York: Crown Publishers, 1979), 244.

[3] For an interesting description of the London's journey and indication of how *The Valley of the Moon* arises from it, see Howard Lachtman, "Four Horses, a Wife, and a Valet: Up the California Coast with Jack London," *The Pacific Historian*, 21 (1977), 103-34.

[4] Jack London, *The Letters of Jack London*, ed. Earle Labor, Robert C. Leitz, III, and I. Milo Shepard, 3 vols. (Stanford, CA: Stanford UP, 1988), 1313.

[5] *Letters*, 1007-08.

[6] *Letters*, 1064.

[7] Sadly, another letter dated one month later than the day London finished *The Valley of the Moon*, in August, 1912, is one of bereavement and consolation to Charmian, who had miscarried their child the night before and noted in her diary, "Another Hope Lost" (*Letters*, 1079).

[8] Clarice Stasz, "Androgyny in the Novels of Jack London," *Western American Literature*, 11 (1976), 121, 127, 132. See also Clarice Stasz, *American Dreamers: Charmian and Jack London* (New York: St. Martin's Press, 1988).

[9] Leroy Armstrong, "The Man Who Came Back: Two Twentieth Century Pilgrims and Where They Landed, *The Saturday Evening Post*, (November 12, 1910), 42. See also Jack London, [Notes and annotations for *The Valley of the Moon*.] Jack London Collection, MS. 1369, Henry E. Huntington Library, San Marino, CA.

[10] Earle Labor has identified London's novel, along with much of his other work, as addressed to the American dream "in the mainstream of our cultural history." *The Valley of the Moon* "dramatize[s] the archetypal tensions between civilization and the wilderness, the machine versus the garden" (Labor, *Jack London* [New York: Twayne, 1974], 149). Elsewhere he finds that in *The Valley of the Moon* and the other novels set in Sonoma, *White Fang* (1906), *Burning Daylight* (1910), *The Abysmal Brute* (1913), and *The Little Lady of the Big House* (1916), the California wilderness is distinguished from London's previous wildernesses of the Klondike, Melanesia, and Polynesia. Prior to the transformative Jungian "wilderness" London encountered in Hawaii in 1916, in the California version of the landscape London allows characters to make a satisfactory long-term adjustment to their natural environment. The problem is how to place human beings in the wilderness and allow them to "partake of its restorative essence without contaminating the crystal springs" from which they drink. In the American West such *aqua vitae* was "accessible and pure." London required that the wilderness be unspoiled and tractable, its would-be human inhabitants purified before entering it, and any changes people would make would have to improve their surroundings without desecrating the wilderness: "the initiate must become a self-appointed guardian of the wilderness, protecting it against all attempts to assault and corrupt morally or materialistically." Sonoma offered a pastoral romance "alien to the White Silence and the tropics" ("Jack London's Symbolic Wilderness: Four Versions," *Nineteenth-Century Fiction*, 17 [1962], 149-61). In this context, Saxon, who embodies in her small frame the drive to live in such an Eden, seemingly acts as an American Eve who leads her husband back into the garden.

[11] Joseph McElrath of Florida State University first discussed with me how much Billy and Saxon talk to each other as they make their journey.

[12] Jack London, *The Valley of the Moon* (New York: Macmillan, 1913), 48. All subsequent references cited in text.

[13] My thanks to Tanya Walsh of the University of Kansas for pointing out this interesting detail. It occurs within a larger image pattern in the novel of enclosure versus open space.

[14] Without quoting lengthy passages, one cannot adequately convey the beauty and fun of the Roberts' fictional journey through California eighty years ago, but these passages and the couple's reactions to the landscape, are, I would guess, most readers' favorite parts. These passages are interesting to compare and contrast with another novel of the West published a few years before London's: Owen Wister's *The Virginian* (New York: Macmillan, 1902). This book's best sections occur towards the end when the hero and his bride journey into the Northwestern wilderness. But the sentimentality of *The Virginian's* conclusion and its promise of eternal bliss contrast sharply with London's conclusion, highlighting London's essential modernism and feminism.

The Valley of the Moon: **A Reassessment**

Laurent Dauphin

When *The Valley of the Moon* was published in 1913, it was an immediate success. The novel sold extremely well and received favorable reviews in the press.

Yet, more than seventy years after its publication, *The Valley of the Moon* is sometimes but briefly mentioned in the various studies dealing with Jack London; its importance as a work of art is often minimized, whereas biographical details are developed at full length; comparatively, much more importance is given to such well-known works as *Martin Eden*, *The Sea-Wolf*, or *The Call of the Wild*.

In his correspondence, however, Jack London never failed to assert that *The Valley of the Moon* was one of his favorites among the several novels he had written—a work he was proud of and always defended with great enthusiasm.

So the question is: how can we account for this paradoxical situation? What prevented *The Valley of the Moon* from being remembered as a work of major importance in Jack London's production?

Perhaps a first answer simply lies in the plot of *The Valley of the Moon*: Experiencing poverty and despair in Oakland, Saxon and Billy Roberts, the two main characters of the novel, live in a world which has many common points with the one depicted in *The Jungle* by Upton Sinclair. As the city threatens to destroy and crush them, they decide to leave Oakland and spend more than two years on the road; they are looking for an ideal valley they call "The Valley of the Moon." After a long wandering, they eventually find this valley in Sonoma, California—Sonoma which, they will later discover, is the Indian name for "Valley of the Moon." Relying on such a brief summary many critics and readers saw the novel as a nostalgic one, indulging in a vain longing for America's rural past.

This leads us to the second problem linked with *The Valley of the Moon*: those who were interested in Jack London primarily as a committed writer considered the novel to be the work of a weary man who had given up the fight against capitalism to settle in Glen Ellen. As remarked by Walter Rideout: "The generation of radicals who came after him preferred to forget *The Valley of the Moon* and to remember *The Iron Heel*".[1]

As is often the case concerning Jack London, this interpretation springs, it seems, from an erroneous use of biographical data. Rather than trying to draw a parallel between Saxon and Billy's discovery of Sonoma Valley and Jack London's situation in 1913, we should ask ourselves if the valley itself or the American countryside are not present in the works that preceded *The Valley of the Moon*; by doing so, we would discover that *The Valley of the Moon*, far from being a turning point or expressing a sudden conversion, is on the contrary the last stage of a long process.

The first significant occurrence is to be found in *White Fang* in 1906; the novel ends in a valley which is not that of Sonoma but of Santa Clara, bathed in radiant sunshine; there, White Fang finds peace and love again; but it is a new space, which has yet to be mastered, as shown by the intrusion of Jim Hall, a dangerous criminal.

It is then in 1907, with the short story "When God Laughs" that the theme of the valley as a refuge is developed at full length; the whole story consists in a long dialogue between a narrator living in California and Carquinez, a gifted dialectician who tells him: "You refuse to play; you have thrown your cards under the table and run away to hide, here amongst your hills".[2]

But it is with *The Iron Heel*, the following year, that the real valley is fully included in fiction. Avis, the wife of the working class leader Ernest Everhard, hides in a cave somewhere in the Sonoma Valley—a valley which becomes synonymous with harmony and protection. It is also in the Sonoma Valley that Elam Harnish, the main character of *Burning Daylight*, escapes greed and corruption and finds happiness with the woman he loves.

Not only is the theme of nature as a sacred place, a redeeming force ever present in London's work, this approach also goes hand in hand with the vision of the city as hell. In the city, one finds the monster-like machines that crush young Johnny in "The Apostate"; in the city, men such as Ross Shanklin in *The Hobo and The Fairy* or Elam Harnish in *Burning Daylight* lose their strength and dignity. Martin Eden, trapped in the city of hypocrisy and false values, dreamt of a remote. . . valley, somewhere in Polynesia. And even as early as 1903 with *The People of the Abyss*, Jack London drew conclusions from his stay in the East End of London that proved valid ten years later in America: what he saw was a rural England which lost its strongest individuals, looking for jobs in the nearby cities; but the city turned them into slaves and beasts doomed to a life of hardship and suffering.

So when in May 1911 Jack London wrote to the editor of *Cosmopolitan Magazine* that he intended to write a novel entitled *The Valley of the Moon* based on the return to the land, there was nothing in that project which could be attributed to a new fancy or a sudden conversion on his part. Avis Everhard, Martin Eden, Elam Harnish and the numerous anonymous characters present in Jack London's novels are but the ancestors of Saxon and Billy Roberts.

The second problem we selected concerning *The Valley of the Moon* was its reputation as a utopian or nostalgic novel suggesting a return to the values of the Jeffersonian Era.

On the one hand, there is no use denying that *The Valley of the Moon* is indeed teeming with references to American history; its characters are also rooted in a long tradition. Whereas Sinclair in *The Jungle* had concentrated his analysis on the existence of Jurgis, a Lithuanian immigrant, London makes us share the daily life of two Americans whose parents fought in the Civil War and whose grand-parents belonged to a proud lineage of pioneers. As a consequence, Saxon and Billy, confronted with poverty and despair, come to perceive the harsh contrast existing between the conditions of their life and that of their ancestors. "Things weren't like that in the old days when our folks crossed the plains," Billy says; "sure, they worked for themselves," Saxon answers.[3] Later on, as riots and demonstrations take place in Oakland, Saxon is said to be "dreaming of the Arcadian days of her people, when they did not live in cities" (60); and once she and Billy have taken the decision to leave, the young woman announces that they are going to travel the way their people came into the West.

The second part of the novel, that is the odyssey of Saxon and Billy, is then totally in keeping with that literary tradition of the American novel showing characters threatened by civilization seeking refuge in the wilderness. The expression "on the road," which will become so important more than forty years later, recurs over and over in the dialogues (155, 160). Nature is described as a temple of innocence and purity, and several descriptive passages are evocative of the paintings by Thomas Burnham or William Hays. Finally, what may have led some critics to see *The Valley of the Moon* as a simplistic work is the extensive use of religious imagery. Saxon herself says she will surely find the valley "just as the Jews found the promised land" (163); both she and Billy state that their long wandering is akin to a pilgrimage.

Yet, Saxon's and Billy's approach to nature and agriculture is not a merely idealistic one—and so is Jack London's; it could have been that: after several unsuccessful attempts at finding the Valley of the Moon, Billy is tempted to remain on the road forever, to be just a rootless traveller. But what prevents the novel from being a mere piece of anachronistic nostalgia is precisely the structure of the odyssey that we have mentioned.

Each village, each county crossed by Saxon and Billy coincides with a new step towards maturity. To take up Thoreau's words, the long wandering serves to put foundations under their castles in the air. As Saxon herself remarks: "we are getting an education" (134). The characters become progressively aware that many things have changed since the time of their glorious ancestors; in San Jose, they discover that many young people have deserted their native villages; Chinese and Japanese then take over, thus beating the American farmer at his own game. Thanks to Benson, a landowner for whom Billy worked, they realize that agriculture is no longer just a matter of hard work and good will; one has to use the latest scientific discoveries in order to be competitive. Then comes Mrs. Mortimer, one of the most important characters encountered by the couple. According to her, American farmers are too ambitious, buying too much land and making quantity prevail over quality.

Finally, the stay in Carmel is also the occasion to improve on the individual point of view. In Oakland, Saxon and Billy were just slaves and lived in a world which turned them into beasts. In the colorful Bohemian Colony, their innate qualities can fully express themselves, far from any oppressive social structure. There is in the novel a subtle blend of innocence and pragmatism, of idealism and realism which is best summed up by Saxon's words: "We started out prepared to go any distance; and if it's to the moon, I expect we can make it" (140).

So the more we read *The Valley of the Moon*, the more we come to understand the specificity and uniqueness of Jack London's approach. For Saxon and Billy, the contact with nature is the occasion to escape alienation, to purify themselves and to find again that lost energy of their ancestors; but this energy, although it is derived from the past, is to be integrated into the present and will be used to build a better future. There is no question of an ideal return to the nineteenth century, no need to look backward except to draw lessons from the past. For instance, it is significant that even more than any other, the traditional American farmer should be severely and constantly criticized in the novel; Mrs. Mortimer sets the tone at the time of her first encounter with Saxon and Billy: "I went almost entirely on the basis that whatever the old-type farmer did was wrong. . . it's almost unthinkable, the stupidity of the old-fashioned farmer" (124).

The old fashioned farmer, as London calls him, is said to run counter to modern and rational methods: reluctant to introduce new fertilizers or to keep accounts, he knows but few alternatives to single-crop farming or the practice of fallowing land; he thus exhausts the soil, fails to prevent erosion and is submitted to the fluctuations of a single market; as a consequence, he becomes indebted, leaves his native village and sells to businessmen and speculators. So, there is nothing static or nostalgic in London's approach; what he stands for is a major change in mentalities.

Moreover, *The Valley of the Moon* is a work which goes even beyond simple antithesis. Saxon and Billy learn something from the various characters encountered on the road, but these characters themselves are later criticized and the values they embody are transcended after they have been integrated into the heroes' consciousness. The members of the Carmel colony, for instance, are caricatured as dreaming intellectuals who can never achieve anything concrete; later, Saxon and Billy even come to doubt that the life conditions of the hard working immigrants or of Mrs. Mortimer are in keeping with their ideal; theirs is a life which has many common points with what the two young people thought they had left behind them—a life in which work enslaves man instead of providing him with an increased mastery over his own existence. Returning to the values of the past for their own sakes is of no interest; the return to the land must bring about new aims and new ideals; and as Saxon asserts, "All the times, I didn't envy the San Leandro Portuguese. . . or even Mrs. Mortimer. What we want is a valley of the moon with not too much work, and all the fun we want" (147).

Rather than an antithesis, *The Valley of the Moon* is a work which offers a synthesis of Jack London's life-long reflection on man and economy. The themes it develops are totally in keeping with those present in the author's essay, from "What the Communities Lose by the Competitive System" in 1900 to *The Human Drift* in 1911. Mark Hall, a poet encountered by Saxon and Billy, is used as London's mouthpiece: Americans are responsible for an enormous waste; theirs was a new country, bordered by oceans and with a wealth of natural resources; greed and ambition prevented modern men from living a better life than that of their ancestors. And once again, the situation is summed up by Saxon with great simplicity and concreteness, "They're always talking about how much more is made by machinery than by the old ways. . . then, with all the machinery we've got now, why don't we get more" (61)?

There must be a reorganization of productive forces so that science becomes man's ally and not his opponent—and this is exactly what Jack London tried to achieve in his own ranch in Glen Ellen. But of course, as we said before, the fact that Saxon and Billy should leave all their friends behind them and that Jack London should have resigned from the socialist party one year after *The Valley of the Moon* led many readers to see the work as a farewell to socialism; London is said to have lost faith in his revolutionary ideals and to have attempted a return to the conditions that were supposed to prevail at the time of the Founding Fathers; this is for instance the thesis developed by Stoddard Martin in *California Writers*, who makes a comparison with other writers: "Steinbeck's position is like London's in *The Valley of the Moon* or Norris. . . the ideal Jeffersonian democracy that every family should have a plot of land."[4]

The reference to Jefferson is also present in several other critical works. Yet this interpretation is far from being satisfactory because a study of Jack London's essays and correspondence reveals that there is one thing he never failed to assert: his constant hostility to any nostalgic, populist or purely reformist ideology. Let us just mention the letter sent to William Walling in 1909, in which he asserts that a cooperation of the Socialist party with the American Federation of Labor would mean a victory of the Iron Heel, or the well-known essay "Revolution," in which biting irony is levelled at the reformist impulses of the middle class: "Little remains for it but to wail as it passes into oblivion, just as it has already begun to wail in accents populistic and Jeffersonian-democratic."[5]

Similarly, if we wish to mention Jack London's resignation from the socialist party, it is worth bearing in mind that in the open-letter he wrote on this occasion, the writer stated that he could not remain a party member "since the whole trend of socialism in the United States of recent years has been one of peaceableness and compromise".[6]

So we can say that *The Valley of the Moon* does not express a lack of faith in socialism—but in socialists. Around Saxon and Billy, each character is emblematic of the contradictory trends which were that of American socialism at the time of Jack London: Bert, the man who lives with Saxon's best friend, has lapsed into anarchy and terrorism; his is a negative violence which does nothing but justify repression; Saxon's brother, Tom, is an orthodox socialist, passively waiting for the day when the working class will break its chains; at the beginning of a strike in Oakland, Billy himself is tempted by unionism; but unionism, he discovers, is just a means to protect certain interests and does not provide global solutions.

Jack London, of course, could not be content with any of these three approaches. After his stay in London in 1903, he had already expressed his disillusions concerning the men of the abyss, who did not seem to be able to shape their own destiny; later, in *The Iron Heel*, he showed socialist leaders executed by the ruling class after they had been elected in congress; his science-fiction stories are likewise characterized by pessimistic visions: works such as "A Curious Fragment" describe men subject to alienation and mass exploitation. As Saxon says to Billy, it seems that "the stupid must always be under the heels of the clever ones" (98).

So this is perhaps why many socialist friends of Jack London preferred to forget *The Valley of the Moon*: Because the novel brought a most disquieting note, running counter to blind optimism and false certitudes. If we look back at America's political and cultural history, we realize that many of Jack London's intuitions were actually justified.

The period going from the publication of *The Son of the Wolf* to London's death, that is 1900-1916, is characterized by the irresistible rise and then the sudden fall of American Socialism. And the main reason given by historians for the decline of the socialist party is precisely the appearance of movements such as populism or progressivism—which aimed at reforming society without changing it.

When John Dos Passos studied that period in the first volume of *U.S.A.* he came to similar conclusions. Dos Passos blames the lack of political maturity of American socialists, who either tried to impose European models in the United States or lapsed into gratuitous violence. And Dos Passos adds that before changing the world, one has to change oneself—and such is Jack London's message in *The Valley of the Moon*.

As Saxon and Billy cannot change the world, they will try to recreate it after their long education. Just before leaving, the two young people had seen a film about the Middle West, a film which gave them a glimpse of their ideal. And the best way to end a study of *The Valley of the Moon* is to quote the very last lines of this passage, "Since its fulfillment had not come to them, they were going away to fulfill it for themselves and make the moving picture come true" (62).

NOTES

[1] Rideout, Walter B. *The Radical Novel in the United States*. (Cambridge: Harvard UP, 1970), 46.

[2] London, Jack. "When God Laughs" in *When God Laughs*. (London: Mills & Boon, 1915), 17.

³ London, Jack. *The Valley of the Moon*. (Los Angeles: Rejl, 1988), 35. Further references in text.

⁴ Martin, Stoddard. *California Writers*. (New York: Macmillan, 1983), 39.

⁵ London, Jack. "Revolution" in *Revolution: Stories and Essays*. (London: Journeyman Press, 1979), 36.

⁶ Labor, Earle, Robert C. Leitz and I. Milo Shepard, eds. *The Letters of Jack London*. 3 vols. (Stanford: Stanford UP, 1988), 3:1537-38.

General Criticism

Jack London's Quest: "The Red One"

James Kirsch

It is with some hesitation that I have chosen to write about Jack London. I am not one of the lucky few amongst the living who have personally known this radiant, extraordinary human being. Nor can I by any means claim to have an expert knowledge of his life and books. I have not even read all his books. I am simply a psychologist who was fascinated by some of his stories, because they revealed the psychological processes which were going on in his own soul and that of his time in a form with which the analytical psychologist is well acquainted.

To explain this a little further I wish to mention that analysts, under certain conditions, employ a method which C. G. Jung has called "active imagination." In its simplest form, it is a method in which a person is asked to use his imagination and to write a fairy tale or a story. Frequently, a motif which previously occurred in a dream may be used to invent or spin out a story. Without fail, the person will discover that the contents, the plots and motifs of his story reveal the psychic processes going on at the time in his unconscious, that they are not a product of chance but follow certain laws, and that it is possible to make essential aspects of his inner life conscious to him. Even more than dreams does such an active imagination permit an integration of unconscious material into consciousness and thus re-establishes the flow of life in the person.

Under the helpful guidance of an analyst, such a process has a healing effect. Our daily work has given us analysts ample proof that the method of active imagination is never irrelevant, because it always releases great amounts of libido—for good or for bad.

With this I have touched upon the problem of the creative artist, especially that of the writer and poet. It will always remain a mystery what the creative act and the creative process are. Nothing I shall write will "explain" the nature of creative genius. All I can do is point out that Jack London, by writing his stories, contacted levels of the unconscious which Jung called "the collective unconscious," and that towards the end of his life the great vision of the Self was bestowed upon him. This was his greatness, but it was also his tragedy.

He was born January 12, 1876, in San Francisco, California. His real father, Professor W. H. Chaney, a full-blooded Irishman, by profession an itinerant astrologer, always denied his fatherhood. So Jack London grew up in the family of John London. He suffered extreme poverty throughout his childhood. At a very early age he had to work, and his wages at many times during his youth represented an important part of the family income. At one time, for instance, he worked in a cellar shoveling coal for $30.00 a month, with one day off a month.

He never received a formal education. There was nothing in his surroundings which, at any time, could have stimulated him to develop his mind, but the flame of the spirit was burning in him. With iron energy he taught himself. For a time he went to school, and even took classes at the University of California at Berkeley. It is one of the sagas of modern American life how this poverty-stricken youth, with no formal education, acquired a profound, comprehensive and thorough grounding in many fields. He was a voracious reader in the fields of history, social science, literature, philosophy, and psychology. Very early he made up his mind to write a thousand words a day. He was always sure that he was a great writer. Success was bound to come his way—and it did in great measure.

He was deeply and wildly in love with life. He lived it to the full, always risking himself and giving himself fully to life as he found it on the outside. And with the same devotion, he gave himself to writing almost every day of his life. The conflict which necessarily arose due to this powerful extraversion as well as this introversion is reflected in many of his books and in the stories themselves.

For a time he lived in Carmel, California. It was during the summer of 1913 that he spent happy weeks there, visiting his life-long friend, George Sterling, swimming in the surf and sunbathing on the sand, hunting for abalone and eating abalone steaks cooked over a wood fire on the beach. It was a happy and creative time, but a time in which the great conflicts of his life had reached a climax. He was writing stories such as *Valley of the Moon*, was active in the Socialist movement of his day and was building his magnificent Wolf House into which he poured his seemingly inexhaustible creative powers and all his money; a house which everyone referred to as a castle, resembling a palace of Justinian or Caesar.

Fate had, however, determined that he should never live in it. On August 19th of the same year, the Wolf House went up in flames. Something in his soul burnt out that night, says Irving Stone, one of his biographers. The Jack London of *Call of the Wild* and many other great stories died in that inferno. A new one was born, but Jack London's vitality was spent, and thus the new personality never had a chance to develop. It died in the bud.

Was this conflagration which destroyed Jack London's dream house a symbol or an event synchronistic with that conflagration which only a year later should engulf more than half the world? There have always been human beings who, seized by an archetype, experience in their individual life that which happens to the collective or even to the whole of mankind.

It becomes clear that after the fire of his dream house, which symbolized to him his conquest of the world, Jack London was finally captured by the inner world. A profound and complete introversion began just when he was thirty-seven years of age, which was only occasionally interrupted by heavy drinking bouts and a few trips.

In Jungian terms we would say he identified the ego with the Self. The definition which Jung gives to these two terms is that the ego is the center of consciousness and the Self the center of the unconscious. The Self as an archetype is in possession of tremendous creative energies. Any identification of ego and Self is dangerous. If the ego is the representative and servant of the Self, a much healthier psychic balance is established. Jack London did not notice that his prolific creative work came out of the Self. He even denied the existence of the soul as is evidenced by supporting Haeckel's rationalistic and materialistic position. He said, for instance,

> "I have always inclined toward Haeckel's position. In fact, 'inclined' is too weak a word. I am a hopeless individualist. I see the soul as nothing else than the sum of the activities of the organism plus personal habits, memories and experiences of the organism, plus inherited habits, memories, and experiences of the organism. *I believe that when I am dead, I am dead. I believe that with my death I am just as much obliterated as the last mosquito you or I have smashed.*
>
> "I have no patience with fly-by-night philosophers such as Bergson. I have no patience with the metaphysical philosophers, with them, always, the wish is parent to the thought, and their wish is parent to their profoundest philosophical conclusions. I join with Haeckel in being. . .'a positive scientific thinker.'"

On the other hand he wrote the most imaginative and lively stories we have known in American literature. He writes, for instance, in "The White Silence":

> Nature has many tricks wherewith she convinces man of his finity—the ceaseless flow of the tides, the fury of the storm, the shock of the earthquake, the long roll of heaven's artillery—but the most tremendous, the most stupefying of all is the passive phase of the White Silence. All movement ceases, the sky clears, the heavens are as brass; the slightest whisper seems sacrilege, and man becomes timid, affrighted at the sound of his own voice. Sole speck of life journeying across the ghostly wastes of a dead world, he trembles at his audacity, realizes that his is a maggot's life, nothing more. Strange thoughts arise unsummoned, and the mystery of all things strives for utterance. And fear of death, of God, of the universe, comes over him—the hope of resurrection and the life, the yearning for immortality, the vain striving of the imprisoned essence—it is there, if ever, man walks alone with God.

How great the conflict was we can see from these two quotations. On one side, he was a staunch materialist of Haeckel's persuasion so characteristic of the end of the nineteenth century; on the other hand, he was a poet, living with incorruptible sincerity and unquestioned devotion in the service of his inner voice. As this quotation from "The White Silence" shows, the numinous[1] experience of the unconscious seized him. This pair of opposites, the scientific materialist and the poet, open to thoughts of God and yearning for immortality, is difficult to carry for any human being. As one of his obituaries said:

> The inner struggle of London is the key to his work. His biography is a record of privation in its first phase, and a diary of individual daring in its second and last phase. He died at the age of forty—left his playground of the world at large as he had lived his short life—left at full speed—took ill in the morning and crossed the tall hill as the sun went down on his mountain ranch.

We could, of course, deduce from the outer events of his life, his marriage, for instance, his friendships, his monetary problems, his relationship to his publishers or to the Socialist movement of his day, what his fundamental problem was, but we are enabled to see the development and denouement of his fate from the rich material of the unconscious which he left us in his writings. Unfortunately, we know only two dreams of Jack London, but practically every story which Jack London ever wrote is "active imagination" and therefore a valid self-representation of the psyche. They allow us an amazing insight into his psychological problems, and also into the problems of his time. Let us turn first to these two dreams. The first is a childhood dream, which throws a significant light on Jack London's outstanding character traits. It is told by George Wharton James. He says that Jack London told him:

> My other childish victory was over a peculiar nightmare. I have lived in the country and was one day brought to town and stood on a railway platform as a railway engine came in. Its ponderous size, its easy and restless onward movement, its panting, its fire and smoke, its great noises, all impressed me so powerfully that that night I dreamt of it, and when the dream turned to a nightmare I was filled with the dread and horror at what seemed to be the fact that this locomotive was pursuing me and that I could not get out of its way. For weeks thereafter I was haunted by this dreadful fear, and night after night I was run down. But, strange to say, I always rose up again after suffering the pangs of horrible death, to go over it all again. The tortures those nightmares gave me none can understand except those who have gone through a similar experience. Then one night came release. In the distance, as the mighty modern juggernaut came towards me, I saw a man with a stepladder. I was unable to cry out, but I waved my hand to him. He hailed me and bid me come. That broke the spell. I ran to him, climbed to the top of the stepladder and thereafter lost all terror at the sight of a locomotive. But the victory gained in climbing the ladder was as real as any I ever had in my waking life.

This dream, as a frequently recurring dream, is very important. It indicates young Jack London's fear of the unconscious. The locomotive symbolizes the tremendous energy which is contained in the unconscious. It comes as a terrific threat against him. For a certain time conflict continues and no solution seems possible, but at last he succeeds in climbing on top of it. In other words, his solution is getting on top of it, a mastering of the unconscious—and thereby achieving a complete identification with it. The fruit of it is an increase in libido and power of imagination. It was this tremendous energy which moved him throughout the first phase of his life. The energy which radiated from him through his work, in his actions, in his many ideas, in his working out of new plans and strivings in many fields—was characteristic for him throughout his life. It was only through the burning of the Wolf House that this enormous vitality received a shock and that his libido definitely turned inward.

The other dream we know is reported by Charmian Kittredge, his second wife, in *The Book of Jack London*. She says there:

> In Jack's dream, at widely separated intervals, appeared the *Man* who would contest Jack's self-mastership, to whom he would eventually bend

a vanquished intelligence. He never saw such a one in the flesh, yet that
entity stalked through more than the hallucinations of sleep. It was long ago
he first told me of the ominous figure in his consciousness. The last
manifestation was within a very few years of his death. The Man, imperial,
inexorable, with destiny, strangely human, descended along a vast cascade
of stairways, and Jack at the foot looked up and waited, as imperially, for
the meeting that was to be his unknown fate. But the nemesis never, in that
form at least, overtook him.

Kittredge spoke very true words in saying this. The figure, as we understand it
today, was certainly the archetype of the Self, and Jack London was a man who,
through his constant active imaginations and the writing of his many books, was
confronted with the Self—had called up the Self. It is sad to think, but it was
tragically unavoidable that Jack could not find any positive aspect in this figure.
We don't know how much he realized that the archetype of the Self had
established itself in him. We know that in the story "The Red One" he certainly
describes in large details his meeting with the Self. We don't know, however,
how much he realized that in writing the story he was writing all about himself
and that he had met the objective Psyche.

He died at the age of forty under circumstances which never made it
quite clear whether he had committed suicide or died of natural causes. There
is, however, no doubt that toward the end of his life he was a very sick man.

On one of his trips to Hawaii in May of 1916, he wrote the story "The
Red One." It was preceded by stories like "The Hussy," in which a man finds
the Tower of Jewels, the gold of the Incas, on a high mountain, and is followed
by a story "Argus of the Ancient Times," in which an old man is in quest of the
Great Treasure and finds it. He writes there:

> It was in the dusk of Death's fluttery wings that Tarwater thus crouched
> and, like his remote forebear, the child-man, went to myth-making, the
> sun-heroizing, himself hero-maker and the hero in quest of the
> immemorable treasure difficult of attainment. Either he must attain the
> treasure—for so ran the inexorable logic of the shadow-land of the
> unconscious—or else sink into the all-devouring sea, the blackness eater of
> the light that swallowed to extinction the sun each night. . .the sun that
> arose in rebirth next morning in the east, and that had become to man
> man's first symbol of immortality through rebirth.

"The Red One," written on the 22nd of May, 1916, exactly six months before
his untimely death, was originally entitled "The Message." Bassett, the hero of
the story, is a young English scientist and botanist who is in search of the
mythical jungle butterfly, one which is more than one foot from wing-tip to

wing-tip and lives in the roof of the jungle. In quest of this butterfly, he hears one day from the island of Ringmanu a marvelous sound which he likens to the trump of an archangel. He determines at once to discover the mysterious instrument which creates this sound. Throughout the story Jack London gives abundant and beautiful descriptions of this sound: "Sonorous as thunder, mellow as a golden bell, thin and sweet as a thrummed taut cord of silver." "Walls of cities might well fall down before so vast and compelling a summons." "It is like the mighty cry of some Titan of the Elder World vexed with misery or wrath." In almost every word of this magnificent story one feels the extreme fascination which the mysterious Red One exerts on Bassett—pardon me, on Jack London. The Self truly inspired this story; there is not a superfluous word in it.

Fascinated by the magic of the tone, Bassett enters the jungle, accompanied by his boy, Sagawa, who carries the shotgun and all the naturalist's gear. Immediately upon moving into the jungle, Sagawa is decapitated—and Bassett, in his fight with the primitive natives, has a terrible struggle to survive. He loses two fingers of his hand. He spends several nights in the jungle, is bitten by insects, becomes very sick and shakes with fever. Finally he succeeds in getting out of the jungle into wonderful grassland. He enters a village and finds there a woman who becomes for him a representation of what Jung called the anima, a symbol of the feminine in a man's psyche. He resolves to shoot her, but can never remember whether or not he had; nor can he remember how he chanced to be in that village or how he succeeded in getting away from it.

At last, however, he fights his way into another village. This one happens to be the principle village in a federation of twelve. Their god is the Red One whom all worship, and to whom they bring bloody sacrifices. He, the Red One, has subdued the gods of all the other tribes on the island of Guadalcanal. Gngngn is the weak chief, Ngurn is the medicine-man whose main occupation is the curing of heads over a fire. The head-hunters bring to him the heads of their victims and through curing these Ngurn receives the wisdom contained in these heads.

Bassett is increasingly possessed by the magic peal of the Red One and now bends every effort to find out its secret and then bring it back to civilization. He is very sick, and the natives know that he will never be able to leave them. Therefore, they give him permission to roam in the three quadrants of the compass, but the fourth quadrant in which the Red One is located is declared taboo to him. In order to satisfy this consuming curiosity imposed upon him by the numinous sound of the Red One and to find a way to set his eyes upon it, he decides to make love to Balatta, the girl who has saved him and has herself fallen in love with the whiteness of his skin. She is just as frightened of breaking the taboo as he is attracted to it by the numinosity of its sound. He succeeds, however, is persuading her to lead the way to the mysterious Red One.

He discovers that the Red One is a perfect sphere, fully two hundred feet in diameter, with the color quality of lacquer, brighter than bright cherry red. On closer investigation it appears that it is no longer lacquer, nor does the Red One have a smooth surface. The substance is metal, but of no metal or combination of metals he had ever known. On the slightest touch it quivered a sound,

> so elusive thin that it was shimmeringly sibilant, piping like an elfin horn, like a peal from some bell of the gods reaching earthward from across space.
>
> Amongst its many names were The Lord Shouter, The God-Voiced, The Bird-Throated, The Sun Singer, and The Star Born. The Star Born was certainly the most fitting one. It was a creation of artifice and mind, a perfect form, a child of intelligence. Bassett laughed aloud at the thought of the wonderful messenger, winged with intelligence across space to fall into a bushman stronghold. It was as if God's word had fallen into the muck mire underlying the bottom of hell; as if the Sermon on the Mount had been preached in a rolling bedlam of lunatics.

So Jack London describes this wonderful discovery. "Who were they?" he asks. "What were they—those far distant superior ones who had bridged the sky with their gigantic, red-iridescent, heaven-singing message?" This sounding sphere contained the speech and wisdom of the stars, it could contain vast histories, profounds of research. It was Time's greatest gift to blindfold, insatiable and sky aspiring man. And to him, Bassett, had been vouchsafed the lordly fortune to be the first to receive this message from man's interstellar kin.

After his return to the village, Bassett renews his plans for going back to civilization. Soon, however, he realizes that his fevers continue to weaken him and that death is inevitable. He continues to make love to Balatta, but with utter reluctance and loathing. He escapes from her as much as possible into the hut of Ngurn, the medicine man who spends his time with curing heads and incantations. He assures Bassett that it will not be very long before he will also cure his head, because Bassett will certainly die from his illness. On a day when his mind is unclouded by fevers, Bassett therefore proposes a contract to Ngurn. He wants to see and hear the Red One once more and die with this wonderful peal in his ears. He will accept to be ritually killed by Ngurn while seeing and hearing the Red One. This is agreed. At the last moment, Bassett considers that he could still kill Ngurn with his shotgun, but he rejects this idea.

But why cheat him? Head-hunting cannibal, beast of a human, nevertheless old Ngurn had played squarer than square. It would be a ghastly pity and an act of dishonor to cheat the old fellow at the last. His head was Ngurn's, and Ngurn's head to cure it would be.

And so as agreed, Bassett—bending his head forward—forgot Balatta who was merely a woman—and undesired.—And for that instant, ere the end, there fell upon Bassett the shadow of the Unknown.—It seemed that he gazed upon the serene face of the Medusa, Truth—and he saw the vision of his head turning slowly, always turning, in the devil-devil house beside the breadfruit tree.

These quotations will convey to you the full poetry and inspired quality of this story. But behind this poetry the story of Jack London's tragedy appears in stark relief.

Let us remember that as a child he climbed on the locomotive, and carried by the magic power of the unconscious, he developed a fascinating personality; he wrote an incredible amount of great and also mediocre stories, was always driven to over-demand himself, strove to achieve the impossible in many fields, always living life to the fullest and fearlessly and sometimes wantonly risking more than even his powerful organism could stand. So illness overtook him, catastrophe broke upon him in the fire of his beloved Wolf House. His daughters from his first marriage refused to live with him. In the midst of thousands of friends, men and women, he was lonely. He did not and could not realize that by his daring adventures into the life of the spirit, he had come into the neighborhood of the Self, nor could he realize that the might of his genius did not originate in his ego, but came from the Self. For a long time, he could afford to identify with the Self and feel himself as a superman. Sooner or later, the *Auseinandersetzung* between himself and the Self had to begin. And that is what the second dream tries to tell him. The *Man*, the ominous figure, the Anthropos who descended, was destiny and became his nemesis. As Ngurn says in "The Red One," paraphrasing the Old Testament, "No white man could see him, and live." (Exodus 33.20: "No man shall see me, and live.") And yet Jack London, in the person of Bassett, looked upon him and lived. He was even able to touch it and to awaken its marvelous voice and then return to the village. This he was able to accomplish because he went down to see him accompanied by the primitive anima, that anima so despised by Bassett. He has actually acquired his fatal illness practically at the instant at which he entered the jungle. And yet he did not die from his illness. His illness rather gave him the chance to experience the miraculous sphere again, to expose himself once more to the greatest risk and grace which can be bestowed upon man. That is, to meet the

Self in its fullness, whose other name is TRUTH. He was driven to it in the hopelessness of his psychic condition, but paradoxically enough he also volunteered. It was a contract he made with the Self. At the last moment he was indeed tempted to cheat God but rejected it, because he acknowledged that the Self had played squarer than square with him. This was different from Faust, the story of another man who was granted a meeting and association with the Self and upon whom the Self bestowed its richest gift—and whom he cheated at the last. Jack London's hero, in contrast, was true to himself at the end. He recognized that the Self had given him both spiritual and material riches, had played squarer than square with him and he, Jack London, must needs play fair as well with the Self to the end.

For Faust, his "immortal" soul is carried to Heaven and his redemption takes place in the beyond. His last achievement is the discovery of the moment in its fullness. But Jack London's fulfillment is the vision of Truth, the Zen experience at the moment of his death, and slow turning of the head in the devil-devil house, in the post-mortal state.

While the Self is the all pervading motif of the story, we discover other classical archetypes of the collective unconscious in this story, and even in their classical sequence: shadow, anima, old wise man and Self. By its very beauty of language, it is obvious that it is not thought out, but truly inspired. The patterns of the unconscious have dictated the story.

In Bassett we find the ego, or to be more correct, the representative of Jack London's ego. It is in Bassett that we see the scientist, the rationalist who, however, carries in himself the longing for the non-rational which is symbolized in his quest for the mythical butterfly, a fitting symbol for the psyche. In his quest he encounters something that transcends by far the value and meaning of this butterfly. It is the magic sound of the mysterious Red One.

Like so many classical journeys, this one also begins as an adventure of a hero and his companion. But in contrast, for instance, to Dante's journey with Virgil or Moses' with Dulquarnein, this second figure, the servant, is described with a remarkable degree of contempt: "He has a queer little monkeyish face, eloquent with fear." Yet he is faithful and—as it turned out—he foresees that this adventure must have a tragic end. Though a companion on this quest, he is not invested with the qualities of a superior guide like Virgil in the Divine Comedy. He has much more the characteristics of Jack London's inferior personality, or what Jung called his shadow. His advice is not listened to, his common sense is not appreciated, and actually this shadow figure has no chance to interact with the ego. The ego at this point has already fallen victim to the spell of the Red One, and there is nothing, not even a trace of common sense which would give the ego fair warning of the dangers awaiting it on this quest, thus permitting it to equip itself for the hazards of the journey.

Thus, poorly prepared Bassett enters the unconscious like a curious adolescent, without much realization of the dangers of such a journey, and Sagawa is immediately killed, that is: he is decapitated, and the hero is assailed by primitives with poison arrows and falls victim to the insects of the jungle, thus catching his fatal illness.

He had irrevocably been captured by the process of individuation, Jung's term for a series of psychological events in which conscious and unconscious meet and a continual change of the personality occurs; it ends in bringing about a unique individual. The fascination issuing from the archetypes, especially from the Self, has caught him, but the loss of the shadow—the archetype that refers to the qualities, habits and feelings most human beings suppress and do not care to know about allowed the unconscious to invade him as poison and infection. Thus the ego is forced to fight a courageous battle, but without the possibility of an ultimate victory or accomplishment of the task. Translated into actual reality, this psychological condition in Jack London meant, for instance, that he undertook his adventure on the outside, that he built the "Snark" and made the famous journey to the South Sea Islands. He overestimated his stamina and powers, his physical and financial resources by far and actually contracted the illness which fatally sapped his strength.

In this way, one could consider Jack London as a tragic victim of the process of individuation. He certainly is, but still not a failure, because he lived his life fully and without reservation, because like a man, he courageously accepted the challenge of the Self, and as a human being he was granted the vision of God in his voluntary sacrifice.

The second of the classical figures, the anima, actually saves his life, but nevertheless she is treated by him with an amazing hostility and loathing. In remembering his first encounter with her he cannot even make sure whether he killed her or not. In her second and more permanent form, he heaps contempt on her, calls her quite frankly the inferior sex, expresses the same sentiments as Nietzsche. Quite obviously this anima is to a large extent contaminated with the shadow. Not only is she described as primitive in the sense of primeval or original, but in the sense of being barbaric, dirty, ugly and smelly. Furthermore, she is predominantly Nature to him only in the sense of sex without any positive feeling tone attached to her. In order to make contact, he has to teach her how to bathe, even to the point of giving her frequent scrubbings. When he meets her for the first time, he tells us that "her sex was advertised by the one article of finery with which she was adorned, namely a pig's tail, thrust through a hole in her left ear lobe." His relationship to her is simply that of making use of her and of exerting power over her. He needs her because there is a taboo which forbids a stranger to see the Red One, because the Red One is hidden in a gorge within the Fourth Quadrant. He can find this place only with the help of a native, and Balatta, because of her love for him, would break the taboo. For this reason only he is forced to make up to her. He uses the charm of his white skin and his masculinity as assets in the deal to achieve his overriding ambition of gaining access to the mysterious Red One. At no point in the story is she treated as an equal, to say nothing of consideration or love. Therefore, we find in Jack London's hero qualities like fascination by the Red One to an unlimited degree; acknowledgement of its power, superiority and transcendental quality. We find submission to it and ecstasy in completely surrendering to it, but never love. And this is probably one important reason why in the same way as the anima is contaminated with the shadow, the Self appears contaminated with an important aspect of the anima, i.e., why it has the transmundane color, this unearthly red.

As is to be expected, the third classical figure is that of the old wise man. Bassett is genuinely attracted to Ngurn, the primitive medicine-man of the tribe, but he also spends as much time as possible with him in order to escape from the loathsome anima. Again we find that this figure has a great deal of negative qualities. Though he certainly is very wise and he conveys his wisdom to Bassett, he is after Bassett's head nevertheless; not in order to re-establish his health and return him to life, but to gain his head and cure it. The whole story occurs in the country of headhunting primitives. The atmosphere of head-hunting and the curing of heads pervades it. All the long talks between Bassett and Ngurn take place in Ngurn's hut whilst he is curing heads. He is one of the best curers of heads, having inherited his art from his medicine-man ancestors, an art long lost in other tribes. He promises Bassett to take good care of his head after his death and to make his head his masterpiece. A curious motive! True, Jack London, in his South Sea journey, came across some examples of hunting and curing of heads, but that it turned up just in this story is most significant.

I have met this motif of the wise head in the dreams of my patients. I have met it in dreams, for instance, as the head which continually spoke perfect wisdom—in this way symbolizing the logos principle of the unconscious. I have encountered it in dreams also as the vessel which had to be prepared and worked upon in order to become the perfect vessel. I have most frequently found it as the Round One, in this way being a symbol of the Self, a most suitable symbol since as head it represented the essential and concentrated substance of the human being.

In *Psychology and Alchemy* Jung refers to the "sixth parable" of the Splendor Solis, where a vision of a dismembered body is mentioned, whose head was of fine gold, but separated from the body. Jung also mentions that the Greek alchemists styled themselves: Children of the Golden Head.

In his article "The Visions of Zosimus," Jung speaks in detail about primitive beliefs and rituals in which animal and human sacrifices were made in order to gain a head and to make it white; he mentions other rather gruesome rituals the purpose of which was to gain a specially prepared head giving forth great wisdom. According to Jung, the head can be interpreted as the so-called "round element," since the Liber Quartorum establishes a connection between the vessel and the head. Furthermore, Zosimus mentions several times "the extremely white stone which is in the head."

In addition, he mentions the rumor that Gerbert of Reims possessed a golden skull which revealed oracles to him. According the rabbinical tradition, the "teraphim," the oracle mentioned in the Old Testament, was supposed to have been a cut-off head or skull. Jung also quotes M. I. Bin Gorion *Die Sagen der Juden*, in which it is said that these teraphim were made in the following way: the head of somebody who had to be a native was cut off, and the hair was plucked out. Then the head was sprinkled with salt and anointed with oil. After that a small tablet of copper or gold was inscribed with the name of the god and put under the tongue of the cut-off head. The head was then placed in a room, candles were lit before it, and it happened that when one prostrated oneself before it, the head began to talk and to answer all the questions which one addressed to it.

These examples were a striking parallel to Jack London's story and show that an archetypal pattern imposed itself on Jack London when he wrote at some length about the curing of the head—and that he recognized its true purpose, which was to gain wisdom. It follows an archetypal pattern when, in the end, he sees his own head slowly turning as the serene face of Truth. It is the "veritas efficaciae" which, according to Dorn is the highest power and impregnable fortress wherein the philosopher's stone lies safeguarded.

Ngurn says to Bassett: "I will tell you many secrets, for I am an old man and very wise, and I shall be adding wisdom to wisdom as I turn your head in the smoke." And yet, there is a great difference between the motif of the teraphim of the old alchemists and the curing of the head as described in "The Red One." The alchemists or the Hebrew priests who gained the head did not identify with it. They gained possession of the head and found means to communicate with it. In Jack London's story, it is Bassett's head which will be cured, and wisdom will accrue to it and issue from it only after his death. In other words, it will occur only in the postmortal state. That is: this wisdom will never serve life or Bassett's individual life, but will represent a terminal condition.

The head itself as the Round One certainly symbolizes the Self, as Jung has demonstrated in *Psychology and Alchemy*. In "The Visions of Zosimus," Jung quotes the Liber Platonis Quartorum: "*Vas. . . oportet esse rotundae figurae: ut sit artifex huius (aperis) mutator firmamenti et testae capitis, ut cum sit res qua indigemus, res simplex.*" (The vessel must be of round shape just as the artist of this work is a transformer of the firmament and of the skull, and like the thing which we need is "a simple thing.") As a vessel, however, it has feminine characteristics as well and therefore has a certain anima aspect. One can therefore conclude that it was more the instinctual and emotional aspect of the anima which was so unacceptable to Jack London, whilst her more spiritual aspect, relating him to the Self, could be assimilated to consciousness.

The head as a vessel of wisdom needing a great deal of work represents the alchemical or psychological process, the opus. Yet it has a rather lugubrious aspect in Jack London's story and casts its dark and fatal shadow on his experience. This is certainly essentially different in the great symbol of the Self which has given its name to the whole story, and of which we hear again and again on account of its all encompassing numinosity.

The sphere as a symbol of the Self is one of the most familiar representations of the Self, as Jung has shown in *Psychology and Alchemy*. The cosmogony of Empedocles, for example, calls this spherical being *eudaimonestatos Theos*, the most serene God, just as Jack London calls the Red Sphere the serene face of Truth. The curious thing about it in this story is that it is described as a metal "though unlike any metal or combination of metals he had ever known." He observes that it shows "signs of heat and fusing." It is "a child of intelligence, remote and unguessable, working corporally in metals. It is a far-journeyer which was lacquered by its fiery bath in two atmospheres." In "The Visions of Zosimus," Jung discusses the question of why the inner man and his spiritual being happen to be represented by metals. He answers that nature seems to be concerned to drive consciousness to greater clarity, and therefore uses man's constant desire for metals, especially the precious ones, to search for them and to examine their possibilities. In this occupation, it might dawn upon him that a dangerous demon or a dove of the Holy Ghost might be contained in lead.

It has exactly this effect upon the hero of our story. Entranced by the wonder of the unthinkable and unguessable thing, it makes him reflect and meditate on it. Psychologically speaking, it means that he has become aware of a world of active intelligences beyond the narrow field of human consciousness, that the awe engendered by the archetypes has struck him, and that he who for so long identified with the archetype of the Self, at last recognizes the activity of the archetypes and asks himself: "Who are they?" and significantly "What are they?"—those far superior ones who had bridged the sky with their gigantic, red-iridescent, heaven-singing message. We are reminded of Dorn who says: "Nemo vero potest cognoscere se, nisi sciat quid, et non ipse sit, a quo depedat, vel cuius sit et in quem finem factus sit." (No one can truly know himself, unless he knows *what* he is, and not *who* he is, on what depends, or to what or whom he belongs, and for what purpose he was created.) Jung comments, "This differentiation between 'quid' and 'quis' is extremely significant. Whilst 'quis' has an indubitably personalistic aspect and therefore refers to the ego, the 'quid' is a neuter, and therefore presupposes nothing but an object of which it is not even sure that it has personality." Thus, Jack London experiences the psyche as an objective reality, as a "quid" and not a "quis." It is even possible to gain its extraordinary wisdom. He realizes that it might contain "engines and elements and mastered forces, love and mysteries and destiny controls. What insight! What vision!" Jack London recognized that the archetypes are the factors which arrange and control our fate, and that by contacting them, we establish a relationship to our destiny and no longer remain mere objects of fate. He recognized his destiny, but also his inability to change his destiny at such a late hour. He, Jack London, was the one who "was vouchsafed the lordly fortune to be the first to receive this message from man's interstellar kin."

On account of his unstinted devotion to life as he found it and to the spirit as he experienced it, he was granted the great vision, and this was his fulfillment. His strength was spent, and he could not go beyond this intuition. All his life he was a seeker for the "immemorable treasure difficult of attainment." Through most of his life he had been seeking the progress and salvation of mankind in Socialism. He was one of the great myth-makers of mankind.

So much for Jack London. We, the heirs of his message, must ask ourselves how much of all this is still our problem today. What Jack London observed in discovering the mysterious sphere, The Red One, was an event in the collective unconscious. The story, "The Red One," does not describe Jack London's personal psychology, but is an accurate picture of American psychology and of Western man as a whole. The Self has embedded itself not only on the mythical island of Guadalcanal, but everywhere in mankind. Jack London was not the first one, as he believed, to whom this lordly fortune was vouchsafed. Nietzsche was probably its first tragic victim in modern times. It is worth noting that Jung's great development and discovery of the collective unconscious took place just in these same years. In a commentary on Heinich Zimmer's book, *Art Forms and Yoga*, he mentions the fact that it was at about this time that he discovered the mandala and essential facts about the archetype of the Self.

The world as a whole has been in constant unrest since. In the years that followed the writing of "The Red One," two world wars, revolutions of social, political and religious nature have been fought, and the discovery of the hydrogen bomb has been made. All this due to the all-determining fact that, as Jack London describes it, the Self has embedded itself in our soil. But the soil in which it has been implanted is a "bushman stronghold." We are "man-eating and head-hunting savages." It is "as if God's Word had fallen into the muck mire of the abyss underlying the bottom of hell, as if the Sermon on the Mount had been preached in a roaring bedlam of lunatics."

Bassett's problem is our problem. We are in the same psychological boat. It is a general human attitude to forget the shadow. We need a good and adequate knowledge of the shadow to release his positive values. We cannot afford to maintain an attitude of contempt, hostility or loathing against the anima, i.e., against the non-rational quality of the unconscious. We would do better to accept it as it is, a world of images and of mysterious life. Such an approach will give us new strength and understanding to receive the Self in our midst and thus to release its unlimited sources of wisdom.

The changes necessary for the reception of the Self in our life cannot occur by means of political agreements or economic planning, they cannot take place in institutions or nations, but only through the work and experience of the individual human being to whom they occur in the stillness and storms of his soul. Only that civilization will survive which allows the individual to meet his Self in full freedom. Only thus, as Jack London says, can "man's life on earth, individual and collective, spring up from its present mire to inconceivable heights of purity and power."

NOTE

[1] *Numinous*: derived from the Latin word *numen*: god; it describes the emotion one experiences in the presence of God or a god. Psychologically speaking, a numinous emotion is always an indication that an archetype is present and active.

From the Abyss to the Summit

Roger Chateauneu [Translated from the French by Susan M. Nuernberg]

The literature professor who in the 1930s in Gascogny as well as in the suburbs of Paris, in Brittany as well as in Alsace, would have suggested to take off a few hours from the time devoted to Corneille[1] and Racine[2] to study Jack London would not have been perceived as a leftist—the term was not yet fashionable—but as mad. He would have needed a considerable dose of eccentricity to venture these words: "Instead of going over *Le Cid* which most of you have studied three times without the least benefit, or recite in chorus the lamentation of Andromaque that even the the class dunce knows by heart, let's read a few pages from *The People of the Abyss*.[3]

Jack London (1876-1916) was a writer of entertainment. Still today, his name seldom emerges from academic writing about large concepts such as God, rights and civilization. The wanderer in the snows and the navigator through the gales is certainly not the type of bard whose marble bust crowned with laurel is found in the principal's office. Yet still, he is another Homer.[4] A Homer of these United States whose bicentennial we are celebrating this year. At the same time we celebrate the centennial of Jack London who belongs to that great democratic literature born from the struggle for independence and liberty led by George Washington and Abraham Lincoln.

But we haven't had twenty centuries of university purgatory to cleanse him and to allow him to take his proper position in the good society without the thick smell of the sea and the road, the patched and worn-out clothes and the alcoholic breath.

No matter. He has already been crowned by the highest glory: the one that is gained from small school children. He is in the company of the Kipling of *Kim*, he listens with Hans Christian Anderson to the song that carries the great adventure of the world, made of pains, wonders, and fears. And also of angers and hopes, all mixed into the endless breath of the wind and the tireless passion of the sea. Do we know him? Maybe not. An affirmation may pass for a paradox. They said that Lenin admired him, he is probably translated into all of the written languages of the planet, he holds the universality of the sea, virgin snows, ports, trains, forests crystallized into cathedrals of ice, frozen or flooding rivers, trails of agony and illumination where the gold seeker walks. Sometimes he reminds us of Chekhov,[5] on his way to Sakhaline, sleeping on thousands of pages of mail—the magic sketch book of Siberia whirling with birds, quivering with fish, embalmed with mushrooms, gorged with moss and humus—and to say it all, intoxicated with immense powers of life. At other times he reminds us of the Van Gogh whose life-size wax effigy watches visitors to the underground of a museum in Amsterdam: pale, wild eyed, ragged, and haggard. He frightens and we sympathize with him. But we have not finished piercing the secret of this light that we guess surrounds Jack London, witness of depths, seeker of the impossible, going no one knows where, toward death in any case, and sooner than the others, hearing enigmatic orders whispered in his ear by the great god Pan: the one whose name symbolizes wholeness.

When reread in the last quarter of the twentieth century, Jack London emerges as a novel avatar. At last here comes the moment when *The Road*[6] will take its place beside the *Odyssey*. The legacy of the drama as handed down by Aeschylus, Euripides, Shakespeare, and Racine will not disappear—it contains the same portion of eternity as man himself—but takes on a new order, to include other essential components of tragedy which are space, solitude, fatigue, extreme climates, and the heavens. It is true that exoticism is not new: we have that of Chateaubriand,[7] and that of Pierre Loti.[8] But let us look at the new role that nature and adventure play in the works a Pablo Neruda and an André Malraux,[9] how an exaggerated landscape is necessary to a Steinbeck and a Sholokhov.[10] And already we can hear the call of the Cosmos. It seems that the soul of man has grown. We feel at the same time worthy and obliged to assume this challenge to feel the suffering which permeates all of Saint-Exupery's[11] works and the prayers for mercy in the poetry of Saint-John Perse. We also feel that our destiny and our pride as human beings consists of being a consciousness and a will, by passing through the trial of the abyss: The trapper of the Great North, solitary sailor, explorer of volcanoes, inventer of caves and sea bottoms, pilot of planes and space ships all undergo the trial of the abyss. It is all one and the same. Jack London would have liked and envied Yuri Gagarin[12] in his life as much as in his death. The more so because at this level of communion the journey brings people together rather than apart. A few years ago in England, a collection of poems dedicated to space was published. One of the works, *Man*, (Part IV, Canto 3), by Ronald Duncan[13] is the meditation of an astronaut carefully chosen for the absolute mastery of his nerves. His courage, his physical and moral equilibrium protect him from the unexpected, so that he is, in a way, "abnormally normal." And here he is in his flight catching himself looking from so far away at this humble speck feebly illuminated in the dark of the night, that is our earth. Then an unknown feeling rises in him. Which force is warming his heart? He will never confess this moment of effusion to the space program directors when he returns from his mission: but he succumbs to love, to moving and sweet love, for our earth and all those on it.

This contemporary poem keeps us in the heart of the matter at a time when people ludicrously, and yet seriously, look for omens to see whether the idea of socialism is compatible with the idea of liberty. Pseudo-polemical writers paint the socialist world with the monotonous colors of bleakness and gloom producing a stifling universe deprived of imagination, moderation and a far-sighted vision. We are able to cite for them one hundred Soviet science fiction works and another hundred popularizing science. Take for instance *The Chain of Pluto*, Evgueny Markhinin's fascinating account of an exploration into "the arc of fire" of the Kuriles Islands [editions de progress, Moscow, translated by Marena Mareseniva]. Haroun Tazieff, Thor Heyerdahl,[14] Yuri Gagarin, Alan Shepard,[15] Guerman Titof,[16] John Glenn,[17] Scott Carpenter,[18] Andrian Nikolaiev,[19] Valentina Terechkova[20] and so many others illustrate a new idea of liberty. Love of liberty, love of the earth, love of knowledge, love of men are not separable. More than ever before, we must guard against the confusion and perversion of terms, we would like to correct in regard to Jack London: the love of liberties insisting on the indispensable plural, and not the Liberty which is abstract, hollow and illusory. For there are many liberties: the real effective liberty to find a job according to one's aptitude and preference; the liberty of earning a wage allowing us truly to renew our vital energy; the liberty of obtaining housing adequate to the necessities of rest, the dignity of conjugal and family life, the needs of hygiene, of leisure, of study; the liberty of aging with respect and without worries—and of dying in the same way. Man ceased being an animal on that day way back when a prehistoric tribe understood that every society is established on gratitude and memory, that the community is not composed entirely of the living, that from the first to the last breath, all of existence is one. The spiritual itinerary that made of Jack London a socialist writer offers an exceptional teaching tool. We are not sure even at the present moment that we have seen, felt, and weighed his objectives. His approach is greatly original, remarkably authentic and (at the risk of abusing this word) unusual. Here is a born globe-trotter constantly burning with desire to be somewhere else sniffing out adventure, an American boy that every routine quickly bores who feels caged everywhere. He is a passionate of the compact, cold, lucid kind. At an early age he read enormously, avidly and attentively the masters of literature, and the philosophers, with the fury of the self-taught individual. But he does not know nor does he want to reason any other way except through facts, gesture, purpose and anecdotes. His grave grievances against capitalist society hardly proceed from good intentions. If he happens to moralize in *The People of the Abyss* it is incidental and involuntary—through the nature of things shall we say because it is impossible for him to repress a cry of anger, a curse, at the spectacle of so much distress and infamy. But it is as a traveller that he came to London, lets not forget it. He is a war correspondent—these are his own words—at the heart of the battle that the dominant class is waging upon the proletariat. Better yet, the East End is an ocean. Thus, the same way that one wears the sailor's clothes to navigate, he wears the cast-off clothing of the downtrodden. Then the world changes around him. It was enough for him to slip into the condition of a poor person to see the dividing lines of his former perception of social classes disappear and, for him to see the universe in the same perspective that he shows himself to the humiliated and the offended. To discover, to discover. . . before Jack London La Bruyere described the horror of the peasant condition. Many tears have been shed over the poor, but the most generous thinkers can not totally get rid of the idea that there is redemption in destitution and that there is heavenly grace in malnutrition. A traditional dictation in our teaching method—from Lamartine, or De Vigny, or De Musset[21]—dispenses a bucolic herb tea regarding some lumberjack who is living off nothing in his hut with his raggedy family but soothed by the gracefulness of the setting sun and the nurturing power of bird songs. "Here is a happy man," our thinker tells himself, happy to have practiced true evangelical teaching during a walk in the woods to digest his dinner. Lets not take offense: such nonsense falls here and there from the pen of George Sand, and still today! Sheep folds, Robinson Crusoe fairy tales, and pastoral sensitivity, do they make us forget the gigantic factory of the giant capitalism, the moloch which in vain and in the name of cupidity mutilates and kills? The promethean effort of man, admirable in itself, is a just struggle. England was right to build steam machines and looms. Not to have done it would have been to abdicate. Scholars whose stature is worthy of our admiration had provided in the eighteenth and nineteenth century the tools of mathematics, physics and chemistry. Newton is not the only one to deserve the epitaph: "Through reason he lifted himself above humanity." Let us open a scientific treatise: out of four inventors there would certainly be an Englishman, at a time when there wasn't more than one Englishman out of forty people. Laws, principles, equations, discoveries engendered by the spirits of these heroes and their assistants, gifted mechanics, Jack London shows us what the disease of profit making has done: look into the richest city of all time and of all continents and find the abomination of the East End. That is why everything was brought together, in this century and in this country, for the voice of Karl Marx[22] to speak out.

Vehement heart, Jack London is fired with anger against the actions of the slum landlords who chase workers' families from their homes always shoving them further away, forcing them to pack into a single room, stuffing the rented space to the limit in order to extract from a tenement the maximum profit. He has condemned this usury, always more clever and more implacable, and the process by which the merchants of sleep dole out to the worn out workers a slice of rest limited to a couple of hours a day—in this he is dreadfully accurate. He has stigmatized the plundering, the prostitution, and the disgrace that transformed the suburbs of London into a belt of shame. He ventured an economic theory which wasn't his strong point and offered some theories full of genuine good will. He is not a theoretician of communism. If he has scandalized the well-intentioned critics who wanted to purify him of his stench by limiting him to his Northland adventure stories by sorting through his work and pulling out portions judged inoffensive for the shelves of the children's libraries, it is no less true that the Marxists were unable to follow him in all of his affirmations and conclusions. We should take care to avoid this misunderstanding and injustice: Jack London, as many generous spirits, wishes to reform the world, but the contribution that he brings to this field is the plea of a poet and not that of an economist or a political strategist. This does not diminish in any way the value of his contribution. Far from it: his meditations on the human condition furnish invaluable material for the highest philosophy and the highest political reflection. Concerning the problem of the relationship of thought to reality, we send the reader to the article of Boris G. Koucnetsov, a relativity physicist, president of the Einstein International Committee, "The Question of Dostoyevsky and the Response of Einstein."[23] Or we will cite among many others—these sentences of the science writer Leonid Ponomarev in the last chapter of his book titled *In the Country of the Quanta:*

> Science isn't capable either of answering questions about the meaning of life. It has a more modest task. Dazzled by the success of science, we tend to forget that for future generations our rationalism and our faith in science will seem as laughable and incomprehensible to them as the rites of Egyptian priests seem to us. Knowledge is limitless but its historical forms are another matter.[24]

Indeed knowledge goes further and by other ways than by manipulation of a table of integral calculus. All scientists worthy of this fine name know now that poetry is one of the most powerful tools of knowledge, equal to mathematics, with which we wonder if it won't soon constitute a common empire. And all of this helps us to better understand today the depth and impact of the last of the great works of Jack London, *John Barleycorn,*[25] the confession of a drinker, the chronicle of alcoholism, which is perhaps his spiritual legacy, which is the equivalent of Plato's Pheidon. Through these pages written non-stop, in a concise, passionate, tense style illuminated by admirable passages, we can feel the life and torments of humanity—the chill rising from the depth of the night and of death to which Hamlet is drawn. To be or not to be. The question of questions.

> The one event happeneth to all alike. There is no new thing under the sun, not even that yearned-for bauble of feeble souls—immortality. But he knows, *he* knows, standing upright on his two legs unswaying. He is compounded of meat and wine and sparkle, of sun-mote and world-dust, a

> frail mechanism made to run for a span, to be tinkered at by doctors of divinity and doctors of physic, and to be flung into the scrap-heap at the end.[26]

The accusation of complacent pessimism and romanticism is too easy. No doubt that Jack London had read Ecclesiastes: all of America is impregnated with the Bible. All the West too, whose culture, as Peter Abrahams[27] reminds us, cannot be understood without the Old Testament. But Jack London knew other works: "Then the city of Oakland appeared in my life, and on the shelves of its municipal library I saw an immense world spring out of the horizon. . . ." He doesn't tell us if it is there that he met in he days of his youth Lao-Tzu, Tchoang-Tse and Lie-Tse,[28] who on the other side of the globe have the same importance as Moses, Aristotle and Plato. But often, his words resound with an accent little familiar to Europeans, and the quotation from Chinese classics which appears in Chapter 36 of *John Barleycorn* is certainly not a literary addition. The whole work proves indeed that Jack London, drunk or sober, carries within himself much of this high morality, without hope but without bitterness, profoundly indifferent and disheartened but generous and open to all colors and sounds of the world. When a man has risen to authentic greatness through courage, endeavor and the love of others, his melancholy and sadness is not negative or destructive. The sadness of Jack London is the sadness of the strong. What it supplies even through the blurred vision of alcohol is power and lucidity.

> To the imaginative man, John Barleycorn [a popular American expression designating alcohol] sends the pitiless, spectral syllogisms of the white logic. He looks upon life and all its affairs with the jaundiced eye of a pessimistic German philosopher. He sees through all illusions. He transvalues all values. God is bad, truth is a cheat, and life is a joke. From his clam-mad heights, with the certitude of a god, he beholds all life as evil. Wife, children, friends—in the clear, white light of his logic they are exposed as frauds and shams. . . . So is he. He realizes that. But there is one difference. He sees; he knows. And he knows his one freedom: he may anticipate the day of his death.[29]

But it is from Faustian anguish and mortal doubts that the highest consciousness emerges, it is there that the most resounding forms of action are engendered. At each hour it is necessary to die in order to be reborn. Everything is a problem, everything is sorrow, burden, contradiction, struggle, conflict. At the end of this stormy road, there is a new idea about mankind. From the disgraced, poor, and hideous London proletariat, from the bottom of this pus-pocket and from this stupor will come the greatest forces of humanity and the shiniest dawn of civilization's days like an irresistible ocean. And it is thus that we will see the drunks of the West India dock, the unemployed of Lime House, the 450,000 wretches of the suburbs, with their millions of comrades throughout the earth, begin their long march. Which will lead them, against all forces of oppression and death, from their abyss to the summit of history.

NOTES

[1] Pierre Corneille. 1606-84. Often called the father of French classical tragedy. His *Le Cid* (performed 1637) is commonly regarded as the most significant play in the history of French drama.

[2] Jean Baptiste Racine. 1639-99. French playwright whose play *Andromaque* (first performed in 1667) has the theme of tragic folly and the blindness of passionate love.

[3] *The People of the Abyss* (1903) is a sociological study of the East End of London, England, written by Jack London while he lived there disguised as an American sailor.

[4] Homer, the presumed author of the *Iliad* and *Odyssey*, the two greatest epic poems of ancient Greece.

[5] Anton Chekhov. 1860-1904. Created a story form that develops through impressionistic details in a radial manner and does not seem to end. There is very little action or plot, but there is a lyrical evocation of mood and atmosphere and a provocative insight into character. See London's 1905 story, "The Sun-Dog Trail" in *Love of Life*.

[6] Jack London recorded the experience of "beating" his way across the country on freight trains in 1894 in *The Road* (1907).

[7] François-August Chateaubriand. 1768-1848. One of the first Romantic writers in France whose visit to the United States in 1791 is memorable chiefly for his travels with fur traders through virgin forests and for his firsthand acquaintance with Indians.

[8] Pierre Loti. 1850-1923. French novelist who experienced and diagnosed such obsessions of modern man as the longing to escape; the refusal of constraint; the appeal of the irrational; and the emphasis on "eroticism"—i.e. the value placed upon physical instinct as a challenge to death.

[9] André Malraux. 1901-76. French novelist and art historian whose novels derive their authority from his own participation in the events of his time.

[10] Mikhail Sholokhov. 1905-. Russian novelist whose *Tikhy Don* (4 vol., 1928-40), became the most widely read novel in the Soviet Union.

[11] Antoine Saint-Exupery. 1900-44. French aviator and writer whose works are the unique testimony of a pilot and a warrior who looked at adventure and danger with a poet's eyes.

[12] Yuri Gagarin. 1934-1968. Russian cosmonaut who was the first man to travel into space.

[13] Ronald Duncan. 1914-1982. "Man." *Frontier of Going*. London: Panther Books, 1969.

[14] Thor Heyerdahl. 1914-. Ethnologist and adventurer who organized and led the famous "Kon-Tiki" (1947) and "Ra" (1969) transoceanic scientific expeditions.

[15] Alan Shepard. 1923-. First U. S. astronaut to travel in space (May 5, 1961) 23 days after Yuri Gagarin orbited the Earth.

[16] Guerman Titov. 1935-. Russian cosmonaut who piloted the Vostok 2 spacecraft launched on Aug. 6, 1961, on the first manned space flight of more than a single orbit.

[17] John Glenn. 1921-. The first U. S. astronaut to orbit the earth (Feb 20, 1962).

[18] Scott Carpenter. 1925-. The second U. S. astronaut to make an orbital space flight (May 24, 1962).

[19] Andrian Nikolayev. 1929-. Russian cosmonaut who piloted Vostok 3 spacecraft, launched Aug. 11, 1962.

[20] Valentina Tereshkova. 1937-. Russian cosmonaut, the first woman to travel into space (June 6, 1963, Vostok 6).

[21] Alphonse de Lamartine, Alfred De Vigny, and Alfred De Musset are key figures in the Romantic movement in French literature.

[22] Karl Marx. 1818-83. Together with Engels he published *The Communist Manifesto* (1848), declaring that all history had been a history of class struggles which the working class would eventually win.

[23] Boris G. Koucnetsov. "The Question of Dostoyesky and the Response of Einstein." *Europe* 510 (1971).

[24] Leonid Ponomarev. *In the Country of the Quanta.* Moscow: Edition Mir, no date.

[25] Jack London's autobiographical *John Barleycorn* (1913) is subtitled "Alcoholic Memoirs."

[26] *John Barleycorn* (New York: Century, 1918), 13.

[27] Peter Abrahams. 1919-. Most prolific of South Africa's black prose writers whose early novel *Mine Boy* (1946) emphasized the dehumanizing effect of apartheid upon South African blacks.

[28] Lao-Tzu is the legendary founder of Taoism; Tchoang-Tse [Chuang-tzu] is an early Chinese interpreter of Taoism; Lie-Tse [Lieh-Tzu] is a Taoist philosopher.

[29] *John Barleycorn*, 14.

Jack London and the Working Class

Stephen Conlon

Some recent writers have had problems when they have tried to write about *The People of the Abyss* (1903). Maybe, some of the reasons behind this fact relate to the kind of book London is writing. It is a book about the working class written by a person who saw himself coming from that class. As Jack Lindsay points out, London was the first industrial proletarian to write about the experience of his own people.[1] But this special relationship between London and his material has been missed by those critics who cannot see much of interest in London's view of himself as a member of the working class. Attempts to break London away from his material may lead to readings of *The People of the Abyss* that miss much of the real drama of life that London felt in the East End of London.

Critics such as Clarice Stasz and Andrew Sinclair disparage London's involvement with his material in *The People of the Abyss* by insisting on what is to them a breach of faith, an act of dishonesty. Both critics charge that he went to England with his mind already set about the condition of the English working class. Sinclair asserts:

> Even though Jack London had read Booth's conclusions before his own brief descent into the East End in August of 1902, he was unable to see beyond the lurid curtain of his preconceptions. He had gone to seek there a pit of suffering, and he duly found the Abyss of his desire and his fear.[2]

What Sinclair seems to object to is that it is London's socialism which is being expressed in his insistence on the degradation of the people of the East End: "As a radical socialist, he had preconceived his vision of the East End as the Black Hole of Empire" (88). As evidence for this assertion Sinclair puts forward London's letter to Anna Strunsky, written while he was on the ship to England:

> He wrote to his confidante Anna Strunsky that he would sink out of sight before the Coronation of Edward the Seventh on August 9th, 1902, in order to see that Imperial show "from the standpoint of the London beasts. That's all they are—beast—if they are anything like the slum people of New York—beasts, shot through with stray flashes of divinity." (88)

In a footnote to this quotation, Sinclair makes clear that he is trying to pry London from any association with the working class world when he casually remarks that this material "gave London's socialist comrades and biographers a great deal of trouble" (94). Not only does Sinclair fail to name these embarrassed comrades, but he also chooses to ignore this feature of the whole literature of poverty. Conservatives such as Gissing and Riis are not alone in their insistence on the bestial way of life of the slum dwellers. Marx also uses harsh words to describe the dehumanization of proletarians in capitalist towns: "Tomorrow, like a swarm of locusts, come crowding in masses of ragged Irishmen or decayed English agricultural laborers."[3] In distorting London's feelings into an expression of hatred, Sinclair is responding out of a class position not dissimilar to that of London's contemporary critics who wanted to accuse him of fomenting class hatred—a charge London always denies. This attempt to manipulate London leads Sinclair to miss the whole point of London's decision to write about the East End as a sincere expression of his sympathy with the working class.

Like Sinclair, Clarice Stasz ignores the ways in which London is drawing on his own working class experience in writing about the East End. But she goes one step further than Sinclair when she claims that in writing the book London was rejecting his ties with the working class:

> *The People of the Abyss* allowed London to reject his class experiences in the guise of an attack on British capitalism. He was relieved to be free of the slum life, as is evident by his actual research activities, library research and photography, and his stated need for returns to the lodging house with its warm baths and clean linens.[4]

While not advancing any textual evidence for her claim that the book allowed London to reject his own class by attacking capitalism —with the spurious logic of seemingly confusing an act of class solidarity with its opposite, class disloyalty, simply through the mystical agency of a "guise"—Stasz can work only by innuendo in this area. She leads up to her claim with an unsubstantiated generalization:

> It is characteristic of persons who are socially mobile to turn upon their original class as a way of dissociating their identity from it. Personal stability during successful mobility requires this rejection. (6)

But she goes on to state that he turns on "British capitalism", which is hardly what she would want the reader to see as London's "original class." Another problem in Stasz's opinion is that London continues to identify with the working class after this book—in *The Iron Heel, Martin Eden* and *Revolution*. One problem with Stasz's argument is that she does not explain what she means by the act of dissociation. She could not mean that London is denying his past, his history—the evidence is contrary. One implication she seems to make is that London signals his becoming a member of the middle class, the bourgeoisie, by attacking the working class way of life. Such a conception of class loyalty would be naive in its suggestion that London sought to reject the workers in order to prove to the middle class reader and himself that he was now bourgeois in the Marxist sense of that word.

As with Sinclair, Stasz distorts London's letters to fit her own views. Using London's statement, in a letter to an editor of *Cosmopolitan Magazine*, February 18, 1906, Stasz states that London's parenthetical remarks make obvious that London had little first hand experience of his material in England. In this letter London is trying to get Millard's magazine to back him on his *Snark* voyage. This means that he must stress his capacity to work under even the most adverse conditions:

> I believe too much in fair play to be a good business man, and if my work be rotten I'd be the last fellow in the world to bind any editor to publish it. On the other hand, I have a tremendous confidence, based upon all kinds of work I have already done, that I can deliver the goods. Anybody doubting this has only to read *The People of the Abyss* to find the graphic, reportorial way I have of handling things. (Between ourselves, and not to be passed on, I gathered every bit of the material, read hundreds of books and thousands of pamphlets, newspaper and Parliamentary Reports, composed *The People of the Abyss,* and typed it all out, took two-thirds of the photographs with my own camera, took a vacation of one week off in the country—and did it all in two months. That's going some, now, isn't it?)[5]

Taken in context, London is stressing his work beast capacity to Millard. A reading of the bracketed information which takes the material as a whole shows that London wants Millard to keep to himself the brevity of the overall period spent in producing the book. On Stasz's reading, London would not want passed on the fact that he spent his time only in libraries, away from any physical contact with the working class. But London is simply not saying any such thing. While he did read a lot, he *also* "gathered every bit of the material" himself, took many photographs and wrote the book. All of this was done in two months.

Finally Stasz does not take into account that this was a stock letter—London also sent copies of it to the respective editors of *Collier's Magazine, McClure's Magazine* and *Outing Magazine*.[6] It does not seem likely that if London had anything very sinister to hide he would tell it to the editors of four of the largest circulating magazines of the day. The tone of personal confidence is more than likely at least partly a sales ploy by London. The last thing he would want to admit to an editor he was trying to convince of the strength of his articles would be that he works only from books. Such an admission would hardly inspire confidence in the editor regarding London's capacity to experience the adventures of the *Snark* voyage and to turn such raw material into literature that would be read and appreciated by the mass reading public.

What Sinclair and Stasz both miss in their attempts to declass London is that it is the remaining closeness of his ties with the working class that enables him to produce the book in such a short time. Because they do not allow him any residual knowledge of the working class, there is no time left in these critics' timetables for London to familiarize himself with his material. For them, everything had to happen in those fateful two months as far as London's meeting with workers is concerned. What these critics seem to be unwilling to concede is that what London was bringing to this work was not some superficial notion of point scoring, but the whole emotional and physical structure of experience carried over from his past. In London's avowal, "I think I put more of my heart into *The People of the Abyss* than into any other book,"[7] it may be seen that this close personal identification with his material belies any attempt to distance him from the working class by distorting his intentions in writing the book.

It is the tension between his working class background and his newly won position as a successful writer—with all the destabilizing compromises that would come with that success as it is explored in *Martin Eden* (1909)—which London expresses in his work. In no way would he have reached for or accepted what Stasz sees as the "personal stability" of belonging exclusively to the bourgeoisie. If anything, it is London's struggle to express his actual class relations that takes so much of his heart.

When London states in his preface to *The People of the Abyss,* "I went down into the under-world of London with an attitude of mind which I may best liken to that of the explorer. I was open to be convinced by the evidence of my eyes, rather than by the teachings of those who had not seen, or by the words of those who had seen and gone before,"[8] he is drawing the reader's attention to the distance between his own work and prior literature on working class life in London. He is modifying the image of the writer as explorer by stating at the outset that others have already covered the terrain. What makes London an explorer is that he is the first person from the working class to write about that life. London is careful not to exclude his own experience in the working class when he talks about his avoidance of the danger of distorting his material through the importation of premeditated ideas into his representation of East End life. It is this area of his past experience that he stresses to the reader when he spells out the criteria he uses to "measure the life of the underworld:" "That which made for more life, for physical and spiritual health, was good: that which made for less life, which hurt, and dwarfed, and distorted life, was bad" (vii). These values come out of London's own work experience. In *Martin Eden* (1909) London reemploys this perspective to represent the mutual rejections made by Eden and the bourgeoisie. These values are seen to come out of Eden's life with working class characters such as Lizzie Connolly. It is these working class characters who are seen to have the vitality London and Eden find appealing. Such criteria are unthinkable from the middle class standpoint where stasis and the inner life are seen as values to be contemplated. Ruth's insipid denial of life, her inability to accept change foredooms her failure with Martin.

The dual potentialities for development and regression, the precariousness of life which would be subsumed by a middle class writer such as Henry James as the ambivalence of experience, are put forward by London as typical of life as a worker as he knows it from personal experience. This source of London's perspective needs to be recognized. Because of his personal identification with the working class in the East End he is able to see the people in sympathetic terms. He is not importing alien values into his exploration of the East End working class. As the first industrial worker to explore his own world in print, London has to come to terms with problems different to those faced by James and Riis.

For the middle class investigator—Charles Booth, Greenwood, Wyckoff and others—the question of one's personal relationship to the material did not seem to be problematical. They saw themselves as reporters coming from outside the social life of the working class, who stay in the working class environment only long enough to collect the material. They then retire to their own parts of town to write up their findings. But for London living in the East End, his identity, his relationship to the material was of a different character. Locating his position as a writer in this world was to prove to be the determinate problematical experience: How does a working class person relate to other workers when he comes back to them in success in order to explain them to the middle class readership? This point is also pivotal in *Martin Eden*.

The sealing or closure of these middle class writings works as an affirmation by these writers of the break in their experience which clearly marks off their time spent in the East End. It remains a world other than the one the writer and his comfortable middle class readers inhabit. There was something reassuring in the clear demarcation between the classes in these narratives. Richard Harding Davis' article "The West and East Ends of London" may serve as an instance of the kind of writing London was up against.

Davis delivers his picture of the working class only after he has filled out the West End society to which he easily relates. It is the softness and gentility of this world which is used to put the East End into a context in which it may be distanced in order to be judged and then dismissed. Unlike London,

Davis feels that both worlds may be represented within a single narrative framework by using a method of juxtaposition. This is possible because he sees the East End as only a curiosity, a source of amusement and entertainment for the West End. The middle class perspective may still explain or consume the working class experience to Davis' satisfaction:

> It [the East End] is the back yard of the greatest city in the world, into which all the unpleasant and unsightly things are thrown and hidden away from sight, to be dragged out occasionally and shaken before the eyes of the West End as a warning or a menace.[9]

While this "neighborhood" is a thing to fear, it may also serve as an object of entertainment (289). Petticoat Lane is described as a street Vaudeville. In this personal view of the East End there is no room left for the working class to speak for itself. London's troubled relation to that world is not even considered by Davis. In place of an all embracing acceptance of that world on its own terms, there is a renunciating choice made between the kinds of experience offered to the observer:

> The East End of London is either to be taken seriously by those who study it, and whose aim and hope are to reclaim it as a great and terrible problem, or from the outside by those who with a morbid interest go to walk through it and to pass by on the other side. (292)

The East End is a piece of property to be reclaimed. Roles are apportioned to different middle class observers. Working class experience may be understood from the outside once it is agreed that it has nothing to offer the observer. From where Davis stands there can be no conception of that East End as an independent entity, as a world that within itself may carry a nucleus of future society. Eight years later, Jack London's depiction of that world without any frame or crutch of West End domination will make untenable Davis' refusal to treat the East End inhabitants as human beings. To understand this shift in perception, the newness of London's approach from within the working class in *The People of the Abyss* needs to be appreciated.

What has been missed in the critical attempts to declass London is this affirmation of London's loyalty to the working class world, a loyalty that is expressed in his willingness to deal with this world on its own terms. For a middle class investigator, the baggage of London's detailed record of his transformation into a worker—a transformation deliberately lacking the mystery of a Frankenstein or Jeckell—could only represent wasted activity or narrative time. There is no point in setting up the process by which one takes on a working class appearance if one means only to discard that disguise in a short time. What London is focusing attention on when he deals with the more typical aspects of travel literature at this early point in his narrative is this class distance which is assumed to be permanent and therefore unbridgeable in middle class eyes. London wants the reader to see that there is a way to cross the gulf between these two nations. By familiarizing his readers with the passages into this new world he is ensuring that they will accompany him on what he promises to be a voyage of discovery to the land of the real working class.

The deep personal note that is characteristic of London's prose—that sustains him throughout the intensive period in which he produced the work—comes from the liberating experience he saw as the act of expression of class. This world opened new alternatives of personal and political development. He had regained his origins. As a personal document, *The People of the Abyss* comes across as a quest story. But it is a quest that has no goals, only new experiences. The goal of identity has been achieved at the outset. This sense of liberation is strong in the fiction immediately following this work. Buck and Van Weyden experience similar makings to London in the East End. Like London, who ends his own response to the wilds of the East End with a return to his Northland experience when he refers to the Innuit Indians, so Buck's freedom comes as he enters the mythologies of the Yeehat Indians.

London is always aware—to the point of self consciousness—of the class differences between the readers and himself. Using physical terms that Larsen will later apply to Van Weyden, London complains to his readers that they would not appreciate the anguish of homeless people in the East End:

> But, O dear, *soft* people, full of *meat and blood*, with white beds and airy rooms waiting you each night, how can I make you know what it is to suffer as you would suffer if you spent a weary night on London's streets? (75-76, emphasis added)

Here, London is turning the narrative eye back onto the reader, the passive observer. There is a *camera obscura* inversion effect which leaves this reader stranded in this raw reality, just as Buck and Hump are left alone. London wants to get his reader involved in the life he represents, he wants a committed reader. London does not want to rest with a simple spotting of the differences between his readers and the people of the abyss.

While Davis leaves his readers unmolested in their role as the audience, London wants to unsettle them. He does this by bringing the people of the East End to life. When he relates how Ginger, a workhouse inmate, steals some food from a refuse heap to give to an old woman, London stresses it as an act of altruism, an altruism that would embarrass the middle class philanthropists:

> O Charity, O Philanthropy, descend to the Spike and take a lesson from
> Ginger. At the bottom of the Abyss he performed as purely an altruistic act
> as was ever performed outside the Abyss. It was fine of Ginger, and if the
> old woman caught contagion from the "no end of meat" on the pork ribs,
> it was still fine, though not so fine. But the most salient thing in this
> incident, it seems to me, is poor Ginger, "clean crazy" at sight of so much
> food going to waste. (111)

This identification of the people of the abyss with the readers who see
themselves quarantined in another world is intended to bring home to those
smug readers the fact that behind the mask of savagery held up to cover the East
End by the middle class commentators there is the all too real face of human
misery. By stressing the human connection between the classes, by exploring the
cultural depth to be found in the abyss, London is working out the basis for his
characterization of these people. While James and Gissing relegate them to the
periphery of their work, London sees that they are strong enough to support the
weight of the narrative structure independent of their middle class patrons—there
are no Hyacinth Robinsons or Sidney Kirkwoods to be found in *The People of
the Abyss*. This is the strength of London as an artist; it is by no means a bad
thing. Before exploring how James and Riis distort this world through an
uncompromising loyalty to their own middle class aspirations, it is necessary to
understand the position of London the narrator as a mediator between the reader
and the abyss, and not as an eclipsing alternative.

Like the declassed subjects of middle class representations of the East
End, London knows that his middle class reader would make himself the only
subject of the story if he ever underwent an experience similar to that of the
Carter and the Carpenter for just one night:

> But when the dawn came, the nightmare over, you would hale you home
> to refresh yourself, and until you died you would tell the story of your
> adventure to groups of admiring friends. It would grow into a mighty
> story. Your little eight hour night would become an Odyssey and you a
> Homer. (76)

There would be no room for the Carter and the Carpenter in such an
individualistic curiosity story, just as such characters could not appear in Davis'
article. London does not want his narrative to grow into such a "mighty story"
with himself as the heroic Odysseus—there can be no end to the experience
evoked in the work. This refusal to drown out his subject could be contemplated
by the next critic who wants to complain about London's apparently all-
pervasive monomania. London is not asserting himself onto these people partly
because he is aware that this relationship is precarious and open to change. He

wants to let them speak for themselves. The narrative strategy is worked out around this end.

London's willingness to let his characters breath in the narrative, though they may find it harder to breath in the stultifying atmosphere of the Spike and Mile End Road, may be seen and heard when London shouts the Carter and the Carpenter a meal. To do this, he is forced to drop his disguise. While he has regained his class consciousness, he remains aware of those aspects of himself which are middle class. And he knows that this middle class aspect cuts him off from these two workers:

> Of course I had to explain to them that I was merely an investigator, a social student, seeking to find out how the other half lived. And at once they shut up like clams. I was not of their kind; my speech had changed, the tones of my voice were different, in short, I was a superior, and they were superbly class conscious. (86)

London is anticipating their views of him, he is not explaining himself to the reader. This is suggested when London remains with them after they react with a distancing distrust. He can sympathize: they are "superbly class conscious." The honesty of London's concern to expose himself as the narrator comes through at this point when he is willing to admit that he is not what he seems to these people—Walter Wyckoff never exposes himself to this sense of betrayal.

Perhaps it is at this point in his experiences that London comes to terms with the contradictions of his class position. It happens at a time when he can closely empathize with the people and so can accommodate their distrust of that part of him which is alien to them. He does not insult them or the reader by trying to justify his position. Because he wants to keep the reader's attention focused on the two workers, he recognizes that he must accept this limitation of the narrator. Here, he intentionally describes instead of narrates. It is a mark of London's confidence both as a writer and as member of the working class that he can leave the story alone. He is no one night Homer who egoistically seeks to impose himself as an explicator or as a barrier at this point to hide his rejection by these people.

One reason why middle class narrators would not think of placing anyone other than a kindred spirit at the center of their stories is that they would not recognize the depth and complexity of feeling shared by members of the working class. P. J. Keating sees this fascination with individuals who come from outside the working class in novels such as *The Nether World* and *The Princess Casamassima* in terms of a "process of avoidance."[10] What Keating seems to miss are the misconceptions held by these writers about the capacities of working class characters. For Keating, the failure of James to place such characters at the center of his novel is to be explained in terms of literary and social conventions that keep such people in their places (46). But this is too abstract. Working class people are not given prominence in middle class fiction because the writers do not find them interesting. James cannot contemplate a serious complex working class character, or even a character capable of remaining within the logic of his own situation in the East End. Contrary to Keating's apologetic avoidance of the artistic issues involved here, this silence by writers such as James must be seen as a failure of confidence in their art. Contrary to Keating's assertion that "James acknowledged the problem [of writing about what he saw as uninteresting working class people] but chose the alternative" (47), there are no options open to James. There was no alternative to James' depiction of a superior individual in decayed circumstances. In London's view, one night Homers would not even consider such alternatives. More than one perverse reviewer of London's book insists on stressing the overpowering interest in one of his own class: "The really interesting part of the story is the author's account of how he did all this."[11]

Defending the impressionistic vagueness of his representation of East End life James sees this world only in terms of it being "beneath the vast smug surface" of the society he knows as the actual world:

> Shouldn't I find it [a defence of his artistic position] in the happy contention that the value I wished most to render and the effect I wished most to produce were precisely those of our not knowing, of society's not knowing, but only guessing and suspecting and trying to ignore, what "goes on" irreconcilably, subversively, beneath the vast smug surface?[12]

Working class life is a world apart, a world in which James, speaking also for his readers, has no connivance. It is not expected of these people that they be conversant with the lived details of this underworld, this world of "mysteries abysmal" (23). What James does choose to ignore is the work of Mayhew, Greenwood, Dickens and Booth in this area. The knowledge that James lacked was available to London through his working class background, it had been felt. As one of them, these people are interesting to London, while James gives them peripheral importance when he complains that drama narrative can be interesting only insofar as the consciousness of the character in it is also interesting:

> This in fact I have ever found rather terribly the point—that the figures in any picture, the agents in any drama, are interesting only in proportion as they feel their respective situations; since the consciousness, on their part, of the complication exhibited forms for us their link of connection with it. But there are degrees of feeling—the muffled, the faint, the just sufficient,

the barely intelligent, as we may say; and the acute, the intense, the complete, in a word—the power to be finely aware and richly responsible. It is those in this latter fashion who "get most" out of all that happens to them and who in so doing enable us, as readers of their record, as participators by a fond attention, also to get most. (9)

Implicit in James' view of the individual character's consciousness as the central narrative concern is the belief that society—including that world beneath its surface which is knowable in the same terms as all is one—may adequately be reflected through a single character's history. This is how the process of avoidance works to substitute a middle class character for a worker. Here is the ultimate avoidance: the denial of the class basis for this shift to an interesting individual.

With Riis, the anonymity of the denied working class people stems more from their identity as a mass. As a mass it is a blur. In *How the Other Half Lives,* Riis' recourse to historicism as an explanation of what he calls the "genesis of the tenement" is one instance of how middle class moralists sought to evade the question of the typicality of what they saw to be working class experience. Riis explains away the political aspects of this life by couching the experience in metaphorical terms: now the tenement is the problem and not so much the people who live in it. This is a rhetorical depersonalization of working class which serves the purpose of allowing Riis' readers, who may not be that different to James' implied reader, to look at the working class without hurting their eyes. For this view to be held, the workers need to be pacified, or at least kept still in their place. In comparison to Riis and James, London does not want to lead the reader's gaze in a restrictive way.

For the other two writers, London would be doing the unthinkable when he takes a cab into the East End. What London sees there is not to be found in these other writers:

> As far as I could see were the solid walls of brick, the slimy pavements, and the screaming streets; and for the first time in my life the fear of the crowd smote me. (8)

What London does that is novel, what he is making the reader do is look out of the cab's windows at the life around it. The attendant fear is repressed by Riis in his tourist guide tone of narrative. This unexpected act by London could not be contemplated by James' characters. James' concern lies inside the cabs as the Prince follows Christina and Muniment as they rattle from one house to another. London's solitary journey to Stepney would not have caught James' eye:

> There are parts of London in which you may never see a cab at all, but there are none in which you may see only one; in accordance with which fortunate truth Prince Casamassima was able to wave his stick to good purpose as soon as the two objects of his pursuit had rattled away. Behind them now, in the gloom, he had no fear of being seen. (454)

For James, this gloom replaces or blots out the solid walls of brick and slimy pavements seen by London. London seems to be more sensitive to the impact of such visible signs of class difference in a working class area. The West End image of a hansom leads him to a confrontation with the East End world, whereas for James, such narratory vehicles serve only to lubricate his passage through these noisy areas of the city. In London's photographs, this sideways or horizontal perspective suggests the claustrophobic narrowness of the streets. Just as London the narrator is getting onto an eye-to-eye level with the poor, so too the photographs, all taken at street level, display no tendency to point away from the immediate world, in a direction that would lead the reluctant Jamesian reader down the street in the trail of James' speeding cabs.

This horizontal level of perception also distinguishes London's work from that of Riis. In *How the Other Half Lives*, most of the external photographs are taken from an elevated position, from a viewpoint superior to or out of that of his subjects, and the vertical path of the street, directing or deflecting the reader's furtive glance back out of the photograph is used to relieve the reader, to release him from the foreboding social pressures of confrontation which London wants his readers to experience.

The perceived permanence of the class relations which serve to keep the workers in their place provides the starting point for Riis' reformism, the ultimate evasion of the subject of class relations and guilt:

> We know now that there is no way out; that the "system" [of tenement houses] that was the evil offspring of public neglect and private greed has come to stay, a storm-center forever of our civilization. Nothing is left but to make the best of a bad bargain.[13]

Riis' description of the recent creation of tenements as a "genesis" points toward the divine or non-human factor in what he sees would otherwise be a blameworthy blot on the conscience of society. The genesis idea also points up the permanence and naturalness of the creation—it is God given.

While the tenement is to be accepted as a permanent feature, Riis also wants to impress on his tourists that it may be rationally explained. This religious tension between the Biblical and the political realities of the present informs his historicism. Riis attempts to locate the cause of the tenements in the isolated immediate historical present, as a phenomena which has its own traceable history. This makes it possible to claim that there was an identifiable first tenement out of which the rest of the tenements inevitably developed, just as murder and crime came out of Cain's actions. The presence of the Genesis idea in Riis' work on the evils of city life is not as innocent as the religious language would lead the reader to assume. After all, Cain was the father of all cities in his banishment. It is not too big a step to associate Cain's crime with the middle class impression of working class life as violent and criminal. With this mythological framework, guilt is transferred to those who suffer in the slums. Treating the tenement, the symptom of social sickness as the disease itself, Riis explains the first tenement as an historical accident, as a creation unintended by the New York ruling class:

> The first tenement New York knew bore the mark of Cain from its birth, though a generation passed before the writing was deciphered. It was the "rear house," infamous ever after in our city's history. There had been tenement houses before, but they were not built for the purpose. Nothing would probably have shocked their original owners more than the idea of their harboring a promiscuous crowd; for they were the decorous homes of the old Knickerbockers, the proud aristocracy of Manhattan in the early days. (7)

In isolating this first tenement in the living memory of the reader by suggesting it is "infamous ever after in our city's history," Riis is saying that what he admits to be an evil in the present society is only an historical accident: the next batch of tenements "were not built for the purpose." The implication is that as a recent development, these tenements need not be seen as endemic to capitalism. His sense of moral vision which he shares with the "shocked" Knickerbockers, comes into play when the outrage is directed away from the ruling class landlords and bosses who directly benefit from these conditions (as Sinclair shows in *The Jungle*), and is placed squarely against the "promiscuous crowd" who now harbor in these places. It is all the fault of the working class for failing to live up to the aristocratic pretensions of the original owners of the houses. The workers have become this crowd, a mass of people who cannot be differentiated from one another, in the same way that they do not differentiate between themselves in their promiscuity, as far as Riis can see. In the confusing context of this metaphysical disguise of piety, where blame is apportioned on the victims, and where history is used to falsify the causes of misery, Riis effectively depersonalizes the suffering to be found in the tenements. This refusal to represent the tenement dwellers as suffering individuals makes them pariahs in Riis' own narrative. Because the poor are seen to be outside the world of Riis and his readers, because the relationship between the classes is denied, Riis feels absolved of any responsibility to deal with these people on their own terms.

It is in these terms that the debate about London's class loyalties must finally be resolved. If his interest in the people of the abyss had been only skin deep, if he was only interested in making copy, then he would have been led into the same traps that held James, Riis and Davis. Nothing would have been easier than to deny the new Adam, which Frankenstein's monster was intended to be. But London's response to this world is to integrate with it. He is not scared of it once he comes to terms with its continued influence in his life. This is the mark of London's confidence as a writer. He is willing to look at hell and recognize its place within. It is understandable that many of his middle class readers mistakenly took his sincerity to be *machismo*. After all, their insecurity with the workers leads them to over assert themselves, as London knew well when he described them as one night Homers. By identifying with what they see as London's *machismo* they hide their own weakness.

NOTES

[1] This point is made by Jack Lindsay in his introduction to *The People of the Abyss* (London: Journeyman Press, 1977), 3.

[2] Andrew Sinclair, "A View of the Abyss." *Jack London Newsletter* 9 (1976):86. Further references in text.

[3] Karl Marx, *Capital*. vol. 1, 1867. (Moscow: Progress Publishers, 1954), 619.

[4] Clairce Stasz, "Jack London as Photographer: *The People of the Abyss*." *The Wolf '77*, 7.

[5] *Letters From Jack London* (London: Macgibbon and Kee, 1966), 196.

[6] Editorial note by Hendricks and Shepard, *Letters From Jack London*, 197.

[7] Letter to Leon Weilskov, Oct. 16, 1916. *Letters From Jack London*, 479.

[8] Jack London, *The People of the Abyss* (New York: Grosset and Dunlap, 1903), vii. Further references in text.

[9] Richard Harding Davis, "The West and East Ends of London." *Harper's New Monthly Magazine* 88 (1894), 289. Further references in text.

[10] P. J. Keating, *The Working Classes in Victorian Fiction* (London: Routledge and Kegan Paul, 1971), 44. Further references in text.

[11] *Academy and Literature*, Nov. 14, 1903. Jack London's Scrapbooks, no. 2, Henry E Huntington Library.

[12] Henry James, *The Princess Casamassima*. 1886. (Harmondsworth: Penguin, 1977), 22. Further references in text.

[13] J. A. Riis, *How the Other Half Lives: Studies Among the Tenements of New York* (New York: Charles Scribner's Sons, 1890), 2. Further reference in text.

Sea Dog and Sea Wolf at Play in the Valley of the Moon

Finn Haakon Frolich [Compiled and Edited by Margaret Guilford-Kardell]

> *My uncle Finn was a Norwegian, a sailor, a sculptor, an innovator, a builder of monuments, a true contemporary of all his times from 1868 to 1947, intimate of the likes of George Sterling, Jack London, Frederick Grayson Sayre—and an inspirer as well as creator of art, as his following account of his years with the Londons illustrates.*
>
> —Margaret Guilford-Kardell

The Beginning. While I was sculpting monuments and figures in New York at the turn of the century, I always had a "psychological" thought in the back of my head that if I should ever go West, Jack London and I would drift together. And we did. I had first met Jack through reading serially in a magazine his story *Sea Wolf*. Then I went to libraries to read his other stories. And from 1906 on I read all the news stories about his building and sailing his sloop the *Snark*. I felt, since I too had grown up on the sea, that we two would be kindred spirits. And we became so.

I had separated from my first wife, and there didn't seem to be another sculpturing commission for me on the horizon in New York. I came off a drunk one morning in 1908 on 42nd Street in front of Grand Central Station and found myself attempting to give away a brass alarm clock to a cabbyhorse that obviously would have preferred nice yellow hay for breakfast. Free of my last possession, I went into the ticket office and asked the agent what kind of places they had and he asked, "What kind of place do you want?" I said, "The farthest away from here you've got." So he gave me a ticket to Seattle. After Seattle, where I met and married another gorgeous girl and had a baby and a front page divorce and custody fight, and where I wept when I found I lacked the money to sail *The Viking*—the ship I built for the Exposition—around the world, I went down to San Francisco and got a studio at 1705 Harrison Street to be ready to work on the Panama-Pacific Exposition in 1915. But first I had to look up Jack London. Reaching him on the phone at his Glen Ellen ranch, I told him that I would like to meet him, told him my name, and then he asked, "Are you Finn Frolich of *The Viking* ship in Seattle?" Then, of course, he said, "Come right up to my ranch! Come tomorrow night! Someone will be meeting you at the depot." Jack met me.

He seemed phlegmatic when I first met him. I was surprised to see all the various kinds of people at his table, from the lowest of sailors to the millionaire type. There were artists, like the painter Marty Martinez whom I had met in Paris, and the "Road-Town" man, a dreamer who had a wonderful scheme to start a house in San Francisco, and add on to it, and have a community kitchen, truck garden, etc. And when the house was a hundred miles long, it would be put on a train and then have autos on the roof, and it would go from coast to coast. Then the old man would go up 100 miles north and start another such house. Jack would humor the "Road-Town" man and encourage him in his story and then turn to Charmian and wink.

I just listened that first night. It wasn't until the next day, when Jack took me out horseback riding into the mountains, that

I found out what a man he really was—a real man who could write the kinds of things he wrote because he had lived and felt them.

I stayed on for three months. It was 1912. Jack was 36 years old, writing *John Barleycorn,* and I was 44 and sculpting a bas-relief of him. One afternoon, when I had been modeling him for about an hour, he tired of sitting and said, "Come, let's have a drink." I said, "Not before six o'clock!" Later, I noticed that he used this idea in his book, *John Barleycorn.* He also used my experiences in the Latin Quarter; having been disabled in a *pampero* off the River Platte; and running into Buenos Aires, the "Paris of America where men congregated with raised glasses."

That same modeling session Jack went into the house saying in admiration to Charmian, "You ought to see what that damn squarehead has done." He never forgot to josh me about being foreign because he liked me; he liked my work; he liked the ribaldry and fun of my favorite book, Rabelais' *Gargantua and Pantagruel;* and he liked swapping sea stories with me. I was his ready source of Viking lore and as close as his copy of Paul du Chaillu's *Viking Age* at his bedside. He loved my stories and I loved telling them to him and to his guests. Once, although he knew all about my sailing abilities, and he'd seen me figure dimensions for sculpting, he thought I ought to hear what he called his $5,000 lecture on math, and so one night he lectured and read to me about mathematics for over five hours.

Jack would tell me of·his poverty as a child, and I could understand his wanting the grandiose "Wolf House" he was building because I could remember such a big house, in Christiania. Our cook, Marta, was famous for her food, and we had lots of room for entertaining. There was even a special little house for playing cards and an extra dining room into which I peeked with the servants and saw a Norwegian female opera singer smoking a little black cigar and from which room I overheard a conversation between the young explorer, Paul du Chaillu, and my father, Ernest Frolich.

In winter, the fishermen would make holes in the ice and fish, then bring the fish to our house to sell. One evening a fisherman, starting to return to the isle where he lived, tried to cross back over the ice, but the tide was bad and he fell through. All of us children were watching the man drowning and trying to get out on the ice. He called to us, "Get Marta!" She ran out onto the ice, threw a heavy rope to him, and saved him.

Jack London was interested in my stories about the servants because he understood being poor. And by the time I met Jack, I had been poor more often than rich. Jack and I shared our life experiences as we came to know each other those first three months—our childhood adventures, our lives at sea. Jack saw in me more than a chesty, wavy brown-haired Norwegian accordion-playing sculptor who could outwork any of the Italian stonemasons or workmen on the ranch. And as for me, in all my life I never saw a man with more beautiful magnetism than Jack London. If there could be a preacher with that much love and life in his make-up, God, this whole world would go religious!

His hair was bushy, and he wore an eye shade—his eyes were big and expressive. He showed an awful lot of white around his eyes. You know they train actresses to make their eyes big like that, but he had it naturally.

His mouth was just as sensitive and full of expression; and the words would come out of him just a-rippling. It was something coming from inside of him, just like his mind was running 60 miles a minute. He talked better than he wrote. And when he talked, no matter what he talked about, his lips would go up, the humor would come out, and you would find yourself laughing your head off. Jack said, "I love your sea-rolling belly laugh."

And he had such depth of feeling. Once when I asked him if he ever went hunting anymore, he said, "No, Finn, I don't hunt anymore. You go hunting here as much as you want to. But not I!" Then he told me a long story about some bird he had shot on the snow. I think maybe it was when they were all dying of hunger in Alaska, but all he could see was that blood on the snow. And when he told me the story his big eyes stood out and tears rolled down to his chin. He said, "Now, when I think about hunting, I think I would rather go out and shake dice for a drink." You couldn't help but love a man like that, could you?

And love him I did. And I think he loved me for he said to Elsie Martinez, "This is the one man I love the most."

Yes, Jack and I understood each other. Take the time Jack had appendicitis, of which Charmian wrote:

On July 6, [1913] we rushed him to Oakland and into hospital. On the 8th, Dr. William S. Porter operated. Four days later, an important moving-picture conference was held in Jack's room. Other afternoons were filled with callers, and his room was banked with flowers. "Only," the bed-ridden one grumbled sheepishly, "I wish men wouldn't bring me flowers—somehow it makes me feel silly." Frolich, the sculptor, unwittingly mitigated the situation by contributing an absurd corbel, a cowled monk in the ultimate throes of seasickness, and Jack racked himself with mirth. . . .

(I remember this differently. As I told Irving Stone while he was writing *Sailor on Horseback,* "When Jack lay in Merritt Hospital recovering from appendicitis, I sent over a gargoyle on the style of those on the Notre Dame de Paris. And that was the first thing he saw when he woke up, and he puked all over it. Later I went over and visited with him and told him one of my funny stories, and he pulled a stitch laughing, and I was told not to come back.")

Jack knew I would have liked to have been a writer. And I've always been a great reader—one of the reasons Jack and I got on so well. We talked books together. I admire writers: they are doing the educating and the civilizing of the human race. Nobody has ever made a sculpture that could educate. People looking at a piece of sculpture must already be able to think. But a piece of writing can educate a child. All that has come down through the ages are the books. As Jack London once said to me, "It's all right, Finn, the world will only know of the dreamers." We did a lot of dreaming and we talked a lot about books and told stories. He talked better books than he ever wrote. They were far more gutsy than he could write and sell in 1912 [. . .].

Cards, Dice and Cows. Besides tales of the sea, Jack London and I really enjoyed playing cards. Jack's inscription to me in a copy of *The House of Pride* (1916) reads, "Dear Finn: In memory of the many happy days, and red dog nights, and black jack deals, we've had together on the ranch. You are never away from here, for wherever I look, I see your beautiful creations." Of course Jack had been playing cards long before he met me—pinochle was kind of a family game. But mostly Jack played stud poker, which he liked best, then red dog, then pedro and whist.

When we first met, Jack and I played some chess. That first time we played, he played so impetuously he got me all rattled and I lost badly. After that I won, and kept on winning until he didn't want to play chess with me anymore.

When you play poker with the same people often, as we did at Jack's ranch, money doesn't really change hands readily. But when you have a $1,000 baby girl to think about and you've spent your wad you made at the Exposition and there isn't much going on artwise, you'd just better find some action. So, in Seattle poker had become my habit. And while Helen, my wife, rocked Virginia in some boarding house, I made money the best way I could.

At Jack's ranch we had wonderful fun games of poker and red dog. It seemed mostly red dog after Jack came back from Honolulu. He said the ladies wanted to play. Anyone who wanted to sit in could play for pennies. Everyone put in a penny, and the dealer gave three cards to everyone, and then you could bet as much as you wanted and within five minutes there were $40 bets on the table. Among those of us who played poker regularly at the ranch, we would see $100-$500 on the table at one time. Jack would even take I.O.U.s up to $100. Many people forgot to pay and eventually those slips of paper would accumulate and he would just tear them up.

One night when I was sitting in I got four Kings, and it so happened that Jack had four Jacks. We bet and bet, and he ran out of cash. He said, "I'll put a cow on the pile." I agreed, picked up the rest of the money on the table and forgot all about the cow.

Next morning a man came around with a beautiful Jersey cow. Jack said, "How do you like your cow? You won it. Fine, then take it." With my eagle on my shoulder and with that cow trailing behind a ranch flivver we made quite a spectacle wending our way down to the depot in Glen Ellen. Idwal Jones caricatured the story well in *Sunset Magazine* and later in his *Ark of Empire*.

I sent the cow to Burlingame where I was living with Kala, as we had a young son who could use that milk. I forgot to wire her, and I forgot that she was a lady unused to milking, but soon I received a telegram: "What is the cow for?" I wired back, "Milk her fast as you can, she's full of milk." Kala sold the milk and gave it away and made cottage cheese and more cottage cheese.

Every year that cow had a calf and we had meat because I wasn't making much money. Finally I had to sell the cow because I needed a car. Some cow fancier took it home in a padded wagon made just for cows. I got $400 for that cow and that bought a 1912 Model T touring Ford, and I started commuting back and forth to the shipyards.

Of course when you've played poker together for years as Jack and I eventually had done, you could have a lot of fun with it too. Charmian told in *The Book of Jack London* about what she termed ". . . a reckless prank that broke up one noonday meal." She wrote,

> I do not remember how it started, nor whose was the suggestion, but someone was dared to swallow, alive and whole, the tiny goldfish that swam among plants in a low cutglass bowl on the long table. In the babble among the horrified girls, Jack shouted: "We'll play a hand of poker for it, and the fellow who loses must not only swallow the fish, but keep it down, for ten minutes, no matter what is said to him." Remonstrance was in vain—the trio, Jack, Finn Frolich, and Joe Mather were "on their way." Joe, slender, fastidious, was "stuck," and exhibited, in paying the forfeit, the keenest courage I have ever witnessed. "Gee," gasped the chesty Frolich, "I *couldn't* have gotten it down!" "I'd have died if I'd had to do

it!" Jack said in awestruck admiration when confronted by the tragic face of the man who had "put away" the scaly morsel. . . .

When Jack would go into a saloon in Glen Ellen, everyone would rush to the bar as Jack would be shooting craps or joining in any bar house games: cards, arm wrestling, etc. Jack had a reputation for craps since he had been in Cuba in 1910 or so reporting on the war and had stayed in the same hotel with Richard Harding Davis and other celebrities. In one craps game on the billiard table downstairs, when Jack got the dice, Richard Harding Davis said, "I'll shoot a hundred. Ante up another $100!" It came up 8 or 9. Jack had shot a 7. He'd lost. He didn't have enough money to cover and so he said, "I'll leave it." He shot another 7, and again he rolled another 7. The ambassadors playing the table went broke, and the next morning their valets came with their money for Jack.

Children, Horses and Other Sonoma Pleasures. Cards and dice weren't our only games: we both loved simple table tricks and practical jokes and so did the lady guests and the children—Charmian's small relatives, my own children, others' children—who were often among the guests at the Beauty Ranch. Jack delighted in pleasing the children and seeing others laugh. My son still remembers Jack reaching under the house and giving him a newborn kitten. Jack hadn't had much of a childhood and certainly little time for games. Likewise, Elsie Martinez, Marty's wife, intellectually was without peer, having read her way through many a college library. But her childhood had been one of total financial poverty, and she had learned to blow soap bubbles through her fingers. Jack found this fascinating as did the children.

One of the children, Virginia Young [Newton] of Redding, California, remembered me many years later when she saw my picture. Her mother, June Young, Charmian's cousin, had brought Virginia to Glen Ellen for the summers when school was out. Virginia recalled,

> Jack was never with us for breakfast. You just took breakfast when you were ready. Things were laid out. And we children were told not to go near Jack's study and not to play outside his window.
>
> Charmian was always so graceful, so slender, and so full of energy. She would have the horses saddled, and all of us would take a trail ride with Charmian leading, and one of the men from the ranch would bring up the rear. We visited the ruins of Wolf House and the rest of the ranch.
>
> My horse was always Cricket, and one Christmas Jack and Charmian offered it to me through my parents, but they refused and never told me until I was grown.

Jack wasn't always at lunch, but always Charmian presided at lunch. Lunch was *always* a big tossed salad—that was not popular then like now. Charmian would sit and serve it out of a great big bowl. There was always lots of garlic cut up in the salad.

When we children were there, Jack would come out in the afternoon and drive us around with his four horse team.

At night everyone had dinner together. There was no cocktail hour in those days. Everyone sat at the same table. There was no separate table for children.

After dinner there were parlor games. Jack loved them. He particularly liked carrying peanuts across the floor on a knife.

Charmian loved little practical jokes like the one Jack euchred me into when he asked me, "Do you want to play 'kiss of welcome' with Charmian, Stella, and the other ladies?" I had to go out and wait until all was prepared. Three ladies were lined up standing on a bench looking very serious. All had on fedora hats. Jack asked, "Whom do you want to kiss?" To be gracious, I replied, "All of them." At which they all leaned forward at once, and their hats full of water fell on me.

People were always asking Jack to lecture about Socialism. The commandant at Alcatraz came and asked Jack to speak to the prisoners. There were many ladies present, and the warden was a bit of a show-off while Jack was entertaining them and taking them on a tour of the place. They came to where I was making a little statue of Charmian on a thoroughbred horse. Jack introduced me as a Scandinavian sailor who was a little bit fat and flabby now but who had done a little arm wrestling. The warden looked me over and said, "I think I can put him down." I looked at the ladies and agreed to arm wrestle. We got a table and started breaking arms. I thought I was beaten but I pushed little by little and he went down. And he said, "Let's do it again." I apologized about being a sailor and having done a lot of rowing, etc., but I put him down again. Jack laughed and said, "Finn, don't ever get into Alcatraz!"

Our days of fun would begin at lunch. Charmian would ring a little bell, Nakata would come in with a slip of paper and we would plan what to do for the rest of the day.

At lunch table there would sometimes be Alex, and Hamilton, a couple of Reds, rather dirty, unkempt, etc. I delighted in placing them alongside some socialite or one of Mr. Hearst's representatives who had come to get Jack to write an article.

Jack had a regular Tally-ho carriage with sleigh bells, and he'd put on his four horses and we'd go down to Fetter's Hot Springs to take a bath and get into the water to play water games, like each person having another on his shoulder and trying to push his opponent down under the water.

Or at lunch we might decide to go horseback riding, and Jack would put his guests on his thoroughbred horses, and we'd all ride up into the mountains since he had many acres of wild country land. All of his guests weren't qualified as equestrians. I remember one so-called princess who claimed to have lived in a Turkish harem. She was really just an Oakland girl married to a Turk.

I tried to remember all the tricks we did on ship to add to Jack's fun. One was to get someone to ask, "How tall are you?" Jack would take up the questioning and an argument would ensue over who was the tallest. So there was nothing to do but stand against the door to be measured, and someone from the other side would give a hit on the door. God, that's a good one. When Jack went into the hospital for appendicitis he was still rubbing his head from having been measured with someone two days before. For years you could see on the door the height marks and names of famous visitors who had felt the Indian acorn grinding pestle.

For the more fastidious table guests we had a glass with four tiny holes drilled around the rim, and when they would drink, the liquid would run down around their collars, etc. They, of course, would think they had been clumsy and would put the glass down and try to act nonchalant.

For farm hands and guests Jack had made over rooms in the carriage house, lovely rooms atop the old wine cellar. I told Jack, "When you tell people 'good night,' mention that it looks like earthquake weather. Be very serious, warn against panic, etc." Previously I had gone into all the rooms (about nine of them) and drilled two holes under each bed and had threaded a 1/2 inch Manilla rope tied criss-cross under the beds. I went to Hassen and some of the other workmen and showed them how, with two men to a bed, one would first pull one way and then the other way. It would feel like an earthquake since the beds were on rollers. The joke worked but kind of backfired. Some wrong people weren't in the right beds.

Our play was interspersed with work. I remember painting the bunk house a bright yellow and blue, real Norwegian colors. Eliza, Jack's sister and ranch manager, was upset with me about the colors. I responded, "You said you'd buy the paint and I could paint it what I wanted."

Eliza also asked me to prune a tree and I did it so peculiarly that the family kept it just that way [until 1977] as a memory of me. I ripped my only pair of pants pruning the tree, and Eliza mended them for me. She cared for Jack, the ranch, and his friends with love.

Once on the ranch I had a gun in the buggy with me and Eliza's stepdaughter. The gun accidentally discharged and she was scratched. I was so grief-stricken, thinking I might have killed her, that I tried to commit suicide. But the laborers put me up in the loft with a bottle and I got drunk.

Jack enjoyed playing his most practical jokes on me. The San Francisco *Examiner,* 27 October 1915, told the story of how "Finn Frolich, the sculptor, went to spend a few days with Jack London at Glen Ellen last week. He had no hunting license but did some shooting. London had one of his ranch hands represent himself as a deputy sheriff and tell Frolich to report to the sheriff.

"Frolich went to an innocent sheriff, displayed a large roll and suggested squaring things. The sheriff didn't understand. Neither did Frolich. Now London has Frolich believing he is to be indicted for attempted bribery."

I guess that was the big difference between Jack London and myself. When I met him he was, as he later told Ernest J. Hopkins of the San Francisco *Bulletin,* making up for the time he never had to play when he was a kid. And I was just playing at life as I always had.

Hopkins had been sent up to Glen Ellen to interview Jack quite often, and when Jack died, Hopkins tried to express Jack's vitality by relating a story about a canoe incident in August of 1915. He told it this way:

HOW HE "PLAYED"

He lent me a pair of puttees, and put me aboard Sonoma Maid, a finer bay mare than I had ever hoped to ride. For two hours, along with Finn Frolich, the sculptor, and a young Greek artist, named Spiro, we threaded the hillside trails of that beautiful Coast range estate. All the time London's voice was rattling along in the happiest rapid-fire of talk—informal, dramatic, extreme, exuberant. Then we emerged at the side of his lake, found a fully equipped bathhouse, and—again on London's insistence—"went in swimming."

London in a series of water fights proved quite as irresistible as London in conversation. He was brimful of practical jokes. Spiro shortly had enough, retired to the bathhouse and resumed the garb of custom. He found a canoe, however, and launched it; and he and I were unwise enough to get in and paddle into deep water, with Frolich and London still in the lake.

THAT FATAL CANOE

I cannot describe the rest of that tragic affair, because it is too awful for description. That canoe became a plaything in the hands of a couple of reckless Neptunes. Its occupants were as helpless as bullets in a baby's rattle. The air was full of sound, and Jack London was so overcome with delight that he almost forgot to swim. It was an unutterable relief when the canoe, after a terrible ten minutes, overturned—and Spiro had his clothes on!

HE REMEMBERED IT

In my library there is a copy of Jack London's *Revolution,* a book of radical essays, and its fly-leaf is inscribed, "With happy memories of your visit

to our Valley of the Moon—not forgetting the canoe! Yours for the Revolution,
Jack London." The bit of fun had sunk into his memory and had become a
living bit of his experience.

And last week, after fifteen months, he spoke of it again, with joyous
laughter over the recitation and a touch of sadness at the passage of time.
Incidentally, I found that the story had grown. He had dressed me up in a
collar and tie instead of the original bathing suit, and, "Of course it was all
Frolich's doing," he commented. Even so slight a bit of foolery had sunk into
that intense mind of his and had become a part of life.

Art Work. A great deal of my association with Jack and Charmian had
to do with my making art work for them. At my studio in San Francisco I was
making garden statuary since it was quite in vogue at the time, especially with
the newly-affluent, and it was rumored that Jack had coming in about $80,000
a year. Of course I had made $35,000 from the Seattle Exposition, but it was
gone before I ever reached San Francisco.

Charmian was keen to have some garden statuary, and I gave them
some. Jack wrote me a letter about those things so I could use it to advertise my
sculpture and my studio. Lots of sculptors were doing those bread and-butter
sort of things while waiting for the real commissions from the Pan-Pacific
Exposition in San Francisco.

Jack was more understanding than most about the work of a sculptor.
For a promotion piece for *The Little Lady of the Big House* I made a model of
Charmian where the lady is jumping into the lake on a stallion. Charmian liked
to model for me, but the stallion didn't seem to enjoy posing for so long a time.
The stableboy, who was actually a very scientific stable man, went to Jack and
kicked about the horse posing for such a long time. Jack said, "Look here, that
man is doing his work; he's got to do it. It means something to him, so never
mind the horse."

I was always able to make a piece of sculpture in no time, or have it
take forever if there were other things that interested me more at the time.
Besides, when I worked fast no one seemed to appreciate the results, and there
was less opportunity for publicity[. . .].

The Life Mask before Death. One of the last things I made for Jack
was a life mask. I was at Glen Ellen a few weeks before Jack died. He had
come back from Honolulu and didn't seem to look or act like himself. Much to
my surprise he was nasty to some of his friends, finding fault with them and
criticizing.

He had become suspicious of people. He would argue because he
wanted to win a point, and he got mad when someone was too stupid to see the
point—even with his friends. He didn't gamble as much as he used to. He didn't

want to do the sporting things he used to do like wrestling and playing. He didn't seem to even want to ride horseback up in the mountains any longer.

But he was again talking to me about buying a three-masted schooner and rigging her up as a home; taking the interior space and putting in a deck and placing bulkheads and fitting it as a studio with a galley, and just sailing the world. We had talked about sailing together ever since our first meeting in 1912. And just a few months before, we had been alone together for nearly three weeks, and he had dreamed and talked of sailing all about. He wanted to go on a schooner and just spend the rest of his life writing. Of course I was to go along, and there would have been Charmian and his Oriental cook.

Having sailed the Mediterranean before, I had told him of marvelous places where he could pick up material for his stories. He had gone to San Francisco and purchased charts of all the places he was thinking of going. I was happy then thinking of the adventures we would have.

But in November of 1916, Jack didn't have that gleam in his eyes that he used to have; he didn't have the laughter. And that's how I got the idea to make a cast of his head. I felt that someday it might be too late to do it. I felt he was going down. God, no, I don't mean that wonderful mind of his, that could never go down. But physically, yes. He was going down, and I was sorry for him.

He didn't seem to even want company, but Charmian still invited people up. Lots of grafters came up there. Also, I remember one time when two businessmen came up, and they couldn't get rid of them.

Then, too, there seemed to be quite a bit of domestic trouble. Before, when I rode in the mountains with Jack, he used to tell me how wonderful Charmian was; now, that spirit was gone. But he never once thought of leaving Charmian. He didn't have it in his head that he wanted to leave her, and I think I would have known.

He didn't talk about suicide either. The only time he had ever talked suicide was in his books. Elsie Martinez and Harriet Dean of the *Little Review* and I used to reminisce about this later in Carmel since they too had been up, with Marty Martinez, just a few weeks before Jack died. They didn't remember any talk of suicide. Elsie said that Jack had long talks with Harriet about Freud and a book by Jung which he had been reading. He felt that Jung would change the course of writing.

We all remembered how, toward the last, Charmian had so beautifully turned the darts of his barbed comments to her and others at the dinner table and how she played Rachmaninoff to soothe him. Charmian in her heart was a very good person although she could be and often was catty and nasty. But she knew Jack was sick and that his stomach and kidneys were in a terrible condition, and she managed him well.

It was on my last visit that I thought I should make a life mask of him in case something happened. I had at that time learned how to cast a mask while a person was sitting up and without straws. I suggested to Jack that he let me experiment with him, and we went down into the wine cellar, mixed the plaster, and put the salt on him, Vaselined his eyebrows and tied a rag around his hair. When the plaster was the right consistency, I put it on him and told him to blow a hole so that he could breathe.

The mask was a success, but I had put on too much salt and Jack didn't like the taste of salt, and he had puckered up his mouth. I only made two copies. One I gave to Charmian. Today you can see it on the wall in the study in the House of Happy Walls at Glen Ellen. The other one I kept. At the time Irving Stone wrote *Sailor on Horseback* I loaned him the mask to advertise his book and had a hell of a time getting the mask back.

When Jack died, I was in Burlingame. I came out of my house that morning, and a Swede sailor who was a neighbor said, "Your friend Jack is dead." I didn't believe it. I told Kala I had to go right up to Oakland. I couldn't get to the funeral, but I did get to the Oakland Crematorium.

When Jack had first gone to Glen Ellen he had come upon the graves of two children. He was very impressed and asked that when he died that he be placed alongside the two innocents and that a tremendous boulder be placed there to mark the spot. Years later Charmian asked me to come up and cut Jack's name on the stone: I did, and I took my son along, and he played among the trees while I did my stone cutting and remembered my friend, Jack London.

From author to reader: Finn was Jack London's fun friend because Finn was a catalyst in any group. Finn got things going and shared with everyone. And they shared with me and thus with you. The daughter of Finn's late-life female friend gave me some notes dictated by Finn, the editing of which led me to Russ Kingman, Milo Shepard, Joyce Shepard-Shafer, the Huntington Library, and eventually the late Irving Stone. Irving made available to me his original field interview notes with Finn while he was working on *Sailor on Horseback*, his biography of Jack London. Irving said,"In Finn I'm sure I missed a great story, but then. . . ." He gave me some suggestions and encouraged me in my research as we found we had both begun, at different times, as economics students at the University of California-Berkeley.

I then contacted all of Finn's living friends, visited libraries, even in Washington, D.C., corrected his notes, and edited them into a readable manuscript which I checked with my cousin Guilford Seinga Frolich and others not germane to this excerpt from my book, *Sculptor and Master of Revels: Finn Haakon Frolich (1868-1947)*.

The Humor of Jack London

Jacqueline Tavernier-Courbin

Despite popular opinion to the contrary, humor is not only present in, but a vital part of Jack London's work. In fact, it informs almost every story and novel, even the gloomiest or apparently most cruel. Almost nowhere do we escape London's love of life and humanity, his ability to laugh at human frailty and at the tricks fate will play on mankind, his admiration for the resourcefulness of some superior individuals, or his sense of the absurd and the ridiculous. The forms taken by his humor are infinitely varied, ranging from traditional tall tales, social parodies, religious satire, ironical dramatizations of human fate, to complex and occasionally bitter existential humor.[1] London also uses comic relief and comic reversal in his most tragic tales.

London's lighter forms of humor include tall tales, social parodies, and stories dramatizing reversals of traditional clichés. The tall tales, mainly "A Hyperborean Brew" and "A Relic of the Pliocene" center around the figure of Thomas Stevens, the Mighty Hunter, and good-humoredly stretch the credulity of the reader by skillfully juggling implausibility, outlandishness, and some form of credibility. In "A Relic of the Pliocene," Stevens runs down a mammoth until, out of sheer exhaustion, thirst, hunger, and despair, the poor animal allows itself to be killed. Despite its preposterousness, the topic is not really funny. What is funny are the absurd visual images conjured up by London, especially that of a mammoth having a nervous breakdown at the hands of a single man. In "A Hyperborean Brew," Stevens and his Indian companion Moosu reenact the conflict between temporal and religious powers in a remote and backward tribe living by the rim of the Arctic sea. Seizing temporal power for himself and leaving Moosu to the role of shaman, Stevens finds out quickly that he has made the wrong choice, and sets out to rectify the situation. After setting his trap carefully and making sure there are no loose ends, he tricks Moosu into the untenable position of having to perform a miracle. Unable to perform, Moosu is disgraced and has to run away with his former master, and break trail for his dogs. This is a less far-fetched story than the previous one. It also introduces the elaborate tricks which London was occasionally fond of dramatizing.

"A Daughter of the Aurora," one of London's most amusing social comedies, dramatizes such a trick. Joy Molineau, a pretty and crafty Métis, wants a husband, and a rich one. She informs the two men who have been courting her that she will marry the one who will be the first to jump a rich claim which is about to become available on Eldorado Creek. Both Jack Harrington and Louis Savoy make extensive preparation to jump the claim ahead of another few hundred men. To the end it seems that Jack Harrington will win, with Louis Savoy a close second. At the last relay of dogs, Jack even finds Joy's dog Wolf-Fang at the head of his team. The race, the mine, and Joy are assuredly his. But, as he reaches Forty Miles and passes the assembled crowd, Joy whistles to her dog, who leaves the track, heading for his mistress and toppling Jack in the snow. Louis, then, rushes past to the gold-recorder's office. The traditional joust for the hand of the damsel has been rigged, and the damsel, despite her cute accent and half-grammatical sentences, is a shrewd woman who knows how to get what she wants and help her chosen knight to success. She has also given herself the opportunity to test both men and find out if either was wanting. Both having made a courageous and determined showing (even, in the case of Louis, when the odds seemed against him), she chooses the one she loves best. But to the end, she retains the power to judge and choose.

"The Wife of a King" is a delightful parody of the Pygmalion myth transposed into a northern setting. Three sourdoughs, including Malemute Kid, London's ideal hero of the North, help another young and pretty Métis, Madeline, to recapture her husband who has fallen for the charms of a Greek dancer. They train Madeline into the social graces as roughly as they would train a wolf-dog for the harness. The contrast between the roughness of the setting, the roughness of their method and the eventual aim of the exercise is a major source of humor, added to the simultaneously humorous and tender way in which London describes Madeline's growing awareness of her own beauty. The story climaxes at a masked ball where Madeline steals every heart, including that of her own husband who does not recognize her until she takes off her mask. The story works on several levels, and establishes the link between a primitive and a civilized society in a convincing way.[2]

"The Story of Jees Uck" is another delightful, if perhaps less light-hearted, comedy of the North. An Alaskan "Madame Butterfly," Jees Uck is no frail flower trampled upon by the white man. Abandoned, with child, by her lover, Neil Bonner, she tracks him down in a long and painful Odyssey, and eventually catches up with him in California. Finding him married to one of his own kind, she has a discussion with him behind closed doors, during which she obviously lays down the law, and exacts a heavy price for her renunciation: $5000.00 a year (in early 1900), the firing of another white man who had tried to starve her into his bed, an unlimited supply of foods and goods for which she will never be charged, and the best of American and European educations for her son. A daughter of all the dominant races that have lived in the Northland, Jees Uck appears as the spirit of the North—a spirit that was never seen as soft. Smart enough to know that she could not break Bonner's marriage, she obviously knew enough to play on his fear of exposure and thus dip into a pocket that was very full, indeed. London does not reinforce racial prejudices in this story, as many have believed, nor does he extol superficial values. He merely points out a different way out of a similar predicament than the one chosen by Madame Butterfly—a more productive one, too, for Jees Uck puts her fortune to good use, opens a school for young Indian girls and becomes celebrated as the Jane Addams or Albert Schweitzer of the Northland. Race has nothing to do with it, except perhaps to make Jees Uck stronger. But London, in general, liked strong women, and had little regard for the weak and clinging type—which made him a very unconventional man for his time. By comparison with Jees Uck, Neil Bonner appears as a rather spineless and faithless weakling, who arouses little sympathy and certainly no admiration.

Of the stories which reverse traditional clichés, "That Spot," "Chun Ah Chun," and "Goliah" are among the most amusing despite the fact that the last two make a sharp comment on human nature. "That Spot" hilariously reverses the cliché that the dog is man's best friend. That Spot is a magnificent and intelligent dog who turns out to be a walking disaster for his masters. He refuses to work, and sticks to them like glue, creating endless problems for them:

> *He could steal and forage to perfection; he had an instinct that was positively gruesome for divining when work was to be done and for making a sneak accordingly; and for getting lost and not staying lost he was nothing short of inspired.*[3]

His masters can neither get rid of him nor escape him. They cannot kill him because of the intelligence they read in his eyes; they cannot abandon him because he always finds them and returns; they cannot run away from him because he tracks them down and finds them against all odds; he costs them a fortune and they nearly starve because of him. Clearly the dog's love for and faithfulness to his masters is their worst nightmare. The humor of the story is also emphasized by the disingenuous narrative voice, and the outrage of the narrator when his partner, Stephen Mackaye, pulls on him the same trick he has himself pulled on Stephen a few months previously—i.e. leaving him alone with, and at the mercy of That Spot. Thus the traditionally moving story of a dog's love and utter devotion to his master becomes here a case of ruthless persecution. But it is difficult not to admire That Spot for his amazing persistence.

"Chun Ah Chun" reverses the traditional concept that family and children are an old man's (or woman's) consolation. Chun Ah Chun, a prosperous Chinese living in Hawaii, devotes much of his energy and enormous fortune to ridding himself of his family. "He was essentially a philosopher. . . [and] lived always in the high equanimity of spiritual repose, undeterred by good fortune, unruffled by ill fortune."[4] Having risen from coolie to multi-millionaire, he finds that marrying off his twelve beautiful daughters to appropriate husbands is difficult because of their being "one thirty-second Polynesian, one-sixteenth Italian, one-sixteenth Portuguese, one-half Chinese, and eleven thirty-seconds English and American" (365). However, Chun Ah Chun knows human nature for what it is, and that even racism has a price. He lets it be known that his eldest daughter will have a three-hundred-thousand-dollar dowry. The future rear admiral Captain Higginson forgets his high family and takes the money along with a pretty wife. Ned Humphreys, the United States immigration commissioner takes the next one, but is disappointed to get only two hundred thousand dollars. "Ah Chun explained that his initial generosity had been to break the ice, and that after that his daughters could not expect otherwise than to go more cheaply" (371). Still, in 1900, this was the equivalent of several million dollars of today's money, and the suitors were queuing at the gate. By the time he is only left with two daughters to marry, Ah Chun has also managed to call in all his investments and prepared his exit from Honolulu back to China. Moreover, problems are about to arise, as he well knows. His sons-in-law are squandering much of their wives' dowries and are bickering among themselves. Ah Chun dowers his last two daughters with one hundred thousand dollars each before they even have suitors, gives his wife half a million in money well invested as well as three houses, and announces his departure. Despite attempts at having him declared insane to prevent his leaving, he escapes safely his "loving family" and lives happily thereafter, far away from them in Canton, in a palace, surrounded by the delights of the Orient and listening to the turmoil overseas. While his family are fighting like cats and dogs, he lives in peace and content, advising them to live in harmony. "At times he chuckles and rubs his hands, and his slant little black eyes twinkle merrily at the thought of the funny world" (373).

One cannot help wondering how much wishful thinking London expressed in this story, for he was saddled with a number of dependents who did little to help themselves but felt it their due to be financially taken care of by him, to the point of ludicrousness, and showed absolutely no appreciation for his generosity: a first wife who would not remarry unless he helped support her second husband and herself; a mother who badmouthed him continually and ostentatiously sided with his first wife; Johnnie Miller, his mother's adopted son, who developed the same traits; his former nannie, Jennie Prentiss, who also sided with the opposition but lived off Jack, and Ninetta Eames who constantly manipulated herself into Jack's and Charmian's lives and pocket books, even paying part of her debt to Jack with Charmian's money instead of her own. Little wonder that Jack was dreaming of discarding family ties and living as far away from them as possible. As George Sterling wrote Jack on 5 February

1915, he could see the day when Jack and Charmian would get a submarine and escape their friends (and, one might add, family) altogether.

"Goliah" reverses the cliché that it is society and social inequality which makes men unhappy, and that men would be happy if they were free. The statement made by London in this story is that it is not in human nature to be happy, and that men will accept happiness only if it costs them their lives to be unhappy. In this truly visionary tale, Goliah, a scientist who has mastered ultimate power and holds every country at his mercy, uses selective murder to force the world to be free and happy. His catch phrase is "I want laughter not slaughter. Those of you who stand in the way of laughter will get slaughter,"[5] and he is true to his word. Feeling that man is not a slave to any one form of government or ideology but a slave to his own collective stupidity, Goliah concludes that a society must be created where men have no other choice but to be happy. He therefore convenes the ten greatest captains of industry to a meeting with him in order to take the world-ship in hand and start work on reducing human suffering, misery, and degradation. Except for one, they all think he is a crackpot, ignore his invitation, and promptly die as he had warned them they would if they disregarded it. After the ten chief politicians of the United States have also disregarded Goliah's next invitation, with the same results, the battleship *Alaska* is dispatched to destroy Goliah's yacht. The *Alaska* is destroyed; so are several vessels of the United States and Japan war fleets which have ignored Goliah's warnings, as well as most of San Francisco. Finally, the world having begun to take him seriously, the ten scientists he convenes obey to a man and meet him on Palgrave Island. Then the world begins to straighten itself out. "With the exception of putting a stop to war, and of indicating the broad general plan, Goliah did nothing. By putting the fear of death into the hearts of those who sat in high places and obstructed progress, Goliah made the opportunity for the unshackled intelligence of the best social thinkers of the world to exert itself" (104). The ideal world thus brought about is a composite of socialism and Nietscheistic selection.

Clearly, the basic premise of this story is hardly optimistic. It holds that the mass of idiocy and selfishness in the world is far greater than the mass of intelligence and selflessness, and that the only way to put intelligence and selflessness in power is not through democracy but through force, since the mass of people will elect their like to power, thus perpetrating their own mediocrity. At the same time the whole tone of the story is casual and humorous, and its message bitterly ironical. It invites the readers to meditate on whether enlightened men have the right to force their superior understanding on the world, even if it is to make it happy despite itself, or whether mediocre minds have the right to rule and make a mess of the world merely because they are the most numerous. Other moral issues involved are that of "the end versus the means" and that of "the economy of suffering." It is a very complex story, and delving into the major issues it raises could lead to lengthy discussion.

In his introduction to the story, Dale L. Walker comments that London "showed a basic misunderstanding of the tenets of Socialism, which rejected all terrorist, anarchistic, individualistic policies. . ." (87). This suggests that Walker missed the point of the story, for what it dramatizes in bitterly humorous terms is London's disenchantment with the American Labor movement and his belief that socialism would neither come about peacefully nor by a revolution in the United States. He always believed in the ideals of socialism, but he eventually concluded that one could not help people who would not help themselves.

One also finds in much of London's work an ironical view of life and an ironical treatment of fate which remind one of his contemporary, Stephen Crane. The two writers had, in fact, more in common than a short, flamboyant life, if a more subdued one for Crane. Both were highly unconventional in their thinking and their ways of life, both had a deep love for humanity, and both, perhaps, took refuge in irony to deal with much of the ugly and unfair in life and man. Irony pervades most of London's work and his whole humorous approach. Although only two stories are discussed here, "War" and "To Build a Fire," London's ironical treatment of fate is present in the social parodies and the religious satires, as well as in some of the more bitter tales which dramatize, for instance, the horror of vengeance.

"War" is by no means an amusing story. It takes place in war-time, when a young soldier is traveling alone though the woods, on horseback. "He was appalled by his own loneliness. The pulse of war that beat from the West suggested the companionship of battling thousands; here was naught but silence, and himself, and possible death-dealing bullets from a myriad ambushes. And yet his task was to find what he feared to find."[6] Coming to a stream, he sees on the other side an enemy about to fill a bottle. It would have been impossible for him to miss his shot, and, as he sighted, he "knew that he was gazing at a man who was as good as dead." But he did not shoot, and the other man "passed into the shelter of the woods beyond." Another day, after having picked apples, he is spotted by a group of enemy soldiers, and, as he is galloping to the safety of the woods, the very man with the ginger beard whom he has spared by the stream, "[kneels] down on the ground, level[s] his gun, and coolly take[s] his time for the long shot" (493), killing the young man instantly. "They, watching at the house, saw him fall, saw his body bounce when it struck the earth, and saw the burst of red-cheeked apples that rolled about him. They laughed at the unexpected eruption of apples, and clapped their hands in applause of the long shot by the man with the ginger beard" (493).

There is nothing light-hearted about this story, and the irony is overwhelming. The recognition of their common humanity which leads the young soldier to spare the ginger-bearded man is absent in the other man. For him it is just a long shot at a target. The situations are parallel and neither is life-threatening, but one man allows another to live while the other does not. The eruption of apples which should make the others aware of the pathos of the situation merely amuses them, further dehumanizing them and their victim. The bitter irony is that the young soldier is a victim of his own humanity and is killed by the very man he has spared.

"To Build a Fire," is the story of a man who dies as a result of his inflated sense of his own knowledge and power. Disregarding the basic law of the North which says that no man should travel alone when outside temperature is colder than fifty. below zero—a law he was reminded of before he left by an old timer—, he sets out alone for Henderson Creek. The man's smugness is matched by his ignorance and his lack of imagination. Fifty degrees below means nothing to him in abstract terms, and it does not lead him to ponder on the frailty of man and on the various mishaps which can, and do, befall him. Throughout, London parallels this man's educated and limited knowledge with the deep, instinctive knowledge of the dog. The man's death is therefore a harsh but ironically suited punishment for his crime. Disregarding the laws of nature because of senseless pride, he falls a victim to these very laws.

London often relies on comic relief to make his stories bearable. "The Red One" is particularly successful in that respect. A profoundly mythical and archetypal story, it dramatizes the night journey of a scientist lost in the jungle of the Solomons and, later, a prisoner of a primitive tribe which worships a red globe and makes human sacrifices to it. In his fear, sickness, and obsessive search for knowledge, Bassett is eventually more dehumanized than the primitive savages he lives with, becoming impervious to death, torture and suffering, especially others'. He is eventually quite willing to sacrifice the woman who loves him and has saved his life, and risk her dying a slow and incredibly painful death in order to satisfy his own curiosity concerning the Red One. However, there is humor in this Guadalcanal Heart of Darkness, which arises mainly from two characters: Balatta and Ngurn, the shaman. Balatta, who has saved Bassett's life because she fell instantly in love with him, and whom he must court in order to see the Red One, is quite horrible to look at:

> *if by nothing else, her sex was advertized by the one article of finery with which she was adorned, namely a pig's tail, thrust through a hole in her left earlobe. So lately had the tail been severed, that its raw end still oozed blood that dried upon her shoulder like so much candle-droppings. And her face! A twisted and wizened complex of apish features, perforated by up-turned, sky-open, Mongolian nostrils, by a mouth that sagged from a huge*

> *upper lip and faded precipitately into a retreating chin, and by peering*
> *querulous eyes that blinked as blink the eyes of denizens of monkey-cages.*[7]

But she is very much in love, and Bassett sacrifices himself on the altar of his own greed for knowledge. A fastidious man who had never been a very passionate lover, he "shuddered" as he put his arm around her dirt-encrusted shoulders and felt the contact of her rancid-oily and kinky hair with his neck and chin. But he nearly screamed when she succumbed to that caress so at the very first of the courtship and mowed and gibbered and squealed little, queer, pig-like gurgly noises of delight. It was too much. And the next thing he did in the singular courtship was to take her down to the stream and give her a vigorous scrubbing" (588-89).

If Bassett survives, he will have to marry Balatta. If he dies, he will become the property of Ngurn at whose hands after-death delights await him. Ngurn is the devil-devil doctor who has befriended Bassett and to whose quarters Bassett retreats when escaping the amorous ardor of Balatta. But Ngurn's specialty is head-shrinking, and he ardently covets Bassett's head. Trying to convince Bassett, he promises to do a wonderful job on his head, selecting the materials himself for the curing smoke, and taking months to cure it so that the skin should remain smooth and not wrinkle. Also, he promises to share with him the knowledge Bassett is yearning for:

> *"And I promise you, in the long days to come when I turn your head in the*
> *smoke, no man of the tribe shall come in to disturb us. And I will tell you*
> *many secrets, for I am an old man and very wise, and I shall be adding*
> *wisdom to wisdom as I turn your head in the smoke. . . . And I promise*
> *you that never will a head be so well cured as yours,. . . Your head shall*
> *be my greatest piece of work in the curing of heads."* (596-97)

The promise of such long nights of intimacy is not quite what Bassett had in mind when seeking the friendship and protection of Ngurn. But, ironically, Ngurn is the more human and kind of the two[. . .].

Jack London's humor is a topic toward which critics have only recently turned their attention. The essays in this volume form the first concerted effort to deal with this aspect of his work and provide distinctive critical insight into his achievement. Five novels—*The Star Rover, The Little Lady of the Big House, The Iron Heel, The Scarlet Plague,* and *Adventure*—as well as a number of short stories are analyzed here. However, it does not mean that the rest of London's novels, as well as the bulk of his short stories, are devoid of humor, much to the contrary. It would, in fact, be difficult to find a novel or a short story entirely devoid of any form of humor. This is a beginning, a first exploration of a wide and varied topic.

NOTES

[1] See Jacqueline Tavernier-Courbin, "The Many Facets of Jack London's Humor," *Critical Essays on Jack London,* ed. J. Tavernier- Courbin (Boston: G. K. Hall, 1983), 89-101; "Social Myth as Parody in Jack London's Northern Tales," *Thalia: Studies in Literary Humor 9,*2 (1986), 3-15; and "Translating Jack London's Humor," *META (Humor and Translation),* 34,1 (1989), 63-72.

[2] For a more detailed reading of this story, see Jacqueline Tavernier-Courbin, "'The Wife of a King': A Defense," *Jack London Newsletter* 10,1 (1977), 34-38.

[3] "That Spot," in *Jack London's Stories for Boys* (New York: Cupples & Leon, 1936), 103.

[4] "Chun Ah Chun," in *Jack London's Short Stories,* eds. Earle Labor, Robert C. Leitz III, and I. Milo Shepard (New York: Macmillan, 1990), 363. Further references will be included in the text.

[5] "Goliah," in *Curious Fragments,* ed. Dale L. Walker (Port Washington, N.Y.: National University Publications, 1975), 94. Further references will be included in the text.

[6] "War", in *Short Stories*, 490. Further references will be included in the text.

[7] "The Red One," in *Short Stories,* 583. Further references will be included in the text.

Selected Bibliography

Suggestions for Further Reading

This checklist of further readings includes works by Jack London, special Jack London issues of journals, bibliographies, and selected biographies. The sections titled *Books* and *Selected Critical Articles* contain listings up to 1980. Items published on London from 1981-1992 are listed in the *Bibliography* which follows these suggestions for further reading.

Works by Jack London

Novels

The Cruise of the Dazzler. New York: Century, 1902.
A Daughter of the Snows. Philadelphia: J.B. Lippincott, 1902.
The Kempton-Wace Letters. New York: Macmillan, 1903.
The Call of the Wild. New York: Macmillan, 1903.
The Sea-Wolf. New York: Macmillan, 1904.
The Game. New York: Macmillan, 1905.
White Fang. New York: Macmillan, 1906.
Before Adam. New York: Macmillan, 1907.
The Iron Heel. New York: Macmillan, 1908.
Martin Eden. New York: Macmillan, 1909.
Burning Daylight. New York: Macmillan, 1910
Adventure. New York: Macmillan, 1911.
The Abysmal Brute. New York: Century, 1913.
The Valley of the Moon. New York: Macmillan, 1913.
The Mutiny of the Elsinore. New York: Macmillan, 1914.
The Scarlet Plague. New York: Macmillan, 1915.
The Star Rover. New York: Macmillan, 1915.
The Little Lady of the Big House. New York: Macmillan, 1916.

Jerry of the Islands. New York: Macmillan, 1917.
Michael, Brother of Jerry. New York: Macmillan, 1917.
Hearts of Three. New York: Macmillan, 1920.
The Assassination Bureau, Ltd. New York: McGraw-Hill, 1963. Completed by Robert
      L. Fish.

Short Stories

The Son of the Wolf: Tales of the Far North. Boston: Houghton, 1900.
The God of His Fathers and Other Stories. New York: McClure, Phillips, 1901.
Children of the Frost. New York: Macmillan, 1902.
The Faith of Men and Other Stories. New York: Macmillan, 1904.
Tales of the Fish Patrol. New York: Macmillan, 1905.
Moon-Face and Other Stories. New York: Macmillan, 1906.
Love of Life and Other Stories. New York: Macmillan, 1907.
Lost Face. New York: Macmillan, 1910.
When God Laughs and Other Stories. New York: Macmillan, 1911.
South Sea Tales. New York: Macmillan, 1911.
The House of Pride and Other Tales of Hawaii. New York: Macmillan, 1912.
A Son of the Sun. Garden City, N.Y.: Doubleday, Page, 1912.
Smoke Bellew. New York: Century, 1912.
The Night Born. New York: Century, 1913.
The Strength of the Strong. New York: Macmillan, 1914.
The Turtles of Tasman. New York: Macmillan, 1916.
The Red One. New York: Macmillan, 1918.
On the Makaloa Mat. New York: Macmillan, 1919.
Dutch Courage and Other Stories. New York: Macmillan, 1922.

Essays and Travel Sketches

The People of the Abyss. New York: Macmillan, 1903.
War of the Classes. New York: Macmillan, 1905.
Revolution and Other Essays. New York: Macmillan, 1910.
The Cruise of the Snark. New York: Macmillan, 1911.
The Human Drift. New York: Macmillan, 1917.

Plays

Scorn of Women. New York: Macmillan, 1906.
Theft. New York: Macmillan, 1910.
The Acorn-Planter: A California Forest Play. New York: Macmillan, 1916.
Daughters of the Rich. Ed. James E. Sisson. Oakland, CA: Holmes Book Co., 1971.
Gold. Ed. James E. Sisson. Oakland, CA: Holmes Book Co., 1972. Written with
      Herbert Heron.

Autobiographies

The Road. New York: Macmillan, 1907.
John Barleycorn. New York: Century, 1913.

Letters

Letters from Jack London. Ed. King Hendricks and Irving Shepard. New York: Odyssey
Press, 1965.
The Letters of Jack London. 3 vols. Ed. Earle Labor, Robert C. Leitz, III, and I. Milo
Shepard. Stanford, CA: Stanford UP, 1988.

Additional Works

Curious Fragments: Jack London's Tales of Fantasy Fiction. Ed. Dale L. Walker. Port
Washington, N.Y.: Kennikat Press, 1975.
Jack London in The Oakland High School Aegis. Ed. James Sisson III. Oakland, CA.:
Star Rover House, 1980.
Jack London: No Mentor But Myself. Ed. Dale L. Walker. Port Washington, N.Y.:
Kennikat Press, 1979.
Jack London on the Road: The Tramp Diary and Other Hobo Writings. Ed. Richard W.
Etulain. Logan: Utah State UP, 1979.
Jack London Reports: War Correspondence, Sports Articles, and Miscellaneous Writings.
Ed. King Hendricks and Irving Shepard. Garden City, N.Y.: Doubleday, 1970.
Jack London's California. Ed. Sal Noto. New York: Beaufort, 1986.
The Portable Jack London. Ed. Earle Labor. New York: Penguin, 1994.
The Science Fiction of Jack London: An Anthology. Ed. Richard Gid Powers. Boston:
G.K. Hall, 1975.
The Social Writings of Jack London. Ed. Philip S. Foner. New York: Citadel, (1947)
1964.
Sporting Blood: Selections from Jack London's Greatest Sports Writing. Ed. Howard
Lachtman. Novato, CA: Presidio Press, 1981.

Special Editions

The Bodley Head Jack London. 4 vols. Ed. Arthur Calder-Marshall. London: The
Bodley Head, 1963-66.
The Complete Short Stories of Jack London. 3 vols. Ed. Earle Labor, Robert C. Leitz,
III, and I. Milo Shepard. Stanford, CA: Stanford UP, 1993.
Jack London: Short Stories. Ed. Earle Labor, Robert C. Leitz, III, and I. Milo Shepard.
New York: Macmillan, 1990.
Novels and Stories, Novels and Social Writings. 2 vols. The Library of America. New
York: Viking, 1982.

Special Issues of Journals

American Book Collector 17, 3 (November 1966): 7-35.
American Literary Realism 24, 2 (Winter 1992): 3-54.
Europe 54, 561-62 (Janvier-Février 1976): 3-160.
Modern Fiction Studies 22, 1 (Spring 1976): 3-125.
Overland Monthly 68, 5 (May 1917): 357-450.
Pacific Historian 22, 2 (Summer 1978): 1-45.
Thalia: Studies in Literary Humor 12, 1 & 2 (1992): 3-110.
Western American Literature. 11, 2 (August 1976): 83-164.

Works about Jack London

Bibliographies

"Bibliographical Update." In *Critical Essays on Jack London*, ed. Jacqueline Tavernier-
        Courbin. Boston: G.K. Hall, 1983, 281-91.
Lachtman, Howard. "Criticism of London: A Selected Checklist," *Modern Fiction
        Studies*, 22 (1976): 107-125.
Sherman, Joan. *Jack London: A Reference Guide*. Boston: G.K. Hall, 1977.
Walker, Dale L., comp. *The Fiction of Jack London: A Chronological Bibliography*.
        Research and editing by James E. Sisson, III. El Paso: Texas Western Press,
        1972.
Woodbridge, Hensley C., John London, and George H. Tweney, comps. *Jack London:
        A Bibliography*. Georgetown, CA: Talisman Press, 1966; revised and expanded
        edition Millwood, N.J.: Kraus Reprint, 1973.

Biographies

Kingman, Russ. *A Pictorial Life of Jack London*. Glen Ellen, CA: Jack London Research
        Center, 1979.
London, Charmian. *The Book of Jack London*. 2 vols. New York: Century, 1921.
London, Joan. *Jack London and His Times*. New York: Doubleday, 1939. Reissued with
        an introduction by the author. Seattle: U of Washington P, 1968.
Walker, Franklin. *Jack London and the Klondike: The Genesis of an American Writer*.
        San Marino, CA: Huntington Library, 1966: reprinted with an introduction by
        Earle Labor, 1994.

Books

Berton, Pierre. *The Klondike Fever*. Toronto: McClelland and Stewart, 1958.
Day, A. Grove. *Jack London in the South Seas*. New York: Four Winds Press, 1971.
Feied, Frederick. *No Pie in the Sky: The Hobo as American Cultural Hero in the Works
        of Jack London, John Dos Passos, and Jack Kerouac*. New York: Citadel,
        1964.
Foner, Philip S. *American Rebel*. New York: Citadel, (1947) 1964.

Henricks, King. *Jack London: Master Craftsman of the Short Story*. Logan: Utah State UP, 1966.

Johnson, Martin E. *Through the South Seas With Jack London*. New York: Dodd, Mead, 1913.

Labor, Earle and Jeanne Campbell Reesman. *Jack London*. Rev. ed. New York: Twayne, 1994.

_____, ed. *The Portable Jack London*. New York: Penguin, 1994.

London, Charmian. *Our Hawaii*. New York: Macmillan, 1917.

McClintock, James I. *White Logic: Jack London's Short Stories*. Grand Rapids, MI: Wolf House Books, 1975.

Tavernier-Courbin, Jacqueline. *The Call of the Wild: A Naturalistic Romance*. New York: Twayne, 1994.

Walcutt, Charles Child. *Jack London*. Pamphlets on American Writers no. 57. Minneapolis: U of Minnesota P, 1966.

Walker, Dale L. *The Alien Worlds of Jack London*. Grand Rapids, MI: Wolf House Books, 1973.

Wilcox, Earl J. *The Call of the Wild: A Casebook*. Chicago: Nelson-Hall, 1980.

Collections of Essays

Ownbey, Ray Wilson, ed. *Jack London: Essays in Criticism*. Santa Barbara, CA: Peregrine Smith, 1978.

Tavernier-Courbin, Jacqueline, ed. *Critical Essays on Jack London*. Boston: G.K. Hall, 1983.

Twentieth-Century Literary Criticism. Vol. 9. Ed. Dennis Poupard. Detroit: Gale Research, 1883, 252-285.

Selected Critical Articles

Baskett, Sam S. "A Brace for London Criticism: An Essay Review." *Modern Fiction Studies* 22 (1976): 101-105.

_____. "Jack London's Heart of Darkness." *American Quarterly* 10 (1958): 66-77.

Benoit, Raymond. "Jack London's *The Call of the Wild*." *American Quarterly* 20 (1968): 246-48.

Bosworth, L. A. M. "Is Jack London a Plagiarist?" *Independent* 62 (1906): 373-75.

Brooks, Van Wyck. "Frank Norris and Jack London," in his *The Confident Years: 1885-1915*. New York: Dutton, 1952, 217-37.

Buck, Philo M. "The American Barbarian." *Methodist Review* 28 (1912): 714-24. See *Creator and Critic: A Controversy Between Jack London and Philo M. Buck, Jr.*, ed. King Hendricks, Logan, Utah, 1961.

Bykov, Vil. "Jack London in the Soviet Union." *Quarterly News Letter* (Book Club of California) 24 (1959): 52-58.

Cambell, Jeanne. "Falling Stars: Myth in 'The Red One'." *Jack London Newsletter* 11 (1978): 86-96.

Courbin, Jacqueline M. "Jack London's Portrayal of the Natives in His First Four Collections of Arctic Tales." *Jack London Newsletter* 10 (1977): 127-37.

Denko, Charles W. "Jack London; A Modern Analysis of His Mysterious Disease." *Journal of Rheumatology* 20 (1993): 1760-63.

Fleming, Beck London. "Memories of My Father, Jack London." *Pacific Historian* 18 (1974): 5-10.

Forrey, Robert. "Male and Female in London's *The Sea-Wolf.*" *Literature and Psychology* (University of Hartford) 24 (1974): 135-43.

Geismar, Maxwell. "Jack London: The Short Cut," in his *Rebels and Ancestors: The American Novel 1890-1915.* Boston: Houghton, 1953.

Hensley, Dennis E. "Jack London's Use of Maritime History in *The Sea Wolf.*" *Pacific Historian* 23,2 (1979): 1-8.

Hicks, Granville. "The Years of Hope," in his *The Great Tradition: An Interpretation of American Literature since the Civil War.* New York: Macmillan, 1933, 1935. Rev. ed. Quadrangle Books, 1969, 164-206.

Kardell, Margaret M. "The Acorn Planter." *Pacific Historian,* 21,2 (1977): 189-95.

Kazin, Alfred. "Progressivism: The Superman and the Muckrake," in his *On Native Grounds: An Interpretation of Modern American Prose Literature.* New York: Harcourt, 1942, 1970, 91-126.

Labor, Earle. "From 'All Gold Canyon' to *The Acorn Planter*: Jack London's Agrarian Vision." *Western American Literature* 11 (1976): 83-101.

_____. "Jack London, 1876-1976: A Centennial Recognition." *Modern Fiction Studies* 22 (1976): 3-7.

_____. "Jack London's 'Planchette': The Road Not Taken." *Pacific Historian* 21,2 (1977): 138-46.

_____. "Jack London's Symbolic Wilderness: Four Versions." *Nineteenth-Century Fiction* 17 (1962): 149-161.

Lachtman, Howard. "Jack and George: Notes on a Literary Friendship." *Pacific Historian* 22,2 (1978): 27-42.

_____. "Reconsideration: *The Valley of the Moon* by Jack London." *New Republic,* Sept. 6, 1975, 27-29.

_____. "Revisiting Jack London's Valley of the Moon." *Pacific Historian* 24,2 (1980): 145-56.

Martinez, Elsie Whittaker. "Jack London," in her *San Francisco Bay Area Writers and Artists.* Berkeley: U of California Bancroft Library, Regional Oral History Office. Bound Typescript, 1969.

Menken, H. L. "Jack London," in his *Prejudices.* New York: Knopf, 1919, 236-39.

Mills, Gordon H. "The Symbolic Wilderness: James Fenimore Cooper and Jack London." *Nineteenth Century Fiction* 13 (1959): 329-340.

Orwell, George. "Introduction to *Love of Life and Other Stories* by Jack London," in *The Collected Essays, Journalism and Letters of George Orwell: In Front of Your Nose.* Ed. Sonia Orwell and Jan Angus. Vol. 4. New York: Harcourt, 1968.

Peterson, Clell T. "The Jack London Legend." *American Book Collector* 9 (1959): 15-22.

Rothberg, Abraham. "Land Dogs and Sea Wolves: A Jack London Dilemma." *Massachusetts Review* 21 (1980): 569-93.

_____. "Old Stock: Jack London and His Valley of the Moon." *Southwest Review* 62 (1977): 361-368.

Sandburg, Carl. "Jack London: A Common Man." *Tomorrow* 2,4 (1906): 35-9.

Shivers, Alfred S. "Jack London: Not a Suicide." *Dalhousie Review* 49 (1969): 43-57.

_____. "Jack London's Mate-Women." *American Book Collector* 15 (1964): 17-21.

Siegel, Paul N. "Jack London's *Iron Heel*: Its Significance for Today." *International Socialist Review* (July-August 1974): 18-29.

Sinclair, Upton. "About Jack London." *Masses* 9 (1917): 17-20.

Stasz, Clarice. "Androgyny in the Novels of Jack London." *Western American Literature* 11 (1976): 121-33.

_____. "The Social Construction of Biography: The Case of Jack London." *Modern Fiction Studies* 22 (1976): 51-71.

Stein, Paul. "Jack London's *The Iron Heel*: Art as Manifesto." *Studies in American Fiction* 6 (1978): 77-92.

Strunsky, Anna. "*The Son of the Wolf*: A Review of Jack London's Book." *Dilettante* 7,8 (1901): 179-84. Rpt. in *Jack London and the Amateur Press*, ed. Robert H. Woodward (1983): 39-43.

Tambling, Victor R. S. "Following in the Footsteps of Jack London: George Orwell, Writer and Critic." *Jack London Newsletter* 11 (1978): 63-70.

Tsujii, Eiji. "Jack London and the Yellow Peril." *Jack London Newsletter* 9 (1974): 96-99.

Van Doren, Carl. "Toward the Left: Naturalism," in his *The American Novel: 1789-1939*. Rev. ed. New York: Macmillan, 1940, 256-71.

Walling, Anna Strunsky. "Memoirs of Jack London." *Masses* 9 (1917): 13-17.

Wilcox, Earl. "Jack London's Naturalism: The Example of *The Call of the Wild*." *Jack London Newsletter* 2 (1969): 91-101.

_____. "*Le milieu, le moment, la race*: Literary Naturalism in Jack London's *White Fang*." *Jack London Newsletter* 3 (1970): 42-45.

"Wild and Tame." [Review of *The Call of the Wild*] *Times Literary Supplement*, March 14, 1968: 263.

Wilding, Michael. "The Iron Heel," in his *Political Fictions*. Boston: Routledge, 1980, 91-126.

Jack London: A Bibliography of Material in English for 1981-1992

Hensley C. Woodbridge

Our purpose is to produce a classified bibliography of London studies which would supplement that of Jacqueline Tavernier-Courbin's in CEJL. The bibliography of Jack London has grown so in slightly more than a decade that we have limited ourselves to material in English. Reviews have been listed if they are 300 words or more.

Bibliographers of all scholars probably need the help of others more. It is therefore with great pleasure that I gladly acknowledge the assistance of Russ and Winnie Kingman who on January 8-9, 1993 allowed me to consult the outstanding Jack London Research Center. While there I worked with Eiji Tsujii of Japan who provided me with a list of his works in English and with Earl Wilcox. On January 11-12 Earle Labor made available much of his personal material concerning London and did everything possible to make our stay on the Centenary College campus profitable. Tony Williams of Carbondale contributed over a dozen items that I might have missed, while Susan Nuernberg not only kindly agreed that I should produce this bibliography but has also contributed to it. Chieko Tachihata, Hawaiian Curator, University of Hawaii Library provided data on several items published in Hawaii. Jeanne Campbell Reesman kindly let me examine an annotated bibliography that she had compiled for another project.

Reviews found in periodicals and newspapers have not been given their titles in an effort to save space. Individuals who desire fuller bibliographical details concerning these should consult the Earl Wilcox bibliography of annotated criticism, which is in progress.

As usual those who helped bear no responsibility for errors either of omission or commission, those are my own.

I have included only those items from *Jack London Echoes* that I feel would be of the most scholarly interest.

The following abbreviations are used:

AL   *American Literature*
ALR   *American Literary Realism*
CEJL   *Critical Essays on Jack London*, ed. Jacqueline Tavernier-
        Courbin, Boston: G.K. Hall, 1983, 298 pp.
JAC   *Journal of American Culture*
JLE   *Jack London Echoes*
JLN   *Jack London Newsletter*
MFS   *Modern Fiction Studies*
PaH   *Pacific Historian*
RALS   *Resources for American Literary Study*
SSF   *Studies in Short Fiction*
WAL   *Western American Literature*

Bibliographies

Hamilton, David Mike. *'Tools of My Trade': The Annotated Books in Jack London's Library*. Seattle, WA: U of Washington P, 1986, xiv, 326 pp.
  Reviews: Sam S. Baskett, *The Centennial Review* 32,1 (1988): 93-94; Sue Irwin Gatti, *Studies in the Humanities* 14 (1987): 60-61; Earle Labor, RALS, 16 (1986-1989): 151-155; John Sunderland, *Huntington Library Quarterly* 51 (1988): 147-49; Jacqueline Tavernier-Courbin, *Analytical and Enumerative Bibliography* 2,2 (1988): 90-93; George H. Tweney, WAL 23 (1988): 61-62; Tony Williams, JLN 21 (1988): 126-27.
Harty, Kevin J. "Dissertations on Jack London, 1936-1987: Evidence for Canonicity," JLN 20 (1987): 58-62.
Tavernier-Courbin, Jacqueline. "Bibliographical Update," CEJL, 281-91.
Taylor, Harvey. "Selections from *The Jack London Bibliography*." *The Wolf '86*, 5-20.
Woodbridge, Hensley C. *"WLT:* Supplement 17," JLN 16 (1981): 35-39.

Biographical Studies

Besant, Larry X. "Jack London and Luther Burbank: Friends and Neighbors?" JLN 21 (1988): 66-73.
Bradshaw, Margaret Flanagan and Virginia Young Newton as told to Margaret Guilford-Kardell. "Jack London drank from our well." *The Covered Wagon* (Shasta Historical Society) 1982, 23-26.
Bykov, Vil. "On the Trail of Jack London," JLE 4 (1984): 41-51.
Conlon, Stephen. "Some Aspects of Jack London in Australia," JLE 4(1984): 24-29.
Davie, John L. "Jack London," in *His Honor, The Buckaroo. The Autobiography of John L. Davie*. Ed. and rev. Jack W. Herzberg. Reno, NV: Jack Herzberg, 1988, 128-30.
Denko, Charles W. "On Jack London's Medical History," *Jack London Foundation Newsletter* 4,1 (1992): [2-5].
Fenady, Andrew J. *The Summer of Jack London*. New York: Walker, 1985, 173 pp. Novel.
Flink, Andrew. *"Our Hawaii* Index," JLN 18 (1985): 1-35.
Gershenowitz, Harry. "Luther Burbank, Jack London and Cacti," *The Wolf '85*, 9-14.
_____. "Mencken and Jack London," *Menckeniana*, no. 116 (1990): 8-9.
Haughey, Homer L. and Connie Kate Johnson. *Jack London Ranch Album*. Stockton, CA: Heritage Pub., 1985, 48 pp. "Foreword" by Earle Labor, 3.
_____. *Jack London Homes Album*. Stockton, CA: Heritage Pub., 1987, 48 pp.
Hedrick, Joan D. *Solitary Comrade: Jack London and His Work*. Chapel Hill, NC: U of North Carolina P, 1982, xviii, 265 pp.
  Reviews: Robert C. Leitz, AL 55 (1983): 108-109; Gorman Beauchamp, ALR 16 (1983): 138-42; Charles N. Watson, Jr., JLN 15 (1983): 128-31; Carolyn Johnston, WAL 18 (1983): 77-78; Jacqueline Tavernier-Courbin, *Studies in American Fiction* 13 (1985): 115-17; Earle Labor, MFS 28 (1982-83): 670-71.
Herron, Don. "Jack London" in *Literary World of San Francisco and Its Environs*. San Francisco: City Lights Books, 1990, 163-76.
Holtz, William. "Jack London's First Biographer," WAL 27,1 (1992): 21-36.

Johnston, Carolyn. *Jack London: An American Radical.* Westport, CT: Greenwood Press, 1984, xvii, 205 pp.
> Reviews: Earle Labor, RALS 16 (1986-1989): 155-157; Dale L. Walker, WAL 20 (1985): 255-56; Tony Williams, JLN 17 (1985): 52-56.

Juron, Joe. "Jack London and Anna Strunsky," JLN 17 (1984): 95-100.

Kingman, Russ. *Jack London: A Definitive Chronology* for the Jack London Research Center. Los Angeles: David Rejl, 1992, 274 pp.
_____. "Kingman's Corner," JLE 1,2 (1981): 56-60; 1,3 (1981): 44-47; 1,4 (1981): 52-56; 2,2 (1982): 56-59; 2,3 (1982): 52-55; 2,4 (1982): 56-59; 3,1 (1983): 56-59; 3,2 (1983): 44-45; 3,3 (1983): 52-55; 3,4 (1983): 56-59.

Lartemy, Eugene P. and Mary Ridge. *For Love of Jack London: His Life with Jennie Prentiss—a True Love Story.* New York: Vantage Press, 1991, xvi, 196 pp. Fiction.

London, Becky. "From My Mailbox," JLE 2,3 (1982): 18-21; 2,4 (1982): 48-59; 3,1 (1983): 42-45; 3,2 (1983): 34-36; 3,3 (1983): 46-49; 3,4 (1983): 48-50.
_____. "Some Memories of Daddy—Jack London," JLE 1,2 (1981): 18-20; 1,3 (1981): 21-25; 1,4 (1981): 35-40.

London, Joan. *Jack London and His Daughters.* Introd. Bart Abbot. Berkeley, CA: Heyday Books, 1990, vi, 200 pp. See Jacqueline Tavernier-Courbin, "A Daughter's Last Message," *Thalia* 12 (1992): 90-99.
> Reviews: Jesse F. Knight, *The Californians* 17 (1992): 53-54; Jackie Koenig, *The Wolf* '91, 9-11; Dale Walker, *Rocky Mountain News* (Denver), July 15, 1990 and July 22, 1990, reprinted in *The Wolf* '91, 5-9.

Lundquist, James. *Jack London: Adventures, Ideas and Fiction.* New York: Ungar, 1987, x, 212 pp.

Middagh, Winifred M. "Jack London, *Sailor on Horseback:* Biography or Fiction?" JLN 15,3 (1982): 132-57.

Nakada, Sachiko. "Jack London in Yokohama, 1893," JLE 3,2 (1983): 3-5.

Nan Loillen, L. "Becky London: The Quiet Survivor Talks About Her Father," *Californians* 9,4 (1992): 34-39.

Noble, Valerie. *Hawaiian Prophet: Alexander Hume Ford.* Smithtown, N.Y.: Exposition Press, 1980, 45-49, 76-77, 80-81, 203.

Noto, Sal. "Jack London, Burlesque and the 'Big Apple,'" JLN 16 (1983): 41-44.
_____. *Jack London's California.* New York: Beaufort, 1986.
_____. "On the Trail of Jack London on Maui," JLE 1,1 (1981): 22-27.
_____. *With a Heart Full of Love: Jack London's Presentation Inscriptions to the Women in His Life.* Berkeley: Two Windows Press, 1986, xi-xiii, 103 pp. Includes "Eliza and Charmian: Stabilizing Forces at Work," 3-13; "Flora Wellman London: Betwixt and Between," 48-56; "Mabel Applegarth: Jack London's Golden Girl," 69-85.

O'Neill, James P. "Jack London: Rebel with a Soul," *Second Spring* 9,11 (1982): 17-21.

Perry, John. *Jack London: An American Myth.* Chicago: Nelson Hall, 1981, 351 pp.
> Reviews: Earle Labor, MFS 28 (1982): 669-70; Dale L. Walker, JLN 15 (1982): 92-96; Victor Tambling, JLN 15 (1982): 97-99.

Redding, Robert H. "The Jack London Connection," *Roundup* 33,1 (1985): 5-14.

Rewak, William J. "Three Graves," *Commonweal* 119,21 (Dec. 4, 1992): 11-15.

Schlottman, David H. "A Stroll through the Park," *The Wolf* '92, 7-17.
_____. "The Jack London Stamp," *The Wolf* '89, 7-17.

_____. "Jack London's Dawson," *The Wolf '82*, 4-23.

_____. "2183: The First Day," *The Wolf '87*, 12-27.

Schoenecke, Michael K., "The Ranch as World View: Jack London's Attempt," *Journal of Regional Cultures* 1 (1981): 131-139.

Schroeder, Alan. *Jack London*. New York: Chelsea House, 1992, 127 pp.

Shillingsburg, Mirian. "Jack London, Socialist, in Sydney," *Australian Literary Studies* 13,2 (1987): 223-26.

Sisson, James E., III. "Jack London and Lieutenant-Colonel Vlachislov Petrovsky of the Imperial Army of Nicholas II, Czar of All the Russians," *The Wolf '83*, 23-24. "Special Issue: A Tribute to Becky," JLE 2,1 (1982): 55 pp. Twenty-three contributors with an original contribution by Becky London.

Stanley, David H. "Jack London's Biographical Legend," ALR 17 (1984): 67-86.

Stasz, Clarice. *American Dreamers: Charmian and Jack London*. New York: St. Martin's Press, 1988, xiii, 302 pp.

Reviews: Emily Leider, *San Francisco Review of Books* 14 (1989): 3,7; Emily Toth, *The Woman's Review of Books* 6,9 (1989): 24; Charles N. Watson, Jr. AL 61 (1989): 684-86.

_____. "London and Eucalyptus: Not a Folly," JLN 19 (1986): 69-77.

Walker, Dale L. "Jack London, Western Writer," *Roundup* 33,1 (1985): 3-4.

_____. "Jack London: An Appreciation," *Firsts: Collecting Modern First Editions* 2,12 (1992): 24-27.

_____. "Jack London's War," JLE 3,4 (1983): 22-23.

Watson, Charles N., Jr. "An Index to *The Book of Jack London* by Charmian London (1921)," JLN 16 (1983): 47-95.

Watson, Toby J. "A Voyage of the Snark," *The Wolf '85*, 15-19.

Weistein, Jerry. "Collecting Jack London," *Firsts: Collecting Modern First Editions* 2,12 (1992): 28-29.

Williams, Tony. "Memories of Jack: An Interview with Becky London," JLN 19,1 (1986): 1-10.

General Studies on London's Novels

Allen, Mary. "The Wisdom of the Dogs in Jack London," in her *Animals in American Literature*. Urbana: U of Illinois P, 1983, 77-96.

Asselineau, Roger. "Jack London as a Crypto-Transcendentalist," CEJL, 86-88.

Beauchamp, Gorman. *Jack London*. Mercer Island, WA: Starmont House, 1984, 96 pp.

Review: Tony Williams, JLN 20 (1987): 36-40.

_____. "What to See in London," *Canadian Review of American Studies* 17,1 (1986): 69-80.

Bender, Bert. "Jack London in the Tradition of American Sea Fiction," *American Neptune* 46 (1986): 188-99; reprinted in his *Sea Brothers*, Philadelphia: U of Pennsylvania P, 1988, 83-98.

Bennett, Kenneth I. "Julio Cortázar and Jack London," JLN 18 (1985): 47-48.

Blackman, Gordon N., Jr. "Jack London: Visionary Realist, Part II," JLN 14 (1981): 1-12.

Boe, John. "Jack London, the Wolf and Jung," *Psychological Perspectives* 11,2 (1980): 133-36.

Booss, Claire. "Introduction," *Jack London: Series II*. Ed. Claire Booss and Paul J. Horowitz, New York: Avenel Books, 1982, ix-xii.

Bush, Glen Paul. "Rebellion, Death and Time as Archetypal Structures in Jack London's Novels: *Martin Eden, The Iron Heel* and *The Star Rover*." Ph.D dissertation, St. Louis U, 1987, 129 pp. *DAI* 49 (1988): 253A.

————. "The Pastoral and the Violent: Jack London's Literary Dialectic," JLN 20 (1987): 52-57.

Callihan, John C. Foreword and Afterword. *Jack London: Farther North*. Tales of the Yukon by Jack London. New York: Westvaco, 1989.

Chessey, Bob. "Jack London's Influence on the Life-style of Jack Kerouac," JLN 15 (1982): 158-65.

Christopulus, Diana K. "American Radicals and the Mexican Revolution 1900-1925." Ph.D. dissertation, State U of New York (Binghampton), 1980, 521 pp. *DAI* 41 (1980): 2732A.

Crews, Brian. "Fate, Naturalism and the Individual in Jack London's Fiction." *Revista canaria de estudios ingleses* 18 (1989): 205-220.

Crow, Charles L. "Homecoming in the California Visionary Romance," WAL 24 (1989): 1-19.

Day, A. Grove. "Introduction," Jack London, *Stories of Hawaii*. Honolulu, HI: Mutual Pub. Paperback Series, Tales of the Pacific, 1990, 5-20.

————. "Jack London and Hawaii," *Honolulu* 19,5 (1984): 70-73, 124-127.

————. "Jack London's 'Heart of Darkness'" in his *Mad About Islands,* Honolulu, HI: Mutual Pub. of Honolulu, 1987, 162-72; *Aloha* 9,2 (1988): 38-41, 76; used as introduction to Jack London, *South Sea Tales,* Honolulu, HI: Mutual Pub. Paperback Series, Tales of the Pacific, 1985, i-xxviii.

————. "Jack London, Pacific Voyager" introduction to Jack London, *The Mutiny of the Elsinore,* Honolulu, HI: Mutual Pub. Paper Back Series, Tales of the Pacific, 1987, [i-iii, unpaginated]

————. "Sailor from California: Jack London." In his *Mad About Islands,* Honolulu, HI: Mutual Pub. of Honolulu, 1987, 144-61.

De Ville, Peter. "In or Out of the Camp Fire: Lawrence and Jack London's Dogs," *Notes and Queries* 38,3 (1991): 339-41.

Edmunds, Lowell. *The Silver Bullet: The Martini in American Civilization*. Westport, CT: Greenwood Press, 1981, 13-16.

Fatzinger, Greg. "Jack London: Rebel, Rambler, Rifhter [sic]," *The Wolf '84*, 19-21.

Fish, Robert L. "About *The Assassination Bureau*," JLE 1,1 (1981): 8.

Fraser, John. "Crane, Norris, and London." *American Literature*. Ed. Boris Ford. Vol. 9 of *The New Pelican Guide to English Literature*. 9 vols. London: Penguin, 1988: 194-98.

Gatti, Susan Irwin. "Jack London on Boxing: The Manly Art of Making It," JLN 21 (1988): 77-85.

————. "Jack London on the Job: A Writer's Representation of Work." Ph.D. dissertation, U of Pittsburgh, 1989, 219 pp. *DAI* 50,6 (Dec. 1989): 1656-1657A.

Gershenowitz, Harry. "Did Lecomte du Nouy Misinterpret Jack London and Why," *The Wolf '84*, 11-13.

————. "Jack London's Influence on Harry Bridges," *The Wolf '87*, 4-12.

————. "Lewis Mumford's Oversight of Emerson's Influence on Jack London," *The Wolf '84*, 9-10.

————. "The Natural History Controversy between Theodore Roosevelt and Jack London: A Life Scientist's View," JLN 14 (1981): 80-82.

————. "The Sustained Misrepresentation of London's Spencerism," *The Wolf '89*, 17-23.

Hamilton, David. "Jack London," *Critical Studies on Short Fiction*, Englewood Cliffs, NJ: Salem Press, 1985, 5: 1809-1813.

Hays, Peter L. "Hemingway and London," *The Hemingway Review* 4,1 (1984): 54-56.

Hensley, Dennis E. "Jack London's Use of the Linguistic Style of the King James Bible," JLE 3,3 (1983): 4-11.

Honberger, Eric. "Jack London," in his *American Writers and Radical Politics, 1900-192: Equivocal Commitments*, New York: St. Martin's Press, 1986, 1-33.

Hornung, Alfred. "Evolution and Expansion in Jack London's Personal Accounts: *The Road* and *John Barleycorn.*" In Serge Ricard, ed., *An American Empire Expansionist Culture and Politics, 1881-1917*, Aix-en-Provence, Université de Provence, 1990, 197-213.

Howard, June. *Form and History in American Literary Naturalism*, Chapel Hill: U of North Carolina P, 1985. Numerous scattered references.

Jackson, Crispin. "The Novels and Stories of Jack London," *Book Collector*, no. 103 (1992): 16-24.

Kaufman, Alan. "We're Saxons. . . and not Dagoes: The Role of Racism in Jack London's Late Novels," JLN 16 (1983): 96-103.

————. "Foreigners, Aliens, Mongrels: Literary Responses to American Immigration, 1880-1920." Ph.D. dissertation, Indiana U, 1982, 195 pp. DAI 43 (1983): 3596A.

Khouri, Nadia. "The Other Side of Otherness: Forms of Fictional Utopianism in the U.S.A. from Mark Twain to Jack London." Ph.D. dissertation, McGill U, 1983. DAI 44 (1984): 2767A.

Kroll, Keith. "Index to James I. McClintock's *White Logic*," JLN 19 (1986): 47-54.

Kummings, Donald. "London and the American Tradition in Literature," JLN 19 (1986): 105-107.

Labor, Earle. "Jack London." *Bénet's Reader's Encyclopedia of American Literature*. Eds. George Perkins, Barbara Perkins, and Phillip Leininger. New York: Harper Collins, 1991, 633-35.

————. "Jack London," *American Short Story Writers, 1880-1910*, ed. Bobby Ellen Kimbel. *Dictionary of Literary Biography* 78. Detroit, MI: Gale, 245-71.

————."Jack London," *Literary History of the American West*, ed. Thomas J. Lyon, et al. Fort Worth, TX: Texas Christian UP, 1987, 381-97.

————. "Jack London's Mondo Cane: 'Batard,' *The Call of the Wild*, and *White Fang*," CEJL, 114-30.

————. "Jack London's Pacific World," CEJL, 205-22.

————. "The Making of a Major Author: Jack London and the Politics of Literary Reputation," JLN 19 (1986): 100-104.

Lewis, Ward B. "The Politics of Jack London During the Weimar Republic," *Germanisch-Romanische Monatschrift* 37,2 (1987): 187-98.

Li, Shuyan. "Jack London in China," JLN 19 (1986): 42-46.

"Literary Vagabond," *American Heritage* 42,7 (1991): 42-43.

Littell, Katherine M. "The 'Nietzschean' and the Individualist in Jack London's Socialist
    Writings," JLN 15 (1982): 76-91.
London, Jack. *The Call of the Wild, White Fang and Other Stories*. Ed. and introd. Earle
    Labor and Robert C. Leitz, III. Oxford and New York: Oxford UP, 1990.
    Of interest are: "Introduction," ix-xxii. "Note on the Text," xxiii-xxv.
    "Explanatory Notes," 358-362.
MacDonald, Marie. "On Rereading Jack London," JLN 15 (1982): 37-39.
Majkut, Paul Theodore. "From Daydream to Nightmare: Utopian Fiction in the late
    Nineteenth and Early Twentieth Centuries." Ph.D. dissertation, Indiana U,
    1986, 278 pp. DAI 48 (1987): 645A.
Martin, R.E. "Jack London: Radical Individualism and Social Justice in the Universe of
    Force," in his *American Literature and the Universe of Force,* Durham, NC:
    Duke UP, 1991, 184-214.
Martin, Stoddard. "Jack London," in his *California Writers: Jack London, John
    Steinbeck, The Tough Guys*. New York: St. Martin's Press, 1983, 17-66.
    Divided into I. "The Underman and the Cause," 17-34. II. "Woman, Race and
    the Land," 34-51. III. "The Little Lady and the Tradition," 51-66.
_____. "The Novels of Jack London," JLN 14 (1981): 48-71.
Moreland, David Allison. "Jack London's South Sea Narratives." Ph.D. dissertation,
    Louisiana State U, 1980, 228 pp. DAI 41 (1980): 1598A.
_____. "Violence in the South Sea Fiction of Jack London," JLN 16 (1983): 1-35.
Nakada, Sachicho. "Jack London and the Japanese Reader: Now and Then," JLE 2,2
    (1982): 16-17.
_____. *Jack London and the Japanese. An Interplay between the West and the East.*
    Uyede: The Central Institute, 1986, 114 pp.
Naso, Anthony. "Jack London and Herbert Spencer," JLN 14 (1981): 13-14.
Nuernberg, Susan Marie. "The Call of Kind: Race in Jack London's Fiction." Ph.D.
    dissertation, U of Massachusetts, 1990, ix, 270 pp. DAI 51,3 (Sept. 1990):
    853A. See "The Call of Kind: A Dialogue" between Hensley C. Woodbridge
    and Susan Nuernberg, *The Wolf '93* 10-17 (HCW), 17-21 (SMN).
Pagnucci, Robyn. "From Thrilling Adventures to Great Stories," *The Wolf '84*, 14-19.
Pizer, Donald. "Jack London: The Problem of Form," *Studies in the Literary
    Imagination 16* (1983): 107-15; rpt. in his *Realism and Naturalism in
    Nineteenth Century American Literature*, Carbondale, IL: Southern Illinois UP,
    1984, 166-79.
Porter, Gerald. "The Art of the Impossible: Two Early American Utopias," in *'News
    that Stays News,'* ed. Gerald Porter, Vassa, Finland: U of Vassa (Proceedings
    of the U of Vassa, 137), 1989, 42-54.
Praetzellis, Adrian and Mary Praetzellis. "'Utility and Beauty Should Be One: ' The
    Landscape of Jack London's Ranch of Good Intentions," *Journal of the Society
    for Historical Archaeology* 23,1 (1989): 33-44.
Rapport, Mirion. "Introduction," London's *Tales of Hawaii,* Kailu: Press Pacifica, 1984,
    v-ix.
Reesman, Jeanne Campbell. "Irony and Feminism in *The Little Lady of the Big House,"
    Thalia* 12 (1992): 34-46.
_____. "Jack London's New Woman in a New World: Saxon Brown Roberts'
    Journey into *The Valley of the Moon*," ALR 24,2 (1992): 40-54.
_____. "Jack London's Popular and Political Masks," JLN 20 (1987): 63-71.

_____. "Knowledge and Identity in Jack London's Hawaiian Fiction," JLN 19 (1986): 91-95.

Roberts, Garyn R. "Humor and the Apocalypse: A Note on Jack London's *The Scarlet Plague," Thalia* 12 (1992): 77-81.

Robillard, Douglass. "Introduction," *The Kempton Wace Letters*, ed. Douglas Robillard, Albany, N.Y.: NCUP, 1990, i-xxi.

Ross, Dale H. "Jack London: An American Dilemma," JAC 5,4 (1982): 57-62.

Schoenecke, Michael Keith. "The Science Fiction of Jack London: Scientific Theories and Three Fictional Extrapolations, *The Sea Wolf* (1904), *Before Adam* (1906), and *The Iron Heel* (1908)." Ph.D. dissertation, Oklahoma State U, 1979, 156 pp. DAI 40 (1980): 6295A.

Sinclair, Andrew. "Afterword: Jack London's Life and Works," in London's *Tales of the Pacific*, New York: Penguin, 1989, 228-32.

_____. "Introduction," London's *Tales of the Pacific,* New York: Penguin, 1989, 7-15.

Smith, Mel. "Jack London and Racial Mongrelism: His Dispute with Spiro Orfans," *Manuscripts*, 63,4 (1991): 281-91.

Stanley, David Hamilton. "Multiple Selves in American Autobiography." Ph.D. dissertation, U of Texas, 1980, 263 pp. DAI 41 (1980): 1600A.

Stasz, Clarice. "Sarcasm, Irony and Social Darwinism in Jack London's *Adventure,*" *Thalia* 12 (1992): 82-89.

Tambling, Victor R.S. "Jack London and George Orwell: A Literary Kinship," in *George Orwell,* Courtney T. Wemyss and Alexej Ugrinsky, eds., New York: Greenwood Press, 1987, 171-75.

Tavernier-Courbin, Jacqueline. "Introduction," *Thalia*, 12 (1992): 3-14.

_____. "Jack London: A Professional," CEJL, 1-21.

_____. "Jack London's Science Fiction," JLN 17 (1984): 71-78.

_____. "The Many Facets of Jack London's Humor," CEJL, 253-79.

_____. "Notes and Documents," CEJL 253-79.

_____. "Translating Jack London's Humor," *META* (Humor and Translation), 34,1 (1989): 63-72.

Tietze, Thomas R. and Gary Rield. "'Saints in Slime': The Ironic Use of Racism in Jack London's *South Sea Tales,*" *Thalia* 12 (1992): 59-66.

Tsujii, Eiji. "For the Promotion of Jack London and His Works in Japan," Jack London Foundation *Newsletter* 3,4 (1991): n.p.

_____. "The Publication of Jack London's Great Prophecy," JLE 4(1984): 110-13.

_____. "Thinking Back upon My Study of Jack London," JLE 2,3 (1982): 22-23.

_____. "To Make Jack London More Popular in Japan," JLN 19 (1986): 116-18.

Walker, Dale L. *Jack London and Conan Doyle: A Literary Kinship*. Bloomington, IN: Gaslight Publications, 1981, 70 pp.
    Review: Victor R.S. Tambling, JLN 14 (1981): 113-15.

Ware, Elaine. "Jack London's *Before Adam:* Social Criticism in the Guise of Fantasy," JLN 19 (1986): 109-15.

Watson, Charles N. Jr. *The Novels of Jack London: A Reappraisal*. Madison, WI: U of Wisconsin P, 1983, xv, 304 pp.
    Reviews: Tony Williams, JLN 18,3 (1985): 77-90,; Earle Labor, AL 55 (1983): 656-58; Carolyn Johnston, WAL 18 (1983): 365-67; Sam S. Baskett,

MFS 29 (1983): 713-14; Jacqueline Tavernier-Courbin, *Western Humanities Review* 38 (1984): 286-88.

————. "Jack London up from Spiritualism," *The Haunted Dusk: American Supernatural Fiction, 1820-1920,* Howard Kerr and Charles L. Crow, eds., Athens, GA: U of Georgia, 1983, 193-207.

Whittemore, Reed. "Jack London's Best Seller Impieties," in his *Six Literary Lives: The Shared Impiety of Adams, London, Sinclair, Williams, dos Passos, and Tate.* Columbia: U of Missouri P, 1993 [published end of 1992] 49-86.

Williams, James. "The Composition of Jack London Writings," *American Literary Realism, 1870-1910* 23 (1991): 64-86.

————. "An Essay upon the Supposed Influence of Herbert Spencer's Philosophy of Style," JLN 20 (1987): 22-30.

Williams, Tony. "Jack London and the Dialogic Imagination," JLN 21 (1988): 128-38.

————. *"Jerry of the Islands* and *Michael, Brother of Jerry,"* JLN 17 (1984): 28-60.

————. *"The Mutiny of the Elsinore:* A Re-Evaluation," JLN 19 (1986): 13-14.

Wilson, Christopher P. "The Brain Worker. Jack London." In his *The Labor of Words.* Athens, GA: U of Georgia P, 1983, 77-96.

Wolf, Dietrich. "The Soul of Jack London (I)," *National Vanguard,* no. 109 (1988): 19-24. White supremacy periodical.

————. "The Soul of Jack London (II). *National Vanguard,* (1989): 18-24.

Woodbridge, Hensley C. "Reflections: *WLT:* A Note," JLE 3,1 (1983): 24-25.

————. "Reflections: Library of America Includes London," JLE 3,2 (1983): 24.

————. "Reflections: A Plea to Publishers," JLE 2,4 (1982): 8-9.

Woodward, Robert H. "Notes on London's Early Writing," JLE 2,2 (1982): 22-23.

Woodward, Servanne. "The Nature of the Beast in Jack London's Fiction," *Bestia* 1 (1989): 661-66.

Studies on Individual Novels

The Call of the Wild:

Bödeker, Birgit. "Terms of Material Culture in Jack London's *The Call of the Wild* and Its German Translations," in Harald Kittle, et al., *Interculturality and the Historical Study of Literary Translation,* Berling: Schmidt, 1991, 64-74.

The Call of the Wild: A Casebook with Text, compiled and introd. Earl J. Wilcox. Chicago: Nelson-Hall, 1980, 245 pp.
        Review: Earle Labor, JLN 14 (1981): 119-21.

Doctorow, E.L. "Introduction," *The Call of the Wild,* New York: Vintage Books/The Library of America, 1990, vi-xviii.

Dyer, Daniel. "Answering The Call of the Wild," *English Journal* 77, 4 (1988): 57-62.

Fusco, Richard. "On Primitivism in *The Call of the Wild,"* ALR 20 (1987): 76-80.

Kumin, Michael. *"The Call of the Wild*: London's Seven Stages of Allegory," JLN 21 (1988): 86-98.

Levi, Primo. "Jack London's Buck," in *The Mirror Maker,* New York: Schocken Books, 1989, 149-53.

Reed, A. Paul. "Running with the Pack: Jack London's *The Call of the Wild* and Jesse Stuart's *Mongrel Mettle,"* JLN 18 (1985): 96-98.

Sisk, J.P. *"Call of the Wild,"* in his *The Tyrannies of Virtues,* ed. and introd. Chris Anderson. Norman, OK: U of Oklahoma P, 1990, 83-104.

The Iron Heel:

Beauchamp, Gorman. "Jack London's Utopian Dystopia and Dystopian Utopia," in *America as Utopia,* Kenneth M. Roemer, ed., New York: Franklin, 1981, 91-107.

France, Anatole. "Preface to *The Iron Heel*," tr. Jacqueline Tavernier-Courbin, CEJL, 35-37.

Portelli, Alessandro. "Jack London's Missing Revolution: Notes on *The Iron Heel,"* *Science Fiction Studies* 9 (1982): 180-94.

Ward, Susan. "Ideology for the Masses: Jack London's *The Iron Heel*," CEJL, 166-79.

Whalen-Bridge, John. "Dual Perspectives in *The Iron Heel,"* *Thalia* 12 (1992): 67-76.

John Barleycorn:

Crowley, John W. "Drunk Descending a Staircase: *John Barleycorn*," *Dionysus: The Literature and Intoxication TriQuarterly*, 3,1 (1991): 3-10.

Hall, James B. "Afterword" to Jack London, *John Barleycorn*. Santa Cruz, CA: Western Tanager Press, 1981, 345-59.

Leonard, Linda Schurse. "The Trickster," in her *Witness to the Fire: Creativity and the Veil of Addiction,* Boston: Shambhala, 1989, 95-113.

Stasz, Clarice. "Introduction," *John Barleycorn*. New York: Signet, 1990, 5-13.

Sutherland, John. "Introduction," *John Barleycorn*. Oxford: Oxford UP, 1989, vli-xxxiv.

Martin Eden:

DiMiceli, Caroline and Noel Mauberret. "Exchange, Gift and Death in Jack London's *Martin Eden,"* JLN 20 (1987): 31-35.

Gair, Christopher. "'A Trade, Like Anything Else': *Martin Eden* and The Literary Marketplace." *Essays in Literature*, 19, 2 (1992): 246-259.

Martin, John E. *"Martin Eden,* a London Superman Adventurer: A Study of the Americanization of European Ideology," in *Die amerikanische Literatur in der Weltliteratur.* Berlin: Schmidt, 1982, 218-30.

Miller, Judith Graves. "From Novel to Theatre: Contemporary Adaptations of Narrative to the French Stage." *Theatre Journal* 33 (1981): 434-440.

Moreland, Kim. "The Attack on the Nineteenth-Century Heroine Women in Jack London's *Martin Eden,"* *Markham Review* 13 (1983-1984): 16-20.

Rachid, Amina. "Popular Voice in the Novel: A Comparative Study of Fikry El-Kholy's *Al-Rihl a* (The Journey), Jack London's *Martin Eden*, and Jules Vallès *Trilogy,"* in Hoda Gindi, ed., *Images of Egypt in Twentieth Century Literature*. Cairo: Dept. of English Language & Literature, Faculty of Arts, U of Cairo, 1991, 355-366.

Sinclair, Andrew. "Introduction," *Martin Eden*. New York: Penguin, 1985, 7-21.

Walsh, Joy. "Visions of Martin Eden as Jack Kerouac," in her *Jack Kerouac: Statement in Brown: Selected Essays.* Clarence Center, New York: The Textile Bridge Press, 1984, 29-39 rpt. from JLN 14 (1981): 105-12.

Watson, Charles N., Jr. "The Composition of *Martin Eden*," AL 53 (1981): 397-408.

The Sea Wolf:

Baskett, Sam S. "Sea Change in *The Sea Wolf*," ALR 24 (1992): 5-22.

Boone, J.A. "Male Independence and the American Quest Genre: Hidden Sexual Politics in the All-Male Worlds of Melville, Twain and London," in *Gender Studies: New Direction in Feminist Criticism,* ed. Judith Spector, Bowling Green, OH: Bowling Green State U Popular P, 1986, 189-217.

_____. "Male Independence and the American Quest Romance as Countertraditional Genre Hidden Sexual Politics in the Male Worlds of *Moby-Dick, Huckleberry Finn, Billy Budd,* and *The Sea Wolf,*" in his *Tradition Counter Tradition, Love and the Force of Fiction,* Chicago: U of Chicago P, 1987, 226-77.

Cobbs, John L. "Afterword" to *The Sea Wolf.* Pleasantville, N.Y.: The Reader's Digest Association, 1989, 297-304.

Lessa, Richard. "Character and Perception in *The Sea Wolf*," JLN 15,3 (1982): 119-27.

London, Jack. *The Sea-Wolf.* Ed. and introd. John Sutherland. New York: Oxford UP, 1992. Of interest are the following items by Sutherland: "Introduction," vii-xxvi. "Note on the Text," xxvii-xxxiv. "Select [annotated] bibliography," xxxv-xxxvi. "Appendix 2: Film Versions of *The Sea-Wolf*," 343-346. "Explanatory Notes," 347-366. "Glossary," 367-375.

Miner, Madonna M. "It Will Be the [Un]masking of You: Manhood Besieged in Jack London's *The Sea Wolf*," JLN 21 (1988): 106-16.

Noto, Sal. *"The Sea Wolf:* A Myth Dispelled - Some First Issue Hairsplitting over Jack London's Most Famous Sea Narrative," JLN 15 (1982): 53-56.

Ostap, Martine Elizabeth. "Jack London's *The Sea Wolf:* A Critical Analysis of Wolf Larsen and Humphrey Van Weyden," JLN 15 (1982): 109-14.

Qualtiere, Michael. "Nietzchean Psychology in London's *The Sea Wolf*," WAL 16 (1982): 261-78.

Robinson, Forrest G. "The Eyes Have It: An Essay on Jack London's *The Sea Wolf*," ALR 18 (1986): 178-95.

Rothberg, Abraham. "Land Dogs and Sea Wolves: A Jack London Dilemma," *Massachusetts Review* 21,3 (1980): 569-93.

Tintner, Adeline R. "Jack London's Use of Joseph Conrad's *The End of the Tether* in *The Sea Wolf*," JLN 17 (1984): 61-65.

Ward, Susan. "Social Philosophy as Best-Seller: Jack London's *The Sea Wolf*," WAL 17 (1983): 321-32.

Williams, Tony. "Charley Furuseth—*The Sea Wolf's* Absent Father," JLN 20 (1987): 1-21.

The Star Rover:

Lacassin, Francis. "On the Roads of Night: A Search for the Origins of *The Star Rover*," trans. Margaret Stanley, CEJL, 180-94.

Savater, Fernando. "The Endless Pilgrimage," in his *Childhood Regained*. Trans. Frances M. López-Morillas. New York: Columbia UP, 1982, 113-121.

Sulphen, Dick. "The Story behind *The Star Rover*," epilogue to London's *The Star Rover*. Malibu, CA: Valley of Sun Pub., 1983, 311-33.

Tambling, Victor R. "Adam Strang in Cho-sen: The Korean Episode in *The Star Rover*," JLN 15 (1982): 1-36.

Williams, James. "Authorial Choice and Textual Meaning: The Sources of *The Star Rover*," JLN 20 (1987): 80-119; JLN 21 (1988): 1-65.

————. "The Composition of Jack London's *The Star Rover*." PhD. dissertation, Columbia U, 1990, 1140 pp. DAI 51 (1991): 2748A.

————. "Jack London's *The Star Rover*: A Case of Wrongful Neglect," JLN 19,3 (1986): 96-99.

————. "Two Sources for *The Star Rover*," JLN 17 (1984): 1-10.

Woodward, Robert H. "The Three 'Coined' Words in London's *The Star Rover*: Errata," JLN 17 (1984): 66.

Woodward, Robert H. and Charles Ludlum. "The Three 'Coined' Words in London's *The Star Rover*," JLN 16 (1983): 106-108.

Short Stories

Bain, Joe S., III. "Interchapter: Jack London's 'The Mexican,'" JLN 15 (1982): 115-18.

Berkove, Lawrence I. "A Parallax Correction in London's 'The Unparalleled Invasion,'" ALR 24,2 (1992): 33-39.

Clasby, Nancy. "Jack London's 'To Build a Fire,'" JLN 20 (1987): 48-51.

Dauphin, Laurent. " 'Moon-face' or the Rhetoric of the Absurd," *Thalia* 12 (1992): 55-58.

Echevarria, E.A. "Jack London and the Spanish American Regional Short Story," JLN 18 (1985): 57-60.

Graham, Don. "Madness and Comedy: A Neglected Jack London Vein," CEJL 223-29.

Guerin, Wilfred L., et al. "The Red One." *Instructor's Manual*. New York: Harper, 1986, 22-26.

Hattenhauer, Darryl. "The Shadow in Three Short Stories by Jack London," JLN 21 (1988): 74-76.

Hensley, Dennis Edward. "Jack London's Real and Fictional Women: A Study of Attributes." Ph.D. dissertation, Ball State U, 1981, 284 pp. DAI 43 (1982): 445-446A.

"Introduction," (unsigned) Jack London, *Short Stories:* Authorized Edition with Definitive Texts. Ed. Earle Labor, Robert C. Leitz III, and I. Milo Shepard. New York: Macmillan, 1990, xiii-xxxiv.

Review: Roscoe L. Buckland, SSF 27,3 (1990): 420-21.

Kirsch, James. "Jack London's Quest: 'The Red One,'" *Psychological Perspectives* 11,2 (1980): 137-54.

Labor, Earle. "The Archetypal Woman at 'Martyr to Truth': Jack London's 'Samuel,'"
        ALR 24,2 (1992): 23-32.
_____. "Introduction," *Jack London: A Trilogy. All Gold Cañon, The Night-Born*
        [and] *The Red One.* Stockton, CA: Minute Man Press, 1985, 1-3.
        Review: Tony Williams, JLN 19 (1986): 11-12.
Lachtman, Howard. "Introduction: Jack London, American Sportsman" to *Sporting
        Blood: Selections from Jack London's Greatest Sports Writing,* Howard
        Lachtman, ed., Novato, CA: Presidio Press, 1981, xi-xvii.
        Review: Earle Labor, JLN 15 (1982): 100-102.
_____. "Introduction: Jack London: The Vein of Gold," to *Young Wolf: The Early
        Adventure Stories of Jack London,* Howard Lachtman, ed., Santa Barbara:
        Capra Press, 1984, 7-13.
London, Jack. *Stories of Boxing*, James Bankes, ed., Dubuque, IA: Wm. C. Brown,
        1992. Of interest are: London, Becky. "Preface," iv; Kingman, Russ.
        "Foreword," v-xi; Bankes, James. "Introduction," xii-xvi; "The Game," 3-5;
        "The Abysmal Brute," 38-41; "A Piece of Steak," 98; "The Mexican," 116-
        17; "Tommy Burns versus Jack Johnson," 142-44; "Jack Johnson versus James
        Jeffries," 155-53.
London, Jack. *Thirteen Tales of Terror,* John Perry, ed., New York: Popular Library,
        1978.
Review: Howard Lachtman, JLN 14 (1981): 42-44.
McIntyre, John C. "Horacio Quiroga and Jack London Compared: 'A la deriva,' 'El
        hombre muerto' and 'To Build a Fire,'" *New Comparison* 7 (1989): 143-59.
Mitchell, Lee Clark. "'Keeping His Head': Repetition and Responsibility in London's
        'To Build a Fire,'" *Journal of Modern Literature* 13,1 (1986): 76-96; rpt. in
        his *Determined Fictions: American Literary Naturalism,* New York: Columbia
        UP, 1989, 34-54.
Moreland, David A. "The Quest That Failed: Jack London's Last Tales of the South
        Seas," *Pacific Studies* 8,1 (1984): 48-70.
Peters, John Gerald. "Nihilism in 'The Law of Life,'" JLN 17 (1984): 92-94.
Peterson, Per Serritslev. "Science-Fictionalizing the Paradox of Living: Jack London's
        'The Red One' and the Ecstasy of Regression," in *Inventing the Future Science
        Fiction in the Context of Cultural History and Literary Theory,* Ib Johansen and
        Peter Ronnon-Jessen, eds., Aarhus, Denmark: Seklos, Dept. of English, U of
        Aarhus, 1985, 35-58.
Reesman, Jeanne Campbell. "Jack London—Kama'aina," JLN 18 (1985): 71-76.
_____. "The Problem of Knowledge in Jack London's 'The Water Baby,'" WAL 23
        (1988): 201-15.
Sisson, James, III. "Introduction," *Jack London's Articles and Short Stories in the Aegis.*
        Oakland, CA: Star Rover House, 1980, xiii-xlv.
Walker, Dale L. "Introduction," *In a Far Country: Jack London's Tales of the West.* Ed.
        and introd. Dale L. Walker. Ottawa, IL: Jameson Books, 1987, 9-10.
Wilcox, Earl J. "Overtures of Literary Naturalism in *The Son of the Wolf* and *The God
        of His Fathers*," CEJL, 105-113.
Woodward, Servanne. "'The Wife of a King' from a Bergsonian Perspective," *Thalia*
        12 (1992): 47-54.

Other Prose Works

Jack London on the Road: The Tramp Diary and Other Hobo Writings. Ed. Richard W. Etulain. Logan, Utah: Utah State UP, 1979.
    Review: Howard Lachtman, JLN 14 (1981): 40-41.
Labor, Earle and Robert C. Leitz, III. "Jack London on Alexander Berkman: An Unpublished Introduction," AL 61 (1989): 447-56.
Moreland, David A. "The Author as Hero: Jack London's *The Cruise of the Snark*," JLN 15 (1982): 57-75.
Nicolson, Colin. "Jack London's *The People of the Abyss*," JLN 17 (1984): 18-27.
O'Connor, Kaori. "Introduction," *The Cruise of the Snark*. New York: KPI, 1986, 13 unnumbered pp.
Stasz, Clarice. "Foreword," *The People of the Abyss. n.p.:* Joseph Simon, 1980, vii-xii.

London as a Letter Writer, a Dramatist, and an Orator

Ennis, Stephen. "The Circuit Rider's Wife and 'Hobo Novelists: ' The Corra Harris/Jack London Correspondence," RSAL 15,2 (1985): 197-204.
Kingman, Russ. "Jack London Playwright," JLE 4 (1984): 8-19.
Labor, Earle, Robert C. Leitz, III and Milo Shepard, eds. *The Letters of Jack London*. Stanford, CA: Stanford UP, 1988. 3 vols.
    Reviews: Joseph H. Brown, *Humanities* 9,5 (1988): 36-38; William E. Cain, *American Literary History* 3 (1991): 603-13; Don L. Cook, *South Central Review* 7,1 (1990): 96-98; E.L. Doctorow, New York *Times Book Review,* Dec. 11, 1988, 1, 39, 41; Joan D. Hedrick, RALS 18 (1992): 146-153; Jesse F. Knight, *Californians* (1990); Joseph R. McElrath, Jr., *Documentary Editing* 12,3 (1990): 49-52; Herbert Mitgang, *The Progressive* 53,3 (1989): 41-42; Virgil Mogel, *New Poetics* 5 (1990): 187-92; Donald Pizer, *Book World,* Nov. 20, 1988, 5; John Sutherland, *London Review of Books* 11 (July 27, 1989): 17-19; Tony Williams, MFS 35 (1989): 272-74; Tony Williams, JLN 21 (1988): 124-25.
Newlin, Keith. "Portrait of a Professional: The Plays of Jack London," ALR 20,2 (1988): 65-84.
Ward, Susan. "Jack London and the Blue Pencil: London's Correspondence with Popular Editors," ALR 14,1 (1981): 16-25.
Zamen, Mark E. "Jack London, Orator," *PaH* 30,2 (1986): 34-49.
_____. *Standing Room Only: Jack London's Controversial Career as a Public Speaker*. Introd. Earle Labor. New York: Peter Lang, 1990, xix, 275 pp.
    Review: Tony Williams, WAL 26 (1991): 156.

Jack London, the Movies and Television

Birchard, Robert S. "Jack London and the Movies," *Film History* 1 (1987): 15-38.
_____. "London and Hollywood," *The Wolf '88,* 16-18.
Bosworth, Mrs. Hobart. "Some Notes on American Film History," *The Wolf '88,* 3.
Walker, Dale L. "Jack London - The Movie," JLE 1 (1981): 48-50.
Williams, Tony. "Alexander Knox on the Warner Brothers' Version of *The Sea Wolf:* Extracts from an Interview," JLN 18 (1985): 49-51.
_____. "Bosworth Incorporated Presents Jack London," *The Wolf '88,* 5-20.
_____. "Cinematic Echoes in the Work of Jack London," JLE 4 (1984): 32-39.
_____. "From London's 'The Unexpected' to Kuleshov's *By the Law*," JLN 19 (1986): 55-68.
_____. "History and Interpretation in the 1941 Version of Jack London's *The Sea Wolf*," JLN 19 (1986): 78-88.
_____. *Jack London. The Movies. An Historical Survey.* Los Angeles: David Rejl, 1992, 260 pp.
_____. "Literature, Film and the Dynamics of Exchange: An Analysis of the Legend of *The Sea Wolf*," JLN 18 (1985): 67-69.
_____. "The War of the Wolves: Filming Jack London's *The Sea Wolf* 1917-1920," *Film History* 4 (1990): 199-217.
_____. "Wolf Larsen. An Allied Artists Production," JLN 18 (1985): 91-95.

Index

About the Editor

SUSAN M. NUERNBERG is an Assistant Professor in the Department of English at the University of Wisconsin at Oshkosh.

ISBN 0-313-28927-1

EAN

90000>

9 780313 289279

HARDCOVER BAR CODE